Ulrike Golas

Analysis and Correctness of Algebraic Graph and Model Transformations

VIEWEG+TEUBNER RESEARCH

Ulrike Golas

Analysis and Correctness of Algebraic Graph and Model Transformations

With a foreword by Prof. Dr. Hartmut Ehrig

VIEWEG+TEUBNER RESEARCH

Bibliographic information published by the Deutsche Nationalbibliothek
The Deutsche Nationalbibliothek lists this publication in the Deutsche Nationalbibliografie;
detailed bibliographic data are available in the Internet at http://dnb.d-nb.de.

Dissertation Technische Universität Berlin, 2010

D 83

1st Edition 2011

Editorial Office: Ute Wrasmann | Anita Wilke

Vieweg+Teubner Verlag is a brand of Springer Fachmedien.
Springer Fachmedien is part of Springer Science+Business Media.
www.viewegteubner.de

Cover design: KünkelLopka Medienentwicklung, Heidelberg
Printing company: STRAUSS GMBH, Mörlenbach
Printed on acid-free paper
Printed in Germany

ISBN 978-3-8348-1493-7

Foreword

The area of web grammars and graph transformations was created about 40 years ago. 10 years later, the algebraic approach of graph grammars was well established as a concrete theory of graph languages. This was the time when also Ulrike Prange was born. Both of them had a smooth childhood for a period of about 20 years.

This smooth period was continued by a highly active one: Computing by graph transformation was adopted as an EC-child leading to the grown-up international conference on graph transformation ICGT, when Ulrike started to study computer science and mathematics. In her master's thesis, she successfully transformed the LS-baby "adhesive category" into the TFS-child "adhesive HLR category", which was educated in functional behavior.

Meanwhile she transformed herself from Ulrike Prange to Ulrike Golas.

The final step is now done in her PhD thesis on two levels: On the abstract level, from adhesive HLR systems to $\mathcal{M}$-adhesive systems with general application conditions, and on the concrete level as a model transformation between different visual languages like statecharts and Petri nets.

Altogether, she has successfully established a bidirectional transformation between categorical and graph transformation techniques as well as between mathematics and computer science concerning her professional degrees. This is an excellent basis for a promising scientific career.

Hartmut Ehrig
Technische Universität Berlin

Abstract

Graph and model transformations play a central role for visual modeling and model-driven software development. It is important to note that the concepts of graphs and their rule-based modification can be used for different purposes like the generation of visual languages, the construction of operational semantics, and the transformation of models between different visual languages.

Within the last decade, a most promising mathematical theory of algebraic graph and model transformations has been developed for modeling, analysis, and to show correctness of transformations, where different basic case studies have already been handled successfully.

For more sophisticated applications, however, like the specification of syntax, semantics, and model transformations of complex models, a more advanced theory is needed including the following issues:

1. Graph transformations based on an advanced concept of constraints and general application conditions in order to extend their expressive power without loosing the available analysis techniques.

2. Extension of concepts for parallelism, synchronization, and binary amalgamation to multi-amalgamation as an advanced modeling technique for operational semantics.

3. Model transformations based on triple graph grammars with general application conditions for adequate modeling and analysis of correctness, completeness, and functional behavior.

4. General framework of graph and model transformations in order to handle transformation systems based on interesting variants of graphs and nets, including typed attributed graphs and high-level Petri nets, in a uniform way.

The main contribution of this thesis is to formulate such an advanced mathematical theory of algebraic graph and model transformations based on $\mathcal{M}$-adhesive categories satisfying all the above requirements. Within this framework, model transformations can successfully be analyzed regarding syntactical correctness, completeness, functional behavior, and semantical simulation and correctness. The developed methods and results are applied to the non-trivial problem of the specification of syntax and operational semantics for UML statecharts and a model transformation from statecharts to Petri nets preserving the semantics.

Zusammenfassung

Graph- und Modelltransformationen spielen in der visuellen Modellierung und der modellgetriebenen Softwareentwicklung eine zentrale Rolle. Graphen und deren regelbasierte Modifikation können insbesondere für unterschiedliche Zwecke wie die Erzeugung visueller Sprachen, die Konstruktion operationaler Semantiken und die Transformation von Modellen zwischen verschiedenen visuellen Sprachen eingesetzt werden.

In den letzten zehn Jahren wurde eine höchst vielversprechende mathematische Theorie der algebraischen Graph- und Modelltransformationen zur Modellierung, Analyse und dem Beweis der Korrektheit von Transformationen entwickelt, mit der verschiedene elementare Fallstudien erfolgreich bearbeitet wurden.

Für anspruchsvollere Anwendungen allerdings, wie die Spezifikation von Syntax, Semantik und Modelltransformationen von komplexen Modellen, wird eine weiterentwickelte Theorie benötigt, die die folgenden Punkte umfasst:

1. Auf fortgeschrittenen Konzepten von Constraints und allgemeinen Anwendungsbedingungen basierende Graphtransformationen, um deren Ausdrucksmächtigkeit zu erhöhen, ohne die verfügbaren Analysetechniken zu verlieren.

2. Erweiterung von Konzepten für Parallelismus, Synchronisation und binäre Amalgamierung auf Multi-Amalgamierung als fortschrittliche Modellierungstechnik für operationale Semantik.

3. Auf Triple-Graphgrammatiken basierende Modelltransformationen mit allgemeinen Anwendungsbedingungen für eine adäquate Modellierung und die Analyse der Korrektheit, Vollständigkeit und des funktionalen Verhaltens.

4. Ein allgemeines Rahmenwerk für Graph- und Modelltransformationen, um Transformationssysteme für verschiedene Varianten von Graphen und Netzen, inklusive getypter attributierter Graphen und High-Level-Petrinetze, einheitlich zu behandeln.

Der wichtigste Beitrag dieser Arbeit ist der Entwurf solch einer weiterentwickelten mathematischen Theorie der algebraischen Graph- und Modelltransformationen aufbauend auf $\mathcal{M}$-adhäsiven Kategorien, die die obigen Anforderungen erfüllt. In diesem Rahmenwerk können Modelltransformationen erfolgreich bezüglich syntaktischer Korrektheit, Vollständigkeit, funktionalem Verhalten und semantischer Simulation und Korrektheit analysiert werden. Die entwickelten Methoden und Ergebnisse werden auf das nichttriviale Problem der Spezifikation von Syntax und operationaler Semantik von UML Statecharts und einer semantik-bewahrenden Modelltransformation von Statecharts zu Petrinetzen angewendet.

Contents

List of Figures

1 Introduction

The research area of graph grammars or graph transformations is a discipline of computer science which dates back to the 1970s. Methods, techniques, and results from this area have already been studied and applied in many fields of computer science, such as formal language theory, pattern recognition, the modeling of concurrent and distributed systems, database design and theory, logical and functional programming, model and program transformation, syntax and semantics of visual languages, refactoring of programs and software systems, process algebras, and Petri nets. This wide applicability is due to the fact that graphs are a very natural way of explaining complex situations on an intuitive level. Hence, they are used in computer science almost everywhere.

In this thesis, the following areas of computing by graph transformation play a special role, where we describe the impact of graphs and graph transformation in more detail:

- *Visual modeling and specification.* Graphs are a well-known, well-understood, and frequently used means to represent system states. Class and object diagrams, network graphs, entity-relationship diagrams, and Petri nets are common graphical representations of system states or classes of system states; there are also many other graphical representations. Rules have proven to be extremely useful for describing computations by local transformations of states. In object-oriented modeling, graphs occur at two levels: the type level (defined on the basis of class diagrams) and the instance level (given by all valid object diagrams). Modeling by graph transformation is visual, on the one hand, since it is very natural to use a visual representation of graphs; on the other hand, it is precise, owing to its formal foundation. Thus, graph transformations can also be used in formal specification techniques for state-based systems.

- *Model transformation.* In recent years, model-based software development processes have evolved. Models are no longer mere (passive) documentation, but are used for code generation, analysis, and simulation as well, where model transformations play a central role. An important question is how to specify such model transformations. Using algebraic graph transformation concepts to specify and verify model transformations offers a visual approach combined with formal, well-defined foundations and proven results and analysis methods. Starting from visual models as discussed above, graph transformations are certainly a natural choice. On the basis of the underlying structure of such visual models, the abstract syntax graphs, the model transformation is defined. Owing to the formal foundation, the correctness of model transformations can be formulated on a solid mathematical basis and verified using the theory of graph transformations.

- *Concurrency and semantics.* When graph transformations are used to describe a concurrent system, graphs are usually taken to describe static system structures. System behavior expressed by state changes is modeled by rule-based graph manipulations, i. e. graph transformations. The rules describe preconditions and postconditions of single transformation steps. In a pure graph transformation system, the order of the steps is determined by the causal dependency of actions only, i. e. independent rule applications can be executed in an arbitrary order. The concept of rules in graph transformations provides a clear concept for defining system behavior. In particular, for modeling the intrinsic concurrency of actions, graph rules provide a suitable means, because they explicate all structural interdependencies.

Since graph transformations are used for the description of development processes, we can argue that we program on graphs. But we do so in a quite abstract form, since the class of structures is some class of graphs and not specialized to a specific one. Furthermore, the elementary operations on graphs are rule applications. Graph transformations advocate for the whole software development life cycle. Our concept of computing by graph transformations is not focused only on programming but includes also specification and implementation by graph transformation, as well as graph algorithms and computational models, and software architectures for graph transformations.

Graph transformation allows one to model the dynamics of systems describing the evolution of graphical structures. Therefore, graph transformations have become attractive as a modeling and programming paradigm for complex-structured software and graphical interfaces. In particular, graph transformation is promising as a comprehensive framework in which the transformation of different structures can be modeled and studied in a uniform way.

Based on formal foundations, graph transformation represents a mathematical theory well-suited for modeling and analysis of dynamic processes in computer science. The concepts of adhesive and weak adhesive high-level replacement (HLR) categories have been a break-through for the double pushout approach of algebraic graph transformations. Almost all main results could be formulated and proven in these categorical frameworks and instantiated to a large variety of HLR systems, including different kinds of graph and Petri net transformation systems [EEPT06]. These main results include the Local Church-Rosser, Parallelism, and Concurrency Theorems, the Embedding and Extension Theorem, completeness of critical pairs, and the Local Confluence Theorem.

For more sophisticated applications, however, like the specification of syntax, semantics, and model transformations of complex models, a more advanced theory is needed including the following issues:

- *General application conditions.* The introduction of an advanced concept of constraints and application conditions allows to enhance the expressiveness and practicability of graph transformation. For a consistent and uniform approach to model transformation based on graph transformation, the concept of graph transformation has to be extended in this direction.

- *Multi-Amalgamation.* Amalgamation is a generalization of parallelism, where the assumption of parallel independence is dropped and pure parallelism is generalized to synchronized parallelism. The main idea of amalgamation is that a certain number of actions has to be performed which are similar for each step, but the concrete occurrences and quantity differ. In [BFH87], the Amalgamation Theorem has been developed only on a set-theoretical basis for a pair of standard graph rules without application conditions. However, in our applications we need amalgamation for n rules, called multi-amalgamation, based not only on standard graph rules, but on different kinds of typed and attributed graph rules including application conditions. The concept of amalgamation plays a key role in the modeling of the operational semantics for visual languages. Up to now, there are two main approaches for the specification of the operational semantics of complex models by graph transformation: either a lot of additional helper structure is needed to synchronize the rule applications depending on the system states, or the rules are constructed depending on the actual model instance leading to infinite many rules for a general semantical description. With amalgamation, the specification of operational semantics becomes easier and analyzable.

- *Triple graph transformation with application conditions.* For the specification of model transformations, triple graph grammars (TGGs) are a well-established concept in praxis, but so far only few formal theory and results are available. Triple rules, which allow the simultaneous construction of source and target models, lead to derived source and forward rules describing the construction of a source model and the actual model transformation from this source to a target model, respectively. Formal properties concerning information preservation, termination, correctness, and completeness of model transformations have been studied already based on triple rules without application conditions, where the decomposition and composition theorem for triple graph transformation sequences plays a fundamental role. In [EHS09], this theorem has been extended to triple rules with negative application conditions, but not yet to general application conditions. Our goal is to define model transformations based on triple graph grammars with general application conditions for adequate modeling and analysis of correctness, completeness, and functional behavior.

- *General framework.* A common foundation is needed to apply the rich theory not only to graphs, but also to different graph-like models as typed attributed graphs and different kinds of Petri nets, such that all kinds of transformation systems can be handled in a uniform way.

The main contribution of this thesis is to formulate such an advanced mathematical theory of algebraic graph and model transformations based on $\mathcal{M}$-adhesive categories satisfying all the above requirements. This allows to instantiate the theory to a large variety of graphs and corresponding graph transformation systems and especially to typed attributed graph transformation systems. We show that also algebraic high-level nets, a variant of Petri nets equipped with data, form an $\mathcal{M}$-adhesive category and that certain properties necessary for the main results of graph transformation are preserved under categorical constructions. In recent work, all the main results of graph transformation have been shown to be valid also for graph transformation based on rules with application conditions.

We develop the theory of multi-amalgamation for graph transformation systems based on rules with application conditions in the context of $\mathcal{M}$-adhesive categories. Basically, the synchronization of rules, so-called multi rules, is expressed by a kernel rule whose application determines how to apply the multi rules. With maximal matchings, all multi rule applications are constructed in parallel. This technique is useful to guide an unknown number of rule applications using the known application of the kernel rule. Combined with the concept of maximal matchings we obtain a mechanism to apply a certain number of rules simultaneously as a semantical step depending on the actual state of a model. With this technique, we are able to describe the operational semantics of models without the need for additional helper structure or infinite many rules. This leads to a clear and vivid rule set suitable for analysis.

Moreover, we lay the foundations for model transformations with application conditions broadening the expressiveness of model transformations based on triple graphs. We show a composition and decomposition theorem for triple transformations with consistent application conditions. Based on this result for triple graph transformations and the semantics defined by amalgamation we can successfully analyze syntactical correctness, completeness, functional behavior, and semantical simulation and correctness of model transformations. For the construction and the analysis of model transformations, different results and methods of graph transformations can be applied. Using TGGs we obtain sufficient and necessary criteria for the existence of model transformations, but these do not help for the actual construction. In this thesis, we define a more elaborated technique of an on-the-fly construction to make the construction of model transformations more efficient.

With this framework, we obtain general methods how model transformations can be successfully analyzed regarding syntactical correctness, completeness, functional behavior, and semantical simulation and correctness. The developed methods and results are applied to the non-trivial problem of the specification of syntax and operational semantics for UML statecharts and a model transformation from statecharts to Petri nets preserving the semantics. The thorough specification and analysis of this complex case study completes this work.

This thesis is organized as follows:

- In Chapter 2, we give a general introduction to model transformation, graph transformation, and show general concepts for model transformations based on graph transformations. Moreover, other existing work is related to our concepts.

- In Chapter 3, we introduce the main concepts of $\mathcal{M}$-adhesive categories and systems. The formal foundations for transformations and their main results are explained. As the main result in this chapter we show how $\mathcal{M}$-adhesive categories can be constructed categorically from given ones and that in addition certain properties are preserved. As an example, different categories of algebraic high-level Petri nets are shown to form $\mathcal{M}$-adhesive categories.

- In Chapter 4, we define multi-amalgamation for an arbitrary number of rules including application conditions. As a first main result in this chapter, we show how to construct a complement rule such that the application of the kernel and complement rule is equivalent to that of the multi rule. The second main result is the Amalgamation Theorem which states that amalgamated transformations are equivalent to the application of a multi rule and a combined complement rule for all other multi rules. The third main result shows that the parallel independence of amalgamated transformations can be reduced to that of the multi rule applications. As examples, we define the operational semantics for elementary Petri nets and statecharts using amalgamation.

- In Chapter 5, we enhance triple graph transformation with application conditions. As the main result in this chapter we show that for a special kind of application conditions the composition and decomposition of transformation sequences can be handled analogously to the case without application condition. As an example, we elaborate a model transformation from statecharts to Petri nets.

- In Chapter 6, we analyze model transformations regarding syntactical correctness, completeness, behavior preservation, termination, functional behavior, and semantical correctness. Moreover, we define the on-the-fly construction to enhance the efficiency of model transformations. Our example from Chapter 5 is analyzed with respect to all these properties.

- In Chapter 7, we summarize our work and give an outlook to future research interests and challenges.

2 Introduction to Graph and Model Transformation, and Related Work

The concept of model transformations is of increasing importance in software engineering, especially in the context of model-driven development. Although many model transformation approaches are implemented in various tools and utilized by a wide range users, often these implementations are quite ad-hoc and without any proven correctness. Thus, in the last years the need for analysis and verification of model transformations has emerged. As a basis, a formal framework is needed which allows to obtain respective results. In this thesis, we use graph transformation to define model transformations and verify certain correctness properties. In this chapter, the basic concepts of graph and model transformations are introduced and a survey of recent literature is given.

In Section 2.1, we introduce the main concepts of model transformations and discuss different model transformation languages and results. Graph transformation as a suitable framework is described in Section 2.2. We give a short overview over different graph transformation approaches and results. In Section 2.3, model transformation by graph transformation is explained, with a focus on triple graph transformation and correctness analysis.

2.1 Model Transformation

In modern software engineering, model driven software development (MDSD) plays an important role [BBG05, SV06]. The idea and ultimate goal is to generate the complete code from high-level system models without the need to program any line of code directly, since programming needs a lot of testing and still is often accompanied by bugs and failures, budget problems, and unstable programs and environments. In MDSD, the system is modeled in an abstract, platform-independent way and refined step by step to platform-specific executable code. Thus, the focus of software engineering moves from direct coding tasks to the design, analysis, and validation of high-level models. When system requirements and design are modeled with high-level visual engineering model languages such as UML [OMG09b], SysML [OMG08], or BPMN [OMG09a], the analysis of these models prior to implementation leads to a further improvement and refinement of the models and, in the end, hopefully to automatic code generation from correct and proven models. This improves software quality and reduces costs.

A part of the modeling is done in domain-specific modeling languages (DSMLs) which define structure, behavior, and requirements in specific domains. A meta-model, often equipped with some constraints, describes which model elements may occur in a correct DSML model. This approach is declarative and it is relatively easy to check if a model conforms to its meta-model. But there is no constructive description how to obtain valid DSML models. For this purpose, graph grammars (see Section 2.2) can be used as a high-level visual specification mechanism for DSMLs [BELT04], where the grammar directly induces the language defined by all possible derivable models.

Model transformations play an important role in MDSD, since models are everywhere in the software development process. In general, a model transformation MT is a relation $MT \subseteq VL_S \times VL_T$ connecting models of a source language VL_S and a target language VL_T. Moreover, such a relation can be seen as bidirectional [Ste08b], i.e. also interpreted as connecting target models to source models. In [CH03, MG06], model transformations are classified into endogenous and exogenous transformations. Endogenous model transformations work within one modeling language, typically used for refactoring [EEE09] or other kinds of optimizations, i.e. $VL_S = VL_T$. Exogenous model transformations translate models of different languages, i.e $VL_S \neq VL_T$.

In [BKMW09], a general mathematical framework of multi-modeling languages and model transformations based on MOF (Meta Object Facility) metamodels and institutions is defined, including the definition of semantics and correctness issues. In [Ste08a], different properties important for model transformations are discussed which will mark main issues in future work. Among specification, composition, and maintenance of model transformations, also verification and correctness properties are advised.

For the correctness of model transformations, we distinguish between syntactical correctness, functional behavior, and semantical correctness. Syntactical correctness means that the resulting target model is a valid model of the target language, i.e. the typing is correct and it satisfies potential constraints. Functional behavior describes that the model transformation MT behaves like a function, i.e. that for each source model a unique target model is found [BDE+07]. Semantical correctness expects that the behavior of the target model is somehow equivalent to that of the source model, where the required semantical properties have to be defined explicitly.

Also a wide range of tools [TEG+05] supports the design and execution of model transformations using languages like XSLT [W3C07], QVT [OMG05], BOTL [MB03], ATL [JAB+06, JABK08], or graph transformation [Roz97, EEKR99, EEPT06]. XSLT (Extensible Stylesheet Language Transformation) is a declarative, text-based transformation language that can be used to transform XML-documents. It handles tree-structures, but is difficult to use for visual models and complex, graph-like models, because the additional tree structure has to be added and makes the definition of the transformation more difficult. Further problems concern modularity, efficiency, reusability, and maintainability for complex transformations. QVT (Query/View/Transformation) is a specification describing the requirements for model transformation languages. There are different implementations of QVT, although many tools only realize some part of the specification. BOTL (Bidirectional Object-oriented Transformation Language) is a rule-based language for model transformations in an object-oriented setting, with a special focus on bidirectional transformations. ATL (ATLAS Transformation Language) is a hybrid of a declarative and imperative model transformation language specified both as a meta-model and as a textual concrete syntax. Although the main transformation is written in a declarative style, imperative constructs are provided for more complex mappings. The main advantage of graph transformation as described in the next chapter is its intuitive rule-based approach and its precise mathematical definition with a lot of applicable results available for the analysis of model transformations.

2.2 Graph Transformation

Graph transformation originally evolved in the late 1960s and early 1970s [PR69, Pra71, EPS73] as a reaction to shortcomings in the expressiveness of classical approaches to rewriting, such as Chomsky grammars and term rewriting, to deal with nonlinear structures. It combines the important concepts of graphs, grammars, and rewriting. A detailed presentation of various graph grammar approaches and application areas of graph transformation is given in the handbooks [Roz97, EEKR99, EKMR99].

The main idea of graph transformation is the rule-based modification of graphs, as shown in Fig. 2.1. The core of a rule p is a pair of graphs (L, R), called the left-hand side L and the right-hand side R. Applying the rule $p = (L, R)$ means finding a match of L in the source graph G and replacing L by R, leading to the target graph H of the graph transformation. The main technical problems are how to delete L from G and how to connect R with the remaining context leading to the target graph H. In fact, there are several different solutions how to handle these problems, leading to several different graph transformation approaches.

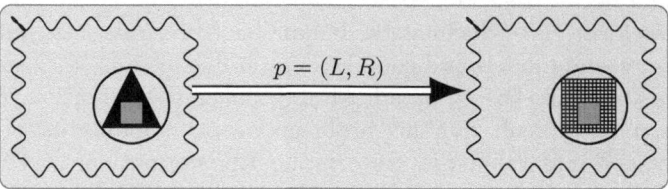

Figure 2.1: Rule-based modification of graphs

The main graph grammar and graph transformation approaches developed in the literature so far are, as presented in [Roz97]:

1. The *node label replacement approach*, developed mainly by Rozenberg, Engelfriet, and Janssens, allows a single node, as the left-hand side L, to be replaced by an arbitrary graph R. The connection of R with the context is determined by an embedding relation depending on node labels. For each removed dangling edge incident with the image of a node n in L and each node n' in R, a new edge (with the same label) incident with n' is established provided that (n, n') belongs to the embedding relation.

2. The *hyperedge replacement approach*, developed mainly by Habel, Kreowski, and Drewes, has as the left-hand side L a labeled hyperedge, which is replaced by an arbitrary hypergraph R with designated attachment nodes corresponding to the nodes of L. The gluing of R to the context at the corresponding attachment nodes leads to the target graph without using an additional embedding relation.

3. The *algebraic approach* is based on pushout constructions, where pushouts are used to model the gluing of graphs. In fact, there are two main variants of the algebraic approach, the double- and the single-pushout approach. In both cases, there is no additional embedding relation.

4. The *logical approach*, developed mainly by Courcelle and Bouderon, allows graph transformation and graph properties to be expressed in monadic second-order logic.

5. The *theory of 2-structures* was initiated by Rozenberg and Ehrenfeucht, as a framework for the decomposition and transformation of graphs.

6. The *programmed graph replacement approach* of Schürr combines the gluing and embedding aspects of graph transformation. Furthermore, it uses programs in order to control the nondeterministic choice of rule applications.

In this thesis, we use the double-pushout (DPO) approach, where pushouts are used to model the gluing of two graphs along a common subgraph. Intuitively, we use this common subgraph and add all other nodes and edges from both graphs. Two gluing constructions are used to model a graph transformation step, which is the reason for the name.

Roughly speaking, a rule is given by $p = (L, K, R)$, where L and R are the left- and right-hand side graphs and K is the common interface of L and R, i.e. their intersection. The left-hand side L represents the preconditions of the rule, while the right-hand side R describes the postconditions. K describes a graph part which has to exist to apply the rule, but is not changed. $L \backslash K$ describes the part which is to be deleted, and $R \backslash K$ describes the part to be created.

A direct graph transformation via a rule p is defined by first finding a match m of the left-hand side L in the current host graph G and then constructing the pushouts (1) and (2) in Fig. 2.2. For the construction of the first pushout, however, a gluing condition has to be satisfied which allows us to construct D such that G is the gluing of L and D via K. The second pushout means that H is the gluing of R and D via K. This means that a direct graph transformation $G \Rightarrow H$ in Fig. 2.2 consists of two gluing constructions, which are pushouts in the category of graphs and graph morphisms.

The algebraic approach to graph transformation is not restricted to (standard) graphs, but has been generalized to a large variety of different types of graphs and other kinds of high-level structures, such as labeled graphs, typed graphs, hypergraphs, attributed graphs, Petri nets, and algebraic specifications. This extension from graphs to high-level structures – in contrast to strings and trees, considered as low-level structures – was initiated

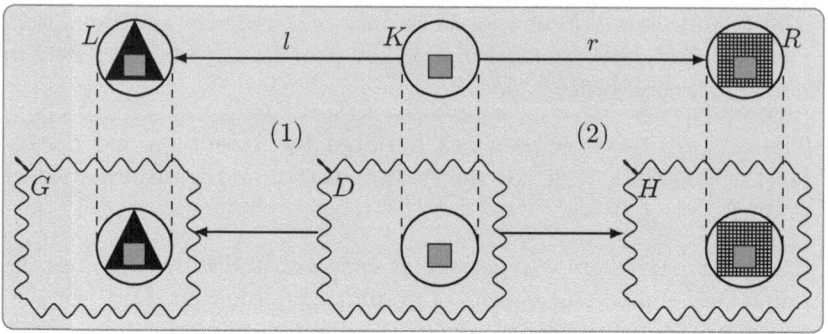

Figure 2.2: DPO graph transformation

in [EHKP91a, EHKP91b] leading to the theory of high-level replacement (HLR) systems based on category theory. In [EHPP04, EEPT06], the concept of high-level replacement systems was joined to that of adhesive categories introduced by Lack and Sobociński in [LS04], leading to the concept of $\mathcal{M}$-adhesive categories and systems (see Section 3.2). There are several interesting instantiations of $\mathcal{M}$-adhesive systems, including not only graph and typed graph transformation systems, but also hypergraph, Petri net, algebraic specification, and typed attributed graph transformation systems.

For graph transformations, many interesting results are available. The Local Church-Rosser Theorem allows us to apply two graph transformations $G \Rightarrow H_1$ via a rule p_1 and $G \Rightarrow H_2$ via a rule p_2 in an arbitrary order, provided that they are parallel independent. In this case they can also be applied in parallel, leading to a parallel graph transformation $G \Rightarrow H$ via the parallel rule $p_1 + p_2$. This result is called the Parallelism Theorem. If the transformations are not independent, the Concurrency Theorem provides a way to define a concurrent rule $p_1 *_E p_2$ which leads to a direct transformation $G \Rightarrow H$ even in the case of dependence. The Embedding and Extension Theorem handles the embedding of a whole transformation sequence into a larger context. In addition, the Local Confluence Theorem shows the local confluence of pairs of direct transformations provided that all critical pairs, which describe conflicts in a minimal context, fulfill a corresponding confluence property.

There are certain extensions of standard graph transformations to allow modeling on a reasonable level of abstraction and to ease the effort for the modeler. Some of them are explained in the following.

To further enhance the expressiveness of graph transformations, application conditions have been introduced. Negative application conditions forbid to apply a rule if a certain structure is present. As a generalization, nested application conditions [HP09], which are only called application conditions in this thesis, provide a more powerful mechanism to control the rule application. While application conditions are as powerful as first order logic on graphs, we can still obtain most of the interesting results available for graph transformations without application conditions for transformations with application conditions [EHL10a, EHL+10b], if certain additional properties hold (see Subsection 3.4.3).

Amalgamation [Tae96] is used for the parallel execution of synchronized rules. We can model an arbitrary number of parallel actions, which are somehow linked, at different places in a model, where the number of actions is not known beforehand. To model this situation with standard graph transformation, we had to apply the rules sequentially with an explicitly coded iteration, but this is neither natural nor efficient and often complicated. For example, for the firing semantics of Petri nets, with amalgamation we only need one rule where we can collect all pre- and post-places and execute the complete firing step. Without amalgamation, one would have to thoroughly remember which places have been already handled to remove or add the tokens place by place.

There are some other approaches dealing with the problem of similar parallel actions: in [GKM09], a collection operator, and in [HJE06], multi-objects are used for cloning the complete matches. In [RK09], an approach based on nested graph predicates is introduced which define a relationship between rules and matches. While nesting extends the expressiveness of these transformations, it is quite complicated to write and understand these predicates and it seems to be difficult to relate or integrate them to the theoretical results for graph transformation.

In [BFH87], the theory of amalgamation for the double-pushout approach has been developed on a set-theoretical basis for pairs of standard graph rules without application conditions. The Amalgamation Theorem is a generalization of the Parallelism Theorem [EK76] where rules do not have to be completely parallel independent, but only outside the synchronization parts. The concepts of amalgamation are applied to communication based systems and visual languages in [BFH87, TB94, HMTW95, Tae96, Erm06] and transferred to the single-pushout approach of graph transformation in [Löw93].

Graph transformation is not only useful for the definition of languages using a graph grammar, but also for the rule-based description of the semantics of a visual language. A semantical step within the model can be executed by one or more rule applications. For the definition of rule-based semantics of visual languages, known approaches use rule schemes leading to infinite many rules or complex control and helper structure. Using amalgamation for the specification of semantics leads to a more compact and understandable rule set.

2.3 Model Transformation Based on Graph Transformation

For model transformations based on graph transformation, typed graphs are used, often equipped with additional attributes leading to typed attributed graphs. A type graph defines the available types for nodes and edges of the graph models. There is a clear correspondence between meta-models and type graphs, where classes correspond to node types, associations to edge types, the conformity of a model to the meta-model corresponds to the existence of a typing morphism into the type graph, and OCL constraints correspond to graph constraints. To simplify the modeling of graph transformations, type graphs have been extended with node type inheritance [LBE+07]. Such a type graph with inheritance can be flattened leading to an equivalent flattened system, which can be analyzed using the standard results for graph transformation.

For model transformations based on graphs, the type graphs ATG_S of the source and ATG_T of the target language have to be integrated into a common type graph ATG. Starting the model transformation for a source model M_S typed over ATG_S, it is also typed over ATG. During the model transformation process, the intermediate models are typed over ATG. This type graph may contain not only ATG_S and ATG_T, but also additional types and relations which are needed for the transformation process only. The resulting model M_T is automatically typed over ATG. If it is not already typed over ATG_T, a restriction is used as the last step of the transformation to obtain a valid target model [EEPT06].

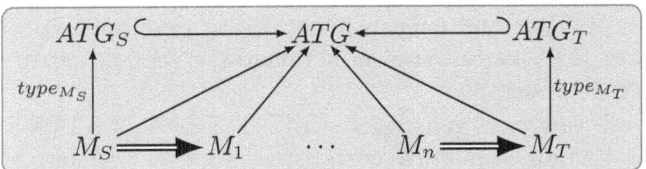

Different tools exist for the specification, simulation, and analysis of graph transformations. While some of them are general graph transformation tools like AGG [AGG] and GrGen [GBG+06], others are specifically designed for model transformations in software engineering based on graph transformation like VIATRA2 [VB07], GReAT [BNBK06], and Fujaba [GZ06].

Verifying model transformations is as difficult as verifying compilers for high-level languages. But the knowledge of the domain-specific nature of the models may help to perform verification with reasonable effort. In [Erm09], a conceptual overview on model transformations based on graph transformations is given, especially regarding research activities and future work for the analysis and verification of model transformations.

For the verification of model transformations, some results for syntactical correctness are available. Using the above mechanism, the correct typing of the target model is implied by the graph transformation approach. Moreover, for the satisfaction of certain structural constraints, these can be translated to application conditions to ensure that all derived target models respect the constraints [TR05].

For specific model transformations, functional behavior can be guaranteed [EEEP07]. In general, functional behavior can be obtained for graph transformations showing termination and local confluence of the transformations. For a given set of rules, sometimes arranged in layers or equipped with a more complex control structure, termination checks if there is no infinite transformation sequence. Together with local confluence, termination leads to global confluence of a graph transformation system. In [Plu95], it is shown that termination is undecidable in general. Nevertheless, termination can be ensured if the rules can be structured into layers, which are either deleting or non-deleting with special negative application conditions [EEL+05]. Extending this result in [VVE+06], the rules are translated into a Petri net, where the analysis of this net leads to a sufficient criterion for the termination of the transformations. Also the restriction of the matches to be injective helps to determine termination [LPE07]. Critical pair analysis is used to determine local confluence. Although critical pairs can be computed, the main task of deciding their confluence has to be done by hand, which can be a difficult and lengthy task. Using essential critical pairs reduces this effort [LEO08] but still an automatic or semi-automatic decision process would be preferable.

Some approaches use test case generation [BKS04, FSB04, EKTW06, KA06] to show syntactical and semantical correctness of model transformations, but for models it is even harder to define suitable test cases then for code, since it is not clear which criteria represent good test cases. Especially to define test cases for constraints is a difficult task, and the evaluation of the results, i. e. if a test is passed or failed, is difficult to be decided automatically.

Also model checking can be used for the analysis and verification of model transformations. In [RSV04], two different approaches are compared: translating graphs and rules into a traditional model checker suits more static problems, while model checking directly on the level of graphs and rules is better for dynamic systems. In [VP03], a simple model transformation from statecharts to Petri nets is analyzed with model checking, but the state explosion problem limits the practical applicability of this approach.

Moreover, certification as used for code generation [DF05] may be a chance to verify at least certain model transformations. In this case, semantical correctness is only analyzed and certified for the actual model on which the certificate depends. Different certification methods are analyzed in [KN07, NK08b, NK08a], mainly certification via bisimilarity and by semantic anchoring. The application to different case studies shows that even for simple models and model transformations certification is quite costly and still difficult to prove.

In [EE08], a first step is made towards the semantical correctness of model transformations, where both source and target models are equipped with an operational semantics based on graph transformations. The rules of the source semantics are transformed by translation rules to semantical rules on the target model and compared to the defined semantics. This approach is only successful under strict preconditions restricting the translation of the source semantics. There, a railway system is simulated by runs in a corresponding Petri net, where the semantical rules of the railway system are translated and analyzed to be correct.

The semantical correctness of a model transformation from a class of automata to PLC-code using triple graph grammars and specified in the tool FUJABA is proven in [GGL$^+$06] utilizing the theorem prover Isabelle/HOL. This work is based on [Lei06], where it is shown that the resulting source and target rules lead to semantical equivalence, i. e. if a source model S and a target model T are semantically correct then also the models S' and T' are semantically correct, where S' and T' can be derived from S and T using the source and target part of the same rule and some induced match. This result has to be shown for each of the triple rules which is a very difficult and lengthy task and can only be done semi-automatically, where a lot of manual interaction is necessary.

Two different approaches are used in [EKR$^+$08, HKR$^+$10], where semantical correctness is shown by weak bisimilarity of the corresponding transition systems of the semantics. As an example, a model transformation from a very simplified version of activity diagrams to TAAL, a textual language, is analyzed, where both languages are equipped with a formal semantics defined by graph transformation. The first proof strategy uses triple graph grammars and an explicit bisimulation relation, while the second one is based on an in-situ model transformations and an extension of the operational semantics using borrowed contexts. Even for this simple example the proofs are quite difficult.

For exogenous model transformations, triple graphs and triple transformations are a common and successful approach [Sch94, KS06]. Within a triple graph, both the source and target models are stored, together with some connections between them. A model transformation can be obtained from the triple rules, which create both source and target models together. These forward and backward transformations can be deduced automatically, requiring only one description for both directions. This eases the specification of bidirectional model transformations. In [KS06] it is shown how to split a triple rule tr into a source rule tr_S, describing the changes in the source graph, and a forward rule tr_F, describing the corresponding update of the target graph. It follows that also transformations can be split up into a source and forward transformation. As a result, the forward rules specify the actual forward model transformation.

These results have been extended in [EEE$^+$07] to show that under the condition of a source consistent forward transformation the bidirectional model transformations are information preserving. Source consistency of a sequence $G_1 \xRightarrow{tr_F^*} G_2$ means that G_1 is constructed by the application of the source rules corresponding to the forward rules in the forward transformation. In [EHS09], triple rules have been enriched with negative application conditions to enhance the expressiveness of the triple transformations. If the negative application conditions are source-target application conditions,

i. e. defined either on the source or the target component, all the results can be transferred to this extension [EHS09].

In [LG08], triple patterns are defined which are used similarly to constraints and specify model transformations in a declarative way, where positive and negative patterns declare what is allowed and forbidden for the transformation. Triple graphs are extended to triple algebras, triple patterns, and transformation patterns, which are more constructive than triple patterns, in [OW09]. For the verification of such a model transformation, a verification specification of positive patterns is defined that characterizes correctness properties. A transformation specification TSP is then correct w. r. t. such a verification specification VSP if $A \in TSP$ implies that $A \in VSP$. Minimal gluings of transformation patterns are analyzed to ensure the correctness. This approach works well for the analysis of syntactical correctness, but is difficult to adopt for semantical correctness.

3 $\mathcal{M}$-Adhesive Transformation Systems

$\mathcal{M}$-adhesive categories constitute a powerful framework for the definition of transformations. The double–pushout approach, which is based on categorical constructions, is a suitable description of transformations leading to a great number of results as the Local Church-Rosser, Parallelism, Concurrency, Embedding, Extension, and Local Confluence Theorems. Yet the rules and transformations themselves are easy and intuitively to understand.

In this chapter, we introduce the main theory of $\mathcal{M}$-adhesive categories and $\mathcal{M}$-adhesive transformation systems. In Section 3.1, we give a short introduction to graphs, typed graphs, and typed attributed graphs as used throughout this thesis. Then we introduce $\mathcal{M}$-adhesive categories in Section 3.2. In addition to [EEPT06], we extend the Construction Theorem to general comma categories, which cover many categorical constructions as, for example, Petri nets. We show that some additional properties stated for $\mathcal{M}$-adhesive categories and needed for the transformation framework are preserved via the constructions. In Section 3.3, we give explicit proofs that certain categories of algebraic high-level schemas, nets, and net systems, which are extensions of Petri nets combining these with actual data elements, are indeed $\mathcal{M}$-adhesive categories. In Section 3.4, we introduce transformations with application conditions in $\mathcal{M}$-adhesive transformation systems and give an overview of various analysis results valid in this framework.

In this chapter, only a short overview over the used notions and categorical terms is given. We expect the reader to be familiar with category theory, see [EEPT06] for an overview, and, for example, [Mac71, AHS90] for more thorough introductions. Moreover, only a short outline of the theory of $\mathcal{M}$-adhesive transformation systems is given here. For the entire theory with all definitions, theorems, proofs, and examples see [EEPT06, EP06, PE07].

3.1 Graphs, Typed Graphs, and Typed Attributed Graphs

Graphs and graph-like structures are the main basis for (visual) models. Basically, a graph consists of nodes, also called vertices, and edges, which link two nodes. Here, we consider graphs which may have parallel edges as well as loops. A graph morphism then maps the nodes and edges of the domain graph to these of the codomain graph such that the source and target nodes of each edge are preserved by the mapping.

Definition 3.1 (Graph and graph morphism)
A *graph* $G = (V_G, E_G, s_G, t_G)$ consists of a set V_G of nodes, a set E_G of edges, and two functions $s_G, t_G : E_G \to V_G$ mapping to each edge its source and target node.

Given graphs G_1 and G_2, a *graph morphism* $f : G_1 \to$ G_2, $f = (f_V, f_E)$ consists of two functions $f_V : V_{G_1} \to$ V_{G_2}, $f_E : E_{G_1} \to E_{G_2}$ such that $s_{G_2} \circ f_E = f_V \circ s_{G_1}$ and $t_{G_2} \circ f_E = f_V \circ t_{G_1}$.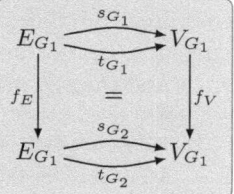

Graphs and graph morphisms form the category **Graphs**, together with the component-wise compositions and identities.

An important extension of plain graphs is the introduction of types. A type graph defines a node type alphabet as well as an edge type alphabet, which can be used to assign a type to each element of a graph. This typing is done by a graph morphism into the type graph. Type graph morphisms then have to preserve the typing.

Definition 3.2 (Typed graph and typed graph morphism)
A *type graph* is a distinguished graph TG.

Given a type graph TG, a tuple $G^T = (G, type_G)$ of a graph G and a graph morphism $type_G : G \to TG$ is called a *typed graph*.

Given typed graphs G_1^T and G_2^T, a *typed graph morphism* $f : G_1^T \to G_2^T$ is a graph morphism $f : G_1 \to G_2$ such that $type_{G_2} \circ f = type_{G_1}$.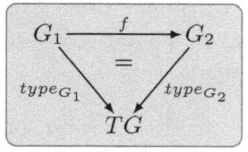

Given a type graph TG, typed graphs and typed graph morphisms form the category **Graphs$_{TG}$**, together with the component-wise compositions and identities.

If the typing is clear in the context, we may not explicitly mention it and consider only the typed graph G with implicit typing $type_G$.

The main idea of an attributed graph is that one has an underlying data structure, given by an algebra, such that nodes and edges of a graph may carry attribute values. For the formal definition, these attributes are represented by edges into the corresponding data domain, which is given by a node set. An attributed graph is based on an E-graph that has, in addition to the standard graph nodes and edges, a set of data nodes as well as node and edge attribute edges.

Definition 3.3 (Attributed graph and attributed graph morphism)
An *E-graph* $G^E = (V_G^G, V_D^G, E_G^G, E_{NA}^G, E_{EA}^G, (s_i^G, t_i^G)_{i \in \{G, NA, EA\}})$ consists of graph nodes V_G^G, data nodes V_D^G, graph edges E_G^G, node attribute edges E_{NA}^G, and edge attribute edges E_{EA}^G, according to the following signature.

For E-graphs G_1^E and G_2^E, an *E-graph morphism* $f : G_1^E \to G_2^E$ is a tuple $f = ((f_{V_i} : V_i^{G_1} \to V_i^{G_2})_{i \in \{G, D\}}, (f_{E_j} : E_j^{G_1} \to E_j^{G_2})_{j \in \{G, NA, EA\}})$ such that f commutes with all source and target functions.

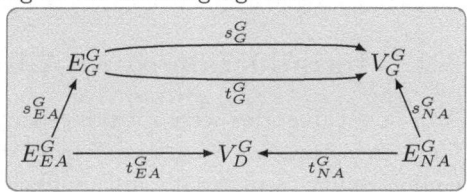

An *attributed graph* G over a data signature $DSIG = (S_D, OP_D)$ with attribute value sorts $S_D' \subseteq S_D$ is given by $G = (G^E, D_G)$, where G^E is an E-graph and D_G is a $DSIG$-algebra such that $\cup_{s \in S_D'} D_{G,s} = V_D^G$.

For attributed graphs $G_1 = (G_1^E, D_{G_1})$ and $G_2 = (G_2^E, D_{G_2})$, an *attributed graph morphism* $f : G_1 \to G_2$ is a pair $f = (f_G, f_D)$ with an E-graph morphism $f_G : G_1^E \to G_2^E$ and an algebra homomorphism $f_D : D_{G_1} \to D_{G_2}$ such that $f_{G, V_D}(x) = f_{D,s}(x)$ for all $x \in D_{G_1, s}$, $s \in S_D'$.

Attributed graphs and attributed graph morphisms form the category **AGraphs**, together with the component-wise compositions and identities.

As for standard typed graphs, an attributed type graph defines a set of types which can be used to assign types to the nodes and edges of an attributed graph. The typing itself is done by an attributed graph morphism between the attributed graph and the attributed type graph.

Definition 3.4 (Typed attributed graph and morphism)
An *attributed type graph* is a distinguished attributed graph $ATG = (TG, Z)$, where Z is the final $DSIG$-algebra.

A tuple $G^T = (G, type)$ of an attributed graph G together with an attributed graph morphism $type : G \to ATG$ is then called a *typed attributed graph*.

Given typed attributed graphs $G_1^T = (G_1, type_1)$ and $G_2^T = (G_2, type_2)$, a *typed attributed graph morphism* $f : G_1^T \to G_2^T$ is a graph morphism $f : G_1 \to G_2$ such that $type_2 \circ f = type_1$.

For a given attributed type graph, typed attributed graphs and typed attributed graph morphisms form the category **AGraphs$_{ATG}$**, together with the component-wise compositions and identities.

3.2 $\mathcal{M}$-Adhesive Categories

For the transformation of not only graphs, but also high-level structures as Petri nets and algebraic specifications, high-level replacement (HLR) categories were established in [EHKP91a, EHKP91b], which require a list of so-called *HLR properties* to hold. They were based on a morphism class $\mathcal{M}$ used for the rule morphisms. This framework allowed a rich theory of transformations for all HLR categories, but the HLR properties were difficult and lengthy to verify for each category.

3.2.1 Introduction to $\mathcal{M}$-Adhesive Categories

Adhesive categories were introduced in [LS04] as a categorical framework for deriving process congruences from reaction rules. They require a certain compatibility of pushouts and pullbacks, called the *van Kampen property*, for pushouts along monomorphisms in the considered category. Later, they were extended to quasiadhesive categories in [JLS07] where the van Kampen property has to hold only for pushouts along regular monomorphisms.

Adhesive categories behave well also for transformations, but interesting categories as typed attributed graphs are neither an adhesive nor a quasiadhesive category. Combining adhesive and HLR categories lead to adhesive HLR categories in [EHPP04, EPT04], where a subclass $\mathcal{M}$ of monomorphisms is considered and only pushouts over $\mathcal{M}$-morphisms have to fulfill the van Kampen property. They were slightly extended to weak adhesive HLR categories in [EEPT06], where a weaker version of the van Kampen property is sufficient to show the main results of graph and HLR transformations also for transformations in weak adhesive HLR categories. Not only many kinds of graphs, but also Petri nets and algebraic high-level nets are weak adhesive HLR categories which allows to apply the theory to all these kinds of structures. In [EEPT06], the main theory including all the proofs for transformations in weak adhesive HLR categories can be found, while a nice introduction including motivation and examples for all the results is given in [PE07].

In this thesis, for simplicity and easier differentiation, we call weak adhesive HLR categories $\mathcal{M}$-adhesive categories. Their main property is the van Kampen property, which is a special compatibility of pushouts and pullbacks in a commutative cube. The idea of a van Kampen square is that of a pushout which is stable under pullbacks, and, vice versa, that pullbacks are stable under combined pushouts and pullbacks.

Definition 3.5 (Van Kampen square)
A commutative cube (2) with pushout (1) in the bottom face and where the back faces are pullbacks fulfills the *van Kampen property* if the following statement holds: the top face is a pushout if and only if the front faces are pullbacks.

A pushout (1) is a *van Kampen square* if the van Kampen property holds for all commutative cubes (2) with (1) in the bottom face.

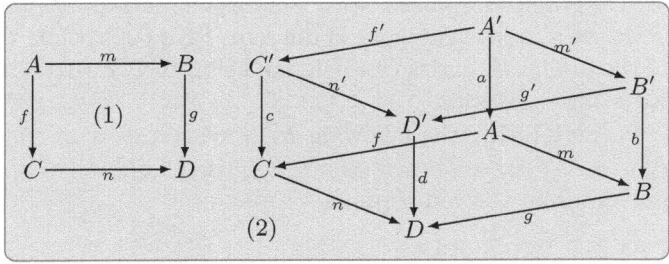

Given a morphism class $\mathcal{M}$, a pushout (1) with $m \in \mathcal{M}$ is an *$\mathcal{M}$-van Kampen square* if the van Kampen property holds for all commutative cubes (2) with (1) in the bottom face and $f \in \mathcal{M}$ or $b, c, d \in \mathcal{M}$.

It might be expected that, at least in the category **Sets**, every pushout is a van Kampen square. Unfortunately, this is not true, but at least pushouts along monomorphisms are van Kampen squares in **Sets** and several other categories.

For an $\mathcal{M}$-adhesive category, we consider a category **C** together with a morphism class $\mathcal{M}$ of monomorphisms. We require pushouts along $\mathcal{M}$-morphisms to be $\mathcal{M}$-van Kampen squares, along with some rather technical conditions for the morphism class $\mathcal{M}$ which are needed to ensure compatibility of $\mathcal{M}$ with pushouts and pullbacks.

Definition 3.6 ($\mathcal{M}$-adhesive category)
A category **C** with a morphism class $\mathcal{M}$ is called an *$\mathcal{M}$-adhesive category* if:

1. $\mathcal{M}$ is a class of monomorphisms closed under isomorphisms, composition ($f : A \to B \in \mathcal{M}, g : B \to C \in \mathcal{M} \Rightarrow g \circ f \in \mathcal{M}$), and decomposition ($g \circ f \in \mathcal{M}, g \in \mathcal{M} \Rightarrow f \in \mathcal{M}$).
2. **C** has pushouts and pullbacks along $\mathcal{M}$-morphisms, and $\mathcal{M}$-morphisms are closed under pushouts and pullbacks.
3. Pushouts in **C** along $\mathcal{M}$-morphisms are $\mathcal{M}$-van Kampen squares.

Examples for $\mathcal{M}$-adhesive categories are the categories **Sets** of sets, **Graphs** of graphs, **Graphs$_{TG}$** of typed graphs, **Hypergraphs** of hypergraphs, **ElemNets** of elementary Petri nets, and **PTNets** of place/transition nets, all together with the class $\mathcal{M}$ of injective morphisms, as well as the category **Specs** of algebraic specifications with the class $\mathcal{M}_{strict}$ of strict injective specification morphisms, the category **PTSys** of place/transition systems with the class $\mathcal{M}_{strict}$ of strict morphisms, and the category **AGraphs$_{\textbf{ATG}}$** of typed attributed graphs with the class $\mathcal{M}_{D-iso}$ of injective graph morphisms with isomorphic data part. The proof that **Sets** is an $\mathcal{M}$-adhesive category is done in [EEPT06], while the proofs for most of the other categories can be done using the Construction Theorem in the following subsection.

In [EHKP91b], the following *HLR properties* were required for HLR categories. All these properties are valid in $\mathcal{M}$-adhesive categories and can be proven using the van Kampen property.

Fact 3.7

The following properties hold in $\mathcal{M}$-adhesive categories:

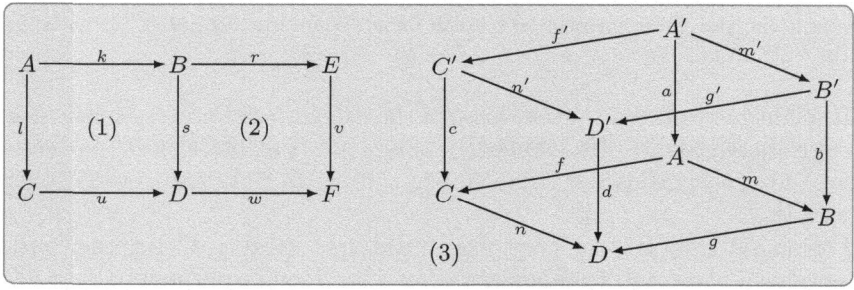

1. *Pushouts along $\mathcal{M}$-morphisms are pullbacks.* Given the above pushout (1) with $k \in \mathcal{M}$, then (1) is also a pullback.

2. *$\mathcal{M}$-pushout–pullback decomposition.* Given the above commutative diagram, where (1) + (2) is a pushout, (2) is a pullback, $w \in \mathcal{M}$, and ($l \in \mathcal{M}$ or $k \in \mathcal{M}$), then (1) and (2) are pushouts and also pullbacks.

3. *Cube pushout–pullback property.* Given the above commutative cube (3), where all morphisms in the top and bottom faces are $\mathcal{M}$-morphisms, the top face is a pullback, and the front faces are pushouts, then the following statement holds: the bottom face is a pullback if and only if the back faces of the cube are pushouts:

4. *Uniqueness of pushout complements.* Given $k : A \to B \in \mathcal{M}$ and $s : B \to D$, then there is, up to isomorphism, at most one C with $l : A \to C$ and $u : C \to D$ such that (1) is a pushout.

PROOF See [EEPT06].

For the main results of transformations in $\mathcal{M}$-adhesive categories we need some additional properties, which are collected in the following.

Definition 3.8 (Additional properties)
Given an $\mathcal{M}$-adhesive category $(\mathbf{C}, \mathcal{M})$, it fulfills the additional properties, if all of the following items hold:

1. *Binary coproducts:* $\mathbf{C}$ has binary coproducts.

2. *Epi–$\mathcal{M}$ factorization:* For each $f : A \to B$ there is a factorization over an epimorphism $e : A \to K$ and $m : K \to B \in \mathcal{M}$ such that $m \circ e = f$, and this factorization is unique up to isomorphism.

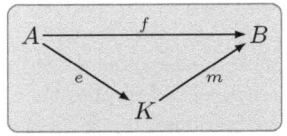

3. *$\mathcal{E}'$–$\mathcal{M}'$ pair factorization:* Given a morphism class $\mathcal{M}'$ and a class of morphism pairs with common codomain $\mathcal{E}'$, for each pair of morphisms $f_1 : A_1 \to B$, $f_2 : A_2 \to B$ there is a factorization over $e_1 : A_1 \to K$, $e_2 : A_2 \to K$, $m : K \to B$ with $(e_1, e_2) \in \mathcal{E}'$ and $m \in \mathcal{M}'$ such that $m \circ e_1 = f_1$ and $m \circ e_2 = f_2$

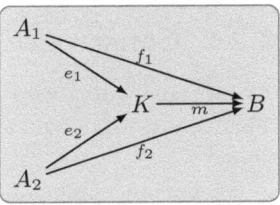

4. *Initial pushouts over $\mathcal{M}'$:* Given a morphism class $\mathcal{M}'$, for each $f : A \to D \in \mathcal{M}'$ there exists an initial pushout (1)

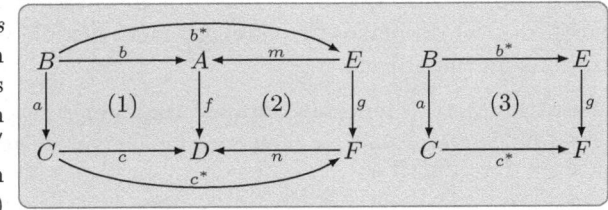

with $b, c \in \mathcal{M}$. (1) is an initial pushout if the following condition holds: for all pushouts (2) with $m, n \in \mathcal{M}$ there exist unique morphisms $b^*, c^* \in \mathcal{M}$ such that $m \circ b^* = b$, $n \circ c^* = c$, and (3) is a pushout.

5. *Effective pushouts:* Given a pullback (4) and a pushout (5) with all morphisms being $\mathcal{M}$-morphisms, then also the induced morphism $e : D \to D'$ is an $\mathcal{M}$-morphism.

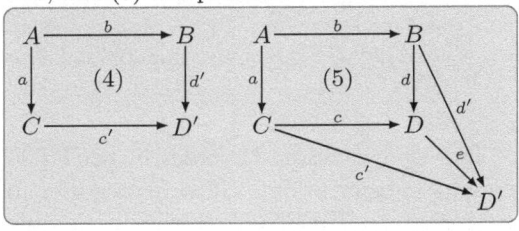

Remark 3.9
In [LS05], it is shown that in the setting of effective pushouts, the morphism e has to be a monomorphism. But up to now we were not able to show that it is actually an $\mathcal{M}$-morphism if the class $\mathcal{M}$ does not contain all monomorphisms.

As shown in [EHL10a], if
$(\mathbf{C}, \mathcal{M})$ has binary coproducts then these are compat-
ible with $\mathcal{M}$, which means
that $f, g \in \mathcal{M}$ implies $f +$
$g \in \mathcal{M}$: For $f : A \to B$,

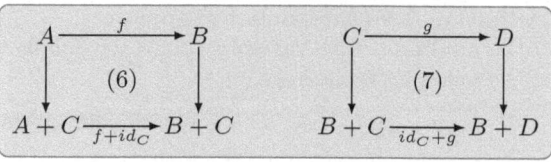

$g : C \to D$, pushout (6) with $f \in \mathcal{M}$ implies that $f + id_C \in \mathcal{M}$ and pushout (7)
with $g \in \mathcal{M}$ implies that $id_B + g \in \mathcal{M}$. Thus, also $f + g = (f + id) \circ (id + g) \in \mathcal{M}$
by composition of $\mathcal{M}$-morphisms.

3.2.2 Construction of $\mathcal{M}$-Adhesive Categories

$\mathcal{M}$-adhesive categories are closed under different categorical constructions.
This means that we can construct new $\mathcal{M}$-adhesive categories from given
ones.

We use an extension of comma categories [Pra07], where we loosen the
restrictions on the domain of the functors compared to standard comma
categories, which makes the category more flexible to describe different operations on the objects.

Definition 3.10 (General comma category)
Given index sets $\mathcal{I}$ and $\mathcal{J}$, categories $\mathbf{C}_j$ for $j \in \mathcal{J}$ and $\mathbf{X}_i$ for $i \in \mathcal{I}$, and for
each $i \in \mathcal{I}$ two functors $F_i : \mathbf{C}_{k_i} \to \mathbf{X}_i$, $G_i : \mathbf{C}_{\ell_i} \to \mathbf{X}_i$ with $k_i, \ell_i \in \mathcal{J}$, then the
general comma category $GComCat((\mathbf{C}_j)_{j \in \mathcal{J}}, (F_i, G_i)_{i \in \mathcal{I}}; \mathcal{I}, \mathcal{J})$ is defined by

- objects $((A_j \in \mathbf{C}_j)_{j \in \mathcal{J}}, (op_i)_{i \in \mathcal{I}})$, where $op_i :$
  $F_i(A_{k_i}) \to G_i(A_{\ell_i})$ is a morphism in $\mathbf{X}_i$,
- morphisms $h : ((A_j), (op_i)) \to ((A'_j), (op'_i))$
  as tuples $h = ((h_j : A_j \to A'_j)_{j \in \mathcal{J}})$ such that
  for all $i \in \mathcal{I}$ we have that $op'_i \circ F_i(h_{k_i}) = G_i(h_{\ell_i}) \circ op_i$.

$$F_i(A_{k_i}) \xrightarrow{\ op_i\ } G_i(A_{\ell_i})$$
$$\downarrow{\scriptstyle F_i(h_{k_i})} \qquad {\scriptstyle G_i(h_{\ell_i})}\downarrow$$
$$F_i(A'_{k_i}) \xrightarrow{\ op'_i\ } G_i(A'_{\ell_i})$$

The Construction Theorem in [EEPT06] has been extended to general
comma categories and full subcategories in [Pra07], which directly implies
the results in [EEPT06]. Basically, it holds that, under some consistency
properties, if the underlying categories are $\mathcal{M}$-adhesive categories so are the
constructed ones.

Theorem 3.11 (Construction Theorem)
If $(\mathbf{C}, \mathcal{M}_1)$, $(\mathbf{D}, \mathcal{M}_2)$, and $(\mathbf{C}_j, \mathcal{M}_j)$ for $j \in \mathcal{J}$ are $\mathcal{M}$-adhesive categories, then
also the following categories are $\mathcal{M}$-adhesive categories:

1. the *general comma category* $(\mathbf{G}, (\times_{j \in \mathcal{J}} \mathcal{M}_j) \cap Mor_{\mathbf{G}})$ with $\mathbf{G} =$
   $GComCat((\mathbf{C}_j)_{j \in \mathcal{J}}, (F_i, G_i)_{i \in \mathcal{I}}; \mathcal{I}, \mathcal{J})$, where for all $i \in \mathcal{I}$ F_i preserves

pushouts along $\mathcal{M}_{k_i}$-morphisms and G_i preserves pullbacks along $\mathcal{M}_{\ell_i}$-morphisms,

2. any *full subcategory* $(\mathbf{C}', \mathcal{M}_1|_{\mathbf{C}'})$ of $\mathbf{C}$, where pushouts and pullbacks along $\mathcal{M}_1$ are created and reflected by the inclusion functor,

3. the *comma category* $(\mathbf{F}, (\mathcal{M}_1 \times \mathcal{M}_2) \cap Mor_{\mathbf{F}})$, with $\mathbf{F} = ComCat(F, G; \mathcal{I})$, where $F : \mathbf{C} \to \mathbf{X}$ preserves pushouts along $\mathcal{M}_1$-morphisms and $G : \mathbf{D} \to \mathbf{X}$ preserves pullbacks along $\mathcal{M}_2$-morphisms,

4. the *product category* $(\mathbf{C} \times \mathbf{D}, \mathcal{M}_1 \times \mathcal{M}_2)$,

5. the *slice category* $(\mathbf{C} \backslash X, \mathcal{M}_1 \cap Mor_{\mathbf{C} \backslash X})$,

6. the *coslice category* $(X \backslash \mathbf{C}, \mathcal{M}_1 \cap Mor_{X \backslash \mathbf{C}})$,

7. the *functor category* $([\mathbf{X}, \mathbf{C}], \mathcal{M}_1\text{-functor transformations})$.

PROOF For the general comma category, it is easy to show that $\mathcal{M}$ is a class of monomorphisms closed under isomorphisms, composition, and decomposition since this holds for all components $\mathcal{M}_j$.

Pushouts along $\mathcal{M}$-morphisms are constructed component-wise in the underlying categories as shown in Lemma A.1. The pushout object is the component-wise pushout object, where the operations are uniquely defined using the property that F_i preserves pushouts along $\mathcal{M}_{k_i}$-morphisms.

Analogously, pullbacks along $\mathcal{M}$-morphisms are constructed component-wise, where the operations of the pullback object are uniquely defined using the property that G_i preserves pullbacks along $\mathcal{M}_{\ell_i}$-morphisms.

The $\mathcal{M}$-van Kampen property follows, since in a proper cube, all pushouts and pullbacks can be decomposed leading to proper cubes in the underlying categories, where the $\mathcal{M}$-van Kampen property holds. The subsequent recomposition yields the $\mathcal{M}$-van Kampen property for the general comma category.

For a full subcategory $\mathbf{C}'$ of $\mathbf{C}$ define $\mathcal{M}' = \mathcal{M}_1|_{\mathbf{C}'}$. By reflection, pushouts and pullbacks along $\mathcal{M}'$-morphisms in $\mathbf{C}'$ exist. Obviously, $\mathcal{M}'$ is a class of monomorphisms with the required properties. Since we only restrict the objects and morphisms, the $\mathcal{M}$-van Kampen property is inherited from $\mathbf{C}$.

As shown in Lemmas A.2 and A.3, product, slice, coslice, and comma categories are instantiations of general comma categories. Obviously, the final category $\mathbf{1}$ is an $\mathcal{M}$-adhesive category and the functors $!_{\mathbf{C}}$, $!_{\mathbf{D}}$, $id_{\mathbf{C}}$, and X preserve pushouts and pullbacks. Thus, the proposition follows directly from the general comma category for these constructions.

The proof for the functor category is explicitly given in [EEPT06].

3.2.3 Preservation of Additional Properties via Constructions

We now analyze how far also the additional properties for $\mathcal{M}$-adhesive categories defined in Def. 3.8 can be obtained from the categorical constructions if the underlying $\mathcal{M}$-adhesive categories fulfill these properties. This work is based on [PEL08] and extended to general comma categories and subcategories in this thesis. Here, we only state and prove the results, for examples see [PEL08].

3.2.3.1 Binary Coproducts

In most cases, binary coproducts can be constructed in the underlying categories, with some compatibility requirements for the preservation of binary coproducts. Note that we do not have to analyze the compatibility of binary coproducts with $\mathcal{M}$, as done in [PEL08], since this is a general result in $\mathcal{M}$-adhesive categories as shown in Rem. 3.9.

Fact 3.12
If the $\mathcal{M}$-adhesive categories $(\mathbf{C}, \mathcal{M}_1)$, $(\mathbf{D}, \mathcal{M}_2)$, and $(\mathbf{C}_j, \mathcal{M}_j)$ for $j \in \mathcal{J}$ have binary coproducts then also the following $\mathcal{M}$-adhesive categories have binary coproducts:

1. the *general comma category* $(\mathbf{G}, (\times_{j \in \mathcal{J}} \mathcal{M}_j) \cap Mor_{\mathbf{G}})$, if for all $i \in \mathcal{I}$ F_i preserves binary coproducts,

2. any *full subcategory* $(\mathbf{C}', \mathcal{M}_1|_{\mathbf{C}'})$ of $\mathbf{C}$, if
   (i) the inclusion functor reflects binary coproducts or
   (ii) $\mathbf{C}'$ has an initial object I and, in addition, we have general pushouts in $\mathbf{C}'$ or $i_A : I \to A \in \mathcal{M}$ for all $A \in \mathbf{C}'$,

3. the *comma category* $(\mathbf{F}, (\mathcal{M}_1 \times \mathcal{M}_2) \cap Mor_{\mathbf{F}})$, if $F : \mathbf{C} \to \mathbf{X}$ preserves binary coproducts,

4. the *product category* $(\mathbf{C} \times \mathbf{D}, \mathcal{M}_1 \times \mathcal{M}_2)$,

5. the *slice category* $(\mathbf{C} \backslash X, \mathcal{M}_1 \cap Mor_{\mathbf{C} \backslash X})$,

6. the *coslice category* $(X \backslash \mathbf{C}, \mathcal{M}_1 \cap Mor_{X \backslash \mathbf{C}})$, if $\mathbf{C}$ has general pushouts,

7. the *functor category* $([\mathbf{X}, \mathbf{C}], \mathcal{M}_1\text{-functor transformations})$.

PROOF   1. If $\mathbf{C}_j$ has binary coproducts for all $j \in \mathcal{J}$ and F_i preserves binary coproducts for all $i \in \mathcal{I}$, then the coproduct of two objects $A = ((A_j), (op_i^A))$ and $B = ((B_j), (op_i^B))$ in $\mathbf{G}$ is the object $A + B = ((A_j + B_j), (op_i^{A+B}))$, where op_i^{A+B} is the unique morphism induced by $G_i(i_{A_{\ell_i}}) \circ$

op_i^A and $G_i(i_{B_{\ell_i}}) \circ op_i^B$. If also G_i preserves coproducts then $op_i^{A+B} = op_i^A + op_i^B$.

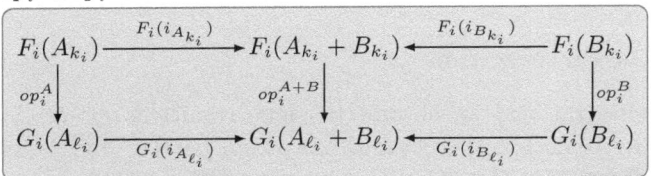

2. If the inclusion functor reflects binary coproducts this is obvious. Otherwise, if we have an initial object I, given $A, B \in \mathbf{C}'$ we can construct the pushout over $i_A : I \to A$, $i_B : I \to B$, which exists because $i_A, i_B \in \mathcal{M}$ or due to general pushouts. In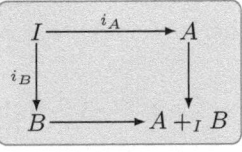
this case, the pushout object is also the coproduct of A and B, because for any object in comparison to the coproduct the morphisms agree via i_A and i_B on I, and the constructed pushout induces also the coproduct morphism.

3. This follows directly from Item 1, since the comma category is an instantiation of general comma categories. The coproduct of objects $(A_1, A_2, (op_i^A))$ and $(B_1, B_2, (op_i^B))$ of the comma category is the object $A + B = (A_1 + B_1, A_2 + B_2, op_i^{A+B})$.

4. Since $\mathbf{C} \times \mathbf{D} \cong ComCat(!_\mathbf{C} : \mathbf{C} \to \mathbf{1}, !_\mathbf{D} : \mathbf{D} \to \mathbf{1}, \varnothing)$ (see Lemma A.3) and $!_\mathbf{C}$ preserves coproducts this follows from Item 3. The coproduct of objects (A_1, A_2) and (B_1, B_2) of the product category is the component-wise coproduct $(A_1 + B_1, A_2 + B_2)$ in $\mathbf{C}$ and $\mathbf{D}$, respectively.

5. Since $\mathbf{C} \backslash X \cong ComCat(id_\mathbf{C} : \mathbf{C} \to \mathbf{C}, X : \mathbf{1} \to \mathbf{C}, \{1\})$ (see Lemma A.3) and $id_\mathbf{C}$ preserves coproducts this follows from Item 3. In the slice category, the coproduct of (A, a') and (B, b') is the ob-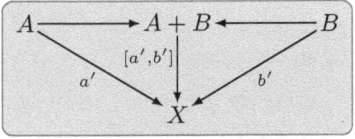
ject $(A + B, [a', b'])$ which consists of the coproduct $A + B$ in $\mathbf{C}$ together with the morphism $[a', b'] : A + B \to X$ induced by a' and b'.

6. If $\mathbf{C}$ has general pushouts, given two objects (A, a') and (B, b') in $X \backslash \mathbf{C}$ we construct the pushout over a' and b' in $\mathbf{C}$. The coproduct of (A, a') and (B, b') is the pushout object $A +_X B$ together with the coslice morphism $b \circ a' = a \circ b'$. For any object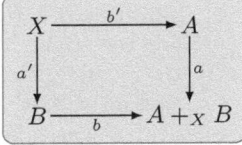
(C, c') in comparison to the coproduct, the coslice morphism c' ensures that the morphisms agree via a' and b' in X such that the pushout also induces the coproduct morphism.

7. If $\mathbf{C}$ has binary coproducts, the coproduct of two functors $A, B : \mathbf{X} \to \mathbf{C}$ in $[\mathbf{X}, \mathbf{C}]$ is the component-wise coproduct functor $A + B$ with $A + B(x) =$

$A(x)+B(x)$ for an object $x \in \mathbf{X}$ and $A+B(h) = A(h)+B(h)$ for a morphism $h \in \mathbf{X}$.

3.2.3.2 Epi–$\mathcal{M}$ Factorization

For Epi–$\mathcal{M}$ factorizations, we obtain the same results as for $\mathcal{E}'$–$\mathcal{M}'$ pair factorizations by replacing the class of morphism pairs $\mathcal{E}'$ by the class of all epimorphisms and $\mathcal{M}'$ by $\mathcal{M}$. We do not explicitly state these results here, but they can be easily deduced from the results in the following.

3.2.3.3 $\mathcal{E}'$–$\mathcal{M}'$ Pair Factorization

For most of the categorical constructions, the $\mathcal{E}'$–$\mathcal{M}'$ pair factorization from the underlying categories is preserved. But for functor categories, we need a stronger property, the $\mathcal{E}'$–$\mathcal{M}'$ *diagonal property*, for this result.

Definition 3.13 (Strong $\mathcal{E}'$–$\mathcal{M}'$ pair factorization)

An $\mathcal{E}'$–$\mathcal{M}'$ pair factorization is called *strong*, if the following $\mathcal{E}'$–$\mathcal{M}'$ diagonal property holds:

Given $(e, e') \in \mathcal{E}'$, $m \in \mathcal{M}'$, and morphisms a, b, n as shown in the following diagram, with $n \circ e = m \circ a$ and $n \circ e' = m \circ b$, then there exists a unique $d : K \to L$ such that $m \circ d = n$, $d \circ e = a$, and $d \circ e' = b$.

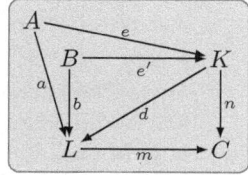

Fact 3.14

In an $\mathcal{M}$-adhesive category $(\mathbf{C}, \mathcal{M})$, the following properties hold:

1. If $(\mathbf{C}, \mathcal{M})$ has a strong $\mathcal{E}'$–$\mathcal{M}'$ pair factorization, then the $\mathcal{E}'$–$\mathcal{M}'$ pair factorization is unique up to isomorphism.

2. A strong $\mathcal{E}'$–$\mathcal{M}'$ pair factorization is functorial, i.e. given morphisms $a, b, c, f_1, g_1, f_2, g_2$ as shown in the right diagram with $c \circ f_1 = f_2 \circ a$ and $c \circ g_1 = g_2 \circ b$, and $\mathcal{E}'$–$\mathcal{M}'$ pair factorizations $((e_1, e_1'), m_1)$ and $((e_2, e_2'), m_2)$ of f_1, g_1 and f_2, g_2, respectively, then 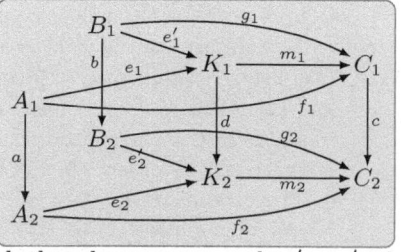 there exists a unique $d : K_1 \to K_2$ such that $d \circ e_1 = e_2 \circ a$, $d \circ e_1' = e_2' \circ b$, and $c \circ m_1 = m_2 \circ d$.

PROOF   See [PEL08].

Fact 3.15

Given $\mathcal{M}$-adhesive categories $(\mathbf{C}_j, \mathcal{M}_j)$, $(\mathbf{C}, \mathcal{M}_1)$, and $(\mathbf{D}, \mathcal{M}_2)$ with $\mathcal{E}'_j$–$\mathcal{M}'_j$, $\mathcal{E}'_1$–$\mathcal{M}'_1$, and $\mathcal{E}'_2$–$\mathcal{M}'_2$ pair factorizations, respectively, then the following $\mathcal{M}$-adhesive categories have an $\mathcal{E}'$–$\mathcal{M}'$ pair factorization and preserve strongness:

1. the *general comma category* $(\mathbf{G}, (\times_{j \in \mathcal{J}} \mathcal{M}_j) \cap Mor_{\mathbf{G}})$ with $\mathcal{M}' = (\times_{j \in \mathcal{J}} \mathcal{M}'_j)$ $\cap\ Mor_{\mathbf{G}}$ and $\mathcal{E}' = \{((e_j,), (e'_j)) \mid (e_j, e'_j) \in \mathcal{E}'_j\} \cap (Mor_{\mathbf{G}} \times Mor_{\mathbf{G}})$, if $G_i(\mathcal{M}'_{\ell_i}) \subseteq Isos$ for all $i \in \mathcal{I}$,

2. any *full subcategory* $(\mathbf{C}', \mathcal{M}_1|_{\mathbf{C}'})$ of $\mathbf{C}$ with $\mathcal{M}' = \mathcal{M}'_1|_{\mathbf{C}'}$ and $\mathcal{E}' = \mathcal{E}'_1|_{(\mathbf{C}' \times \mathbf{C}')}$, if the inclusion functor reflects the $\mathcal{E}'_1$–$\mathcal{M}'_1$ pair factorization,

3. the *comma category* $(\mathbf{F}, (\mathcal{M}_1 \times \mathcal{M}_2) \cap Mor_{\mathbf{F}})$ with $\mathcal{M}' = (\mathcal{M}'_1 \times \mathcal{M}'_2) \cap Mor_{\mathbf{F}}$ and $\mathcal{E}' = \{((e_1, e_2), (e'_1, e'_2)) \mid (e_1, e'_1) \in \mathcal{E}'_1, (e_2, e'_2) \in \mathcal{E}'_2\} \cap (Mor_{\mathbf{F}} \times Mor_{\mathbf{F}})$, if $G(\mathcal{M}'_2) \subseteq Isos$,

4. the *product category* $(\mathbf{C} \times \mathbf{D}, \mathcal{M}_1 \times \mathcal{M}_2)$ with $\mathcal{M}' = \mathcal{M}'_1 \times \mathcal{M}'_2$ and $\mathcal{E}' = \{((e_1, e_2), (e'_1, e'_2))$ $\mid (e_1, e'_1) \in \mathcal{E}'_1, (e_2, e'_2) \in \mathcal{E}'_2\}$,

5. the *slice category* $(\mathbf{C} \backslash X, \mathcal{M}_1 \cap Mor_{\mathbf{C} \backslash X})$ with $\mathcal{M}' = \mathcal{M}'_1 \cap Mor_{\mathbf{C} \backslash X}$ and $\mathcal{E}' = \mathcal{E}'_1 \cap (Mor_{\mathbf{C} \backslash X} \times Mor_{\mathbf{C} \backslash X})$,

6. the *coslice category* $(X \backslash \mathbf{C}, \mathcal{M}_1 \cap Mor_{X \backslash \mathbf{C}})$ with $\mathcal{M}' = \mathcal{M}'_1 \cap Mor_{X \backslash \mathbf{C}}$ and $\mathcal{E}' = \mathcal{E}'_1 \cap (Mor_{X \backslash \mathbf{C}} \times Mor_{X \backslash \mathbf{C}})$, if $\mathcal{M}'_1$ is a class of monomorphisms,

7. the *functor category* $([\mathbf{X}, \mathbf{C}], \mathcal{M}_1\text{-functor transformations})$ with the class $\mathcal{M}'$ of all $\mathcal{M}'_1$-functor transformations and $\mathcal{E}' = \{(e, e') \mid e, e' \text{ functor transformations}, (e(x), e'(x)) \in \mathcal{E}'_1 \text{ for all } x \in \mathbf{X}\}$, if $\mathcal{E}'_1$–$\mathcal{M}'_1$ is a strong pair factorization in $\mathbf{C}$.

PROOF   1. Given objects $A = ((A_j), (op_i^A))$, $B = ((B_j), (op_i^B))$, $C = ((C_j), (op_i^C))$, and morphisms $f = (f_j) : A \to C$, $g = (g_j) : B \to C$ in $\mathbf{G}$, we have an $\mathcal{E}'_j$–$\mathcal{M}'_j$ pair factorization $((e_j, e'_j), m_j)$ of f_j, g_j in $\mathbf{C}_j$.

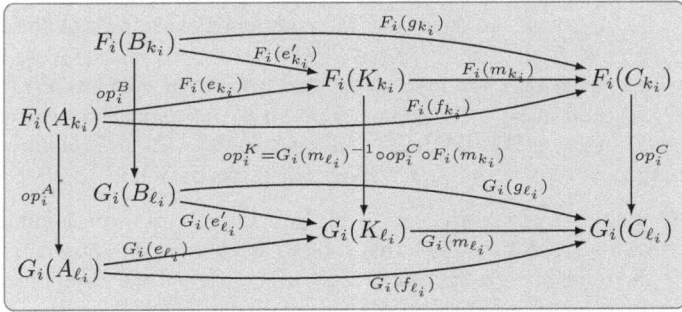

If $G_i(m_{\ell_i})$ is an isomorphism, we have an object $K = ((K_j), (op_i^K = G_i(m_{\ell_i})^{-1} \circ op_i^C \circ F_i(m_{k_i})))$ in $\mathbf{G}$. By definition, $m = (m_j) : K \to C$ is a morphism in $\mathbf{G}$. For $e = (e_j)$ we have $op_i^K \circ F_i(e_{k_i}) = G_i(m_{\ell_i})^{-1} \circ op_i^C \circ$

$F_i(m_{k_i}) \circ F_i(e_{k_i}) = G_i(m_{\ell_i})^{-1} \circ op_i^C \circ F_i(f_{k_i}) = G_i(m_{\ell_i})^{-1} \circ G_i(f_{\ell_i}) \circ op_i^A = G_i(e_{\ell_i}) \circ op_i^A$ and an analogous result for $e' = (e'_j)$, therefore e and e' are morphisms in $\mathbf{G}$. This means that $((e, e'), m)$ is an $\mathcal{E}'$-$\mathcal{M}'$ pair factorization in $\mathbf{G}$.

To show the $\mathcal{E}'$–$\mathcal{M}'$ diagonal property, we consider $(e, e') = ((e_j), (e'_j)) \in \mathcal{E}'$, $m = (m_j) \in \mathcal{M}'$, and morphisms $a = (a_j), b = (b_j), n = (n_j)$ in $\mathbf{G}$. Since $(e_j, e'_j) \in \mathcal{E}'_j$ and $m_j \in \mathcal{M}'_j$, we get a unique mor-

$$
\begin{array}{l}
((A_j), (op_i^A)) \\
\quad\quad\quad \xrightarrow{\quad (e_j) \quad} \\
(a_j) \quad ((B_j), (op_i^B)) \xrightarrow{\quad (e'_j) \quad} ((K_j), (op_i^K)) \\
\quad\quad (b_j) \quad\quad (d_j) \quad\quad\quad\quad\quad\quad (n_j) \\
((L_j), (op_i^L)) \xrightarrow{\quad\quad (m_j) \quad\quad} ((C_j), (op_i^C))
\end{array}
$$

phism $d_j : K_j \to L_j$ in $\mathbf{C}_j$ with $m_j \circ d_j = n_j$, $d_j \circ e_j = a_j$, and $d_j \circ e'_j = b_j$.

It remains to show that $d = (d_j) \in \mathbf{G}$, i.e. the compatibility with the operations. For all $i \in \mathcal{I}$ we have that $G_i(m_{\ell_i}) \circ op_i^L \circ F_i(d_{k_i}) = op_i^C \circ F_i(m_{k_i}) \circ F_i(d_{k_i}) = op_i^C \circ F_i(n_{k_i}) = G_i(n_{\ell_i}) \circ op_i^K = G_i(m_{\ell_i}) \circ G_i(d_{\ell_i}) \circ op_i^K$, and since

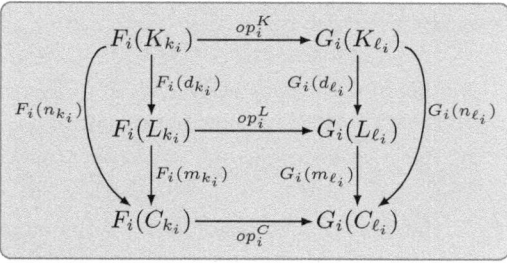

$G_i(m_{\ell_i})$ is an isomorphism it follows that $op_i^L \circ F_i(d_{k_i}) = G_i(d_{\ell_i}) \circ op_i^K$, i.e. $d \in \mathbf{G}$.

2. This is obvious.

3. This follows directly from Item 1, since any comma category is an instantiation of a general comma categories. For morphisms $f = (f_1, f_2)$ and $g = (g_1, g_2)$ in $\mathbf{F}$ we construct the component-wise pair factorizations $((e_1, e'_1), m_1)$ of f_1, g_1 with $(e_1, e'_1) \in \mathcal{E}'_1$ and $m_1 \in \mathcal{M}'_1$, and $((e_2, e'_2), m_2)$ of f_2, g_2 with $(e_2, e'_2) \in \mathcal{E}'_2$ and $m_2 \in \mathcal{M}'_2$. This leads to morphisms $e = (e_1, e_2)$, $e' = (e'_1, e'_2)$, and $m = (m_1, m_2)$ in $\mathbf{F}$, and an $\mathcal{E}'$–$\mathcal{M}'$ pair factorization with $(e, e') \in \mathcal{E}'$ and $m \in \mathcal{M}'$. If the $\mathcal{E}'_1$–$\mathcal{M}'_1$ and the $\mathcal{E}'_2$–$\mathcal{M}'_2$ pair factorizations are strong then also $\mathcal{E}'$–$\mathcal{M}'$ is a strong pair factorization.

4. Since $\mathbf{C} \times \mathbf{D} \cong ComCat(!_{\mathbf{C}} : \mathbf{C} \to \mathbf{1}, !_{\mathbf{D}} : \mathbf{D} \to \mathbf{1}, \varnothing)$ (see Lemma A.3) and $!_{\mathbf{D}}(\mathcal{M}'_2) \subseteq \{id_1\} = Isos$ this follows from Item 3. For morphisms $f = (f_1, f_2)$ and $g = (g_1, g_2)$ in $\mathbf{C} \times \mathbf{D}$ we construct the component-wise pair factorizations $((e_1, e'_1), m_1)$ of f_1, g_1 with $(e_1, e'_1) \in \mathcal{E}'_1$ and $m_1 \in \mathcal{M}'_1$, and $((e_2, e'_2), m_2)$ of f_2, g_2 with $(e_2, e'_2) \in \mathcal{E}'_2$ and $m_2 \in \mathcal{M}'_2$. This leads to morphisms $e = (e_1, e_2)$, $e' = (e'_1, e'_2)$, and $m = (m_1, m_2)$ in $\mathbf{C} \times \mathbf{D}$, and an $\mathcal{E}'$–$\mathcal{M}'$ pair factorization with $(e, e') \in \mathcal{E}'$ and $m \in \mathcal{M}'$. If the $\mathcal{E}'_1$–$\mathcal{M}'_1$ and

the $\mathcal{E}'_2$–$\mathcal{M}'_2$ pair factorizations are strong then also $\mathcal{E}'$–$\mathcal{M}'$ is a strong pair factorization.

5. Since $\mathbf{C}\backslash X \cong ComCat(id_{\mathbf{C}} : \mathbf{C} \to \mathbf{C}, X : \mathbf{1} \to \mathbf{C}, \{1\})$ (see Lemma A.3) and $X(\mathcal{M}'_2) \subseteq X(\{id_1\}) = \{id_X\} \subseteq Isos$ this follows from Item 3. Given morphisms f and g in $\mathbf{C}\backslash X$, an $\mathcal{E}'_1$–$\mathcal{M}'_1$ pair factorization of f and g in $\mathbf{C}$ is also an $\mathcal{E}'_1$–$\mathcal{M}'_1$ of f and g in $\mathbf{C}\backslash X$. If the $\mathcal{E}'_1$–$\mathcal{M}'_1$ pair factorization is strong in $\mathbf{C}$ this is also true for $\mathbf{C}\backslash X$.

6. Given morphisms $f : (A, a') \to (C, c')$ and $g : (B, b') \to (C, c')$ in $X\backslash\mathbf{C}$, we have an $\mathcal{E}'_1 - \mathcal{M}'_1$ pair factorization $((e, e'), m)$ of f and g in $\mathbf{C}$. This is a pair factorization in $X\backslash\mathbf{C}$ if $e \circ a' = e' \circ b'$, because then $(K, e \circ a')$ and $(K, e' \circ b')$ is the same object in $X\backslash\mathbf{C}$. If m is a monomorphism, this follows from $m \circ e \circ a' = f \circ a' = c' = g \circ b' = m \circ e' \circ b'$.

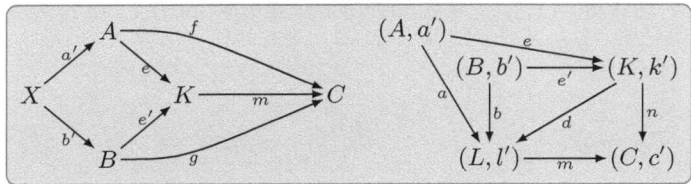

To prove that strongness is preserved we have to show the $\mathcal{E}'_1$–$\mathcal{M}'_1$ diagonal property in $X\backslash\mathbf{C}$. Since it holds in $\mathbf{C}$, given $(e, e') \in \mathcal{E}'$, $m \in \mathcal{M}'$, and morphisms a, b, n in $X\backslash\mathbf{C}$ with $n \circ e = m \circ a$ and $n \circ e' = m \circ b$ we get an induced unique $d : K \to L$ with $d \circ e = a$, $d \circ e' = b$, and $m \circ d = n$ from the diagonal property in $\mathbf{C}$. It remains to show that d is a valid morphism in $X\backslash\mathbf{C}$. Since $m \circ d \circ k' = n \circ k' = c' = m \circ l'$ and m is a monomorphisms it follows that $d \circ k' = l'$ and thus $d \in X\backslash\mathbf{C}$.

7. Given morphisms $f = (f(x))_{x \in \mathbf{X}}$ and $g = (g(x))_{x \in \mathbf{X}}$ in $[\mathbf{X}, \mathbf{C}]$, we have an $\mathcal{E}'_1$–$\mathcal{M}'_1$ pair factorization $((e_x, e'_x), m_x)$ with $m_x : K_x \to C(x)$ of $f(x), g(x)$ in $\mathbf{C}$ for all $x \in \mathbf{X}$.

We have to show that $K(x) = K_x$ can be extended to a functor and that $e = (e_x)_{x \in \mathbf{X}}$, $e' = (e'_x)_{x \in \mathbf{X}}$, and $m = (m_x)_{x \in \mathbf{X}}$ are functor transformations. For a morphism $h : x \to y$ in $\mathbf{X}$ we use the $\mathcal{E}'_1$–$\mathcal{M}'_1$ diagonal property in $\mathbf{C}$ with $(e_x, e'_x) \in \mathcal{E}'_1$, $m_y \in \mathcal{M}'_1$ to define

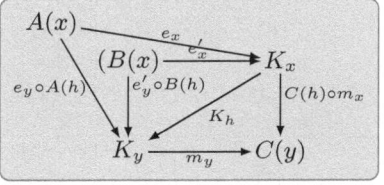

$K_h : K_x \to K_y$ as the unique induced morphism with $m_y \circ K_h = C(h) \circ m_x$, $K_h \circ e_x = e_y \circ A(h)$, and $K_h \circ e'_x = e'_y \circ B(h)$.

Using the uniqueness property of the strong pair factorization in $\mathbf{C}$, we can show that K with $K(x) = K_x$, $K(h) = K_h$ is a functor and by construction e, e', and m are functor transformations. This means that $(e, e') \in \mathcal{E}'$ and $m \in \mathcal{M}'$, i.e. this is an $\mathcal{E}'$–$\mathcal{M}'$ pair factorization of f and g.

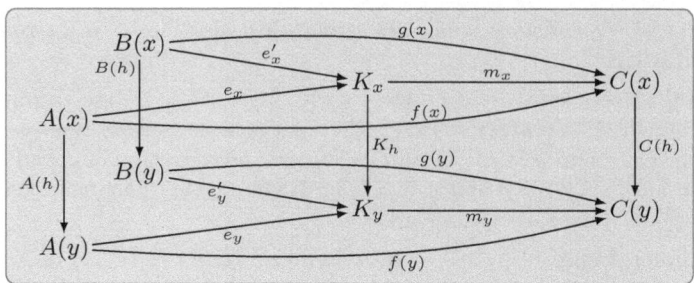

The $\mathcal{E}'$–$\mathcal{M}'$ diagonal property can be shown as follows. Given $(e, e') \in \mathcal{E}'$, $m \in \mathcal{M}'$, and morphisms a, b, n in $[\mathbf{X}, \mathbf{C}]$ from the $\mathcal{E}'_1$–$\mathcal{M}'_1$ diagonal property in $\mathbf{C}$ we obtain a unique morphism $d_x : K(x) \to L(x)$ for $x \in \mathbf{X}$. It remains to show that $d = (d_x)_{x \in \mathbf{X}}$ is a functor transformation, i. e. we have to show for all $h : x \to y \in \mathbf{X}$ that $L(h) \circ d_x = d_y \circ K(h)$.

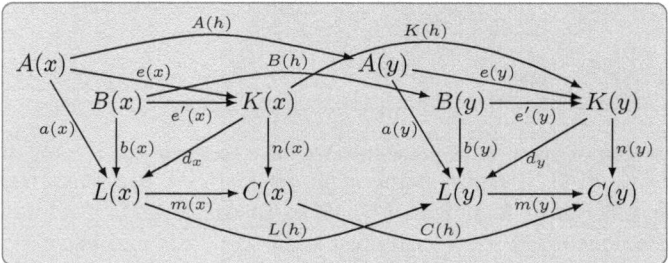

Because $(e(x), e'(x)) \in \mathcal{E}'_1$ and $m(y) \in \mathcal{M}'_1$, the $\mathcal{E}'_1$–$\mathcal{M}'_1$ diagonal property can be applied. This means that there is a unique $k : K(x) \to L(y)$ with $k \circ e(x) = L(h) \circ a(x)$, $k \circ e'(x) = L(h) \circ b(x)$, and $m(y) \circ k = n(y) \circ K(h)$.

For $L(h) \circ d_x$ we have that $L(h) \circ d_x \circ e(x) = L(h) \circ a(x)$, $L(h) \circ d_x \circ e'(x) = L(h) \circ b(x)$ and $m(y) \circ L(h) \circ d_x = C(h) \circ m(x) \circ d_x = C(h) \circ n(x) = n(y) \circ K(h)$. Similarly, for $d_y \circ K(h)$ we have that $d_y \circ K(h) \circ e(x) = d_y \circ e(y) \circ A(h) = a(y) \circ A(h) = L(h) \circ a(x)$, $d_y \circ K(h) \circ e'(x) = d_y \circ e'(y) \circ B(h) = b(y) \circ B(h) = L(h) \circ b(x)$, and

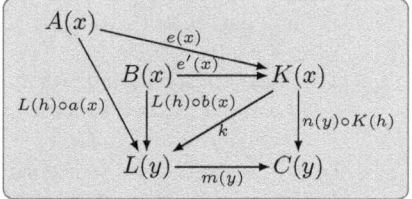

$m(y) \circ d_y \circ K(h) = n(y) \circ K(h)$. Thus, from the uniqueness of k it follows that $k = L(h) \circ d_x = d_y \circ K(h)$ and d is a functor transformation.

3.2.3.4 Initial Pushouts

In general, the construction of initial pushouts from the underlying categories is complicated since the existence of the boundary and context objects have to be ensured. In many cases, this is only possible under very strict limitations.

Fact 3.16

If the $\mathcal{M}$-adhesive categories $(\mathbf{C}, \mathcal{M}_1)$, $(\mathbf{D}, \mathcal{M}_2)$, and $(\mathbf{C}_j, \mathcal{M}_j)$ for $j \in \mathcal{J}$ have initial pushouts over $\mathcal{M}_1'$, $\mathcal{M}_2'$, and $\mathcal{M}_j'$, respectively, then also the following $\mathcal{M}$-adhesive categories have initial pushouts over $\mathcal{M}'$-morphisms:

1. the *general comma category* $(\mathbf{G}, (\times_{j \in \mathcal{J}} \mathcal{M}_j) \cap Mor_\mathbf{G})$ with $\mathcal{M}' = \times_{j \in \mathcal{J}} \mathcal{M}_j'$, if for all $i \in \mathcal{I}$ F_i preserves pushouts along $\mathcal{M}_{k_i}$-morphisms and $G_i(\mathcal{M}_{\ell_i}) \subseteq Isos$,

2. any *full subcategory* $(\mathbf{C}', \mathcal{M}_1|_{\mathbf{C}'})$ of $\mathbf{C}$ with $\mathcal{M}' = \mathcal{M}_1'|_{\mathbf{C}'}$, if the inclusion functor reflects initial pushouts over $\mathcal{M}'$-morphisms,

3. the *comma category* $(\mathbf{F}, (\mathcal{M}_1 \times \mathcal{M}_2) \cap Mor_\mathbf{F})$ with $\mathcal{M}' = \mathcal{M}_1' \times \mathcal{M}_2'$, if F preserves pushouts along $\mathcal{M}_1$-morphisms and $G(\mathcal{M}_2) \subseteq Isos$,

4. the *product category* $(\mathbf{C} \times \mathbf{D}, \mathcal{M}_1 \times \mathcal{M}_2)$ with $\mathcal{M}' = \mathcal{M}_1' \times \mathcal{M}_2'$,

5. the *slice category* $(\mathbf{C} \backslash X, \mathcal{M}_1 \cap Mor_{\mathbf{C} \backslash X})$ with $\mathcal{M}' = \mathcal{M}_1' \cap Mor_{\mathbf{C} \backslash X}$,

6. the *coslice category* $(X \backslash \mathbf{C}, \mathcal{M}_1 \cap Mor_{X \backslash \mathbf{C}})$ with $\mathcal{M}' = \mathcal{M}_1' \cap Mor_{X \backslash \mathbf{C}}$, if for $f : (A, a') \to (D, d') \in \mathcal{M}'$

   (i) the initial pushout over f in $\mathbf{C}$ can be extended to a valid square in $X \backslash \mathbf{C}$ or

   (ii) $a' : X \to A \in \mathcal{M}_1$ and the pushout complement of a' and f in $\mathbf{C}$ exists,

7. the *functor category* $([\mathbf{X}, \mathbf{C}], \mathcal{M}_1$-functor transformations$)$ with $\mathcal{M}' = \mathcal{M}_1'$-functor transformations, if $\mathbf{C}$ has arbitrary limits and intersections of $\mathcal{M}_1$-subobjects.

PROOF   1. Given $f = (f_j) : A \to D \in \mathcal{M}'$ we have initial pushouts $(1)_j$ over

$f_j \in \mathcal{M}_j'$ in $\mathbf{C}_j$ with $b_j, c_j \in \mathcal{M}_j$. Since $G_i(\mathcal{M}_{\ell_i}) \subseteq Isos$, $G_i(b_{\ell_i})^{-1}$ and $G_i(c_{\ell_i})^{-1}$ exist. Define objects $B = ((B_j), (op_i^B = G_i(b_{\ell_i})^{-1} \circ op_i^A \circ F_i(b_{k_i})))$ and $C = ((C_j), (op_i^C = G_i(c_{\ell_i})^{-1} \circ op_i^D \circ F_i(c_{k_i}))$ in $\mathbf{G}$. Then we have that

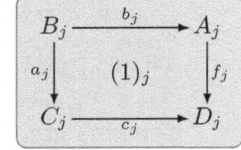

- $G_i(b_{\ell_i}) \circ op_i^B = G_i(b_{\ell_i}) \circ G_i(b_{\ell_i})^{-1} \circ op_i^A \circ F_i(b_{k_i}) = op_i^A \circ F_i(b_{k_i})$,
- $G_i(c_{\ell_i}) \circ op_i^C = G_i(c_{\ell_i}) \circ G_i(c_{\ell_i})^{-1} \circ op_i^D \circ F_i(c_{k_i}) = op_i^D \circ F_i(c_{k_i})$,
- $G_i(c_{\ell_i}) \circ G_i(a_{\ell_i}) \circ op_i^B = G_i(f_{\ell_i}) \circ G_i(b_{\ell_i}) \circ op_i^B = G_i(f_{\ell_i}) \circ op_i^A \circ F_i(b_{k_i}) = op_i^D \circ F_i(f_{k_i}) \circ F_i(b_{k_i}) = op_i^D \circ F_i(c_{k_i}) \circ F_i(a_{k_i}) = G_i(c_{\ell_i}) \circ op_i^C \circ F_i(a_{k_i})$ and $G_i(c_{\ell_i})$ being an isomorphism implies that $G_i(a_{\ell_i}) \circ op_i^B = op_i^C \circ F_i(a_{k_i})$, which means that $a = (a_j)$, $b = (b_j)$, and $c = (c_j)$ are morphisms in $\mathbf{G}$ with $b, c \in \mathcal{M}'$, (1) is a valid square in $\mathbf{G}$, and by Lemma A.1 also a pushout.

$$((B_j),(op_i^B)) \xrightarrow{b} ((A_j),(op_i^A)) \qquad ((A_j),(op_i^A)) \xleftarrow{d} ((E_j),(op_i^E))$$

$$\downarrow a \qquad (1) \qquad \downarrow f \qquad \qquad \downarrow f \qquad (2) \qquad \downarrow g$$

$$((C_j),op_i^C)) \xrightarrow{c} ((D_j),(op_i^D)) \qquad ((D_j),(op_i^D)) \xleftarrow{e} ((F_j),(op_i^F))$$

It remains to show the initiality. For any pushout (2) in $\mathbf{G}$ with $d = (d_j), e = (e_j) \in \mathcal{M}$, Lemma A.1 implies that the components $(2)_j$ are pushouts in $\mathbf{C}_j$. The initiality of pushout $(1)_j$ implies that there are unique morphisms $b_j^* : B_j \to E_j$ and $c_j^* : C_j \to F_j$ with $d_j \circ b_j^* = b_j$, $e_j \circ c_j^* = c_j$, and $b_j^*, c_j^* \in \mathcal{M}_j$ such that $(3)_j$ is a pushout.

$$A_j \xleftarrow{d_j} E_j \qquad B_j \xrightarrow{b_j^*} E_j \qquad ((B_j),(op_i^B)) \xrightarrow{b^*} ((A_j),(op_i^A))$$

$$\downarrow f_j \quad (2)_j \quad \downarrow g_j \qquad \downarrow a_j \quad (3)_j \quad \downarrow g_j \qquad \downarrow a \qquad (3) \qquad \downarrow g$$

$$D_j \xleftarrow{e_j} F_j \qquad C_j \xrightarrow{c_j^*} F_j \qquad ((E_j),(op_i^E)) \xrightarrow{c^*} ((F_j),(op_i^F))$$

With $G_i(d_{\ell_i}) \circ G_i(b_{\ell_i}^*) \circ op_i^B = G_i(b_{\ell_i}) \circ op_i^B = op_i^A \circ F_i(b_{k_i}) = op_i^A \circ F_i(d_{k_i}) \circ F_i(b_{k_i}^*) = G_i(d_{\ell_i}) \circ op_i^E \circ F_i(b_{k_i}^*)$ and $G_i(d_{\ell_i})$ being an isomorphism it follows that $G_i(b_{\ell_i}^*) \circ op_i^B = op_i^E \circ F_i(b_{k_i}^*)$ and therefore $b^* = (b_j^*) \in \mathbf{G}$, and analogously $c^* = (c_j^*) \in \mathbf{G}$. This means that we have unique morphisms $b^*, c^* \in \mathcal{M}'$ with $d \circ b^* = b$ and $e \circ c^* = c$, and by Lemma A.1 (3) composed of $(3)_j$ is a pushout. Therefore (1) is the initial pushout over f in $\mathbf{G}$.

2. This is obvious.

3. Since comma categories are an instantiation of general comma categories, this follows directly from Item 1. The initial pushout of $f = (f_1, f_2) : (A_1, A_2, (op_i^A)) \to (D_1, D_2, (op_i^D)) \in \mathcal{M}_1' \times \mathcal{M}_2'$ is the component-wise initial pushout in $\mathbf{C}$ and $\mathbf{D}$, with $B = (B_1, B_2, op_i^B = G(b_2)^{-1} \circ op_i^A \circ F(b_1))$ and $C = (C_1, C_2, op_i^C = G(c_1)^{-1} \circ op_i^D \circ F(c_1))$.

4. Since $\mathbf{C} \times \mathbf{D} \cong ComCat(!_{\mathbf{C}} : \mathbf{C} \to \mathbf{1}, !_{\mathbf{D}} : \mathbf{D} \to \mathbf{1}, \varnothing)$ (see Lemma A.3), $!_{\mathbf{C}}$ preserves pushouts, and $!_{\mathbf{D}}(\mathcal{M}_2) \subseteq \{id_1\} = Isos$ this follows from Item 3. The initial pushout (3) over a morphism $(f_1, f_2) : (A_1, A_2) \to (D_1, D_2) \in \mathcal{M}_1' \times \mathcal{M}_2'$ is the component-wise product of the initial pushouts over f_1 in $\mathbf{C}$ and f_2 in $\mathbf{D}$.

5. Since $\mathbf{C} \backslash X \cong ComCat(id_{\mathbf{C}} : \mathbf{C} \to \mathbf{C}, X : \mathbf{1} \to \mathbf{C}, \{1\})$, $id_{\mathbf{C}}$ preserves pushouts, and $X(\mathcal{M}_2) = X(\{id_1\}) = \{id_X\} \subseteq Isos$ this follows from Item 3. The initial pushout over $f : (A, a') \to (D, d') \in \mathcal{M}_1'$ in $\mathbf{C} \backslash X$ is given by the initial pushout over f in $\mathbf{C}$, with objects (B, b'), (C, c'), $b' = a' \circ b$, and $c' = d' \circ c$.

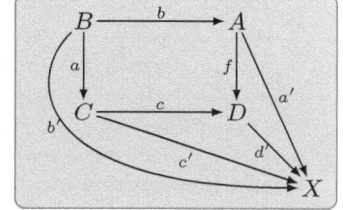

6. Given objects (A, a'), (D, d'), and a morphism $f :$ 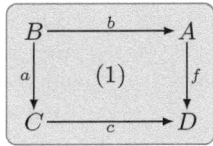 $A \to D$ in $X\backslash\mathbf{C}$ with $f \in \mathcal{M}'_1$, the initial pushout (1) over f in $\mathbf{C}$ exists by assumption. For any pushout (2) in $X\backslash\mathbf{C}$ with $d, e \in \mathcal{M}_1$, the corresponding diagram (3) is a pushout in $\mathbf{C}$. Since (1) is an initial pushout in $\mathbf{C}$ there exist unique morphisms $b^* : B \to E$ and $c^* : C \to F$ such that $d \circ b^* = b$, $e \circ c^* = c$, $b^*, c^* \in \mathcal{M}_1$, and (4) is a pushout in $\mathbf{C}$.

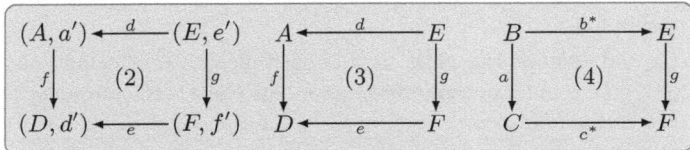

(i) If diagram (1) has valid extension via morphisms $b' : X \to B$, $c' : X \to C$ in $X\backslash\mathbf{C}$, then this is also a pushout in $X\backslash\mathbf{C}$. With $d \circ b^* \circ b' = b \circ b' = a' = d \circ e'$ and d being a monomorphism it follows that $b^* \circ b = e'$ and thus $b^* \in X\backslash\mathbf{C}$, and analogously $c^* \in X\backslash\mathbf{C}$. This means that (4) is also a pushout in $X\backslash\mathbf{C}$.

(ii) If $a' : X \to A \in \mathcal{M}_1$ and the pushout complement of $f \circ a'$ in $\mathbf{C}$ exists, we can construct the unique pushout complement (5) in $\mathbf{C}$, and the corresponding diagram (6) is a pushout in $X\backslash\mathbf{C}$.

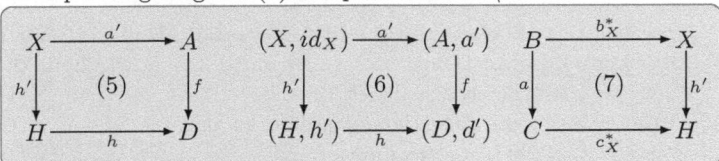

It remains to show the initiality of (6). For any pushout (2), $e' : X \to E$ is unique with respect to $d \circ e' = a'$ because d is a monomorphism.

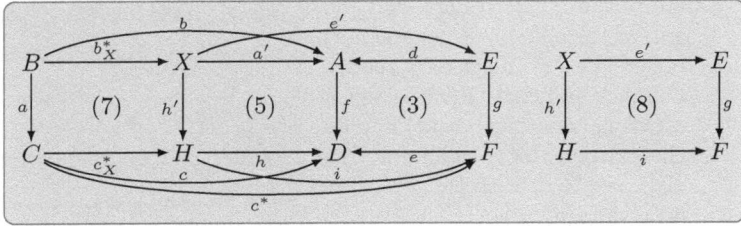

Since (1) is an initial pushout in $\mathbf{C}$ and (5) is a pushout, there are morphisms $b^*_X : B \to X$ and $c^*_X : C \to H$ such that $b^*_X, c^*_X \in \mathcal{M}_1$, $a' \circ b^*_X = b$, $h \circ c^*_X = c$, and (7) is a pushout in $\mathbf{C}$. With $e \circ c^*_X \circ a = c \circ a = h \circ c^*_X \circ a = h \circ h' \circ b^*_X = f \circ a' \circ b^*_X = f \circ d \circ e' \circ b^*_X = e \circ g \circ e' \circ b^*_X$ and e being a monomorphism it follows that $c^* \circ a = g \circ e' \circ b^*_X$. Pushout (7) implies that there is a unique $i : H \to F$ with $c^* = i \circ c^*_X$ and

$i \circ h' = g \circ e'$. It further follows that $e \circ i = h$ using the pushout properties of H. By pushout decomposition, (8) is a pushout in $\mathbf{C}$ and the corresponding square in $X\backslash\mathbf{C}$ is also a pushout. Therefore, (6) is an initial pushout over f in $X\backslash\mathbf{C}$.

7. If $\mathbf{C}$ has intersections of $\mathcal{M}_1$-subobjects this means that given $c_i : C_i \to D \in \mathcal{M}_1$ with $i \in \mathcal{I}$ for some index set $\mathcal{I}$ the corresponding diagram has a limit $(C, (c_i' : C \to C_i)_{i\in\mathcal{I}}, c : C \to D)$ in $\mathbf{C}$ with $c_i \circ c_i' = c$ and $c, c_i' \in \mathcal{M}_1$ for all $i \in \mathcal{I}$.

Let $\mathcal{M}$ denote the class of all $\mathcal{M}_1$-functor transformations. Given $f : A \to D \in \mathcal{M}'$, by assumption we can construct component-wise the initial pushout (1_x) over $f(x)$ in $\mathbf{C}$ for all $x \in \mathbf{X}$, with $b_0(x), c_0(x) \in \mathcal{M}_1$.

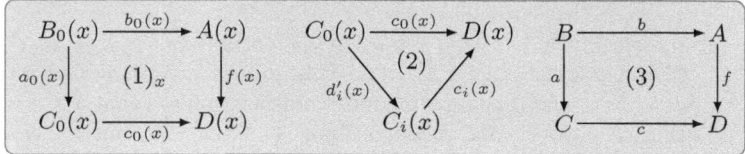

Define $(C, (c_i' : C \to C_i)_{i\in\mathcal{I}}, c : C \to D)$ as the limit in $[\mathbf{X}, \mathbf{C}]$ of all those $c_i : C_i \to D \in \mathcal{M}$ such that for all $x \in \mathbf{X}$ there exists a $d_i'(x) : C_0(x) \to C_i(X) \in \mathcal{M}_1$ with $c_i(x) \circ d_i'(x) = c_0(x)$ (2), which defines the index set $\mathcal{I}$. Limits in $[\mathbf{X}, \mathbf{C}]$ are constructed component-wise in $\mathbf{C}$, and if $\mathbf{C}$ has intersections of $\mathcal{M}_1$-subobjects it follows that also $[\mathbf{X}, \mathbf{C}]$ has intersections of $\mathcal{M}$-subobjects. Hence $c, c_i' \in \mathcal{M}$ and $C(x)$ is the limit of $c_i(x)$ in $\mathbf{C}$. Now we construct the pullback (3) over $c \in \mathcal{M}$ and f in $[\mathbf{X}, \mathbf{C}]$, and since $\mathcal{M}$-morphisms are closed under pullbacks also $b \in \mathcal{M}$.

For $x \in X$, $C(x)$ being the limit of $c_i(x)$, the family $(d_i'(x))_{i\in\mathcal{I}}$ with (2) implies that there is a unique morphism $c'(x) : C_0(x) \to C(x)$ with $c_i'(x) \circ c'(x) = d_i'(x)$ and $c(x) \circ c'(x) = c_0(x)$. Then $(3)_x$ being a pullback and $c(x) \circ c'(x) \circ a_0(x) = c_0(x) \circ a_0(x) = f(x) \circ b_0(x)$ implies the existence of a unique $b'(x) : B_0(x) \to B(x)$ with $b(x) \circ b'(x) = b_0(x)$ and $a(x) \circ b'(x) = c'(x) \circ a_0(x)$. $\mathcal{M}_1$ is closed under decomposition, $b_0(x) \in \mathcal{M}_1$, and $b(x) \in \mathcal{M}_1$

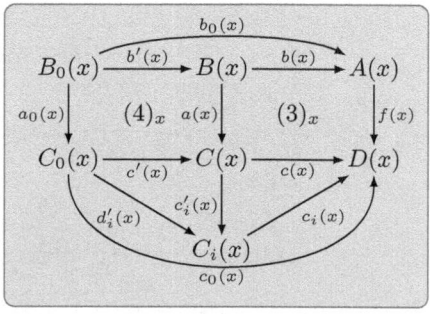

implies that $b'(x) \in \mathcal{M}_1$. Since (1_x) is a pushout, (3_x) is a pullback, the whole diagram commutes, and $c(x), b'(x) \in \mathcal{M}_1$, the $\mathcal{M}_1$ pushout-pullback property implies that (3_x) and (4_x) are both pushouts and pullbacks in $\mathbf{C}$ and hence (3) and (4) are both pushouts and pullbacks in $[\mathbf{X}, \mathbf{C}]$.

It remains to show the initiality of (3) over f. Given a pushout (5) with $b_1, c_1 \in \mathcal{M}$ in $[\mathbf{X}, \mathbf{C}]$, (5_x) is a pushout in $\mathbf{C}$ for all $x \in$

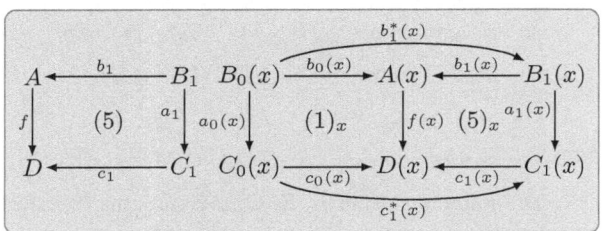

$\mathbf{X}$. Since (1_x) is an initial pushout in $\mathbf{C}$, there exist morphisms $b_1^*(x)$: $B_0(x) \to B_1(x)$, $c_1^* : C_0(x) \to C_1(x)$ with $b_1^*(x), c_1^*(x) \in \mathcal{M}_1$, $b_1(x) \circ b_1^*(x) = b_0(x)$, and $c_1(x) \circ c_1^*(x) = c_0(x)$. Hence $c_1(x)$ satisfies (2) for $i = 1$ and $d_1'(x) = c_1^*(x)$. This means that c_1 is one of the morphisms the limit C was built of and there is a morphism $c_1' : C \to C_1$ with $c_1 \circ c_1' = c$ by construction of the limit C.

Since (5) is a pushout along $\mathcal{M}$-morphisms it is also a pullback, and $f \circ b = c \circ a = c_1 \circ c_1' \circ a$ implies that there exists a unique $b_1' : B \to B_1$ with $b_1 \circ b_1' = b$ and $a_1 \circ b_1' = c_1' \circ a$. By $\mathcal{M}$-decomposition also $b_1' \in \mathcal{M}$. Now using also $c_1 \in \mathcal{M}$ the $\mathcal{M}$ pushout-pullback decomposition property implies that also (6) is a pushout, which shows the initiality of (3).

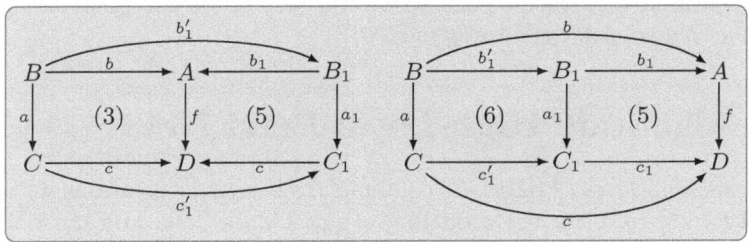

Effective Pushouts

Using Rem. 3.9, we already know for the regarded situation that the induced morphism is a monomorphism. We only have to show that it is indeed an $\mathcal{M}$-morphism. This is obviously the case if pullbacks, pushouts, and their induced morphisms are constructed component-wise.

Fact 3.17
If the $\mathcal{M}$-adhesive categories $(\mathbf{C}, \mathcal{M}_1)$, $(\mathbf{D}, \mathcal{M}_2)$, and $(\mathbf{C}_j, \mathcal{M}_j)$ for $j \in \mathcal{J}$ have effective pushouts then also the following $\mathcal{M}$-adhesive categories have effective pushouts:

1. the *general comma category* $(\mathbf{G}, (\times_{j \in \mathcal{J}} \mathcal{M}_j) \cap Mor_{\mathbf{G}})$,

2. any *full subcategory* $(\mathbf{C}', \mathcal{M}_1|_{\mathbf{C}'})$ of $\mathbf{C}$,

3. the *comma category* $(\mathbf{F}, (\mathcal{M}_1 \times \mathcal{M}_2) \cap Mor_{\mathbf{F}})$,

4. the *product category* $(\mathbf{C} \times \mathbf{D}, \mathcal{M}_1 \times \mathcal{M}_2)$,

5. the *slice category* $(\mathbf{C}\backslash X, \mathcal{M}_1 \cap Mor_{\mathbf{C}\backslash X})$,

6. the *coslice category* $(X\backslash\mathbf{C}, \mathcal{M}_1 \cap Mor_{X\backslash\mathbf{C}})$,

7. the *functor category* $([\mathbf{X}, \mathbf{C}], \mathcal{M}_1\text{-functor transformations})$.

PROOF 1. As shown in Lemma A.1, pushouts over $\mathcal{M}$-morphisms in the general comma category are constructed component-wise in the underlying categories. The induced morphism is constructed from the induced morphisms in the underlying components. Since also pullbacks over $\mathcal{M}$-morphisms are constructed component-wise, the effective pushout property of the categories $(\mathbf{C}_j, \mathcal{M}_j)$ implies this property in $(\mathbf{G}, \mathcal{M})$.

2. This is obvious.

3.-6. This follows directly from Item 1, because all these categories are instantiations of general comma categories.

7. Pushouts and pullbacks over $\mathcal{M}$-morphisms as well as the induced morphisms are constructed point-wise in the functor category, thus the effective pushout property is directly induced.

3.3 Algebraic High-Level Petri Nets

Algebraic high-level (AHL) nets combine algebraic specifications with Petri nets [PER95] to allow the modeling of data, data flow, and data changes within the net. In general, an AHL net denotes a net based on a specification SP in combination with an SP-algebra A, in contrast a net without a specific algebra is called a schema. An AHL net system then combines an AHL net with a suitable marking.

In this section, we show that different versions of AHL schemas, nets, and systems are $\mathcal{M}$-adhesive categories [Pra07, Pra08].

Definition 3.18 (AHL schema)
An *AHL schema* over an algebraic specification SP, where $SP = (SIG, E, X)$ has additional variables X and $SIG = (S, OP)$, is given by $AC = (P, T, pre, post, cond, type)$ with sets P of places and T of transitions, $pre, post : T \to (T_{SIG}(X) \otimes P)^{\oplus}$ as pre- and post-domain functions, $cond : T \to \mathcal{P}_{fin}(Eqns(SIG, X))$ assigning to each $t \in T$ a finite set $cond(t)$ of equations over SIG and X, and $type : P \to S$ a type function. Note that $T_{SIG}(X)$ is the SIG-term algebra with variables X and $(T_{SIG}(X) \otimes P) = \{(term, p) \mid term \in T_{SIG}(X)_{type(p)}, p \in P\}$.

An *AHL schema morphism* $f_{AC} : AC \rightarrow AC'$ is given by a pair of functions $f_{AC} = (f_P : P \rightarrow P', f_T : T \rightarrow T')$ which are compatible with *pre*, *post*, *cond*, and *type* as shown below.

$$\mathcal{P}_{fin}(Eqns(SIG, X)) = \begin{array}{c} \xleftarrow{\quad cond \quad} T \xrightarrow[\quad post \quad]{\quad pre \quad} (T_{SIG}(X) \otimes P)^{\oplus} \quad P \xrightarrow{\quad type \quad} \\ \Big\downarrow f_T \qquad = \qquad \Big\downarrow (id \otimes f_P)^{\oplus} \qquad f_P \Big\downarrow \qquad = \qquad S \\ \xleftarrow{\quad cond' \quad} T' \xrightarrow[\quad post' \quad]{\quad pre' \quad} (T_{SIG}(X) \otimes P')^{\oplus} \quad P' \xrightarrow{\quad type' \quad} \end{array}$$

Given an algebraic specification SP, AHL schemas over SP and AHL schema morphisms form the category **AHLSchemas(SP)**.

As shown in [EEPT06], AHL schemas over a fixed algebraic specification SP are an $\mathcal{M}$-adhesive category. Using the concept of general comma categories, we can rewrite and simplify the proof.

Fact 3.19
The category (**AHLSchemas(SP)**, $\mathcal{M}$) is an $\mathcal{M}$-adhesive category. $\mathcal{M}$ is the class of all injective morphisms, i. e. $f \in \mathcal{M}$ if f_P and f_T are injective.

PROOF We construct an isomorphic general comma category with index sets $\mathcal{I} = \{pre, post, cond, type\}$ and $\mathcal{J} = \{P, T\}$, categories $\mathbf{C}_j = \mathbf{X}_i = \mathbf{Sets}$, and functors $F_{pre} = F_{post} = F_{cond} = id_{\mathbf{Sets}} : \mathbf{C}_T \rightarrow \mathbf{Sets}$, $F_{type} = id_{\mathbf{Sets}} : \mathbf{C}_P \rightarrow \mathbf{Sets}$, $G_{pre} = G_{post} = (T_{SIG}(X) \otimes \_)^{\oplus} : \mathbf{C}_P \rightarrow \mathbf{Sets}$, $G_{cond} = const_{\mathcal{P}_{fin}(Eqns(SIG,X))}$, and $G_{type} = const_S$.

In fact, the identical functors preserve pushouts, and $(T_{SIG}(X) \otimes \_) : \mathbf{Sets} \rightarrow \mathbf{Sets}$, the constant functors, and $\square^{\oplus} : \mathbf{Sets} \rightarrow \mathbf{Sets}$ preserve pullbacks along injective functions, hence also $(T_{SIG}(X) \otimes \_)^{\oplus} : \mathbf{Sets} \rightarrow \mathbf{Sets}$ preserves pullbacks along injective functions. This means that Thm. 3.11 implies that (**AHLSchemas(SP)**, $\mathcal{M}$) is an $\mathcal{M}$-adhesive category.

To represent the actual data space, we combine AHL schemas with algebras to AHL nets. To obtain an $\mathcal{M}$-adhesive category, there are different choices for the algebra part:

1. The category (**Algs(SP)**, $\mathcal{M}_{iso}$) with the class $\mathcal{M}_{iso}$ of isomorphisms, which is useful for systems where only the net part but not the data part is allowed to be changed by rule application.

2. The category (**Algs(SP)**, $\mathcal{M}_{inj}$) with the class $\mathcal{M}_{inj}$ of injective morphisms, where SP is a graph structure algebra, which means that only unary operations are allowed.

Definition 3.20 (AHL net)
An *AHL net* $AN = (AC, A)$ is given by an AHL schema AC over SP and an SP-algebra $A \in \mathbf{A(SP)}$, where $\mathbf{A(SP)}$ is a subcategory of $\mathbf{Algs(SP)}$, the category of all algebras over SP.

An *AHL net morphism* $f_{AN} : AN \to AN'$ is given by a pair $f_{AN} = (f_{AC} : AC \to AC', f_A : A \to A')$, where f_{AC} is an AHL schema morphism and $f_A \in \mathbf{A(SP)}$ an SP-homomorphism.

Given an algebraic specification SP, AHL nets over SP and AHL net morphisms form the category $\mathbf{AHLNets(SP)}$.

Fact 3.21
If $(\mathbf{A(SP)}, \mathcal{M})$ is an $\mathcal{M}$-adhesive category then the category $(\mathbf{AHLNets(SP)}, \mathcal{M}')$ is an $\mathcal{M}$-adhesive category. $\mathcal{M}'$ is the class of all morphisms $f = (f_S, f_A)$ where f_S is injective and $f_A \in \mathcal{M}$.

PROOF The category $\mathbf{AHLNets(SP)}$ is isomorphic to the product category $\mathbf{AHLSchemas(SP)} \times \mathbf{A(SP)}$. According to Thm. 3.11 this implies that $(\mathbf{AHLNets(SP)}, \mathcal{M}')$ is an $\mathcal{M}$-adhesive category.

We get a more powerful variant of AHL schemas, called generalized AHL schemas, if we do not fix the specification. This is especially useful for net transformations such that it is possible to define the rules based on a small specification SP representing only the necessary data. Then these rules can be applied to nets over a larger specification SP'. We define generalized AHL schemas and nets and show that they form $\mathcal{M}$-adhesive categories under certain conditions on the data part.

Definition 3.22 (Generalized AHL schema)
A *generalized AHL schema* $GC = (SP, AC)$ is given by an algebraic specification SP and an AHL schema AC over SP.

A *generalized AHL schema morphism* $f : GC \to GC'$ is a tuple $f_{GC} = (f_{SP} : SP \to SP', f_P : P \to P', f_T : T \to T')$, where f_{SP} is a specification morphism and f_P, f_T are compatible with *pre*, *post*, *cond*, and *type* as shown below. $f_{SP}^{\#}$ is the extension of f_{SP} to terms and equations.

$$
\begin{array}{ccccccc}
\mathcal{P}_{fin}(Eqns(SIG, X)) & \xleftarrow{cond} T & \xrightarrow[post]{pre} & (T_{SIG}(X) \otimes P)^{\oplus} & P & \xrightarrow{type} & S \\
{\scriptstyle \mathcal{P}_{fin}(f_{SP}^{\#})} \downarrow \quad & = \quad {\scriptstyle f_T} \downarrow \quad & = & \downarrow {\scriptstyle (f_{SP}^{\#} \otimes f_P)^{\oplus}} & {\scriptstyle f_P} \downarrow & = & \downarrow {\scriptstyle f_{SP,S}} \\
\mathcal{P}_{fin}(Eqns(SIG', X')) & \xleftarrow{cond'} T' & \xrightarrow[post']{pre'} & (T_{SIG'}(X') \otimes P')^{\oplus} & P' & \xrightarrow{type'} & S'
\end{array}
$$

Generalized AHL schemas and generalized AHL schema morphisms form the category $\mathbf{AHLSchemas}$.

Fact 3.23

The category $(\mathbf{AHLSchemas}, \mathcal{M})$ is an $\mathcal{M}$-adhesive category. $\mathcal{M}$ is the class of all morphisms $f = (f_{SP}, f_P, f_T)$ where f_{SP} is a strict injective specification morphism and f_P, f_T are injective.

PROOF The category $\mathbf{AHLSchemas}$ is isomorphic to a suitable full subcategory of the general comma category $\mathbf{G} = GComCat(\mathbf{C}_1, \mathbf{C}_2, (F_i, G_i)_{i \in \mathcal{I}}; \mathcal{I}, \mathcal{J})$ with

- $\mathcal{I} = \{pre, post, cond, type\}$, $\mathcal{J} = \{1, 2\}$,

- $\mathbf{C}_1 = \mathbf{Specs} \times \mathbf{Sets}$, $\mathbf{C}_2 = \mathbf{Sets}$, $\mathbf{X}_i = \mathbf{Sets}$ for all $i \in \mathcal{I}$,

- $F_i : \mathbf{C}_2 \to \mathbf{X}_i$ for $i \in \{pre, post, cond\}$, $F_{type} : \mathbf{C}_1 \to \mathbf{X}_{type}$, $G_i : \mathbf{C}_1 \to \mathbf{X}_i$ for all $i \in \mathcal{I}$,

where the functors are defined by

- $F_i = Id_{\mathbf{Sets}}$, $G_i(SP, P) = (T_{SIG}(X) \times P)^{\oplus}$, $G_i(f_{SP}, f_P) = (f_{SP}^{\#} \times f_P)^{\oplus}$ for $i \in \{pre, post\}$,

- $F_{cond} = Id_{\mathbf{Sets}}$, $G_{cond}(SP, P) = \mathcal{P}_{fin}(Eqns(SIG, X))$, $G_{cond}(f_{SP}, f_P) = \mathcal{P}_{fin}(f_{SP}^{\#})$,

- $F_{type}(SP, P) = P$, $F_{type}(f_{SP}, f_P) = f_P$, $G_{type}(SP, P) = S$, $G_{type}(f_{SP}, f_P) = f_{SP,S}$.

Since $(\mathbf{Specs}, \mathcal{M}_1)$ with the class $\mathcal{M}_1$ of strict injective morphisms and $(\mathbf{Sets}, \mathcal{M}_2)$ with the class $\mathcal{M}_2$ of injective morphisms are $\mathcal{M}$-adhesive categories, Thm. 3.11 implies that also $(\mathbf{Specs} \times \mathbf{Sets}, \mathcal{M}_1 \times \mathcal{M}_2)$ is an $\mathcal{M}$-adhesive category.

The functors F_i preserve pushouts along $\mathcal{M}_{k_i}$-morphisms, which is obvious for F_{pre}, F_{post}, F_{cond}, and shown in Lemma A.4 for F_{type}, and the functors G_i preserve pullbacks along $\mathcal{M}_{\ell_i}$-morphisms as shown in Lemmas A.5, A.6, and A.7, therefore we can apply Thm. 3.11 such that $\mathbf{G}$ is an $\mathcal{M}$-adhesive category.

Now we restrict the objects $((SP, P), T, pre, post, cond, type)$ in $\mathbf{G}$ to those where

$$(1) \quad pre(t), post(t) \in (T_{SIG}(X) \otimes P)^{\oplus} \text{ for all } t \in T.$$

The full subcategory induced by these objects is isomorphic to $\mathbf{AHLSchemas}$. Since the condition (1) is preserved by pushout and pullback constructions in $\mathbf{G}$ it follows that for morphisms $f, g \in \mathbf{AHLSchemas}$ with the same (co)domain, the pushout (pullback) over f, g in $\mathbf{G}$ is also the pushout (pullback) in $\mathbf{AHLSchemas}$. Using again Thm. 3.11 we conclude that $(\mathbf{AHLSchemas}, \mathcal{M})$ is an $\mathcal{M}$-adhesive category.

As previously, we combine generalized AHL schemas with algebras to generalized AHL nets. We have two possible choices for the algebraic part:

1. The category $(\mathbf{Algs}, \mathcal{M}_{iso})$ with the class $\mathcal{M}_{iso}$ of isomorphisms, which is useful for systems where only the net part but not the data part is allowed to be changed by rule application.

2. The category $(\mathbf{Algs}|_{\mathbf{QTA}}, \mathcal{M}_{sinj})$ of quotient term algebras and unique induced homomorphisms, with the class $\mathcal{M}_{sinj}$ of strict injective morphisms.

Definition 3.24 (Generalized AHL net)
A *generalized AHL net* $GN = (GC, A)$ is given by a generalized AHL schema GC over an algebraic specification SP and an SP-algebra $A \in \mathbf{A}$, where $\mathbf{A}$ is a subcategory of $\mathbf{Algs}$.

A *generalized AHL net morphism* $f_{GN} : GN \rightarrow GN'$ is a tuple $f_{GN} = (f_{GC} : GC \rightarrow GC', f_{GA} : A \rightarrow V_{f_{SP}}(A'))$, where $f_{GC} = (f_{SP}, f_P, f_T)$ is a generalized AHL schema morphism and $f_{GA} \in \mathbf{A}$ a generalized algebra homomorphism. $V_{f_{SP}} : \mathbf{Algs(SP')} \rightarrow \mathbf{Algs(SP)}$ is the forgetful functor induced by f_{SP}.

Generalized AHL nets and generalized AHL net morphisms form the category **AHLNets**.

Fact 3.25
If $(\mathbf{A}, \mathcal{M}_1)$ is an $\mathcal{M}$-adhesive category then also the category $(\mathbf{AHLNets}, \mathcal{M})$ is an $\mathcal{M}$-adhesive category. $\mathcal{M}$ is the class of all injective AHL net morphisms f with $f_A \in \mathcal{M}_1$.

PROOF The category **AHLNets** is isomorphic to the full subcategory $(\mathbf{AHLSchemas} \times \mathbf{A})|_{Ob'}$, where $Ob' = \{((SP, P, T, pre, post, cond, type), A) \mid A \in \mathbf{A(SP)}\}$. In this subcategory, the pushout and pullback objects over $\mathcal{M}$-morphisms are the same as in **AHLSchemas** $\times$ **A**. According to Thm. 3.11 this implies that $(\mathbf{AHLNets}, \mathcal{M})$ is an $\mathcal{M}$-adhesive category.

To show that also the corresponding net systems, which are nets together with a suitable marking, are $\mathcal{M}$-adhesive categories, the more general category of markings is used, together with a result that shows under which conditions nets with markings are $\mathcal{M}$-adhesive categories. We do not go into detail here, but refer to Section A.3 in the appendix.

Combining AHL nets with markings we obtain AHL net systems, with the following choices for the underlying AHL nets:

1. The category $(\mathbf{AHLNets(SP)}, \mathcal{M}_{iso})$ with the class $\mathcal{M}_{iso}$ of isomorphisms.

2. The category $(\mathbf{AHLNets(SP, A_{fin})}, \mathcal{M}_{inj})$ of algebraic high-level nets with a fixed finite algebra A and the class $\mathcal{M}_{inj}$ of injective morphisms with identities on the algebra part.

Unfortunately, choice 1. is not useful for transformations, because the rule morphisms have to be $\mathcal{M}$-morphisms. In the case of isomorphisms, only isomorphic rules and transformations were allowed.

Definition 3.26 (AHL net system)
Given an algebraic specification SP, an *AHL net system* $AS = (AN, m)$ is given by an AHL net $AN = (P, T, pre, post, cond, type, A)$ over SP with $A \in \mathbf{A(SP)}$, where $\mathbf{A(SP)}$ is a subcategory of $\mathbf{Algs(SP)}$, and a marking $m : (A \otimes P) \to \mathbb{N}$.

An *AHL net system morphism* $f_{AS} : AS \to AS'$ is given by an AHL net morphism $f_{AN} = (f_{AC}, f_A) : AN \to AN'$ with $f_{AC} = (f_P, f_T)$ and $f_A \in \mathbf{A(SP)}$ that is marking-preserving, i.e. $\forall (a, p) \in A \otimes P : m(a, p) \leq m'(f_A(a), f_P(p))$.

AHL net systems and AHL net system morphisms form the category **AHLSystems(SP)**.

Fact 3.27
If $(\mathbf{AHLNets(SP)}, \mathcal{M}')$ is an $\mathcal{M}$-adhesive category and the functor $M : \mathbf{AHLNets(SP)} \to \mathbf{Sets}$, defined by $M(P, T, pre, post, cond, type, A) = A \otimes P$ and $M(f_{AN}) = f_A \otimes f_P$ for $f_{AN} = (f_{AC}, f_A)$ and $f_{AC} = (f_P, f_T)$, preserves pushouts and pullbacks along $\mathcal{M}'$-morphisms then the category $(\mathbf{AHLSystems(SP)}, \mathcal{M})$ is an $\mathcal{M}$-adhesive category, where $\mathcal{M}$ is the class of all strict morphisms, i.e. $f_{AS} = (f_{AC}, f_A) : AS \to AS' \in \mathcal{M}$ if $f_A \in \mathcal{M}_1$, $f_{AC} = (f_P, f_T)$ is injective, and f_{AS} is marking-strict, i.e. $\forall (a, p) \in A \otimes P : m(a, p) = m'(f_A(a), f_P(p))$.

PROOF If the category $(\mathbf{AHLNets(SP)}, \mathcal{M}')$ with a suitable choice of algebras is an $\mathcal{M}$-adhesive category we can apply Thm. A.16 to obtain the result that $(\mathbf{AHLSystems(SP)}, \mathcal{M})$ is an $\mathcal{M}$-adhesive category.

Analogously, we can show that generalized AHL net systems form an $\mathcal{M}$-adhesive category if the marking set functor M preserves pushouts and pullbacks along $\mathcal{M}'$-morphisms. Due to the conditions for M there are two suitable choices for the category $(\mathbf{AHLNets}, \mathcal{M}')$:

1. The category $(\mathbf{AHLNets}, \mathcal{M}_{iso})$ with the class $\mathcal{M}_{iso}$ of isomorphisms, which is, analogously to the case $(\mathbf{AHLNets(SP)}, \mathcal{M}_{iso})$, not useful for transformations.

2. The category $(\mathbf{AHLNets_{iso}}, \mathcal{M}_{sinj})$ of algebraic high-level nets with morphisms that are isomorphisms on the algebra part, with the class $\mathcal{M}_{sinj}$ of strict injective morphisms.

Definition 3.28 (Generalized AHL net system)
A *generalized AHL net system* $GS = (GN, m)$ is given by a generalized AHL net $GN = (SP, P, T, pre, post, cond, type, A)$ with $A \in \mathbf{A}$, where $\mathbf{A}$ is a subcategory of **Algs**, and a marking $m : (A \otimes P) \to \mathbb{N}$.

A *generalized AHL net system morphism* $f_{GS} : GS \to GS'$ is given by a generalized AHL net morphism $f_{GN} = (f_{GC}, f_{GA}) : GN \to GN'$ with $f_{GC} = (f_P, f_T)$ and $f_{GA} \in \mathbf{A}$ that is marking-preserving, i.e. $\forall (a, p) \in A \otimes P : m(a, p) \leq m'(f_A(a), f_P(p))$.

Generalized AHL net systems and generalized AHL net system morphisms form the category **AHLSystems**.

Fact 3.29

If (**AHLNets**, $\mathcal{M}'$) is an $\mathcal{M}$-adhesive category and the functor $M :$ **AHLNets** $\to$ **Sets**, with $M(SP, P, T, pre, post, cond, type, A) = A \otimes P$ and $M(f_{GN}, f_{GA}) = f_{GA} \otimes f_P$ for $f_{GN} = (f_{GC}, f_{GA})$ and $f_{GC} = (f_P, f_T)$, preserves pushouts and pullbacks along $\mathcal{M}'$-morphisms then the category (**AHLSystems**, $\mathcal{M}$) is an $\mathcal{M}$-adhesive category, where $\mathcal{M}$ is the class of all strict morphisms, i.e. $f_{GS} = (f_{GC}, f_{GA}) : GS \to GS' \in \mathcal{M}$ if $f_{GA} \in \mathcal{M}_1$, $f_{GC} = (f_P, f_T)$ is strict injective and f_{GS} is marking-strict, i.e. $\forall (a, p) \in A \otimes P : m(a, p) = m'(f_A(a), f_P(p))$.

PROOF By Fact 3.25, (**AHLNets**, $\mathcal{M}'$) with a suitable choice of algebras is an $\mathcal{M}$-adhesive category. Then we can apply Thm. A.16 to obtain the result that (**AHLSystems**, $\mathcal{M}$) is an $\mathcal{M}$-adhesive category.

In the following theorem, we summarize the results in this subsection stating that AHL schemas, nets, and net systems as well as generalized AHL schemas, nets, and net systems form $\mathcal{M}$-adhesive categories.

Theorem 3.30 (Petri net classes as $\mathcal{M}$-adhesive categories)

With suitable choices for the underlying $\mathcal{M}$-morphisms, specifications, and algebras, the following Petri net classes form $\mathcal{M}$-adhesive categories:

- (**AHLSchemas(SP)**, $\mathcal{M}$) of AHL schemas over SP,
- (**AHLNets(SP)**, $\mathcal{M}$) of AHL nets over SP,
- (**AHLSystems(SP)**, $\mathcal{M}$) of AHL net systems over SP,
- (**AHLSchemas**, $\mathcal{M}$) of generalized AHL schemas,
- (**AHLNets**, $\mathcal{M}$) of generalized AHL nets, and
- (**AHLSystems**, $\mathcal{M}$) of generalized AHL net systems.

PROOF This follows directly from Facts 3.19, 3.21, 3.27, 3.23, 3.25, and 3.29.

3.4 Transformations in $\mathcal{M}$-Adhesive Systems

In the double-pushout approach [EEPT06], transformations are defined by the application of a rule to an object, which is provided by two pushouts.

The transformation exists if both pushouts can be constructed. To express a more restricted application of rules, application conditions are a beneficial technique. Throughout this section, we assume to have an $\mathcal{M}$-adhesive category $(\mathbf{C}, \mathcal{M})$.

3.4.1 Conditions and Constraints over Objects

Nested conditions were introduced in [HP05, HP09] to express properties of objects in a category. They are expressively equivalent to first-order formulas on graphs. Later, we will use them to express application conditions for rules to increase the expressiveness of transformations.

Basically, a condition describes the existence or non-existence of a certain structure for an object.

Definition 3.31 (Condition)
A *(nested) condition ac* over an object P is of the form

- $ac = \text{true}$,
- $ac = \exists(a, ac')$, where $a : P \to C$ is a morphism and ac' is a condition over C,
- $ac = \neg ac'$, where ac' is a condition over P,
- $ac = \wedge_{i \in \mathcal{I}} ac_i$, where $(ac_i)_{i \in \mathcal{I}}$ with an index set $\mathcal{I}$ are conditions over P, or
- $ac = \vee_{i \in \mathcal{I}} ac_i$, where $(ac_i)_{i \in \mathcal{I}}$ with an index set $\mathcal{I}$ are conditions over P.

Moreover, false abbreviates $\neg\text{true}$, $\exists a$ abbreviates $\exists(a, \text{true})$, and $\forall(a, ac)$ abbreviates $\neg\exists(a, \neg ac)$.

A condition is satisfied by a morphism into an object if the required structure exists, which can be verified by the existence of suitable morphisms.

Definition 3.32 (Satisfaction of conditions)
Given a condition ac over P a morphism $p : P \to G$ *satisfies ac*, written $p \models ac$, if

- $ac = \text{true}$,
- $ac = \exists(a, ac')$ and there exists a morphism $q \in \mathcal{M}$ with $q \circ a = p$ and $q \models ac'$,

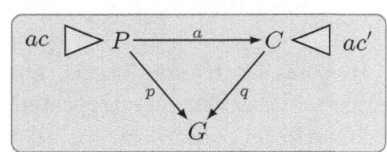

- $ac = \neg ac'$ and $p \not\models ac'$,
- $ac = \wedge_{i \in \mathcal{I}} ac_i$ and $\forall i \in \mathcal{I} : p \models ac_i$, or
- $ac = \vee_{i \in \mathcal{I}} ac_i$ and $\exists i \in \mathcal{I} : p \models ac_i$.

Two conditions ac and ac' over P are *semantically equivalent*, denoted by $ac \cong ac'$, if $p \models ac \Leftrightarrow p \models ac'$ for all morphisms p.

As shown in [HP09, EHL10a], conditions can be shifted over morphisms into equivalent conditions over the codomain. For this shift construction, all epimorphic overlappings of the codomain of the shift morphism and the codomain of the condition morphism have to be collected.

Definition 3.33 (Shift over morphism)
Given a condition ac over P and a morphism $b : P \to P'$, then Shift(b, ac) is a condition over P' defined by

- Shift$(b, ac) = $ true if $ac = $ true,
- Shift$(b, ac) = \bigvee_{(a', b') \in \mathcal{F}} \exists(a', \text{Shift}(b', ac'))$ if $ac = \exists(a, ac')$ and $\mathcal{F} = \{(a', b') \mid (a', b')$ jointly epimorphic, $b' \in \mathcal{M}, b' \circ a = a' \circ b\}$,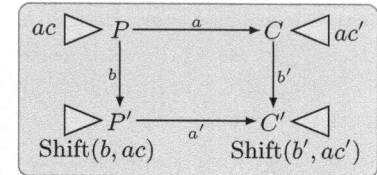
- Shift$(b, ac) = \neg\text{Shift}(b, ac')$ if $ac = \neg ac'$,
- Shift$(b, ac) = \bigwedge_{i \in \mathcal{I}}\text{Shift}(b, ac_i)$ if $ac = \bigwedge_{i \in \mathcal{I}} ac_i$, or
- Shift$(b, ac) = \bigvee_{i \in \mathcal{I}}\text{Shift}(b, ac_i)$ if $ac = \bigvee_{i \in \mathcal{I}} ac_i$.

Fact 3.34
Given a condition ac over P and morphisms $b : P \to P'$, $b' : P' \to P''$, and $p : P' \to G$ then

- $p \models \text{Shift}(b, ac)$ if and only if $p \circ b \models ac$ and
- Shift$(b', \text{Shift}(b, ac)) \cong \text{Shift}(b' \circ b, ac)$.

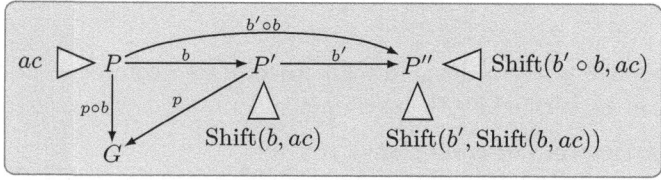

PROOF See [HP09, EHL10a].

In contrast to conditions, constraints describe global requirements for objects. They can be interpreted as conditions over the initial object, which means that a constraint $\exists(i_C, \text{true})$ with the initial morphism i_C is valid for an object G if there exists a morphism $c : C \to G$. This constraint expresses that the existence of C as a part of G is required.

Definition 3.35 (Constraint)
Given an initial object I, a condition ac over I is called a *constraint*.

The satisfaction of a constraint is that of the corresponding conditions, adapted to the special case of a condition over an initial object.

Definition 3.36 (Satisfaction of constraint)
Given a constraint ac (over the initial object I), then an object G *satisfies* ac, written $G \models ac$, if

- $ac = \text{true}$,
- $ac = \exists(i_C, ac')$ and there exists a morphism $c \in \mathcal{M}$ with $c \models ac'$,
- $ac = \neg ac'$ and $G \not\models ac'$,
- $ac = \bigwedge_{i \in \mathcal{I}} ac_i$ and $\forall i \in \mathcal{I} : G \models ac_i$, or
- $ac = \bigvee_{i \in \mathcal{I}} ac_i$ and $\exists i \in \mathcal{I} : G \models ac_i$.

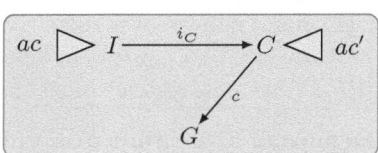

3.4.2 Rules and Transformations

In [EEPT06], transformation systems based on a categorical foundation using $\mathcal{M}$-adhesive categories were introduced which can be instantiated to various graphs and graph-like structures. In addition, application conditions extend the standard approach of transformations. Here, we present the theory of transformations for rules with application conditions, while the case without application conditions is always explicitly mentioned.

A rule is a general description of local changes that may occur in objects of the transformation system. Mainly, it consists of some deletion part and some construction part, defined by the rule morphisms l and r, respectively.

Definition 3.37 (Rule)
A *rule* $p = (L \xleftarrow{l} K \xrightarrow{r} R, ac)$ consists of objects L, K, and R, called left-hand side, gluing, and right-hand side, respectively, two morphisms l and r with $l, r \in \mathcal{M}$, and a condition ac over L, called *application condition*.

A transformation describes the application of a rule to an object via a match. It can only be applied if the match satisfies the application condition.

Definition 3.38 (Transformation)
Given a rule $p = (L \xleftarrow{l} K \xrightarrow{r} R, ac)$, an object G, and a morphism $m : L \to G$, called match, such that $m \models ac$ then a *direct transformation* $G \xRightarrow{p,m} H$ from G to an object H is given by the pushouts (1) and (2).

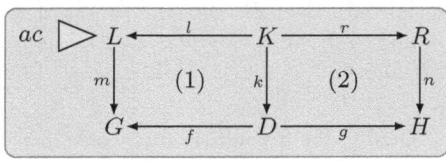

A sequence of direct transformations is called a *transformation*.

Remark 3.39

Note that for the construction of pushout (1) we have to construct the pushout complement of $m \circ l$, which is only possible if the so-called gluing condition is satisfied.

In analogy to the application condition over L, which is a pre-application condition, it is also possible to define post-application conditions over the right-hand side R of a rule. Since these application conditions over R can be translated to equivalent application conditions over L (and vice versa) [HP09], we can restrict our rules to application conditions over L.

Definition 3.40 (Shift over rule)

Given a rule $p = (L \xleftarrow{l} K \xrightarrow{r} R, ac)$ and a condition ac_R over R, then $\mathrm{L}(p, ac_R)$ is a condition over L defined by

- $\mathrm{L}(p, ac_R) = $ true if $ac_R = $ true,

- $\mathrm{L}(p, ac_R) = \exists(b, \mathrm{L}(p^*, ac'_R))$

  if $ac_R = \exists(a, ac'_R)$, $a \circ r$ has a pushout complement (1), and $p^* = (Y \xleftarrow{l^*} Z \xrightarrow{r^*} X)$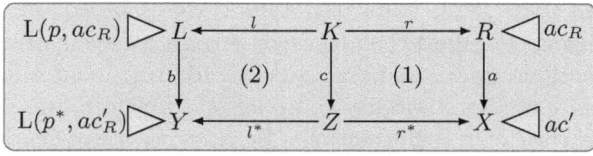

  is the derived rule by constructing pushout (2), $\mathrm{L}(p, \exists(a, ac'_R)) = $ false otherwise,

- $\mathrm{L}(p, ac_R) = \neg \mathrm{L}(p, ac'_R)$ if $ac_R = \neg ac'_R$,

- $\mathrm{L}(p, ac_R) = \wedge_{i \in \mathcal{I}} \mathrm{L}(p, ac_{R,i})$ if $ac_R = \wedge_{i \in \mathcal{I}} ac_{R,i}$, or

- $\mathrm{L}(p, ac_R) = \vee_{i \in \mathcal{I}} \mathrm{L}(p, ac_{R,i})$ if $ac_R = \vee_{i \in \mathcal{I}} ac_{R,i}$.

Dually, for a condition ac_L over L we define $\mathrm{R}(p, ac_L) = \mathrm{L}(p^{-1}, ac_L)$, where the *inverse rule p^{-1}* without application conditions is defined by $p^{-1} = (R \xleftarrow{r} K \xrightarrow{l} L)$.

Fact 3.41

Given a transformation $G \xRightarrow{p,m} H$ via a rule $p = (L \xleftarrow{l} K \xrightarrow{r} R, ac)$ and a condition ac_R over R, then $m \models \mathrm{L}(p, ac_R)$ if and only if $n \models ac_R$ and Shift$(m, \mathrm{L}(p, ac_R)) \cong \mathrm{L}(p', \text{Shift}(n, ac_R))$ for $p' = (G \xleftarrow{f} D \xrightarrow{g} H)$.

Dually, for a condition ac_L over L we have that $m \models ac_L$ if and only if $n \models \mathrm{R}(p, ac_L)$.

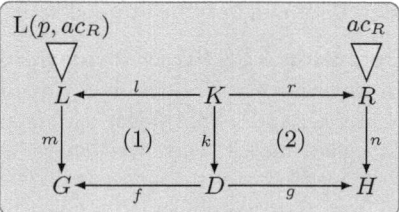

PROOF See [HP09].

A set of rules constitutes an $\mathcal{M}$-adhesive transformation system, and combined with a start object an $\mathcal{M}$-adhesive grammar. The language of such a grammar contains all objects derivable from the start object.

Definition 3.42 ($\mathcal{M}$-adhesive transformation system and grammar)
An $\mathcal{M}$-*adhesive transformation system* $AS = (\mathbf{C}, \mathcal{M}, P)$ consists of an $\mathcal{M}$-adhesive category $(\mathbf{C}, \mathcal{M})$ and a set of rules P.

An $\mathcal{M}$-*adhesive grammar* $AG = (AS, S)$ consists of an $\mathcal{M}$-adhesive transformation system AS and a start object S.

The *language* L of an $\mathcal{M}$-adhesive grammar AG is defined by
$$L = \{G \mid \exists \text{ transformation } S \stackrel{*}{\Rightarrow} G \text{ via } P\}.$$

3.4.3 Main Analysis Results in $\mathcal{M}$-Adhesive Transformation Systems

In [EEPT06], main important results for $\mathcal{M}$-adhesive transformation systems without application conditions were proven. These were extended in [LEOP08, LEPO08] to $\mathcal{M}$-adhesive transformation systems with negative application conditions (NACs), a special variant of application conditions which forbid the existence of a certain structure extending the match. With [EHL10a, EHL$^+$10b], all these results are now available also for transformations with application conditions. Here, we explain and state the results and as far as necessary the underlying concepts, but do not show the proofs. Most of these results are based on the results for transformations without application conditions combined with some additional requirements for the application conditions and based on shifting the application conditions over morphisms and rules.

3.4.3.1 Local Church-Rosser and Parallelism Theorem

The first result is concerned with parallel and sequential independence of direct transformations. We study under what conditions two direct transformations applied to the same object can be applied in arbitrary order, leading to the same result. This leads to the Local Church-Rosser Theorem. Moreover, the corresponding rules can be applied in parallel in this case, leading to the Parallelism Theorem.

First, we define the notion of parallel and sequential independence. Two direct transformations $G \xrightarrow{p_1, m_1} H_1$ and $G \xrightarrow{p_2, m_2} H_2$ are parallel independent if p_1 does not delete anything p_2 uses and does not create or delete anything to invalidate ac_2, and vice versa.

Definition 3.43 (Parallel independence)

Two direct transformations $G \xRightarrow{p_1,m_1} H_1$ and $G \xRightarrow{p_2,m_2} H_2$ are *parallel independent* if there are morphisms $i : L_1 \to D_2$ and $j : L_2 \to D_1$ such that $f_2 \circ i = m_1$, $f_1 \circ j = m_2$, $g_2 \circ i \models ac_1$, and $g_1 \circ j \models ac_2$.

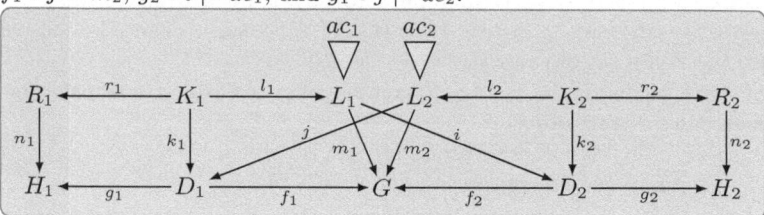

Analogously, two direct transformations $G \xRightarrow{p_1,m_1} H_1 \xRightarrow{p_2,m_2} G'$ are sequentially independent if p_1 does not create something p_2 uses, p_2 does not delete something p_1 uses or creates, p_1 does not delete or create anything thereby initially validating ac_2, and p_2 does not delete or create something invalidating ac_1.

Definition 3.44 (Sequential independence)

Two direct transformations $G \xRightarrow{p_1,m_1} H_1 \xRightarrow{p_2,m_2} G'$ are *sequentially independent* if there are morphisms $i : R_1 \to D_2$ and $j : L_2 \to D_1$ such that $f_2 \circ i = n_1$, $g_1 \circ j = m_2$, $g_2 \circ i \models \mathrm{R}(p_1, ac_1)$, and $f_1 \circ j \models ac_2$.

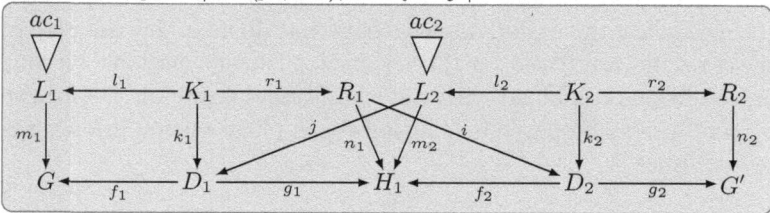

The idea of a parallel rule is, in case of parallel independence, to apply both rules in parallel. For rules p_1 and p_2, the parallel rule $p_1 + p_2$ is the coproduct of the rules, and for the application conditions we have to make sure that both single rules can be applied in any order. For the parallel rule, we require an $\mathcal{M}$-adhesive category with binary coproducts.

Definition 3.45 (Parallel rule)

Given rules $p_1 = (L_1 \xleftarrow{l_1} K_1 \xrightarrow{r_1} R_1, ac_1)$ and $p_2 = (L_2 \xleftarrow{l_2} K_2 \xrightarrow{r_2} R_2, ac_2)$, the *parallel rule* $p_1 + p_2 = (L_1 + L_2 \xleftarrow{l_1+l_2} K_1 + K_2 \xrightarrow{r_1+r_2} R_1 + R_2, ac)$ is defined by the component-wise binary coproducts of the left-hand sides, glueings, and right-hand sides including the morphisms, and $ac =$ Shift$(i_{L_1}, ac_1) \wedge L(p_1 + p_2,$ Shift$(i_{R_1}, R(p_1, ac_1)))$ $\wedge$ Shift$(i_{L_2}, ac_2) \wedge L(p_1 + p_2,$ Shift$(i_{R_2}, R(p_2, ac_2)))$.

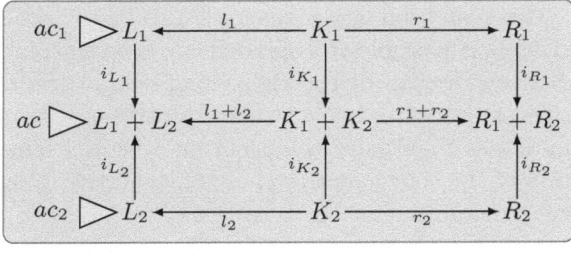

With these notions of independence and the parallel rule, we are able to formulate the Local Church-Rosser and Parallelism Theorem.

Theorem 3.46 (Local Church-Rosser and Parallelism Theorem)
Given two parallel independent direct transformations $G \xRightarrow{p_1, m_1} H_1$ and $G \xRightarrow{p_2, m_2} H_2$ there is an object G' together with direct transformations $H_1 \xRightarrow{p_2, m_2'} G'$ and $H_2 \xRightarrow{p_1, m_1'} G'$ such that $G \xRightarrow{p_1, m_1} H_1 \xRightarrow{p_2, m_2'} G'$ and $G \xRightarrow{p_2, m_2} H_2 \xRightarrow{p_1, m_1'} G'$ are sequentially independent.

Given two sequentially independent direct transformations $G \xRightarrow{p_1, m_1} H_1 \xRightarrow{p_2, m_2'} G'$ there is an object H_2 together with direct transformations $G \xRightarrow{p_2, m_2} H_2 \xRightarrow{p_1, m_1'} G'$ such that $G \xRightarrow{p_1, m_1} H_1$ and $G \xRightarrow{p_2, m_2} H_2$ are parallel independent.

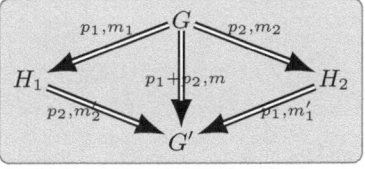

In any case of independence, there is a parallel transformation $G \xRightarrow{p_1 + p_2, m} G'$ and, vice versa, a direct transformation $G \xRightarrow{p_1 + p_2, m} G'$ via the parallel rule $p_1 + p_2$ can be sequentialized both ways.

PROOF See [EHL10a].

3.4.3.2 Concurrency Theorem

In contrast to the Local Church-Rosser Theorem, the Concurrency Theorem is concerned with the execution of transformations which may be sequentially dependent. This means that, in general, we cannot commute subsequent direct transformations, as done for independent transformations in the Local Church-Rosser Theorem, nor are we able to apply the corresponding parallel rule, as done in the Parallelism Theorem. Nevertheless, it is possible to apply both transformations concurrently using a so-called E-concurrent rule and shifting the application conditions of the single rules to an equivalent concurrent application condition.

Given an arbitrary sequence $G \xrightarrow{p_1, m_1} H \xrightarrow{p_2, m_2} G'$ of direct transformations it is possible to construct an E-concurrent rule $p_1 *_E p_2$. The object E is an overlap of the right-hand side of the first rule and the left-hand side of the second rule, where the two overlapping morphisms have to be in a class $\mathcal{E}'$ of pairs of morphisms with the same codomain. The construction of the concurrent application condition is again based on the two shift constructions.

Definition 3.47 (Concurrent rule)
Given rules $p_1 = (L_1 \xleftarrow{l_1} K_1 \xrightarrow{r_1} R_1, ac_1)$ and $p_2 = (L_2 \xleftarrow{l_2} K_2 \xrightarrow{r_2} R_2, ac_2)$ an object E with morphisms $e_1 : R_1 \to E$ and $e_2 : L_2 \to E$ with $(e_1, e_2) \in \mathcal{E}'$ is an E-*dependency relation* of p_1 and p_2 if the pushout complements (1) and (2) of $e_1 \circ r_1$ and $e_2 \circ l_2$, respectively, exist.

Given an E-dependency relation (E, e_1, e_2) of p_1 and p_2 the E-*concurrent rule* $p_1 *_E p_2 = (L \xleftarrow{s_1 \circ w_1} K \xrightarrow{t_2 \circ w_2} R, ac)$ is constructed by pushouts (1), (2), (3), (4), and pullback (5), with $ac = \text{Shift}(u_1, ac_1) \wedge L(p^*, \text{Shift}(e_2, ac_2))$ and $p^* = (L \xleftarrow{s_1} C_1 \xrightarrow{t_1} E)$.

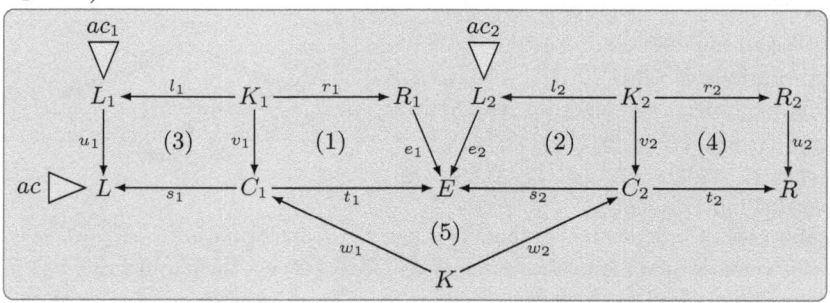

A sequence $G \xrightarrow{p_1, m_1} H \xrightarrow{p_2, m_2} G'$ is called E-*related* if there exist $h : E \to H$, $c_1 : C_1 \to D_1$, and $c_2 : C_2 \to D_2$ such that $h \circ e_1 = n_1$, $h \circ e_2 = m_2$, $c_1 \circ v_1 = k_1$, $c_2 \circ v_2 = k_2$, and (6) and (7) are pushouts.

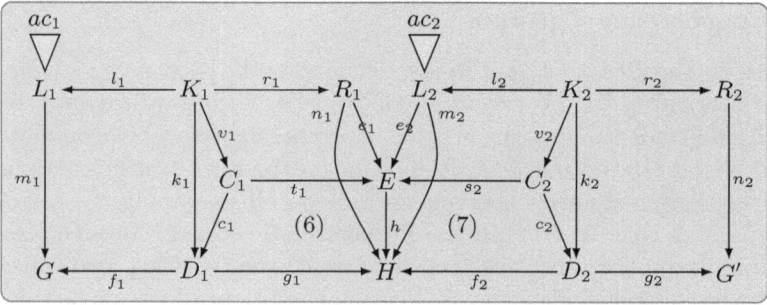

For a sequence $G \xrightarrow{p_1,m_1} H \xrightarrow{p_2,m_2} G'$ of direct transformations we can construct an E-dependency relation such that the sequence is E-related. Then the E-concurrent rule $p_1 *_E p_2$ allows us to construct a direct transformation $G \xrightarrow{p_1*_Ep_2} G'$ via $p_1 *_E p_2$. Vice versa, each direct transformation $G \xrightarrow{p_1*_Ep_2} G'$ via the E-concurrent rule $p_1 *_E p_2$ can be sequentialized leading to an E-related transformation sequence $G \xrightarrow{p_1,m_1} H \xrightarrow{p_2,m_2} G'$ of direct transformations via p_1 and p_2.

Theorem 3.48 (Concurrency Theorem)
For rules p_1 and p_2 and an E-concurrent rule $p_1 *_E p_2$ we have:

- Given an E-related transformation sequence $G \xrightarrow{p_1,m_1} H \xrightarrow{p_2,m_2} G'$ then there is a *synthesis construction* leading to a direct transformation $G \xrightarrow{p_1*_Ep_2,m} G'$ via the E-concurrent rule $p_1 *_E p_2$.

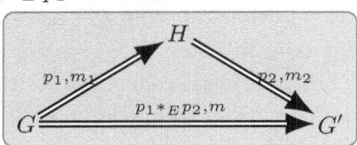

- Given a direct transformation $G \xrightarrow{p_1*_Ep_2,m} G'$ then there is an *analysis construction* leading to an E-related transformation sequence $G \xrightarrow{p_1,m_1} H \xrightarrow{p_2,m_2} G'$.

- The synthesis and analysis constructions are inverse to each other up to isomorphism.

PROOF See [EHL10a].

3.4.3.3 Embedding and Extension Theorem

For the Embedding and Extension Theorem, we analyze under what conditions a transformation $t : G_0 \overset{*}{\Rightarrow} G_n$ can be extended to a transformation $t' : G'_0 \overset{*}{\Rightarrow} G'_n$ via an extension morphism $k_0 : G_0 \to G'_0$. The idea is to obtain an *extension diagram* (1), which is defined by pushouts $(2_i) - (5_i)$ for all $i = 1, \ldots, n$, where the same rules $p_1, \ldots, p_n$ are applied in the same order in t and t'.

$$
\begin{array}{ccccccccc}
G_0 & \xrightarrow{\ t\ *} & G_n & ac_i \triangleright & L_i & \xleftarrow{\ l_i\ } & K_i & \xrightarrow{\ r_i\ } & R_i \\
k_0 \downarrow & (1) & \downarrow k_n & & m_i \downarrow & (2_i)\ \ j_i \downarrow & (3_i) & & \downarrow n_i \\
G'_0 & \xrightarrow[t']{\ *} & G'_n & & G_{i-1} & \xleftarrow{\ f_i\ } & D_i & \xrightarrow{\ g_i\ } & G_i \\
& & & & k_i \downarrow & (4_i)\ \ d_i \downarrow & (5_i) & & \downarrow k_{i+1} \\
& & & & G'_{i-1} & \xleftarrow[f'_i]{} & D'_i & \xrightarrow[g'_i]{} & G'_i
\end{array}
$$

It is important to note that this is not always possible, because there may be some elements in G'_0 invalidating an application condition or forbidding the deletion of something which can still be deleted in G_0. But we are able to give a necessary and sufficient consistency condition to allow such an extension. This result is important for all kinds of applications where we have a large object G'_0, but only small subparts of G'_0 have to be changed by the rules $p_1, \ldots, p_n$. In this case, we choose a suitable small subobject G_0 of G'_0 and construct a transformation $t : G_0 \overset{*}{\Rightarrow} G_n$ via $p_1, \ldots, p_n$ first. Then we compute the *derived span* of this transformation, which we extend in a second step via the inclusion $k_0 : G_0 \to G'_0$ to a transformation $t' : G'_0 \overset{*}{\Rightarrow} G'_n$ via the same rules $p_1, \ldots, p_n$. Since we only have to compute the small transformation from G_0 to G_n and the extension of G_n to G'_n, this makes the computation of $G'_0 \Rightarrow G'_n$ more efficient.

The derived span connects the first and the last object of a transformation and describes in one step, similar to a rule, the changes between them. Over the derived span we can also define a derived application condition which becomes useful later for the Local Confluence Theorem.

Definition 3.49 (Derived span and application condition)
Given a transformation $t : G_0 \overset{*}{\Rightarrow} G_n$ via rules $p_1, \ldots, p_n$, the *derived span* $der(t)$ is inductively defined by

$$der(t) = \begin{cases} G_0 \overset{f_1}{\leftarrow} D_1 \overset{g_1}{\rightarrow} G_1 & \text{for } t : G_0 \xrightarrow{p_1, m_1} G_1 \\ G_0 \overset{d'_0 \circ d}{\leftarrow} D \overset{g_n \circ d_n}{\rightarrow} G_n & \text{for } t : G_0 \overset{*}{\Rightarrow} G_{n-1} \xrightarrow{p_n, m_n} G_n \text{ with} \\ & \quad der(G_0 \overset{*}{\Rightarrow} G_{n-1}) = (G_0 \overset{d'_0}{\leftarrow} D' \overset{d'_{n-1}}{\rightarrow} G_{n-1}) \\ & \quad \text{and pullback } (PB) \end{cases}$$

$$G_0 \overset{d'_0}{\longleftarrow} D' \overset{d'_{n-1}}{\longrightarrow} G_{n-1} \overset{f_n}{\longleftarrow} D_n \overset{g_n}{\longrightarrow} G_n$$
$$(PB)$$
$$D' \overset{d}{\searrow} \quad D \quad \overset{d_n}{\swarrow} D_n$$

Moreover, the *derived application condition* $ac(t)$ is defined by

$$ac(t) = \begin{cases} \text{Shift}(m_1, ac_1) & \text{for } t : G_0 \xrightarrow{p_1, m_1} G_1 \\ ac(G_0 \overset{*}{\Rightarrow} G_{n-1}) & \text{for } t : G_0 \overset{*}{\Rightarrow} G_{n-1} \xrightarrow{p_n, m_n} G_n \\ \wedge \text{L}(p_n^*, \text{Shift}(m_n, ac_n)) & \text{with } p_n^* = der(G_0 \overset{*}{\Rightarrow} G_{n-1}) \end{cases}$$

For the consistency condition, we need the concept of initial pushouts over $\mathcal{M}'$ (see Def. 3.8 Item 4) and require $k_0 \in \mathcal{M}'$. In order to be *boundary consistent*, we have to find a morphism from the boundary of k_0 to the consistent span, which means that no element in the boundary is deleted by the transformation. Moreover, k_0 needs to be *AC-consistent*, therefore it should fulfill a summarized set of application conditions formulated on G_0. This set is equivalent to all application conditions occurring in t and again based on the shift constructions. We say that k_0 is *consistent* with respect to t if it is both boundary consistent and AC-consistent.

Definition 3.50 (Consistency)
Given a transformation $t : G_0 \overset{*}{\Rightarrow} G_n$ via rules $p_1, \ldots, p_n$ with a derived span $G_0 \overset{d_0^*}{\leftarrow} D \overset{d_n^*}{\rightarrow} G_n$ a morphism $k_0 : G_0 \rightarrow G_0' \in \mathcal{M}'$ is called *consistent w. r. t. t* if it is

1. *boundary consistent,* i.e. given the initial pushout (6) over k_0 there is a morphism $b' \in \mathcal{M}$ with $d_0^* \circ b' = b$, and

2. *AC-consistent,* i.e. given the concurrent rule $p = (L \overset{l}{\leftarrow} K \overset{r}{\rightarrow} R, ac)$ of t with match $m : L \rightarrow G_0$ then $k_0 \circ m \models ac$.

The Embedding and Extension Theorem now describes the fact that consistency of a morphism $k_0 : G_0 \rightarrow G_0'$ is both necessary and sufficient to embed a transformation $t : G_0 \overset{*}{\Rightarrow} G_n$ via k_0.

Theorem 3.51 (Embedding and Extension Theorem)
Given a transformation $t : G_0 \overset{*}{\Rightarrow} G_n$ and a morphism $k_0 : G_0 \rightarrow G_0' \in \mathcal{M}'$ which is consistent with respect to t then there is an extension diagram over t and k_0.

Given a transformation $t : G_0 \overset{*}{\Rightarrow} G_n$ with an extension diagram (1) and initial pushout (6) over $k_0 : G_0 \rightarrow G_0' \in \mathcal{M}'$ as above then we have that:

1. k_0 is consistent with respect to $t : G_0 \overset{*}{\Rightarrow} G_n$.

2. There is a rule $der(t) = (G_0 \overset{d_0^*}{\leftarrow} D \overset{d_n^*}{\rightarrow} G_n)$ leading to a direct transformation $G_0' \Rightarrow G_n'$ via $der(t)$.

3. G_n' is the pushout of C and G_n along B, i.e. $G_n' = G_n +_B C$.

PROOF See [EHL$^+$10b].

3.4.3.4 Critical Pairs and Local Confluence Theorem

A transformation system is called *confluent* if, for all transformations $G \overset{*}{\Rightarrow} H_1$ and $G \overset{*}{\Rightarrow} H_2$, there is an object X together with transformations $H_1 \overset{*}{\Rightarrow} X$ and $H_2 \overset{*}{\Rightarrow} X$. *Local confluence* means that this property holds for all pairs of direct transformations $G \overset{p_1,m_1}{\Longrightarrow} H_1$ and $G \overset{p_2,m_2}{\Longrightarrow} H_2$.

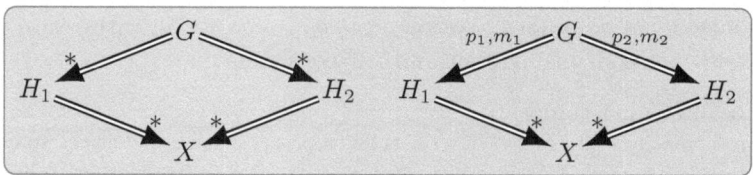

Confluence is an important property of a transformation system, because, in spite of local nondeterminism concerning the application of a rule, we have global determinism for confluent transformation systems. *Global determinism* means that, for each pair of terminating transformations $G \stackrel{*}{\Rightarrow} H$ and $G \stackrel{*}{\Rightarrow} H'$ with the same source object, the target objects H and H' are equal or isomorphic. A transformation $G \stackrel{*}{\Rightarrow} H$ is called *terminating* if no rule is applicable to H anymore. This means that each transformation sequence terminates after a finite number of steps.

The Local Church-Rosser Theorem shows that, for two parallel independent direct transformations $G \xrightarrow{p_1,m_1} H_1$ and $G \xrightarrow{p_2,m_2} H_2$, there is an object G' together with direct transformations $H_1 \xrightarrow{p_2,m_2'} G'$ and $H_2 \xrightarrow{p_1,m_1'} G'$. This means that we can apply the rules p_1 and p_2 with given matches in an arbitrary order. If each pair of productions is parallel independent for all possible matches, then it can be shown that the corresponding transformation system is confluent.

In the following, we discuss local confluence for the general case in which $G \xrightarrow{p_1,m_1} H_1$ and $G \xrightarrow{p_2,m_2} H_2$ are not necessarily parallel independent. According to a general result for rewriting systems, it is sufficient to consider local confluence, provided that the transformation system is terminating.

The main idea is to study critical pairs. The notion of critical pairs was developed first in the area of term rewriting systems (see, e.g., [Hue80]), later introduced in the area of graph transformation for hypergraph rewriting [Plu93], and then for all kinds of transformation systems fitting into the framework of $\mathcal{M}$-adhesive categories [EEPT06, LEPO08, EHL$^+$10b].

Note that the notion of critical pairs for transformations with and without application conditions differs. For transformations without application conditions, a pair $P_1 \xleftarrow{p_1,o_1} K \xrightarrow{p_2,o_2} P_2$ of direct transformations is called a critical pair if it is parallel dependent and minimal in the sense that $(o_1, o_2) \in \mathcal{E}'$, while for transformations with application conditions, the matches o_1 and o_2 are allowed to violate the application conditions, but induce new ones that have to be respected by a parallel dependent extension of the critical pair. These induced application conditions make sure that the extension respects the application conditions of the given rules and that there is indeed a conflict. Here, we only present the Local Confluence Theorem for transformations with application conditions, see [EEPT06] for transformations without application conditions and [LEPO08] for transformations with only negative application conditions.

Definition 3.52 (Critical pair)
Given rules $p_1 = (L_1 \overset{l_1}{\leftarrow} K_1 \overset{r_1}{\rightarrow} R_1, ac_1)$ and $p_2 = (L_2 \overset{l_2}{\leftarrow} K_2 \overset{r_2}{\rightarrow} R_2, ac_2)$ a pair $P_1 \overset{p_1,o_1}{\Longleftarrow} K \overset{p_2,o_2}{\Longrightarrow} P_2$ of direct transformations without application conditions is a *critical pair* (for transformations with application conditions), if $(o_1, o_2) \in \mathcal{E}'$ and there exists an extension of the pair via a monomorphism $m : K \rightarrow G \in \mathcal{M}'$ such that $m \models ac_K = ac_K^E \wedge ac_K^C$, with

- *extension application condition:* $ac_K^E = \mathrm{Shift}(o_1, ac_1) \wedge \mathrm{Shift}(o_2, ac_2)$ and

- *conflict-inducing application condition:* $ac_K^C = \neg(ac_{z_1} \wedge ac_{z_2})$, with
  if $(\exists z_1 : v_1 \circ z_1 = o_2$ then $ac_{z_1} = \mathrm{L}(p_1^*, \mathrm{Shift}(w_1 \circ z_1, ac_2))$ else $ac_{z_1} = \mathrm{false}$,
  $\qquad\qquad\qquad\qquad\qquad$ with $p_1^* = (K \overset{v_1}{\leftarrow} N_1 \overset{w_1}{\rightarrow} P_1)$
  if $(\exists z_2 : v_2 \circ z_2 = o_1$ then $ac_{z_2} = \mathrm{L}(p_2^*, \mathrm{Shift}(w_2 \circ z_2, ac_1))$ else $ac_{z_2} = \mathrm{false}$,
  $\qquad\qquad\qquad\qquad\qquad$ with $p_2^* = (K \overset{v_2}{\leftarrow} N_2 \overset{w_2}{\rightarrow} P_2)$

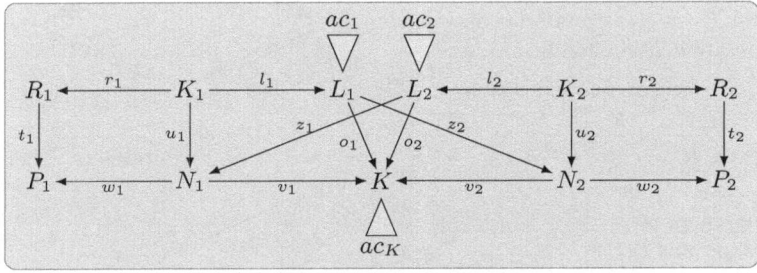

It can be shown that every pair of parallel dependent direct transformations is an extension of a critical pair, which is shown in the Completeness Theorem.

Theorem 3.53 (Completeness Theorem)
For each pair of parallel dependent direct transformations $H_1 \overset{p_1,m_1}{\Longleftarrow} G \overset{p_2,m_2}{\Longrightarrow} H_2$ there is a critical pair $P_1 \overset{p_1,o_1}{\Longleftarrow} K \overset{p_2,o_2}{\Longrightarrow} P_2$ with induced application condition ac_K and a monomorphism $m : K \rightarrow G \in \mathcal{M}'$ with $m \models ac_K$ leading to extension diagrams (1) and (2).

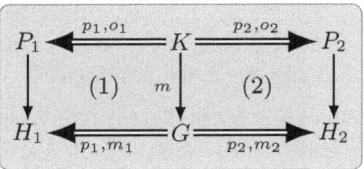

PROOF See [EHL$^+$10b].

In order to show local confluence it is sufficient to show strict AC-confluence of all its critical pairs. As discussed above, confluence of a critical pair $P_1 \Leftarrow K \Rightarrow P_2$ means the existence of an object K' together with transformations $P_1 \overset{*}{\Rightarrow} K'$ and $P_2 \overset{*}{\Rightarrow} \dot{K}'$.

Strictness is a technical condition which means, intuitively, that the parts which are preserved by both transformations of the critical pair are also preserved in the common object K'. In [Plu95], it has been shown that confluence of critical pairs without strictness is not sufficient to show local confluence. For strict AC-confluence of a critical pair, the transformations of the strict solution of the critical pair must be extendable to G, which means that each application condition of both transformations must be satisfied in the bigger context.

Definition 3.54 (Strict AC-confluence)
A critical pair $P_1 \xleftarrow{p_1,o_1} K \xrightarrow{p_2,o_2} P_2$ with induced application conditions ac_K is strictly AC-confluent if it is

1. confluent without application conditions, i. e. there are transformations $P_1 \overset{*}{\Rightarrow} K'$ and $P_2 \overset{*}{\Rightarrow} K'$ eventually disregarding the application conditions, and

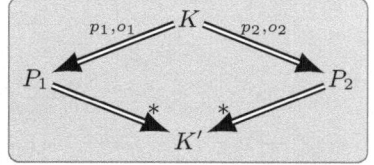

2. strict, i. e. given derived spans $der(P_i \xrightarrow{p_i,o_i} K_i) = (K \xleftarrow{v_i} N_i \xrightarrow{w_i} P_i)$ and $der(P_i \overset{*}{\Rightarrow} K') = (P_i \xleftarrow{v_{i+2}} N_{i+2} \xrightarrow{w_{i+2}} K')$ for $i = 1, 2$ and pullback (1) then there exist morphisms z_3, z_4 such that diagrams (2), (3), and (4) commute, and

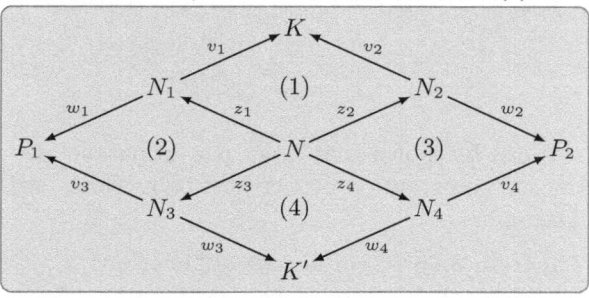

3. for $\bar{t}_i : K \xrightarrow{p_i,o_i} P_i \overset{*}{\Rightarrow} K'$ it holds that $ac_K \Rightarrow ac(\bar{t}_i)$ for $i = 1, 2$.

Based on strict AC-confluent critical pairs we can obtain local confluence of a transformation system.

Theorem 3.55 (Local Confluence Theorem)
A transformation system is locally confluent if all its critical pairs are strictly AC-confluent.

PROOF See [EHL$^+$10b].

4 Amalgamated Transformations

In this chapter, we introduce amalgamated transformations, which are useful for the definition of the semantics of models using transformations. An amalgamated rule is based on a kernel rule, which defines a fixed part of the match, and multi rules, which extend this fixed match. From a kernel and a multi rule, a complement rule can be constructed which characterizes the effect of the multi rule exceeding the kernel rule. An interaction scheme is defined by a kernel rule and available multi rules, leading to a bundle of multi rules that specifies in addition how often each multi rule is applied. Amalgamated rules are in general standard rules in $\mathcal{M}$-adhesive transformation systems, thus all the results follow. In addition, we are able to refine parallel independence of amalgamated rules based on the induced multi rules. If we extend an interaction scheme as large as possible we can describe the transformation for an unknown number of matches, which otherwise would have to be defined by an infinite number of rules. This leads to maximal matchings, which are useful to define the semantics of models.

In Section 4.1, we introduce amalgamated rules and transformations, show some important results, and illustrate our work with a running example. In Section 4.2, we define the firing semantics of elementary Petri nets modeled by typed graphs using amalgamation. Moreover, we introduce statecharts and use amalgamation to define a suitable operational semantics.

4.1 Foundations and Analysis of Amalgamated Transformations

In this section, we introduce amalgamated transformations and show the main results. In the following, a *bundle* represents a family of morphisms or transformation steps with the same domain, which means that a bundle of things always starts at the same object. Moreover, we require an $\mathcal{M}$-adhesive category with binary coproducts, initial and effective pushouts (see Section 3.2).

4.1.1 Kernel, Multi, and Complement Rules

A kernel morphism describes how a smaller rule, the kernel rule, is embedded into a larger rule, the multi rule. The multi rule has its name because it can be applied multiple times for a given kernel rule match as described later. We need some more technical preconditions to make sure that the embeddings of the L-, K-, and R-components as well as the application conditions are consistent and allow to construct a complement rule.

Definition 4.1 (Kernel morphism)

Given rules $p_0 = (L_0 \xleftarrow{l_0} K_0 \xrightarrow{r_0} R_0, ac_0)$ and $p_1 = (L_1 \xleftarrow{l_1} K_1 \xrightarrow{r_1} R_1, ac_1)$, a *kernel morphism* $s_1 : p_0 \to p_1$, $s_1 = (s_{1,L}, s_{1,K}, s_{1,R})$ consists of $\mathcal{M}$-morphisms $s_{1,L} : L_0 \to L_1$, $s_{1,K} :$

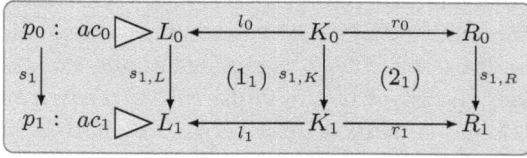

$K_0 \to K_1$, and $s_{1,R} : R_0 \to R_1$ such that in the above diagram (1_1) and (2_1) are pullbacks, (1_1) has a pushout complement $(1'_1)$ for $s_{1,L} \circ l_0$, and $ac_1 \Rightarrow \text{Shift}(s_{1,L}, ac_0)$. In this case, p_0 is called *kernel rule* and p_1 *multi rule*.

ac_0 and ac_1 are *complement-compatible* w.r.t. s_1 if there is some application condition ac'_1 on L_{10} such that $ac_1 \cong \text{Shift}(s_{1,L}, ac_0) \wedge \text{L}(p_1^*, \text{Shift}(v_1, ac'_1))$ for the pushout (3_1) and $p_1^* = (L_1 \xleftarrow{u_1} L_{10} \xrightarrow{v_1} E_1)$.

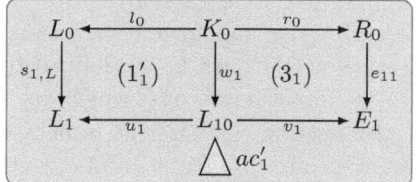

Remark 4.2

The complement-compatibility of the application conditions makes sure that there is a decomposition of ac_1 into parts on L_0 and L_{10}, where the latter ones are used later for the application conditions of the complement rule.

Example 4.3

To explain the concept of amalgamation, in our example we model a small transformation system for switching the direction of edges in labeled graphs, where we

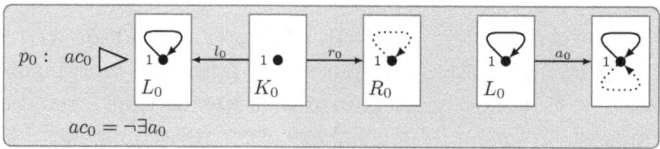

Figure 4.1: The kernel rule p_0 deleting a loop at a node

only have different labels for edges – black and dotted edges. The kernel rule p_0 is depicted in Fig. 4.1. It selects a node with a black loop, deletes this loop, and adds a dotted loop, all of this if no dotted loop is already present. The matches are defined by the numbers at the nodes and can be induced for the edges by their position.

In Figure 4.2, two multi rules p_1 and p_2 are shown which extend the rule p_0 and in addition reverse an edge if no backward edge is present. They also inherit the application condition of p_0 forbidding a dotted loop at the selected node. There is a kernel morphism $s_1 : p_0 \rightarrow p_1$ as shown in the top of Fig. 4.2 with pullbacks (1_1), (2_1) and pushout complement $(1_1')$. Similarly, there is a kernel morphism $s_2 : p_0 \rightarrow p_2$ as shown in the bottom of Fig. 4.2 with pullbacks (1_2), (2_2) and pushout complement $(1_2')$.

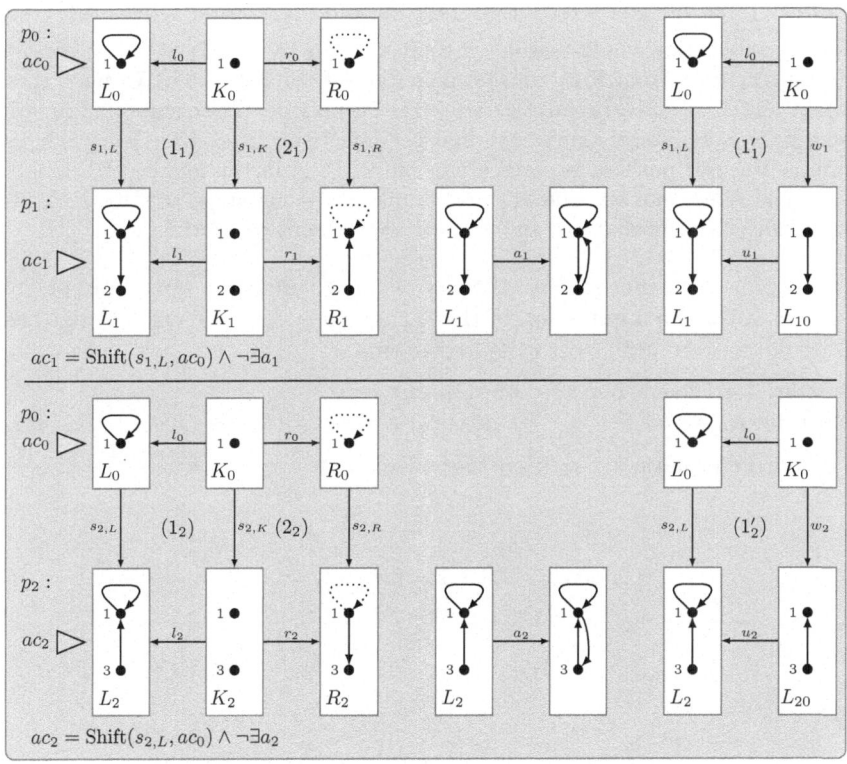

Figure 4.2: The multi rules p_1 and p_2 describing the reversion of an edge

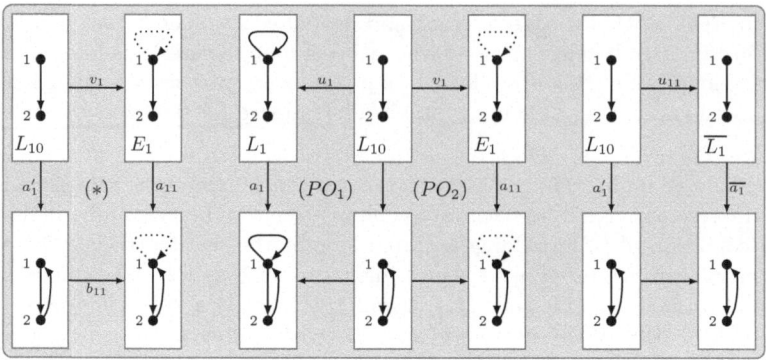

Figure 4.3: Constructions for the application conditions

For the application conditions, $ac_1 = \text{Shift}(s_{1,L}, ac_0) \wedge \neg \exists a_1 \cong \text{Shift}(s_{1,L}, ac_0) \wedge$ $\text{L}(p_1^*, \text{Shift}(v_1, \neg \exists a_1'))$ with a_1' as shown in the left of Fig. 4.3. We have that $\text{Shift}(v_1, \neg \exists a_1') = \neg \exists a_{11}$, because square $(*)$ is the only possible commuting square leading to a_{11}, b_{11} jointly surjective and b_{11} injective. $\text{L}(p_1^*, \neg \exists a_{11}) = \neg \exists a_1$ as shown by the two pushout squares (PO_1) and (PO_2) in the middle of Fig. 4.3. Thus $ac_1' = \neg \exists a_1'$, and ac_0 and ac_1 are complement-compatible w. r. t. s_1. Similarly, it can be shown that ac_0 and ac_2 are complement-compatible w. r. t. s_2.

For a given kernel morphism, the complement rule is the remainder of the multi rule after the application of the kernel rule, i. e. it describes what the multi rule does in addition to the kernel rule.

Theorem 4.4 (Existence of complement rule)
Given rules $p_0 = (L_0 \xleftarrow{l_0} K_0 \xrightarrow{r_0} R_0, ac_0)$ and $p_1 = (L_1 \xleftarrow{l_1} K_1 \xrightarrow{r_1} R_1, ac_1)$, and a kernel morphism $s_1 : p_0 \to p_1$ then there exists a rule $\overline{p_1} = (\overline{L_1} \xleftarrow{\overline{l_1}} \overline{K_1} \xrightarrow{\overline{r_1}}$

$\overline{R_1}, \overline{ac_1}$) and a jointly epimorphic cospan $R_0 \xrightarrow{e_{11}} E_1 \xleftarrow{e_{12}} \overline{L_1}$ such that the E_1-concurrent rule $p_0 *_{E_1} \overline{p_1}$ exists and $p_1 = p_0 *_{E_1} \overline{p_1}$ for rules without application conditions. Moreover, if ac_0 and ac_1 are complement-compatible w. r. t. s_1 then $p_1 \cong p_0 *_{E_1} \overline{p_1}$ also for rules with application conditions.

PROOF First, we consider the construction without application conditions. Since s_1 is a kernel morphism the following diagrams (1_1) and (2_1) are pullbacks and (1_1) has a pushout complement $(1'_1)$ for $s_{1,L} \circ l_0$. Construct the pushout (3_1).

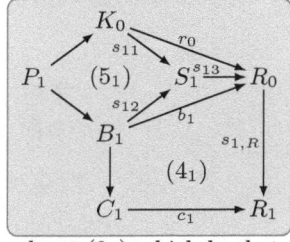

Now construct the initial pushout (4_1) over $s_{1,R}$ with $b_1, c_1 \in \mathcal{M}$, P_1 as the pullback object of r_0 and b_1, and the pushout (5_1) where we obtain an induced morphism $s_{13} : S_1 \to R_0$ with $s_{13} \circ s_{12} = b_1$, $s_{13} \circ s_{11} = r_0$, and $s_{13} \in \mathcal{M}$ by effective pushouts.

Since (1_1) is a pullback Lemma A.17 implies that there is a unique morphism $l_{10} : K_1 \to L_{10}$ with $l_{10} \circ s_{1,K} = w_1$, $u_1 \circ l_{10} = l_1$, and $l_{10} \in \mathcal{M}$, and we can construct pushouts $(6_1) - (9_1)$ as a decomposition of pushout (3_1) which leads to $\overline{L_1}$ and $\overline{K_1}$ of the complement rule, and with $(7_1) + (9_1)$ being a pushout e_{11} and e_{12} are jointly epimorphic.

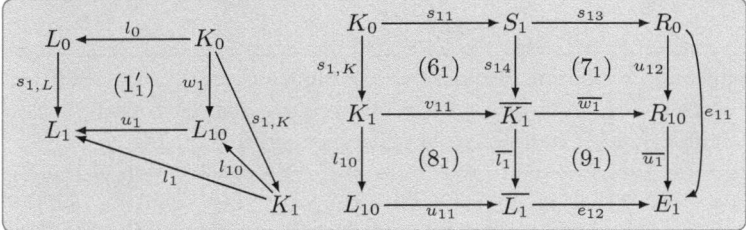

The pushout (4_1) can be decomposed into pushouts (10_1) and (11_1) obtaining the right-hand side $\overline{R_1}$ of the complement rule, while pullback (2_1) can be decomposed into pushout (6_1) and square (12_1) which is a pullback by Lemma A.18.

Now Lemma A.17 implies that there is a unique morphism $\overline{r_1} : \overline{K_1} \to \overline{R_1}$ with $\overline{r_1} \circ s_{14} = u_{13}$, $t_1 \circ \overline{r_1} = v_{12}$, and $\overline{r_1} \in \mathcal{M}$. With pushout (7_1) there is a unique morphism $\overline{v_1} : R_{10} \to R_1$ and by pushout decomposition of $(11_1) = (7_1) + (13_1)$ square (13_1) is a pushout.

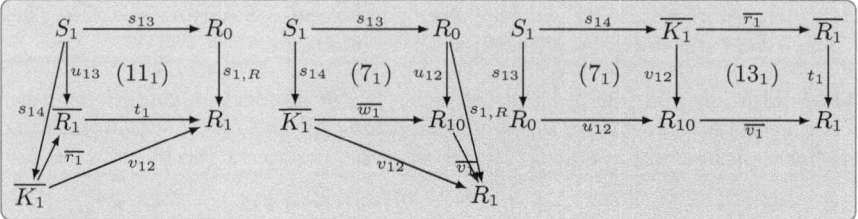

Moreover, $(8_1) + (9_1)$ as a pushout over $\mathcal{M}$-morphisms is also a pullback which completes the construction of the rule and $p_1 = p_0 *_{E_1} \overline{p_1}$ for rules without application conditions.

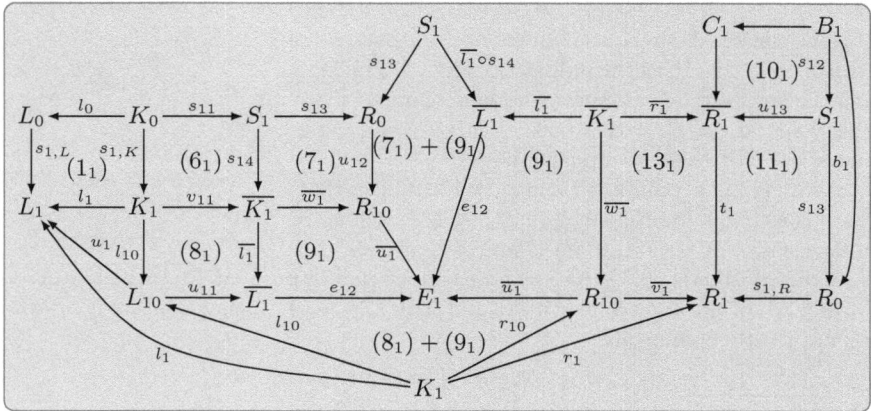

For the application conditions, suppose $ac_1 \cong \mathrm{Shift}(s_{1,L}, ac_0) \wedge \mathrm{L}(p_1^*, \mathrm{Shift}(v_1, ac_1'))$ for $p_1^* = (L_1 \xleftarrow{u_1} L_{10} \xrightarrow{v_1} E_1)$ with $v_1 = e_{12} \circ u_{11}$ and ac_1' over L_{10}. Now define $\overline{ac_1} = \mathrm{Shift}(u_{11}, ac_1')$, which is an application condition on $\overline{L_1}$.

We have to show that $(p_1, ac_{p_0 *_{E_1} \overline{p_1}}) \cong (p_1, ac_1)$. By construction of the E_1-concurrent rule we have that $ac_{p_0 *_{E_1} \overline{p_1}} \cong \mathrm{Shift}(s_{1,L}, ac_0) \wedge \mathrm{L}(p_1^*, \mathrm{Shift}(e_{12}, \overline{ac_1})) \cong \mathrm{Shift}(s_{1,L}, ac_0) \wedge \mathrm{L}(p_1^*, \mathrm{Shift}(e_{12}, \mathrm{Shift}(u_{11}, ac_1'))) \cong \mathrm{Shift}(s_{1,L}, ac_0) \wedge \mathrm{L}(p_1^*, \mathrm{Shift}(e_{12} \circ u_{11}, ac_1')) \cong \mathrm{Shift}(s_{1,L}, ac_0) \wedge \mathrm{L}(p_1^*, \mathrm{Shift}(v_1, ac_1')) \cong ac_1$.

Remark 4.5

Note that by construction the interface K_0 of the kernel rule has to be preserved in the complement rule. The construction of $\overline{p_1}$ is not unique w. r. t. the property $p_1 = p_0 *_{E_1} \overline{p_1}$, since other choices for S_1 with $\mathcal{M}$-morphisms s_{11} and s_{13} also lead to a well-defined construction. In particular, one could choose $S_1 = R_0$ leading to $\overline{p_1} = E_1 \xleftarrow{\overline{u_1}} R_{10} \xrightarrow{\overline{v_1}} R_1$. Our choice represents the smallest possible complement, which should be preferred in most application areas.

Definition 4.6 (Complement rule)

Given rules $p_0 = (L_0 \xleftarrow{l_0} K_0 \xrightarrow{r_0} R_0, ac_0)$ and $p_1 = (L_1 \xleftarrow{l_1} K_1 \xrightarrow{r_1} R_1, ac_1)$, and a kernel morphism $s_1 : p_0 \to p_1$ such that ac_0 and ac_1 are complement-compatible w. r. t. s_1 then the rule $\overline{p_1} = (\overline{L_1} \xleftarrow{\overline{l_1}} \overline{K_1} \xrightarrow{\overline{r_1}} \overline{R_1}, \overline{ac_1})$ constructed in Thm. 4.4 is called *complement rule* (of s_1).

If we choose $\overline{ac_1}$ = true this leads to the *weak complement rule* (of s_1) $\overline{p_1} = (\overline{L_1} \xleftarrow{\overline{l_1}} \overline{K_1} \xrightarrow{\overline{r_1}} \overline{R_1}, \text{true})$, which is defined even if ac_0 and ac_1 are not complement-compatible.

Example 4.7

Consider the kernel morphism s_1 depicted in Fig. 4.2. Using Thm. 4.4 we obtain the complement rule depicted in the top row in Fig. 4.4 with the application condition $\overline{ac_1} = \neg\exists\overline{a_1}$ constructed in the right of Fig. 4.3. The diagrams in Fig. 4.5 show the complete construction as done in the proof. Similarly, we obtain a complement rule for the kernel morphism $s_2 : p_0 \to p_2$ in Fig. 4.2, which is shown in the bottom row of Fig. 4.4.

Each direct transformation via a multi rule can be decomposed into a direct transformation via the kernel rule followed by a direct transformation via the (weak) complement rule.

Fact 4.8

Given rules $p_0 = (L_0 \xleftarrow{l_0} K_0 \xrightarrow{r_0} R_0, ac_0)$ and $p_1 = (L_1 \xleftarrow{l_1} K_1 \xrightarrow{r_1} R_1, ac_1)$, a kernel morphism $s_1 : p_0 \to p_1$, and a direct transformation $t_1 : G \xRightarrow{p_1, m_1} G_1$ then t_1 can be decomposed into the transformation $G \xRightarrow{p_0, m_0}$

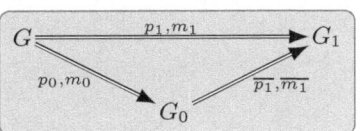

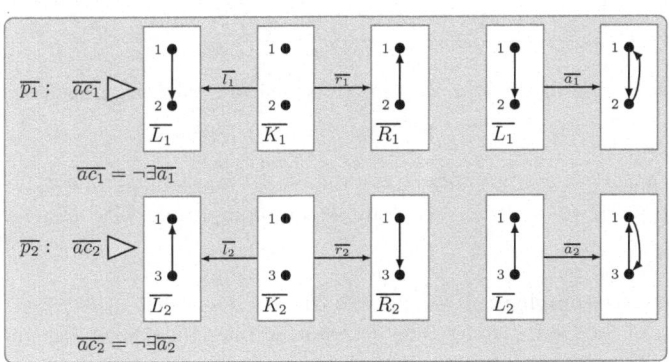

Figure 4.4: The complement rules for the kernel morphisms

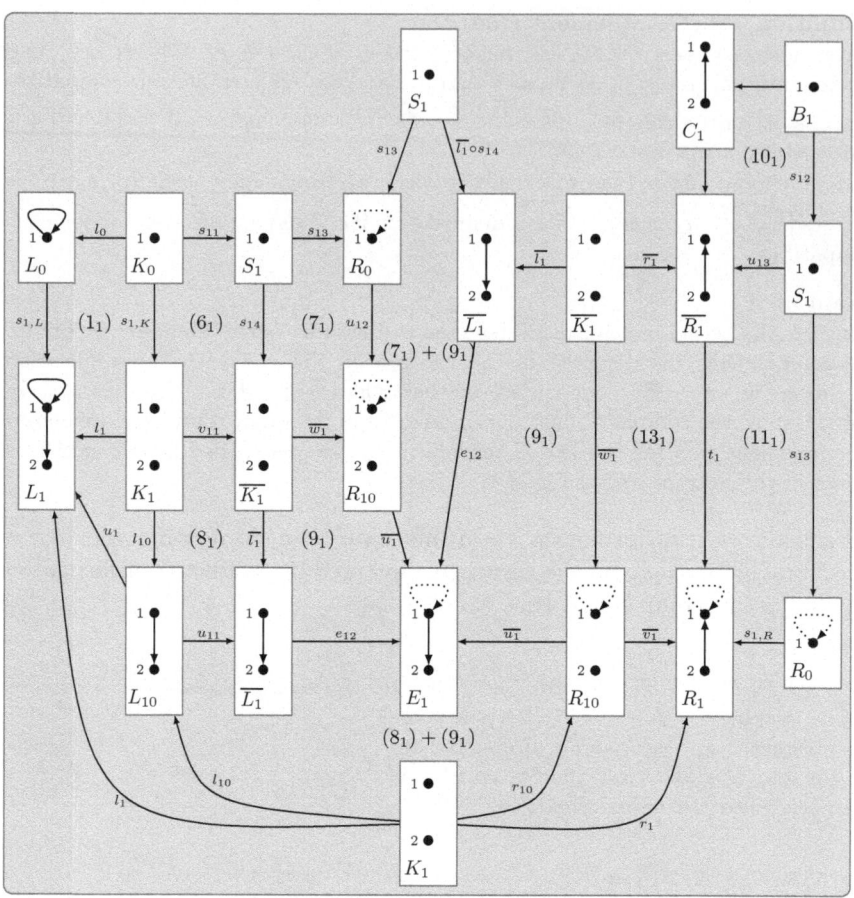

Figure 4.5: The construction of the complement rule for the kernel morphism s_1

$G_0 \xrightarrow{\overline{p_1}, \overline{m_1}} G_1$ with $m_0 = m_1 \circ s_{1,L}$ using either the weak complement rule $\overline{p_1}$ or the complement rule $\overline{p_1}$, if ac_0 and ac_1 are complement-compatible with respect to s_1.

PROOF If ac_0 and ac_1 are complement-compatible then we have that $p_1 \cong p_0 *_{E_1}$ $\overline{p_1}$. The analysis part of the Concurrency Theorem now implies the decomposition into $G \xrightarrow{p_0, m_0} G_0 \xrightarrow{\overline{p_1}, \overline{m_1}} G_1$ with $m_0 = m_1 \circ s_{1,L}$.

If ac_0 and ac_1 are not complement-compatible we can apply the analysis part of the Concurrency Theorem without application conditions leading to a decomposition into $G \xrightarrow{p_0, m_0} G_0 \xrightarrow{\overline{p_1, m_1}} G_1$ with $m_0 = m_1 \circ s_{1,L}$ for rules without application conditions. Since $ac_1 \Rightarrow \mathrm{Shift}(s_{1,L}, ac_0)$ and $m_1 \models ac_1$ we have that $m_1 \models \mathrm{Shift}(s_{1,L}, ac_0) \Leftrightarrow m_0 = m_1 \circ s_{1,L} \models ac_0$. Moreover, $\overline{ac_1} = $ true and $\overline{m_1} \models \overline{ac_1}$. This means that this is also a decomposition for rules with application conditions.

4.1.2 Amalgamated Rules and Transformations

Now we consider not only single kernel morphisms, but bundles of them over a fixed kernel rule. Then we can combine the multi rules of such a bundle to an amalgamated rule by gluing them along the common kernel rule.

Definition 4.9 (Multi-amalgamated rule)

Given rules $p_i = (L_i \xleftarrow{l_i} K_i \xrightarrow{r_i} R_i, ac_i)$ for $i = 0, \ldots, n$ and a bundle of kernel morphisms $s = (s_i : p_0 \to p_i)_{i=1,\ldots,n}$, then the *(multi-)amalgamated rule* $\tilde{p}_s = (\tilde{L}_s \xleftarrow{\tilde{l}_s} \tilde{K}_s \xrightarrow{\tilde{r}_s} \tilde{R}_s, \tilde{ac}_s)$ is constructed as the component-wise colimit of the kernel morphisms.

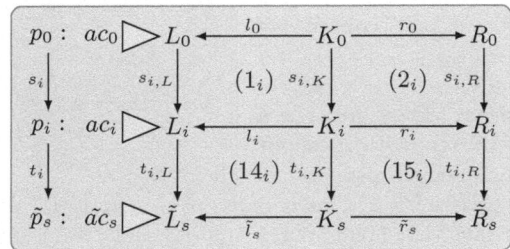

This means that $\tilde{L}_s = Col((s_{i,L})_{i=1,\ldots,n})$, $\tilde{K}_s = Col((s_{i,K})_{i=1,\ldots,n})$, and $\tilde{R}_s = Col((s_{i,R})_{i=1,\ldots,n})$, with $\tilde{l}_s$ and $\tilde{r}_s$ induced by $(t_{i,L} \circ l_i)_{i=0,\ldots,n}$ and $(t_{i,R} \circ r_i)_{0=1,\ldots,n}$, respectively, with $\tilde{ac}_s = \bigwedge_{i=1,\ldots,n} \mathrm{Shift}(t_{i,L}, ac_i)$.

This definition is well-defined. Moreover, if the application conditions of the kernel morphisms are complement-compatible this also holds for the application condition of the amalgamated rule with respect to the morphisms from the original kernel and multi rules.

Fact 4.10

The amalgamated rule as defined in Def. 4.9 is well-defined and we have kernel morphisms $t_i = (t_{i,L}, t_{i,K}, t_{i,R}) : p_i \to \tilde{p}_s$ for $i = 0, 1, \ldots, n$. If ac_0 and ac_i are complement-compatible w. r. t. s_i for all $i = 1, \ldots, n$ then also ac_i and $\tilde{ac}_s$ as well as ac_0 and $\tilde{ac}_s$ are complement compatible w. r. t. t_i and t_0, respectively.

PROOF Consider the colimits $(\tilde{L}_s, (t_{i,L})_{i=0,\ldots,n})$ of $(s_{i,L})_{i=1,\ldots,n}$, $(\tilde{K}_s, (t_{i,K})_{i=0,\ldots,n})$ of $(s_{i,K})_{i=1,\ldots,n}$, and $(\tilde{R}_s, (t_{i,R})_{i=0,\ldots,n})$ of $(s_{i,R})_{i=1,\ldots,n}$, with $t_{0,*} = t_{i,*} \circ s_{i,*}$ for $* \in \{L, K, R\}$. Since $t_{i,L} \circ l_i \circ s_{i,K} = t_{i,L} \circ s_{i,L} \circ l_0 = t_{0,L} \circ l_0$, we get an induced morphism $\tilde{l}_s : \tilde{K}_s \to \tilde{L}_s$ with $\tilde{l}_s \circ t_{i,K} = t_{i,L} \circ l_i$ for $i = 0, \ldots, n$. Similarly, we obtain $\tilde{r}_s : \tilde{K}_s \to \tilde{R}_s$ with $\tilde{r}_s \circ t_{i,K} = t_{i,R} \circ r_i$ for $i = 0, \ldots, n$.

The colimit of a bundle of n morphisms can be constructed by iterated pushout constructions, which means that we only have to require pushouts over $\mathcal{M}$-morphisms. Since pushouts are closed under $\mathcal{M}$-morphisms, the iter-

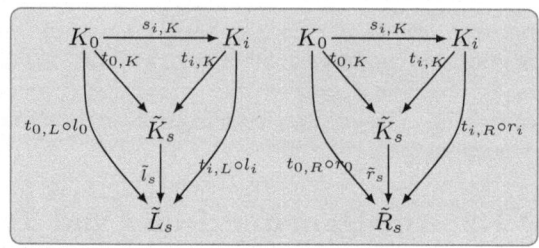

ated pushout construction leads to $t \in \mathcal{M}$.

It remains to show that (14_i) resp. $(14_i) + (1_i)$ and (15_i) resp. $(15_i) + (2_i)$ are pullbacks, and (14_i) resp. $(14_i) + (1_i)$ has a pushout complement for $t_{i,L} \circ l_i$. We prove this by induction over j for (14_i) resp. $(14_i) + (1_i)$, the pullback property of (15_i) follows analogously.

We prove: Let $\tilde{L}_j$ and $\tilde{K}_j$ be the colimits of $(s_{i,L})_{i=1,\ldots,j}$ and $(s_{i,K})_{i=1,\ldots,j}$, respectively. Then (16_{ij}) is a pullback with pushout

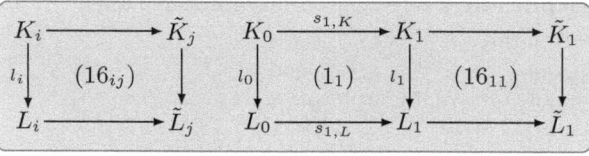

complement property for all $i = 0, \ldots, j$.

Basis $j = 1$: The colimits of $s_{1,L}$ and $s_{1,K}$ are L_1 and K_1, respectively, which means that $(16_{01}) = (1) + (16_{11})$ and (16_{11}) are both pushouts and pullbacks.

Induction step $j \to j + 1$: Construct $\tilde{L}_{j+1} = \tilde{L}_j +_{L_0} L_{j+1}$ and $\tilde{K}_{j+1} = \tilde{K}_j +_{K_0} K_{j+1}$ as pushouts, and we have the right cube with the top and bottom faces as pushouts, the back faces as pullbacks, and by the van Kampen property also the front faces are pullbacks. Moreover, by Lemma A.19 the front faces have the

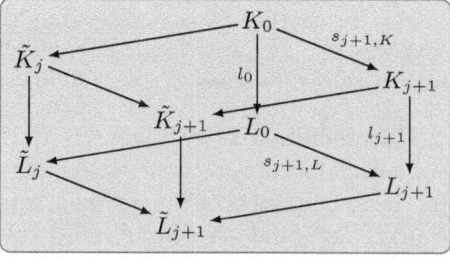

pushout complement property, and by Lemma A.20 this also holds for (16_{0j}) and (16_{ij}) as compositions. Thus, for a given n, (16_{in}) is the required pullback (14_i) resp. $(14_i) + (1_i)$ with pushout complement property, using $\tilde{K}_n = \tilde{K}_s$ and $\tilde{L}_n = \tilde{L}_s$. Obviously, $\tilde{ac}_s = \bigwedge_{i=1,\ldots,n} \text{Shift}(t_{i,L}, ac_i) \Rightarrow \text{Shift}(t_{i,L}, ac_i)$ for all $i = 1, \ldots, n$, which completes the first part of the proof.

If ac_0 and ac_i are complement-compatible we have that $ac_i \cong \text{Shift}(s_{i,L}, ac_0) \wedge \text{L}(p_i^*, \text{Shift}(v_i, ac_i'))$. Consider the pullback (17_i), which is a pushout by $\mathcal{M}$-pushout-pullback decomposition and the uniqueness of pushout complements, and the pushout (18_i). For ac_i', it holds that $\text{Shift}(t_{i,L}, \text{L}(p_i^*, \text{Shift}(v_i, ac_i'))) \cong \text{L}(\tilde{p}_s^*, \text{Shift}(\tilde{k}_i \circ v_i, ac_i')) \cong \text{L}(\tilde{p}_s^*, \text{Shift}(\tilde{v}, \text{Shift}(\tilde{l}_i, ac_i')))$. Define $ac_i^* := \text{Shift}(\tilde{l}_i, ac_i')$ as an application condition on $\tilde{L}_0$. It follows that $\tilde{ac}_s = \bigwedge_{i=1,\ldots,n} \text{Shift}(t_{i,L}, ac_i) \cong$

$\bigwedge_{i=1,\ldots,n}(\text{Shift}(t_{i,L} \circ s_{i,L}, ac_0) \wedge \text{Shift}(t_{i,L}, \text{L}(p_i^*, \text{Shift}(v_i, ac_i')))) \cong \text{Shift}(t_{0,L}, ac_0) \wedge$
$\bigwedge_{i=1,\ldots,n} \text{L}(\tilde{p}_s^*, \text{Shift}(\tilde{v}, ac_i^*)).$

For $i = 0$ define $ac'_{s0} = \bigwedge_{j=1,\ldots,n} ac_j^*$, and hence $\tilde{ac}_s \cong$ Shift$(t_{0,L}, ac_0) \wedge$ L$(\tilde{p}_s^*, \text{Shift}(\tilde{v},$ $ac'_{s0}))$ implies the complement-compatibility of ac_0 and $\tilde{ac}_s$. For $i > 0$, we have that $\text{Shift}(t_{0,L},$ $ac_0) \wedge$ L$(\tilde{p}_s^*, \text{Shift}(\tilde{v}, ac_i^*)) \cong$ Shift$(t_{i,L}, ac_i)$. Define $ac'_{si} = \bigwedge_{j=1,\ldots,n\backslash i} ac_j^*$, and hence $\tilde{ac}_s \cong$

$$
\begin{array}{ccccccc}
p_0: & ac_0 \rhd L_0 & \xleftarrow{\ l_0\ } & K_0 & \xrightarrow{\ r_0\ } & R_0 \\[2pt]
s_{i,L} \downarrow & (1_i') & w_i \downarrow & (3_i) & e_{i1} \downarrow \\[2pt]
p_i^*: & ac_i \rhd L_i & \xleftarrow{\ u_i\ } & L_{i0} & \xrightarrow{\ v_i\ } & E_i \\[2pt]
t_{i,L} \downarrow & (17_i) & \bar{l}_i \downarrow & (18_i) & \tilde{k}_i \downarrow \\[2pt]
\tilde{p}_s^*: & \tilde{ac}_s \rhd \tilde{L}_s & \xleftarrow{\ \tilde{u}\ } & \tilde{L}_0 & \xrightarrow{\ \tilde{v}\ } & \tilde{E}
\end{array}
$$

Shift$(t_{i,L}, ac_i) \wedge$ L$(\tilde{p}_s^*, \text{Shift}(\tilde{v}, ac'_{si}))$ implies the complement-compatibility of ac_i and $\tilde{ac}_s$.

The application of an amalgamated rule yields an amalgamated transformation.

Definition 4.11 (Amalgamated transformation)
The application of an amalgamated rule to a graph G is called an *amalgamated transformation*.

Example 4.12
Consider the bundle $s = (s_1, s_2, s_3 = s_1)$ of the kernel morphisms depicted in Fig. 4.2. The corresponding amalgamated rule $\tilde{p}_s$ is shown in the top row of Fig. 4.6. This amalgamated rule can be applied to the graph G leading to the amalgamated transformation depicted in Fig. 4.6, where the application condition $\tilde{ac}_s$ is obviously fulfilled by the match $\tilde{m}$.

If we have a bundle of direct transformations of an object G, where for each transformation one of the multi rules is applied, we want to analyze if the amalgamated rule is applicable to G combining all the single transformation steps. These transformations are compatible, i.e. multi-amalgamable, if the matches agree on the kernel rules, and are independent outside.

Definition 4.13 (Multi-amalgamable)
Given a bundle of kernel morphisms $s = (s_i : p_0 \to p_i)_{i=1,\ldots,n}$, a bundle of direct transformations steps $(G \xrightarrow{p_i, m_i} G_i)_{i=1,\ldots n}$ is *s-multi-amalgamable*, or short *s-amalgamable*, if

- it has *consistent matches*, i.e. $m_i \circ s_{i,L}$ $= m_j \circ s_{j,L} =: m_0$ for all $i, j = 1, \ldots, n$

- it has *weakly independent matches*, i.e. for all $i \neq j$ consider the pushout complements $(1_i')$ and $(1_j')$, and then there exist morphisms $p_{ij} : L_{i0} \to D_j$ and $p_{ji} : L_{j0} \to D_i$ such that $f_j \circ p_{ij} = m_i \circ u_i$ and $f_i \circ p_{ji} = m_j \circ u_j$.

$$
\begin{array}{ccc}
 & \xrightarrow{s_{i,L}} L_i & \xrightarrow{m_i} \\
L_0 & \Rightarrow\ \ m_0 & G \\
 & \xrightarrow{s_{j,L}} L_j & \xrightarrow{m_j}
\end{array}
$$

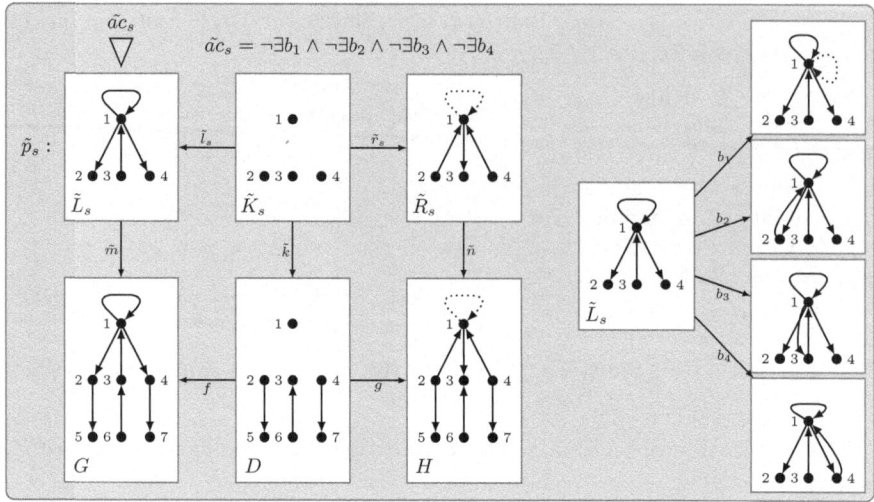

Figure 4.6: An amalgamated transformation

Moreover, if ac_0 and ac_i are complement-compatible we require $g_j \circ p_{ij} \models ac_i'$ for all $j \neq i$.

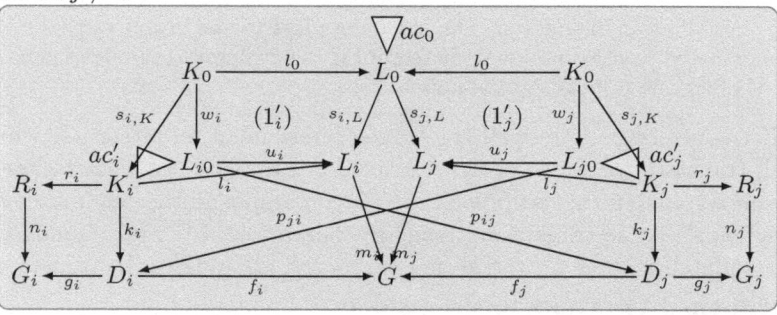

Similar to the characterization of parallel independence in [EEPT06] we can give a set-theoretical characterization of weak independence.

Fact 4.14

For graphs and other set-based structures, weakly independent matches means that $m_i(L_i) \cap m_j(L_j) \subseteq m_0(L_0) \cup (m_i(l_i(K_i)) \cap m_j(l_j(K_j)))$ for all $i \neq j =$

$1, \ldots, n$, i.e. the elements in the intersection of the matches m_i and m_j are either preserved by both transformations, or are also matched by m_0.

PROOF We have to proof the equivalence of $m_i(L_i) \cap m_j(L_j) \subseteq m_0(L_0) \cup (m_i(l_i(K_i)) \cap m_j(l_j(K_j)))$ for all $i \neq j = 1, \ldots, n$ with the definition of weakly independent matches.

"$\Leftarrow$" Let $x = m_i(y_i) = m_j(y_j)$, and suppose $x \notin m_0(L_0)$. Since $(1'_i)$ is a pushout we have that $y_i = u_i(z_i) \in u_i(L_{i0} \backslash w_i(K_0))$, and $x = m_i(u_i(z_i)) = f_j(p_i(z_i)) = m_j(y_j)$, and by pushout properties $y_j \in l_j(K_j)$ and $x \in m_j(l_j(K_j))$. Similarly, $x \in m_i(l_i(K_i))$.

"$\Rightarrow$" For $x \in L_{i0}$, $x = w_i(k)$ define $p_{ij}(x) = k_j(s_{j,K}(k))$, then $f_j(p_{ij}(x)) = f_j(k_j(s_{j,K}(k))) = m_j(l_j(s_{j,K}(k))) = m_j(s_{j,L}(l_0(k))) = m_i(s_{i,L}(l_0(k))) = m_i(n_i(w_i(k))) = m_i(u_i(x))$. Otherwise, $x \notin w_i(K_0)$, i.e. $u_i(x) \notin s_{i,L}(L_0)$, and define $p_{ij}(x) = y$ with $f_j(y) = m_i(u_i(x))$. This y exists, because either $m_i(u_i(x)) \notin m_j(L_j)$ or $m_i(u_i(x)) \in m_j(L_j)$ and then $m_i(u_i(x)) \in m_j(l_j(K_j))$, and in both cases $m_i(u_i(x)) \in f_j(D_j)$. Similarly, we can define p_{ji} with the required property.

Example 4.15
Consider the bundle $s = (s_1, s_2, s_3 = s_1)$ of kernel morphisms from Ex. 4.12. For the graph G given in Fig. 4.6 we find matches $m_0 : L_0 \to G$, $m_1 : L_1 \to G$, $m_2 : L_2 \to G$, and $m_3 : L_1 \to G$ mapping all nodes from the left-hand side to their corresponding nodes in G, except for m_3 mapping node 2 in L_1 to node 4 in G. For all these matches, the corresponding application conditions are fulfilled and we can apply the rules p_1, p_2, p_1, respectively, leading to the bundle of direct transformations depicted in Fig. 4.7. This bundle is s-amalgamable, because the matches m_1, m_2, and m_3 agree on the match m_0, and are weakly independent, because they only overlap in m_0.

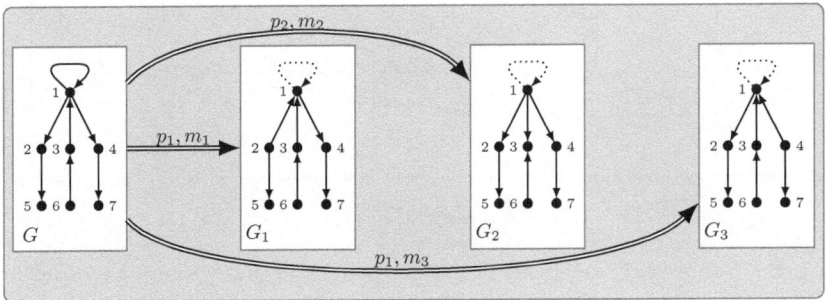

Figure 4.7: An s-amalgamable bundle of direct transformations

For an s-amalgamable bundle of direct transformations, each single transformation step can be decomposed into an application of the kernel rule followed by an application of the (weak) complement rule as shown in Fact 4.8. Moreover, all kernel rule applications lead to the same object, and the following applications of the complement rules are parallel independent.

Fact 4.16

Given a bundle of kernel morphisms $s = (s_i : p_0 \rightarrow p_i)_{i=1,\dots,n}$ and an s-amalgamable bundle of direct transformations $(G \xRightarrow{p_i,m_i} G_i)_{i=1,\dots,n}$ then each direct transformation $G \xRightarrow{p_i,m_i} G_i$ can be decomposed into a transformation $G \xRightarrow{p_0,m_0} G_0 \xRightarrow{\overline{p_i},\overline{m_i}} G_i$, where $\overline{p_i}$ is the (weak) complement rule of s_i. Moreover, the transformations $G_0 \xRightarrow{\overline{p_i},\overline{m_i}} G_i$ are pairwise parallel independent.

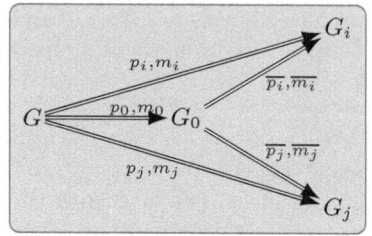

PROOF From Fact 4.8 it follows that each single direct transformation $G \xRightarrow{p_i,m_i} G_i$ can be decomposed into a transformation $G \xRightarrow{p_0,m_0^i} G_0^i \xRightarrow{\overline{p_i},\overline{m_i}} G_i$ with $m_0^i = m_i \circ s_{i,L}$ and, since the bundle is s-amalgamable, $m_0 = m_i \circ s_{i,L} = m_0^i$ and $G_0 := G_0^i$ for all $i = 1,\dots,n$.

It remains to show the pairwise parallel independence. From the constructions of the complement rule and the Concurrency Theorem we obtain the following diagram for all $i = 1,\dots,n$.

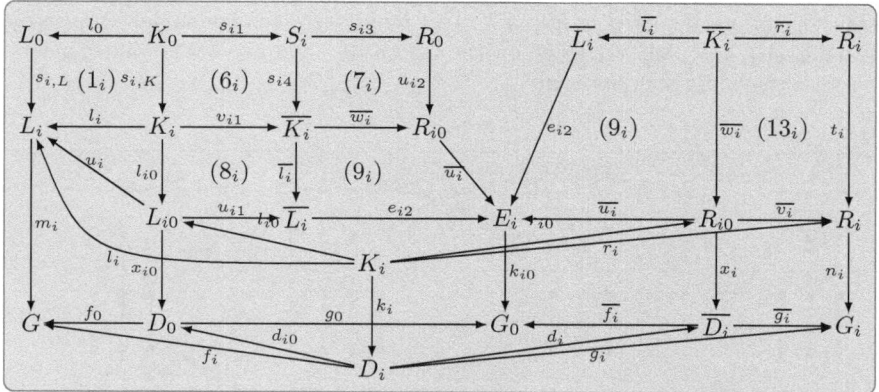

For $i \neq j$, from weakly independent matches it follows that we have a morphism $p_{ij} : L_{i0} \rightarrow D_j$ with $f_j \circ p_{ij} = m_i \circ u_i$. It follows that $f_j \circ p_{ij} \circ w_i = m_i \circ u_i \circ w_i = m_i \circ s_{i,L} \circ l_0 = m_0 \circ l_0 = m_j \circ s_{j,L} \circ l_0 = m_j \circ u_j \circ w_j = m_j \circ u_j \circ l_{j0} \circ s_{j,K} = m_j \circ l_j \circ s_{j,K} = f_j \circ k_j \circ s_{j,K}$ and with $f_j \in \mathcal{M}$ we have that $p_{ij} \circ w_i = k_j \circ s_{jk}$ (*).

Now consider the pushout $(19_i) = (6_i) + (8_i)$ in comparison with object $\overline{D_j}$ and morphisms $d_j \circ p_{ij}$ and $x_j \circ u_{j2} \circ s_{i3}$. We have that $d_j \circ p_{ij} \circ l_{i0} \circ s_{i,K} \overset{(*)}{=} d_j \circ p_{ij} \circ w_i \overset{(*)}{=} d_j \circ k_j \circ s_{j,K} = x_j \circ r_{j0} \circ s_{j,K} = x_j \circ \overline{w_j} \circ v_{j1} \circ s_{j,K} = x_j \circ u_{j2} \circ s_{j3} \circ s_{j1} = x_j \circ u_{j2} \circ r_0 = x_j \circ u_{j2} \circ s_{i3} \circ s_{i1}$. Now pushout (19_i) induces a unique morphism q_{ij} with $q_{ij} \circ u_{i1} = d_j \circ p_{ij}$ and $q_{ij} \circ \overline{l_i} \circ s_{i4} = x_j \circ u_{j2} \circ s_{i3}$.

For the parallel independence of G_0 $\xrightarrow{\overline{p_i},\overline{m_i}} G_i$, $G_0 \xrightarrow{\overline{p_j},\overline{m_j}} G_j$, we have to show that $q_{ij} : \overline{L_i} \to \overline{D_j}$ satisfies $\overline{f_j} \circ q_{ij} = k_{i0} \circ e_{i2} =: \overline{m_i}$.

With $f_0 \in \mathcal{M}$ and $f_0 \circ d_{j0} \circ p_{ij} = f_j \circ p_{ij} = m_i \circ u_i = f_0 \circ c_{i0}$ it follows that $d_{j0} \circ p_{ij} = x_{i0}$ (**). This means that $\overline{f_j} \circ$

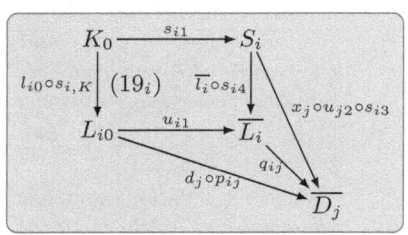

$q_{ij} \circ u_{i1} = \overline{f_j} \circ d_j \circ p_{ij} = g_0 \circ d_0 \circ p_{ij} \overset{(**)}{=}$ $g_0 \circ x_{i0} = k_{i0} \circ e_{i2} \circ u_{i1}$. In addition, we have that $\overline{f_j} \circ q_{ij} \circ \overline{l_i} \circ s_{i4} = \overline{f_j} \circ x_j \circ u_{j2} \circ s_{i3} = k_{j0} \circ \overline{u_j} \circ u_{j2} \circ s_{i3} = k_{i0} \circ \overline{u_i} \circ u_{i2} \circ s_{i3} = k_{i0} \circ e_{i2} \circ \overline{l_i} \circ s_{i4}$. Since (19_i) is a pushout we have that u_{i1} and $\overline{l_i} \circ s_{i4}$ are jointly epimorphic and it follows that $\overline{f_j} \circ q_{ij} \circ e_{i2} = k_{i0} \circ e_{i2}$.

If ac_0 and ac_i are not complement-compatible then $\overline{ac_i} = $ true and trivially $\overline{g_j} \circ q_{ij} \models \overline{ac_i}$ for all $j \neq i$. Otherwise, we have that $g_j \circ p_{ij} \models ac'_i$, and with $g_j \circ p_{ij} = \overline{g_j} \circ d_j \circ p_{ij} = \overline{g_j} \circ q_{ij} \circ u_{i1}$ it follows that $\overline{g_j} \circ q_{ij} \circ u_{i1} \models ac'_i$, which is equivalent to $\overline{g_j} \circ q_{ij} \models \mathrm{Shift}(u_{i1}, ac'_1) = \overline{ac_i}$.

If a bundle of direct transformations of an object G is s-amalgamable we can apply the amalgamated rule directly to G leading to a parallel execution of all the changes done by the single transformation steps.

Theorem 4.17 (Multi-Amalgamation Theorem)
Consider a bundle of kernel morphisms $s = (s_i : p_0 \to p_i)_{i=1,\dots,n}$.

1. *Synthesis.* Given an s-amalgamable bundle of direct transformations $(G \xrightarrow{p_i,m_i} G_i)_{i=1,\dots,n}$ then there is an amalgamated transformation $G \xrightarrow{\tilde{p}_s,\tilde{m}} H$ and transformations $G_i \xrightarrow{q_i} H$ over

   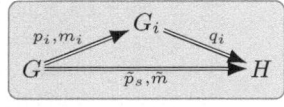

   the complement rules q_i of the kernel morphisms $t_i : p_i \to \tilde{p}_s$ such that $G \xrightarrow{p_i,m_i} G_i \xrightarrow{q_i} H$ is a decomposition of $G \xrightarrow{\tilde{p}_s,\tilde{m}} H$.

2. *Analysis.* Given an amalgamated transformation $G \xrightarrow{\tilde{p}_s,\tilde{m}} H$ then there are s_i-related transformations $G \xrightarrow{p_i,m_i} G_i \xrightarrow{q_i} H$ for $i = 1,\dots,n$ such that the bundle $(G \xrightarrow{p_i,m_i} G_i)_{i=1,\dots,n}$ is s-amalgamable.

3. *Bijective Correspondence.* The synthesis and analysis constructions are inverse to each other up to isomorphism.

PROOF   1. We have to show that $\tilde{p}_s$ is applicable to G leading to an amalgamated transformation $G \xrightarrow{\tilde{p}_s, \tilde{m}} H$ with $m_i = \tilde{m} \circ t_{i,L}$, where $t_i : p_i \to \tilde{p}_i$ are the kernel morphisms constructed in Fact 4.10. Then we can apply Fact 4.8 which implies the decomposition of $G \xrightarrow{\tilde{p}_s, \tilde{m}} H$ into $G \xrightarrow{p_i, m_i} G_i \xrightarrow{q_i} H$, where q_i is the (weak) complement rule of the kernel morphism t_i.

Given the kernel morphisms, the amalgamated rule, and the bundle of direct transformations, we have pullbacks (1_i), (2_i), (14_i), (15_i) and pushouts (20_i), (21_i).

Using Fact 4.16, we know that we can apply p_0 via m_0 leading to a direct transformation

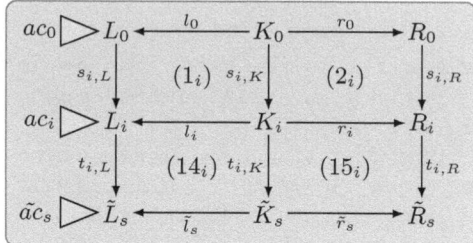

$G \xrightarrow{p_0, m_0} G_0$ given by pushouts (20_0) and (21_0). Moreover, we find decompositions of pushouts (20_0) and (20_i) into pushouts $(1'_i)$ and (22_i) resp. (22_i) and (23_i) by $\mathcal{M}$-pushout pullback decomposition and uniqueness of pushout complements.

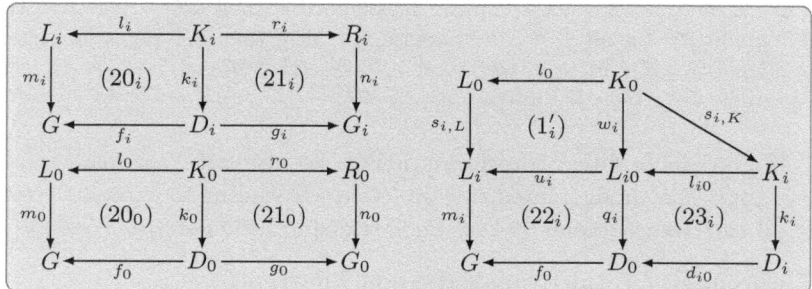

Since we have consistent matches, $m_i \circ s_{i,L} = m_0$ for all $i = 1, \ldots, n$. Then the colimit $\tilde{L}_s$ implies that there is a unique morphism $\tilde{m} : \tilde{L}_s \to G$ with $\tilde{m} \circ t_{i,L} = m_i$ and $\tilde{m} \circ t_{0,L} = m_0$ (a). Moreover, $m_i \models ac_i \Rightarrow \tilde{m} \circ t_{i,L} \models ac_i \Rightarrow \tilde{m} \models \text{Shift}(t_{i,L}, ac_i)$ for all $i = 1, \ldots, n$, and thus $\tilde{m} \models \tilde{ac}_s = \bigwedge_{i=1,\ldots,n} \text{Shift}(t_{i,L}, ac_i)$.

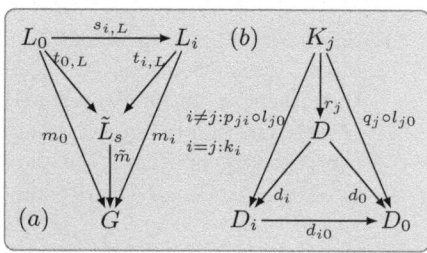

Weakly independent matches means that there exist morphisms p_{ij} with $f_j \circ p_{ij} = m_i \circ u_i$ for $i \neq j$. Construct D as the limit of $(d_{i0})_{i=1,\ldots,n}$ with morphisms d_i. Now f_0 being a monomorphism with $f_0 \circ d_{i0} \circ p_{ji} =$

$f_i \circ p_{ji} = m_j \circ u_j = f_0 \circ q_j$ implies that $d_{i0} \circ p_{ji} = q_j$. It follows that $d_{i0} \circ p_{ji} \circ l_{j0} = q_j \circ l_{j0}$ and, together with $d_{i0} \circ k_i = q_i \circ l_{i0}$, limit D implies that there exists a unique morphism r_j with $d_i \circ r_j = p_{ji} \circ l_{ji}$, $d_i \circ r_i = k_i$, and $d_0 \circ r_j = q_j \circ l_{j0}$ (b).

Similarly, f_j being a monomor-
phism with $f_j \circ p_{ij} \circ l_{i0} \circ s_{i,K} =$
$m_i \circ u_i \circ w_i = m_i \circ s_{i,L} \circ l_0 =$
$m_0 \circ l_0 = m_j \circ s_{j,L} \circ l_0 = m_j \circ l_j \circ$
$s_{j,K} = f_j \circ k_j \circ s_{j,K}$ implies that
$p_{ij} \circ l_{i0} \circ s_{i,K} = k_j \circ s_{j,K}$. Now
colimit $\tilde{K}_s$ implies that there is
a unique morphisms $\tilde{r}_j$ with $\tilde{r}_j \circ$
$t_{i,K} = p_{ij} \circ l_{i0}$, $\tilde{r}_j \circ t_{j,K} = k_j$, and

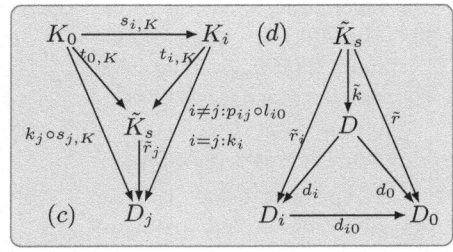

$\tilde{r}_j \circ t_{0,K} = k_j \circ s_{j,K}$ (c). Since $d_{i0} \circ \tilde{r}_i \circ t_{i,K} = d_{i0} \circ k_i = q_i \circ l_{i0} = d_{j0} \circ p_{ij} \circ l_{i0} = d_{j0} \circ \tilde{r}_j \circ t_{i,K}$ and $d_{i0} \circ \tilde{r}_i \circ t_{0,K} = d_{i0} \circ k_i \circ s_{i,K} = k_0 = d_{j0} \circ \tilde{r}_j \circ t_{0,K}$ colimit $\tilde{K}_s$ implies that for all i, j we have that $d_{i0} \circ \tilde{r}_i = d_{j0} \circ \tilde{r}_j =: \tilde{r}$. From limit D it now follows that there exists a unique morphism $\tilde{k}$ with $d_i \circ \tilde{k} = \tilde{r}_i$ and $d_0 \circ \tilde{k} = \tilde{r}$ (d).

We have to show that (20_s) with $f = f_0 \circ d_0$ is a pushout. With $f \circ \tilde{k} \circ t_{i,K} = f_0 \circ d_0 \circ \tilde{k} \circ t_{i,K} = f_0 \circ \tilde{r} \circ t_{i,K} = f_0 \circ d_{i0} \circ \tilde{r}_i \circ t_{i,K} = f_0 \circ d_{i0} \circ k_i = f_i \circ k_i = m_i \circ l_i = \tilde{m} \circ t_{i,L} \circ l_i = \tilde{m} \circ \tilde{l}_s \circ t_{i,K}$, $f \circ \tilde{k} \circ t_{0,K} = f_0 \circ d_0 \circ \tilde{k} \circ t_{0,K} = f_0 \tilde{r} \circ t_{0,K} = f_0 \circ d_{i0} \circ \tilde{r}_i \circ t_{0,K} = f_0 \circ d_{i0} \circ k_i \circ s_{i,K} = f_0 \circ k_0 = m_0 \circ l_0 = \tilde{m} \circ t_{0,L} \circ l_0 = \tilde{m} \circ \tilde{l}_s \circ t_{0,K}$, and $\tilde{K}_s$ being colimit it follows that $f \circ \tilde{k} = \tilde{m} \circ \tilde{l}_s$, thus the square commutes.

Pushout (23_i) can be decomposed into pushouts (24_i) and (25_i). Using Lemma A.21 it follows that D_0 is the colimit of $(x_i)_{i=1,\ldots,n}$, because (23_i) is a pushout, D is the limit of $(d_{i0})_{i=1,\ldots,n}$, and we have morphisms p_{ij} with $d_{j0} \circ p_{ij} = q_i$. Then Lemma A.22 implies that also (25) is a pushout.

$$
\begin{array}{ccccccccccc}
L_s & \xleftarrow{\tilde{l}_s} & K_s & \quad & K_i & \xrightarrow{r_i} & D & \xrightarrow{d_i} & D_i & +K_i \xrightarrow{+l_{i0}} & +L_{i0} \\
\tilde{m}\downarrow & (20_s) & \tilde{k}\downarrow l_{i0} & & \downarrow & (24_i) & \downarrow x_i & (25_i) & \downarrow d_{i0} \quad r & (25) & \downarrow \tilde{d} \\
G & \xleftarrow{f} & D & \quad & L_{i0} & \xrightarrow{x_{i0}} & P_i & \xrightarrow{y_{i0}} & D_0 & D \xrightarrow{d_0} & D_0
\end{array}
$$

Now consider the coequalizers $\tilde{K}_s$ of $(i_{K_i} \circ s_{i,K} : K_0 \to +K_i)_{i=1,\ldots,n}$ (which is actually $\tilde{K}_s$ by construction of colimits), $\tilde{L}_0$ of $(i_{L_{i0}} \circ w_i : K_0 \to +L_{i0})_{i=1,\ldots,n}$ (as already constructed in Fact 4.10), D of $(\tilde{k} \circ t_{0,K} : K_0 \to D)_{i=1,\ldots,n}$, and D_0 of $(k_0 : K_0 \to D_0)_{i=1,\ldots,n}$.

In the right cube, the top square with identical morphisms is a pushout, the top cube commutes, and the middle square is pushout (25). Using Lemma A.23 it follows that also the bottom face (26) constructed of the four coequalizers is a pushout.

In the cube below, the top and middle squares are pushouts and the two top cubes commute. Using again Lemma A.23 it follows that (20_s) in the bottom face is actually a pushout, where $(27) = (1_i') + (17_i)$ is a pushout by composition. Now we can construct pushout (21_s) which completes the direct transformation $G \overset{\tilde{p}_s, \tilde{m}}{\Longrightarrow} H$.

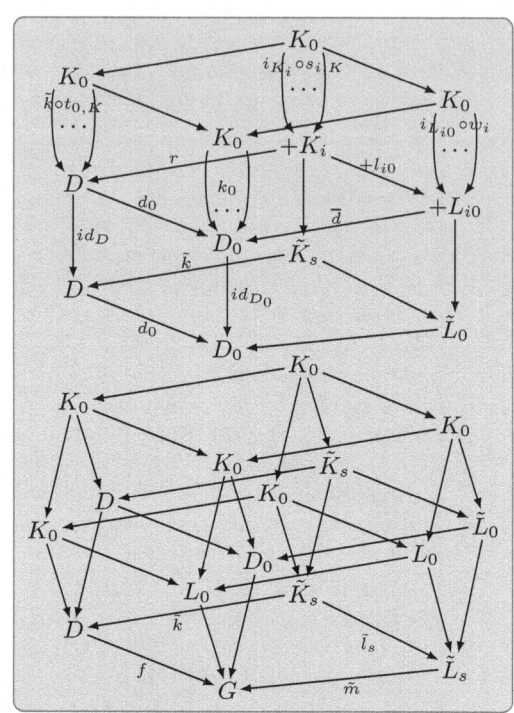

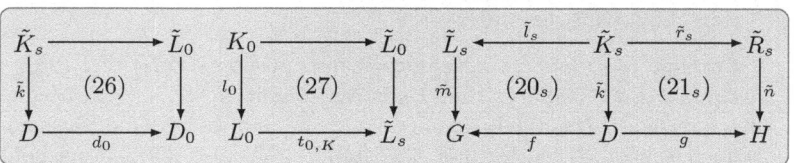

2. Using the kernel morphisms t_i we obtain transformations $G \overset{p_i, m_i}{\Longrightarrow} G_i \overset{q_i}{\Longrightarrow} H$ from Fact 4.8 with $m_i = \tilde{m} \circ t_{i,L}$. We have to show that this bundle of transformations is s-amalgamable.

Applying again Fact 4.8 we obtain transformations $G \overset{p_0, m_0^i}{\Longrightarrow} G_0^i \overset{\overline{p_i}}{\Longrightarrow} G_i$ with $m_0^i = m_i \circ s_{i,L}$. It follows that $m_0^i = m_i \circ s_{i,L} = \tilde{m} \circ t_{i,L} \circ s_{i,L} = \tilde{m} \circ t_{0,L} = \tilde{m} \circ t_{j,L} \circ s_{j,L} = m_j \circ s_{j,L}$ and thus we have consistent matches with $m_0 := m_0^i$ well-defined and $G_0 = G_0^i$. It remains to show the weakly independent matches. Given the above

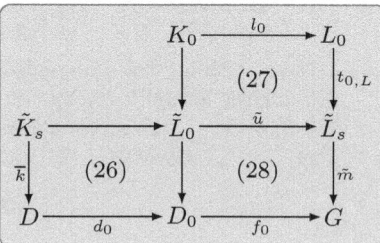

transformations we have pushouts (20_0), (20_i), (20_s) as above. Then we can find decompositions of (20_0) and (20_s) into pushouts $(27) + (28)$ and $(26) + (28)$, respectively. Using pushout (26) and Lemma A.24 it follows that (25) is a pushout, since $\tilde{K}_s$ is the colimit of $(s_{i,L})_{i=1,...,n}$, $\tilde{L}_0$ is the colimit of $(w_i)_{i=1,...,n}$, and id_{K_0} is obviously an epimorphism.

Now Lemma A.22 implies that there is a decomposition into pushouts (24_i) with colimit D_0 of $(x_i)_{i=1,...,n}$ and pushout (25_i) by $\mathcal{M}$-pushout pullback decomposition. Since D_0 is the colimit of $(x_i)_{i=1,...,n}$ and (25_j) is a pushout it follows that D_j is the colimit of $(x_i)_{i=1,...,j-1,j+1,...,n}$ with morphisms $q_{ij} : P_i \to D_j$ and $d_{j0} \circ q_{ij} = y_{i0}$. Thus we obtain for all $i \neq j$ a morphism $p_{ij} = q_{ij} \circ x_{i0}$ and $f_j \circ p_{ij} = f_0 \circ d_{j0} \circ q_{ij} \circ x_{i0} = f_0 \circ y_{i0} \circ x_{i0} = m_i \circ u_i$.

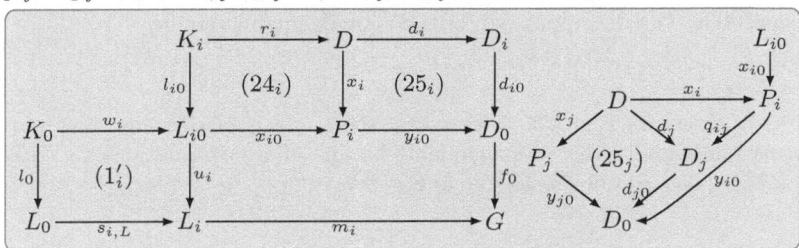

3. Because of the uniqueness of the used constructions, the above constructions are inverse to each other up to isomorphism.

Remark 4.18

Note that q_i can be constructed as the amalgamated rule of the kernel morphisms $(p_{K_0} \to \overline{p_j})_{j \neq i}$, where $p_{K_0} = (K_0 \xleftarrow{id_{K_0}} K_0 \xrightarrow{id_{K_0}} K_0, \text{true}))$ and $\overline{p_j}$ is the complement rule of p_j.

For $n = 2$ and rules without application conditions, the Multi-Amalgamation Theorem specializes to the Amalgamation Theorem in [BFH87]. Moreover, if p_0 is the empty rule this is the Parallelism Theorem in [EHL10a], since the transformations are parallel independent for an empty kernel match.

Example 4.19

As already observed in Ex. 4.15, the transformations $G \xrightarrow{p_1,m_1} G_1$, $G \xrightarrow{p_2,m_2} G_2$, and $G \xrightarrow{p_1,m_3} G_3$ shown in Fig. 4.7 are s-amalgamable for the bundle $s = (s_1, s_2, s_3 = s_1)$ of kernel morphisms. Applying Fact. 4.16, we can decompose these transformations into a transformation $G \xrightarrow{p_0,m_0} G_0$ followed by transformations $G_0 \xrightarrow{\overline{p_1},\overline{m_1}} G_1$, $G_0 \xrightarrow{\overline{p_2},\overline{m_2}} G_2$, and $G_0 \xrightarrow{\overline{p_1},\overline{m_3}} G_3$ via the complement rules, which are pairwise parallel independent. These transformations are depicted in Fig. 4.8.

Moreover, Thm. 4.17 implies that we obtain for this bundle of direct transformations an amalgamated transformation $G \xRightarrow{\tilde{p}_s,\tilde{m}} H$, which is the transformation

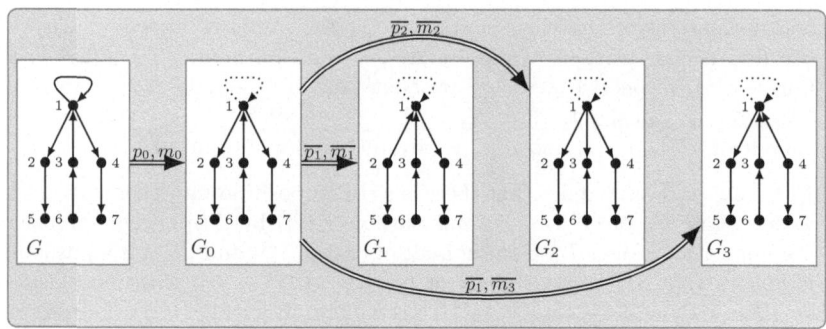

Figure 4.8: The decomposition of the s-amalgamable bundle

already shown in Fig. 4.6. Vice versa, the analysis of this amalgamated transformation leads to the s-amalgamable bundle of transformations $G \xrightarrow{p_1, m_1} G_1$, $G \xrightarrow{p_2, m_2} G_2$, and $G \xrightarrow{p_1, m_3} G_3$ in Fig. 4.7.

For an $\mathcal{M}$-adhesive transformation system with amalgamation we define a set of kernel morphisms and allow all kinds of amalgamated transformations using bundles from this set.

Definition 4.20 ($\mathcal{M}$-adhesive grammar with amalgamation)
An $\mathcal{M}$-*adhesive transformation system with amalgamation* $ASA = (\mathbf{C}, \mathcal{M}, P, \mathcal{S})$ is an $\mathcal{M}$-adhesive transformation system $(\mathbf{C}, \mathcal{M}, P)$ with a set of kernel morphisms $\mathcal{S}$ between rules in P.

An $\mathcal{M}$-*adhesive grammar with amalgamation* $AGA = (ASA, S)$ consists of an $\mathcal{M}$-adhesive transformation system with amalgamation ASA and a start object S.

The language L of an $\mathcal{M}$-adhesive grammar with amalgamation AGA is defined by

$$L = \{G \mid \exists \text{ amalgamated transformation } S \xRightarrow{*} G\},$$

where all amalgamated rules over arbitrary bundles of kernel morphisms in $\mathcal{S}$ are allowed to be used.

Remark 4.21
Note that by including the kernel morphism $id_p : p \to p$ for a rule p into the set $\mathcal{S}$ the transformation $G \xRightarrow{p, m} H$ is also an amalgamated transformation for this kernel morphism as the only one considered in the bundle.

4.1.3 Parallel Independence of Amalgamated Transformations

Since amalgamated rules are normal rules in an $\mathcal{M}$-adhesive transformation system with only a special way of constructing them, we obtain all the results from Subsection 3.4.3 also for amalgamated transformations. Especially for parallel independence, we can analyze this property in more detail to connect the result to the underlying kernel and multi rules.

Parallel independence of two amalgamated transformations of the same object can be reduced to the parallel independence of the involved transformations via the multi rules if the application conditions are handled properly. This leads to two new notions of parallel independence for amalgamated transformations and bundles of transformations.

Definition 4.22 (Parallel amalgamation and bundle independence)
Given two bundles of kernel morphisms $s = (s_i : p_0 \rightarrow p_i)_{i=1,...,n}$ and $s' = (s'_j : p'_0 \rightarrow p'_j)_{j=1,...,n'}$, and two bundles of s- resp. s'-amalgamable transformations $(G \xrightarrow{p_i, m_i} G_i)_{i=1,...,n}$ and $(G \xrightarrow{p'_j, m'_j} G'_j)_{j=1,...,n'}$ leading to the amalgamated transformations $G \xrightarrow{\tilde{p}_s, \tilde{m}} H$ and $G \xrightarrow{\tilde{p}_{s'}, \tilde{m}'} H'$, then we have that

- $G \xrightarrow{\tilde{p}_s, \tilde{m}} H$ and $G \xrightarrow{\tilde{p}_{s'}, \tilde{m}'} H'$ are *parallel amalgamation independent* if they are parallel independent, i.e. there are morphisms $\tilde{r}_s$ and $\tilde{r}_{s'}$ with $f \circ \tilde{r}_{s'} = \tilde{m}'$, $f' \circ \tilde{r}_s = \tilde{m}$, $g \circ \tilde{r}_{s'} \models \tilde{a}c_{s'}$, and $g' \circ \tilde{r}_s \models \tilde{a}c_s$, and in addition we have that $g_i \circ d_i \circ \tilde{r}_{s'} \models \text{Shift}(t'_{j,L}, ac'_j)$ and $g'_j \circ d'_j \circ \tilde{r}_s \models \text{Shift}(t_{i,L}, ac_i)$ for all i, j.

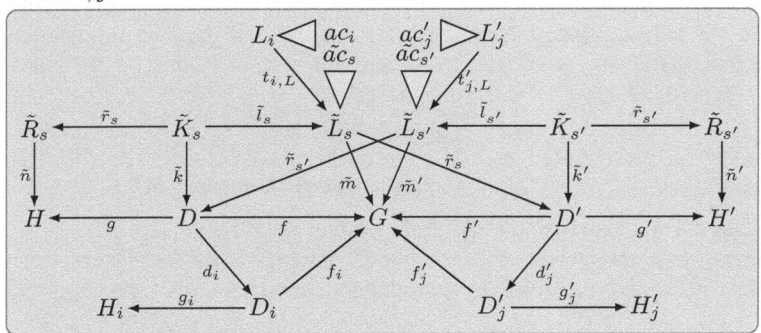

- $(G \xrightarrow{p_i, m_i} G_i)_{i=1,...,n}$ and $(G \xrightarrow{p'_j, m'_j} G'_j)_{j=1,...,n'}$ are *parallel bundle independent* if they are pairwise parallel independent for all i, j, i.e. there are morphisms r_{ij} and r'_{ji} with $f'_j \circ r_{ij} = m_i$, $f_i \circ r'_{ji} = m'_j$, $g'_j \circ r_{ij} \models ac_i$, and $g_i \circ r'_{ji} \models ac'_j$, and in addition we have for the induced morphisms $\tilde{r}_s : \tilde{L}_s \rightarrow D'$ and $\tilde{r}_{s'} : \tilde{L}_{s'} \rightarrow D$ that $g \circ \tilde{r}_{s'} \models \tilde{a}c_{s'}$ and $g' \circ \tilde{r}_s \models \tilde{a}c_s$.

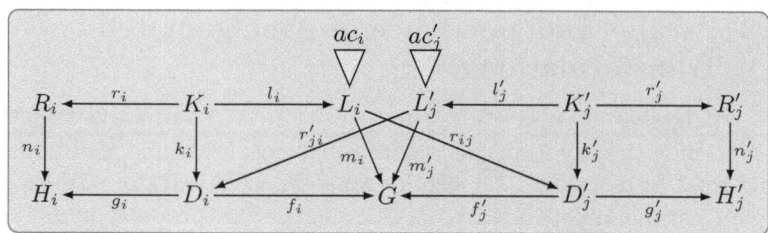

Remark 4.23

Note that all objects and morphisms in the above diagrams originate from the construction in the proof of Thm. 4.17 and the parallel independence.

Two amalgamated transformations are parallel amalgamation independent if and only if the corresponding bundles of transformations are parallel bundle independent.

Theorem 4.24 (Characterization of parallel independence)

Given two bundles of kernel morphisms $s = (s_i : p_0 \to p_i)_{i=1,...,n}$ and $s' = (s'_j : p'_0 \to p'_j)_{j=1,...,n'}$, and two bundles of s- resp. s'-amalgamable transformations $(G \xrightarrow{p_i,m_i} G_i)_{i=1,...,n}$ and $(G \xrightarrow{p'_j,m'_j} G'_j)_{j=1,...,n'}$ leading to the amalgamated transformations $G \xrightarrow{\tilde{p}_s,\tilde{m}} H$ and $G \xrightarrow{\tilde{p}_{s'},\tilde{m}'} H'$ then the following holds: $(G \xrightarrow{p_i,m_i} G_i)_{i=1,...,n}$ and $(G \xrightarrow{p'_j,m'_j} G'_j)_{j=1,...,n'}$ are parallel bundle independent if and only if $G \xrightarrow{\tilde{p}_s,\tilde{m}} H$ and $G \xrightarrow{\tilde{p}_{s'},\tilde{m}'} H'$ are parallel amalgamation independent.

PROOF "if": If $G \xrightarrow{\tilde{p}_s,\tilde{m}} H$ and $G \xrightarrow{\tilde{p}_{s'},\tilde{m}'} H'$ are parallel amalgamation independent define $r_{ij} = d'_j \circ \tilde{r}_s \circ t_{i,L}$ and $r'_{ji} = d_i \circ \tilde{r}_{s'} \circ t'_{j,L}$. It follows that $f_i \circ r'_{ji} = f_i \circ d_i \circ \tilde{r}_{s'} \circ t'_{j,L} = f \circ \tilde{r}_{s'} \circ t'_{j,L} = \tilde{m}' \circ t'_{j,L} = m'_j$, $f'_j \circ r_{ij} = f'_j \circ d'_j \circ \tilde{r}_s \circ t_{i,L} = f' \circ \tilde{r}_s \circ t_{i,L} = \tilde{m} \circ t_{i,L} = m_i$, and by precondition $g_i \circ d_i \circ \tilde{r}_{s'} \models \text{Shift}(t_{j,L}, ac'_j)$, which means that $g_i \circ d_i \circ \tilde{r}_{s'} \circ t'_{j,L} = g_i \circ r'_{ji} \models ac'_j$. Similarly, $g'_j \circ d'_j \circ \tilde{r}_s \models \text{Shift}(t_{i,L}, ac_i)$ implies that $g'_j \circ d'_j \circ \tilde{r}_s \circ t_{i,L} = g'_j \circ r_{ij} \models ac_i$. This means that $G \xrightarrow{p_i,m_i} G_i$ and $G \xrightarrow{p'_j,m'_j} G'_j$ are pairwise parallel independent for all i, j.

The induced morphisms $\tilde{r}_s : \tilde{L}_s \to D'$ and $\tilde{r}_{s'} : \tilde{L}_{s'} \to D$ are exactly the morphisms $\tilde{r}_s$ and $\tilde{r}_{s'}$ given by parallel independence with $g' \circ \tilde{r}_s \models \tilde{a}c_s$ and $g \circ \tilde{r}_{s'} \models \tilde{a}c_{s'}$. This means that $(G \xrightarrow{p_i,m_i} G_i)_{i=1,...,n}$ and $(G \xrightarrow{p'_j,m'_j} G'_j)_{j=1,...,n'}$ are parallel bundle independent.

"only if": Suppose $(G \xrightarrow{p_i,m_i} G_i)_{i=1,...,n}$ and $(G \xrightarrow{p'_j,m'_j} G'_j)_{j=1,...,n'}$ are parallel bundle independent. We have to show that the morphisms $\tilde{r}_s$ and $\tilde{r}_{s'}$ actually exist. D is the limit of $(d_{i0})_{i=1,...,n}$ as already constructed in the proof of Thm. 4.17. f_0 is an $\mathcal{M}$-morphism, and $f_0 \circ d_{i0} \circ r'_{ji} = f_i \circ r'_{ji} = m_i = \tilde{m} \circ t_{i,L} =$

$m_k = f_k \circ r'_{jk} = f_0 \circ d_{k0} \circ r'_{jk}$ implies that $d_{i0} \circ r'_{ji} = d_{k0} \circ r'_{jk} =: r'_{j0}$ for all i, k. Now the limit D implies that there exists a unique morphism r'_{js} such that $d_i \circ r'_{js} = r'_{ji}$ and $d_0 \circ r'_{js} = r'_{j0}$ (a).

Similarly, $\mathcal{M}$-morphism f_i and $f_i \circ r'_{ji} \circ s_{j,L} = m'_j \circ s_{j,L} = m'_0 = m'_k \circ s'_{k,L} = f_i \circ r'_{ki} \circ s'_{k,L}$ implies that $r'_{ji} \circ s'_{j,L} = r'_{ki} \circ s'_{k,L}$ for all i, k. It follows that $d_i \circ r'_{js} \circ s_{j,L} = r'_{ji} \circ s'_{j,L} = r'_{ki} \circ s'_{k,L} = d_i \circ r'_{ks} \circ s'_{k,L}$, and with $\mathcal{M}$-morphism d_i we have that $r'_{js} \circ s_{j,L} = r'_{ks} \circ s_{k,L} =: r'_{0s}$. From colimit $\tilde{L}_{s'}$ we obtain a morphism $\tilde{r}_{s'}$ with $\tilde{r}_{s'} \circ t'_{j,L} = r'_{j,s}$ and $\tilde{r}_{s'} \circ t'_{0,L} = r'_{0,s}$ (b).

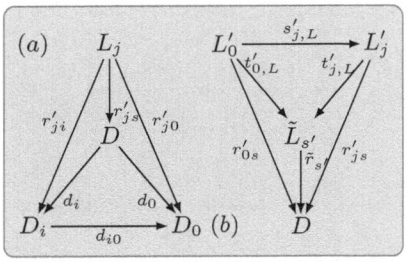

It follows that $f \circ \tilde{r}_{s'} \circ t'_{0,L} = f_i \circ d_i \circ r'_{0s} = f_i \circ d_i \circ r'_{js} \circ s'_{j,L} = f_i \circ r'_{ji} \circ s'_{j,L} = m'_j \circ s_{j,L} = m'_0 = \tilde{m}' \circ t_{0,L}$ and $f \circ \tilde{r}_{s'} \circ t_{j,L} = f_i \circ d_i \circ r'_{js} = f_i \circ r'_{ji} = m'_j = \tilde{m}' \circ t'_{j,L}$. The colimit property of $\tilde{L}_{s'}$ implies now that $f \circ \tilde{r}_{s'} = \tilde{m}'$. Similarly, we obtain the required morphism $\tilde{r}_s$ with $f' \circ \tilde{r}_s = \tilde{m}$.

Since we have already required that $g \circ \tilde{r}_{s'} \models \tilde{ac}_{s'}$ and $g' \circ \tilde{r}_s \models \tilde{ac}_s$, this means that $G \xrightarrow{\tilde{p}_s, \tilde{m}} H$ and $G \xrightarrow{\tilde{p}_{s'}, \tilde{m}'} H'$ are parallel independent. Moreover, from the pairwise independence we know that $g_i \circ r'_{ji} = g_i \circ d_i \circ r'_{js} = g_i \circ d_i \circ \tilde{r}_{s'} \circ t'_{j,L} \models ac'_j$ which implies that $g_i \circ d_i \circ \tilde{r}_{s'} \models \text{Shift}(t'_{j,L} ac'_j)$. Similarly, $g'_j \circ r_{ij} \models ac_i$ implies that $g'_j \circ d'_j \circ \tilde{r}_s \models \text{Shift}(t_{i,L}, ac_i)$, which leads to parallel amalgamation independence of the amalgamated transformations.

Remark 4.25
Note that the additional verification of the application conditions is necessary because the common effect of all rule applications may invalidate the amalgamated application condition, although the single applications of the multi rules behave well. For an example, consider the kernel morphism s'_1 in Fig. 4.9, where the bundles $s = (s'_1, s'_1)$ and $s' = (s'_1, s'_1)$ are applied to the graph X. Although all pairs of applications of the rule p'_1 to X are pairwise parallel independent, the amalgamated transformations are not parallel independent because they invalidate the application condition.

Similarly, a positive condition may be fulfilled for the amalgamated rule, but not for all single multi rules.

Given two amalgamated rules, the parallel rule can be constructed as an amalgamated rule using some component-wise coproduct constructions of the kernel and multi rules.

Fact 4.26
Given two bundles of kernel morphisms $s = (s_i : p_0 \rightarrow p_i)_{i=1,\ldots,n}$ and $s' = (s'_j : p'_0 \rightarrow p'_j)_{j=1,\ldots,n'}$ leading to amalgamated rules $\tilde{p}_s$ and $\tilde{p}_{s'}$, respectively, the

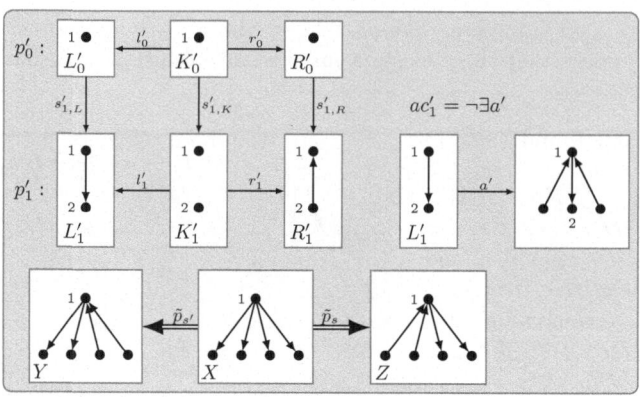

Figure 4.9: A counterexample for parallel independence of amalgamated transformations

parallel rule $\tilde{p}_s + \tilde{p}_{s'}$ is constructed by $\tilde{p}_s + \tilde{p}_{s'} = \tilde{p}_t$ as the amalgamated rule of the bundle of kernel morphisms $t = (t_i : p_0 + p_0' \to p_i + p_0', t_j' : p_0 + p_0' \to p_0 + p_j')$.

PROOF This follows directly from the general construction of colimits.

As in any $\mathcal{M}$-adhesive transformation system, also for amalgamated transformations the Local Church-Rosser and Parallelism Theorem holds. This is a direct instantiation of Thm. 3.46 to amalgamated transformations. For the analysis of parallel independence and the construction of the parallel rule we may use the results from Thm. 4.24 and Fact. 4.26, respectively.

Theorem 4.27 (Local Church-Rosser and Parallelism Theorem)
Given two parallel independent amalgamated transformations $G \xRightarrow{\tilde{p}_s} H_1$ and $G \xRightarrow{\tilde{p}_{s'}} H_2$ there is an object G' together with direct transformations $H_1 \xRightarrow{\tilde{p}_{s'}} G'$ and $H_2 \xRightarrow{\tilde{p}_s} G'$ such that $G \xRightarrow{\tilde{p}_s} H_1 \xRightarrow{\tilde{p}_{s'}} G'$ and $G \xRightarrow{\tilde{p}_{s'}} H_2 \xRightarrow{\tilde{p}_s} G'$ are sequentially independent.

Given two sequentially independent direct transformations $G \xRightarrow{\tilde{p}_s} H_1 \xRightarrow{\tilde{p}_{s'}} G'$ there is an object H_2 with direct transformations $G \xRightarrow{\tilde{p}_{s'}} H_2 \xRightarrow{\tilde{p}_s} G'$ such that $G \xRightarrow{\tilde{p}_s} H_1$ and $G \xRightarrow{\tilde{p}_{s'}} H_2$ are parallel independent.

In any case of independence, there is a parallel transformation $G \xRightarrow{\tilde{p}_t} G'$ via the parallel rule $\tilde{p}_s + \tilde{p}_{s'} = \tilde{p}_t$ and, vice versa, a direct transformation $G \xRightarrow{\tilde{p}_t} G'$ can be sequentialized both ways.

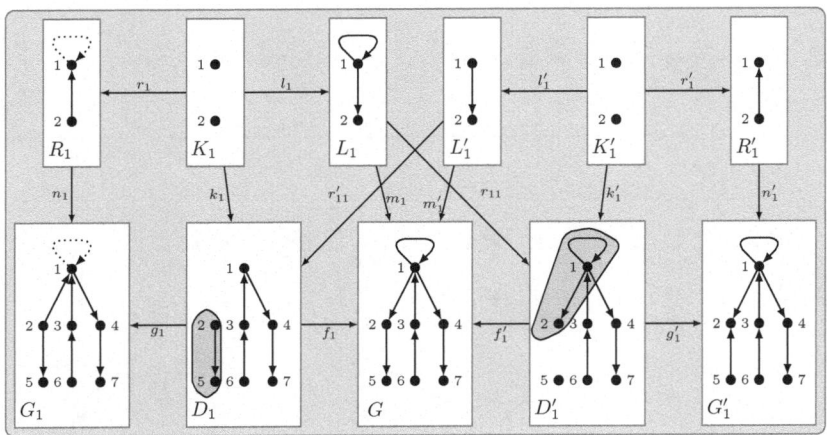

Figure 4.10: Parallel independence of the transformations $G \xrightarrow{p_1,m_1} G_1$ and $G \xrightarrow{p_1',m_1'} G_1'$

PROOF This follows directly from Thm. 3.46.

Example 4.28
Consider the amalgamated transformation $G \xrightarrow{\tilde{p}_s,\tilde{m}} H$ in Fig. 4.6 and the bundle of kernel morphisms $s' = (s_1')$ using the kernel morphism depicted in Fig. 4.9. The amalgamated rule $\tilde{p}_{s'}$ can also be applied to G via match $\tilde{m}'$ matching the nodes 1 and 2 in L_1' to the nodes 2 and 5 in G, respectively. This results in an amalgamated transformation $G \xrightarrow{\tilde{p}_{s'},\tilde{m}'} H'$.

For the analysis of parallel amalgamation independence, we first analyze the pairwise parallel independence of the transformations $G \xrightarrow{p_i,m_i} G_i$ and $G \xrightarrow{p_1',m_1'} G_1'$ for $i = 1, 2, 3$, with $m_1' = \tilde{m}'$ and $G_1' = H'$. This is done exemplarily for $i = 1$ in Fig. 4.10, where we do not show the application conditions. The morphisms r_{11} and r_{11}' are marked in their corresponding domains D_1' and D_1 leading to $f_1' \circ r_{11} = m_1$ and $f_1 \circ r_{11}' = m_1'$. Moreover, $g \circ r_{11}' \models ac_1$, because there are no ingoing edges into node 2, and $g' \circ r_{11} \models ac_1$, because there is no dotted loop at node 1 and no reverse edge. Thus, both transformations are parallel independent, and this follows analogously for $i = 2, 3$. Moreover, the induced morphism $\tilde{r}_{s'} : \tilde{L}_{s'} = L_1' \to D$ leads to $g \circ \tilde{r}_{s'} \models \tilde{ac}_{s'} = ac_1'$. In the other direction, $\tilde{r}_s : \tilde{L}_s \to D' = D_1'$ ensures that $g_1' \circ \tilde{r}_s \models \tilde{ac}_s$. Thus, the two bundles are parallel bundle independent and, using Thm. 4.24, it follows that $G \xrightarrow{\tilde{p}_s,\tilde{m}} H$ and $G \xrightarrow{\tilde{p}_{s'},\tilde{m}'} H'$ are parallel amalgamation independent.

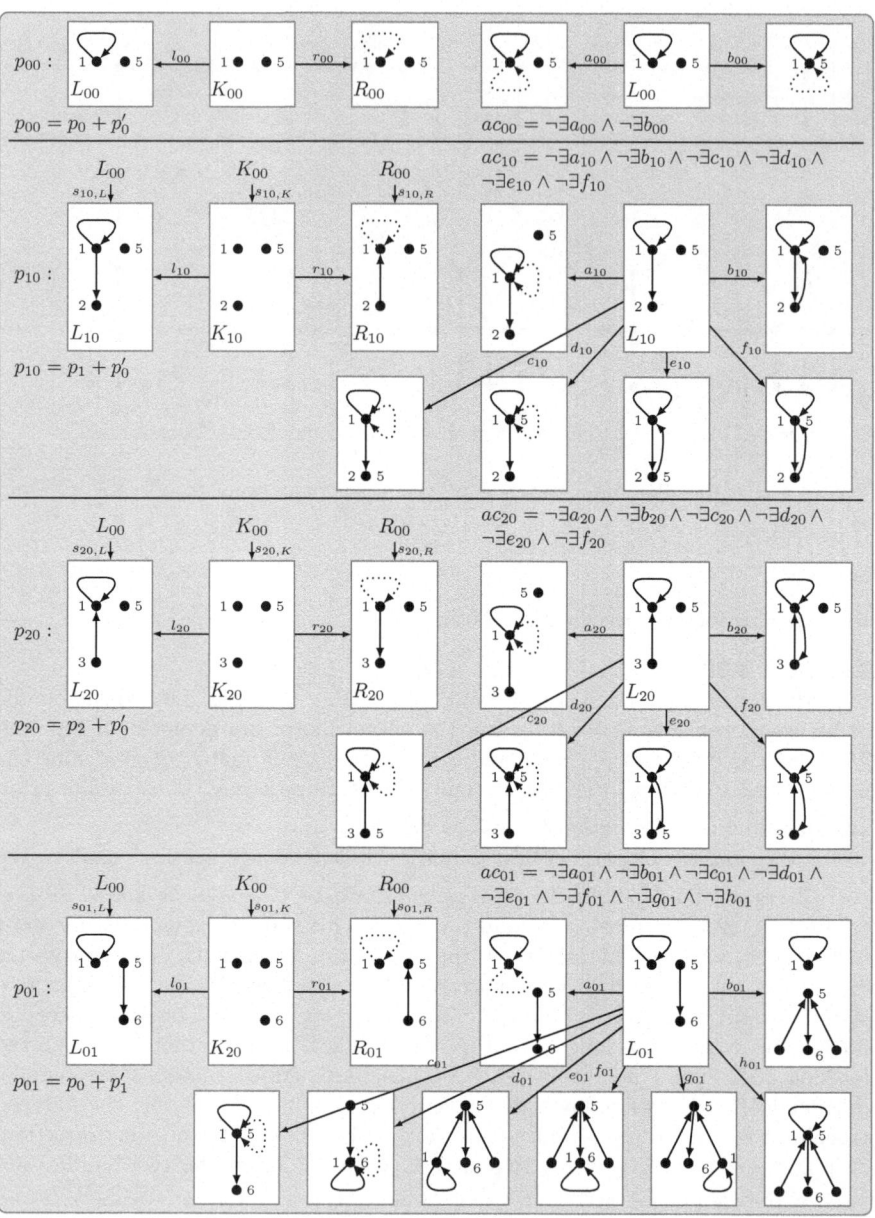

Figure 4.11: The kernel morphisms leading to the parallel rule

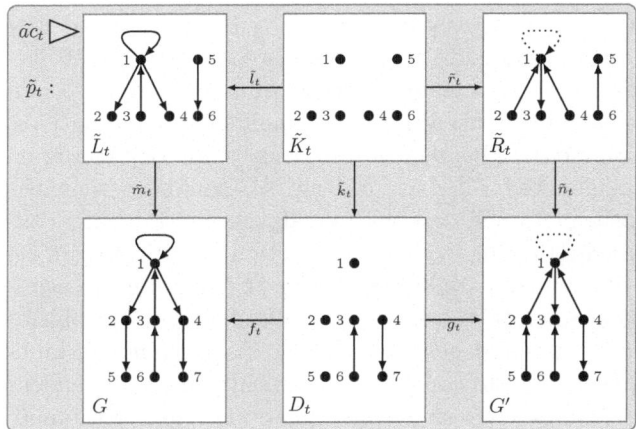

Figure 4.12: A parallel amalgamated graph transformation

The construction of this parallel rules according to Fact 4.26 is shown in Fig. 4.11. The parallel rule $\tilde{p}_s + \tilde{p}_{s'} = \tilde{p}_t$ is the amalgamated rule of the bundle of kernel morphisms $t = (s_{10} = s_1 + id_{p'_0}, s_{20} = s_2 + id_{p'_0}, s_{10} = s_1 + id_{p'_0}, s_{01} = id_{p_0} + s'_1)$. The corresponding parallel rule is depicted in the top of Fig. 4.12, where we omit to show the application condition ac_t due to its length. It leads to the amalgamated transformation $G \xrightarrow{\tilde{p}_t, \tilde{m}_t} G'$ depicted in Fig. 4.12. Moreover, from Thm. 4.27 we obtain also amalgamated transformations $H \xrightarrow{\tilde{p}_{s'}} G'$ and $H' \xrightarrow{\tilde{p}_s} G'$, with $G \xrightarrow{\tilde{p}_s} G \xrightarrow{\tilde{p}_{s'}} G'$ and $G \xrightarrow{\tilde{p}_{s'}} H \xrightarrow{\tilde{p}_s} G'$ being sequentially independent transformations sequences.

4.1.4 Other Results for Amalgamated Transformations

For $\mathcal{M}$-adhesive transformation systems with amalgamation, also the other results stated in Subsection 3.4.3 are valid for amalgamated transformations. But additional results for the analysis of the results for amalgamated rules based on the underlying kernel and multi rules are future work:

- For the Concurrency Theorem, two amalgamated rules leading to parallel dependent amalgamated transformations can be combined to an E-concurrent rule and the corresponding transformation. It would be interesting to analyze if this E-concurrent rule could be constructed as an amalgamated rule based on the underlying kernel and multi rules.

- For the Embedding and Extension Theorem, an amalgamated rule can be embedded if the embedding morphism is consistent. Most likely, consistency w. r. t. an amalgamated transformation can be formulated as a consistency property w. r. t. the bundle of transformations.
- For the Local Confluence Theorem, if all critical pairs depending on all available amalgamated rules are strictly AC-confluent then the $\mathcal{M}$-adhesive transformation system with amalgamation is locally confluent. It would be interesting to find a new notion of critical pairs depending not on the amalgamated rules, but on the kernel morphisms. For arbitrary amalgamated rules, any bundle of kernel morphisms had to be analyzed. It would be more efficient if some kinds of minimal bundles were sufficient to construct all critical pairs or dependent transformations of the $\mathcal{M}$-adhesive transformation system with amalgamation.

4.1.5 Interaction Schemes and Maximal Matchings

For many interesting application areas, including the operational semantics for Petri nets and statecharts, we do not want to define the matches for the multi rules explicitly, but to obtain them dependent on the object to be transformed. In this case, only an interaction scheme is given, which defines a set of kernel morphisms but does not include a count how often each multi rule is used in the bundle leading to the amalgamated rule.

Definition 4.29 (Interaction scheme)
A kernel rule p_0 and a set of multi rules $\{p_1, \ldots, p_k\}$ with kernel morphisms $s_i : p_0 \rightarrow p_i$ form an *interaction scheme is* $= \{s_1, \ldots, s_k\}$.

When given an interaction scheme, we want to apply as many rules occurring in the interaction scheme as often as possible over a certain kernel rule match. There are two different possible maximal matchings: maximal weakly independent and maximal weakly disjoint matchings. For maximal weakly independent matchings, we require the matchings of the multi rules to be weakly independent to ensure that the resulting bundle of transformations is amalgamable. This is the minimal requirement to meet the definition. In addition, for maximal weakly disjoint matchings the matches of the multi rules should be disjoint up to the kernel rule match. This variant is preferred for implementation, because it eases the computation of additional matches when we can rule out model parts that were already matched.

Definition 4.30 (Maximal weakly independent matching)
Given an object G and an interaction scheme $is = \{s_1, \ldots, s_k\}$, a maximal weakly disjoint matching $m = (m_0, m_1, \ldots, m_n)$ is defined as follows:

1. Set $i = 0$. Choose a kernel matching $m_0 : L_0 \to G$ such that $G \xrightarrow{p_0, m_0} G_0$ is a valid transformation.

2. As long as possible: Increase i, choose a multi rule $\hat{p}_i = p_j$ with $j \in \{1, \ldots, k\}$, and find a match $m_i : L_j \to G$ such that $m_i \circ s_{j,L} = m_0$, $G \xrightarrow{p_j, m_i} G_i$ is a valid transformation, the matches $m_1, \ldots, m_i$ are weakly independent, and $m_i \neq m_\ell$ for all $\ell = 1, \ldots, i - 1$.

3. If no more valid matches for any rule in the interaction scheme can be found, return $m = (m_0, m_1, \ldots, m_n)$.

The maximal weakly independent matching leads to a bundle of kernel morphisms $s = (s_i : p_0 \to \hat{p}_i)$ and an s-amalgamable bundle of direct transformations $G \xrightarrow{\hat{p}_i, m_i} G_i$.

Definition 4.31 (Maximal weakly disjoint matching)
Given an object G and an interaction scheme $is = \{s_1, \ldots, s_k\}$, a maximal weakly disjoint matching $m = (m_0, m_1, \ldots, m_n)$ is defined as follows:

1. Set $i = 0$. Choose a kernel matching $m_0 : L_0 \to G$ such that $G \xrightarrow{p_0, m_0} G_0$ is a valid transformation.

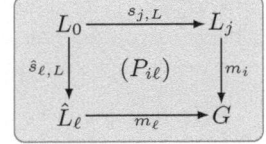

2. As long as possible: Increase i, choose a multi rule $\hat{p}_i = p_j$ with $j \in \{1, \ldots, k\}$, and find a match $m_i : L_j \to G$ such that $m_i \circ s_{j,L} = m_0$, $G \xrightarrow{p_j, m_i} G_i$ is a valid transformation, the matches $m_1, \ldots, m_i$ are weakly independent, and $m_i \neq m_\ell$ and the square $(P_{i\ell})$ is a pullback for all $\ell = 1, \ldots, i - 1$.

3. If no more valid matches for any rule in the interaction scheme can be found, return $m = (m_0, m_1, \ldots, m_n)$.

The maximal weakly disjoint matching leads to a bundle of kernel morphisms $s = (s_i : p_0 \to \hat{p}_i)$ and an s-amalgamable bundle of direct transformations $G \xrightarrow{\hat{p}_i, m_i} G_i$.

Note that for maximal weakly disjoint matchings, the pullback requirement already implies the existence of the morphisms for the weakly independent matches. Only the property for the application conditions has to be checked in addition.

Fact 4.32
Given an object G, a bundle of kernel morphisms $s = (s_1, \ldots, s_n)$, and matches $m_1, \ldots, m_n$ leading to a bundle of direct transformations $G \xrightarrow{p_i, m_i} G_i$ such that $m_i \circ s_{i,L} = m_0$ and square (P_{ij}) is a pullback for all $i \neq j$ then the bundle $G \xrightarrow{p_i, m_i} G_i$ is s-amalgamable for transformations without application conditions.

PROOF By construction, the matches m_i agree on the match m_0 of the kernel rule. It remains to show that they are weakly independent.

Given the transformations $G \xrightarrow{p_i, m_i} G_i$ with pushouts (20_i) and (21_i), consider the following cube, where the bottom face is pushout (20_i), the back right face is pullback (1_i), and the top right face is pullback (P_{ij}). Now construct the pullback of f_i and m_j as the front left face, and from $m_j \circ s_{j,L} \circ l_0 = m_i \circ s_{i,L} \circ l_0 = m_i \circ l_i \circ s_{i,K} = f_i \circ k_i \circ s_{i,K}$ we obtain a morphism p with $\hat{f} \circ p = s_{j,L} \circ l_0$ and $\hat{m} \circ p = k_i \circ s_{i,K}$.

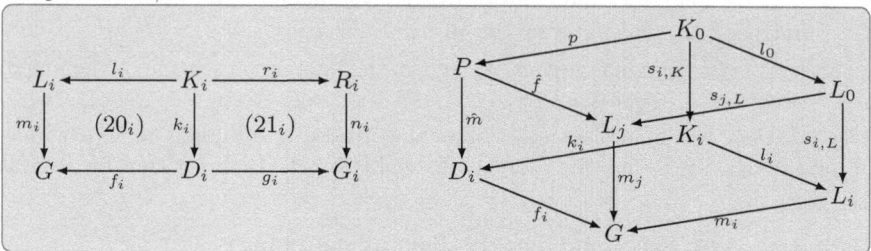

From pullback composition and decomposition of the right and left faces it follows that also the back left face is a pullback. Now the $\mathcal{M}$-van Kampen property can be applied leading to a pushout in the top face. Since pushout complements are unique up to isomorphism, we can substitute the top face by pushout $(1_i')$ with $P \cong L_{j0}$. Thus we have found the morphism $p_{ji} := \hat{m}$ with $f_i \circ p_{ji} = m_j \circ u_i$. This construction can be applied for all pairs i, j leading to weakly independent matches without application conditions.

This fact leads to a set-theoretical characterization of maximal weakly disjoint matchings.

Fact 4.33

For graphs and graph-based structures, valid matches $m_0, m_1, \ldots, m_n$ with $m_i \circ s_{i,L} = m_0$ for all $i = 1, \ldots, n$ form a maximal weakly disjoint matching without application conditions if and only if $m_i(L_i) \cap m_j(L_j) = m_0(L_0)$.

PROOF Valid matches means that the transformations $G \xrightarrow{p_i, m_i}$ are well-defined. In graphs and graph-like structures, (P_{ij}) is a pullback if and only if $m_i(L_i) \cap m_j(L_j) = m_0(L_0)$. Then Fact 4.32 implies that the matches form a maximal weakly disjoint matching without application conditions.

Example 4.34

Consider the interaction scheme $is = (s_1, s_2)$ defined by the kernel morphisms s_1 and s_2 in Fig. 4.2, the graph X depicted in the middle of Fig. 4.13, and the kernel rule match m_0 mapping the node 1 in L_0 to the node 1 in X.

If we choose maximal weakly independent matchings, the construction works as follows defining the following matches, where f is the edge from 1 to 2 in L_1 and g the reverse edge in L_2:

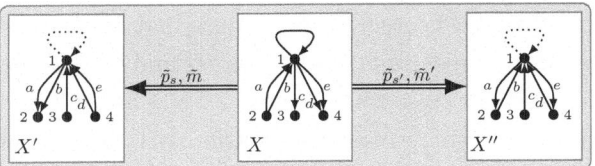

Figure 4.13: Application of an amalgamated rule via maximal matchings

$i = 1 : \hat{p}_1 = p_1, m_1 : 2 \mapsto 3, f \mapsto c,$
$i = 2 : \hat{p}_2 = p_1, m_2 : 2 \mapsto 4, f \mapsto d,$
$i = 3 : \hat{p}_3 = p_2, m_3 : 3 \mapsto 2, g \mapsto a,$
$i = 4 : \hat{p}_4 = p_1, m_4 : 2 \mapsto 4, f \mapsto e,$
$i = 5 : \hat{p}_5 = p_2, m_5 : 3 \mapsto 2, g \mapsto b.$

Thus, we find five different matches, three for the multi rule p_1 and two for the multi rule p_2. Note that in addition to the overlapping m_0, the matches m_3 and m_5 overlap in the node 2, while m_2 and m_4 overlap in the node 4. But since these matches are still weakly independent, because the nodes 2 and 4 are not deleted by the rule applications, this is a valid maximal weakly independent matching. It leads to the bundle $s = (s_1, s_1, s_1, s_2, s_2)$ and the amalgamated rule $\tilde{p}_s$, which can be applied to X leading to the amalgamated transformation $X \xrightarrow{\tilde{p}_s, \tilde{m}} X'$ as shown in the left of Fig. 4.13.

If we choose maximal weakly disjoint matchings instead, the matches m_4 and m_5 are no longer valid because they overlap with m_2 and m_3, respectively, in more than the match m_0. Thus we obtain the maximal weakly disjoint matching (m_0, m_1, m_2, m_3), the corresponding bundle $s' = (s_1, s_1, s_2)$ leading to the amalgamated rule $\tilde{p}_{s'}$ and the amalgamated transformation $X \xrightarrow{\tilde{p}_{s'}, \tilde{m}'} X''$ depicted in the right of Fig. 4.13. Note that this matching is not unique, also (m_0, m_1, m_2, m_4) could have been chosen as a maximal weakly disjoint matching.

4.1.6 Main Results for Amalgamated Transformations Based on Maximal Matchings

If we only allow to apply amalgamated rules via maximal matchings, the main results from Subsection 3.4.3 do not hold instantly as is the case for arbitrary matchings. The main problem is that the amalgamated transformations obtained from the results are in general not applied via maximal matchings. The analysis and definition of properties ensuring these results is future work:

- For the Local Church-Rosser Theorem, it guarantees that for parallel independent amalgamated transformations $G \xrightarrow{\tilde{p}_s} H_1$ and $G \xrightarrow{\tilde{p}_{s'}} H_2$ via maximal matchings there exist transformations $H_1 \xrightarrow{\tilde{p}_{s'}} G'$ and $H_2 \xrightarrow{\tilde{p}_s} G'$. But in general, these resulting transformations will not be via maximal matching, since $\tilde{p}_{s'}$ may create new matchings for s, and vice versa. Thus, one has to find properties that make sure that no new matches, or at least no new disjoint matches, are created.
- For the Parallelism Theorem, the property of maximal weakly independent matchings is transferred to the application of the parallel rule as shown below.
- For the Concurrency Theorem, one first has to formulate results concerning the construction of an E-concurrent rule as an amalgamated rule based on the underlying kernel and multi rules before it can be related to maximal matchings.
- For the Embedding and Extension Theorem, embedding an object G with a maximal matching into a larger context G' in general enables more matches, i. e. the application of the amalgamated rule to G' may not be maximal. One needs to define properties to restrict the embedding to some parts outside the matches of the multi rules to ensure that the same matchings are maximal in G and G'.
- For the Local Confluence Theorem, maximal matchings may actually lead to fewer critical pairs if we have additional information about the objects to be transformed, since some conflicting transformations may not occur at all due to maximal matchings.

In case of parallel independent transformations, the property of a maximal weakly independent matchings is transferred to the application of the parallel rule. Note that for maximal weakly disjoint matchings, we have to require in addition that the matches of the two amalgamated transformations do not overlap.

Theorem 4.35 (Parallelism of maximal weakly independent matchings)
Given parallel independent amalgamated transformations $G \xrightarrow{\tilde{p}_s, \tilde{m}} H_1$ and $G \xrightarrow{\tilde{p}_{s'}, \tilde{m}'} H_2$ leading to the induced transformations $G \xrightarrow{\tilde{p}_t, \tilde{m}_t} G'$ via the parallel rule $\tilde{p}_t = \tilde{p}_s + \tilde{p}_{s'}$ then the following holds: if $G \xrightarrow{\tilde{p}_s, \tilde{m}} H_1$ and $G \xrightarrow{\tilde{p}_{s'}, \tilde{m}'} H_2$ are transformations via maximal weakly independent matchings then also $G \xrightarrow{\tilde{p}_t, \tilde{m}_t} G'$ is a transformation via a maximal weakly independent matching.

PROOF Given parallel independent amalgamated transformations $G \xrightarrow{\tilde{p}_s, \tilde{m}} H_1$ and $G \xrightarrow{\tilde{p}_{s'}, \tilde{m}'} H_2$ via maximal weakly independent matchings $(m_0, m_1, \ldots, m_n)$

with $\tilde{m} \circ t_{i,L} = m_i$ and $(m'_0, m'_1, \ldots, m'_{n'})$ with $\tilde{m}' \circ t'_{j,L} = m'_j$, respectively. Then we have the matching $m = ([m_0, m'_0], ([m_i, m'_0])_{i=1,\ldots,n}, ([m_0, m'_j])_{j=1,\ldots,n'})$ for the parallel transformation $G \xrightarrow{\tilde{p}_t, \tilde{m}_t} G'$, with $[m_i, m'_0] \circ (s_{i,L} + id_{L_0}) = [m_0, m'_0]$ and $[m_0, m'_j] \circ (id_{L_0} + s'_{j,L}) = [m_0, m'_0]$. We have to show the maximality of m.

Suppose m is not maximal. This means that there is, w.l.o.g., some match $\hat{m} : L_k + L'_0 \rightarrow G$ such that $\hat{m} \circ (s_{k,L} + id_{L'_0}) = [m_0, m'_0]$ and $\hat{m} \neq [m_i, m'_0]$ for all $i = 1, \ldots, n$ such that $(m, \hat{m})$ is also weakly independent. Then we find a match $\hat{m}_k := \hat{m} \circ i_{L_k}$ for the rule p_k with $\hat{m}_k \circ s_{k,L} = m_0$ and $\hat{m}_k \neq m_i$ for all i. It follows that $(m_0, m_1, \ldots, m_n, \hat{m}_k)$ are also weakly independent, which is a contradiction to the maximality of $(m_0, m_1, \ldots, m_n)$.

4.2 Operational Semantics Using Amalgamation

In this section, we use amalgamation as introduced before to model the operational semantics of elementary Petri nets and UML statecharts. Using amalgamation allows the description of a semantical step in an unknown surrounding with only one interaction scheme. We do not need specific rules for each occurring situation as is the case for standard graph transformation.

4.2.1 Semantics for Elementary Nets

In the following, we present a semantics for the firing behavior of elementary Petri nets using graph transformation and amalgamation. Elementary Petri nets are nets where at most one token is allowed on each place. A transition

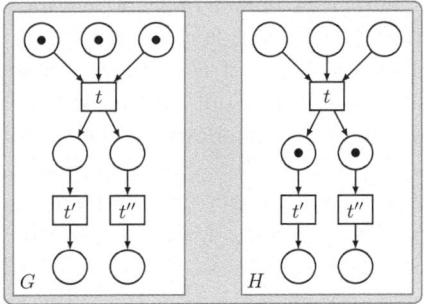

Figure 4.14: The firing of the transition t

t is activated if there is a token on each pre-place of t and all post-places of t are token-free. In this case, the transition may fire leading to the follower marking where the tokens on all the pre-places of t are deleted and at all post-places of t a token appears. An example is depicted in Fig. 4.14, where the transition t in the elementary Petri net G is activated in the left and the follower marking is depicted in the right of Fig. 4.14 leading to the elementary Petri net H.

We model these nets by typed graphs. The type graph is depicted in Fig. 4.15 and consists simply of places, transitions, the corresponding pre- and post-arcs, and tokens attached to their places. For the following examples, we use the well-known concrete syntax of Petri nets, modeling a place by a circle, a transition by a rectangle, and a token by a small filled circle placed on its place.

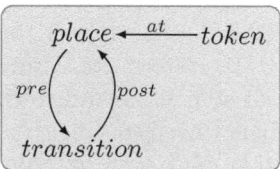

Figure 4.15: The type graph for elementary nets

In Figs. 4.16 and 4.17, three rules p_0, p_1, and p_2 are shown, which will result as an amalgamated rule with maximal weakly disjoint matchings in a firing step of the net. The rule p_0 in Fig. 4.16 selects a transition t which is not changed at all. But note that the application condition restricts this rule to be only applicable if there is no empty pre-place of t and we have only empty post-places. This means, that the transition t is activated in the elementary net. The rule p_1 describes the firing of a preplace, where the token on this place is deleted. It only inherits the application condition of p_0 to guarantee a kernel morphism $s_1 : p_0 \to p_1$ as shown in the top of Fig. 4.17. s_1 is indeed a kernel morphism because (1) and (2) are pullbacks and (3) is the required pushout complement. ac_0 and ac_1 are complement-compatible w.r.t. s_1 with $ac_1' =$ true. Similarly, rule p_2 describes the firing of a post-place, where a token is added on this place. Again, there is a kernel morphism $s_2 : p_0 \to p_2$ as shown in the bottom of Fig. 4.17 with pullbacks (1') and (2)', (1') is already a pushout, and ac_0 and ac_2 are complement-compatible w.r.t. s_2 with $ac_2' =$ true.

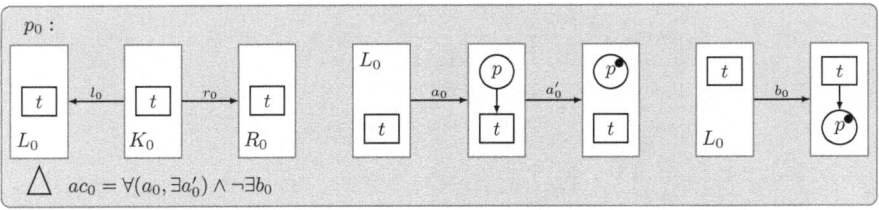

Figure 4.16: The kernel rule selecting an activated transition

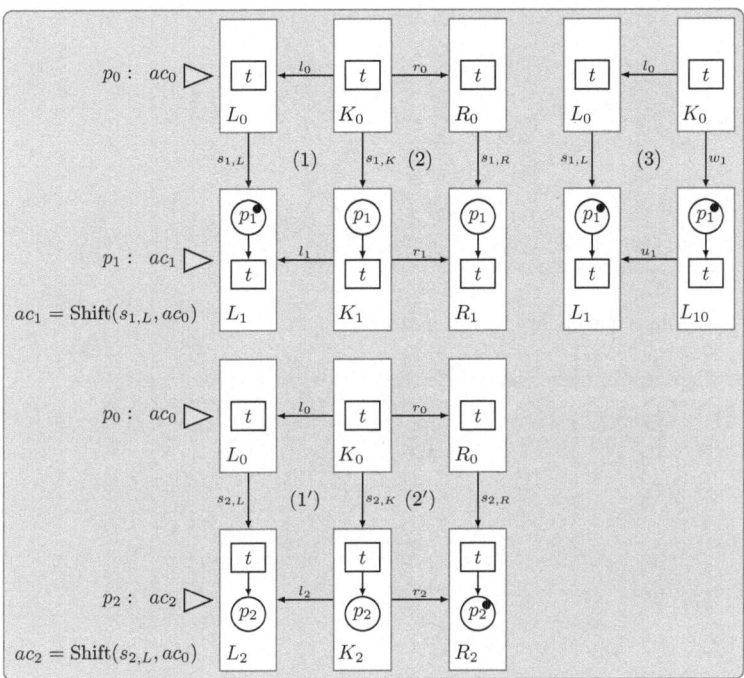

Figure 4.17: The multi rules describing the handling of each place

For the multi rules in Fig. 4.17, the complement rules are the rules p_1 and p_2 themselves but with empty application condition true, because they contain everything which is done in addition to p_0 including the connection with K_0, while the application condition is already ensured by p_0.

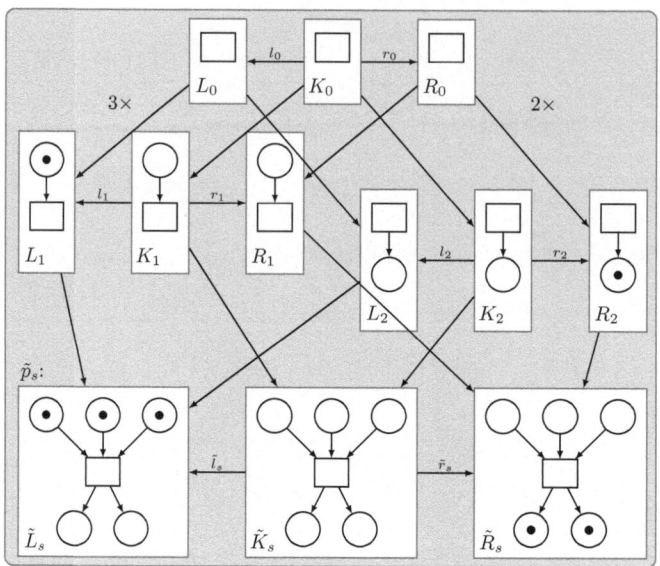

Figure 4.18: The construction of the amalgamated rule

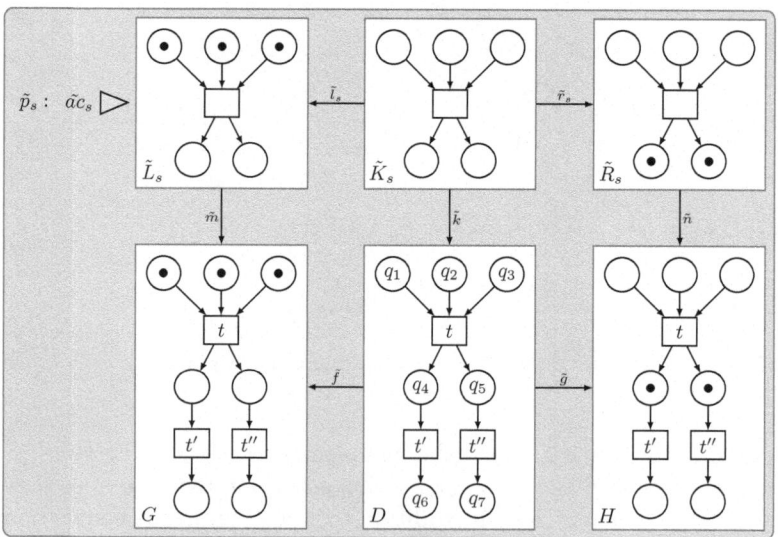

Figure 4.19: An amalgamated transformation

Now consider the interaction scheme $is = \{s_1, s_2\}$ leading to the bundle of kernel morphisms $s = (s_1, s_1, s_1, s_2, s_2)$. The construction of the corresponding amalgamated rule $\tilde{p}_s$ is shown in Fig. 4.18 without application conditions. This amalgamated rule can be applied to the elementary Petri net G as depicted in Fig. 4.19 leading to the amalgamated transformation $G \xrightarrow{\tilde{p}_s, \tilde{m}} H$.

Moreover, we can find a bundle of transformations $G \xrightarrow{m_1, p_1} G_1$, $G \xrightarrow{m_2, p_1} G_2$, $G \xrightarrow{m_3, p_1} G_3$, $G \xrightarrow{m_4, p_2} G_4$, and $G \xrightarrow{m_5, p_2} G_5$ with the resulting nets depicted in Fig. 4.20 and matches $m_0 : t \mapsto t$, $m_1 : p_1 \mapsto q_1$, $m_2 : p_1 \mapsto q_2$, $m_3 : p_1 \mapsto q_3$, $m_4 : p_2 \mapsto q_4$, and $m_3 : p_2 \mapsto q_5$. This bundle is s-amalgamable, because it has consistent matches with m_0 matching the transition t from p_0 to the transition t in G, and all matches are weakly independent, they only overlap in L_0. $(m_0, \ldots, m_5)$ is both a maximal weakly independent and a maximal weakly disjoint matching, because not other match can be found extending the kernel rule match, and all these matches are disjoint up to the selected transition t.

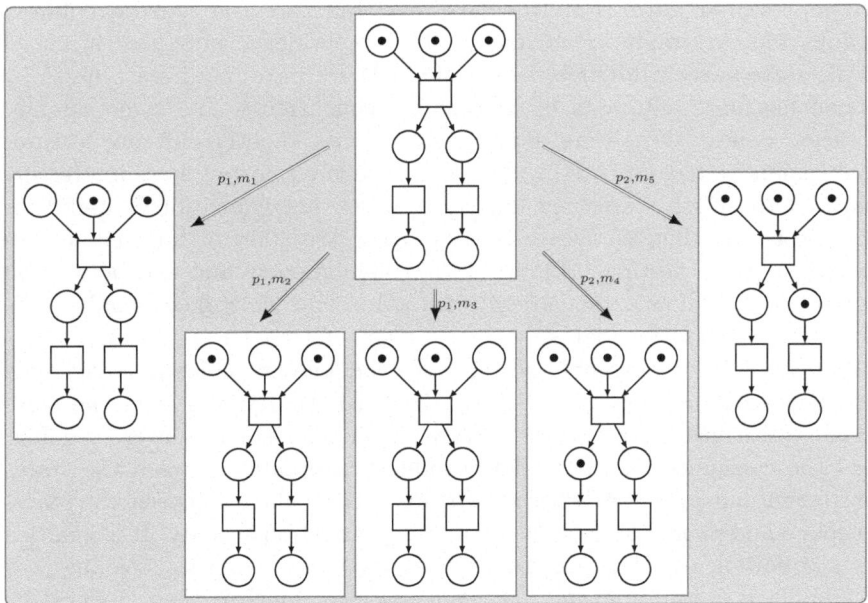

Figure 4.20: An s-amalgamable transformation bundle

If we always use maximal matchings, any application of an amalgamated rule created from the interaction scheme $is = \{s_1, s_2\}$ is a valid firing step of a transition in the elementary net. For example, to fire the transition t' in G the bundle $s' = (s_1, s_2)$ leads to the required amalgamated rule. In general, for a transition with m pre- and n post-arcs, the corresponding bundle $s = ((s_1)_{i=1,...,m}, (s_2)_{j=1,...,n})$ leads to the amalgamated rule firing this transition via a maximal matching. Note that each maximal weakly independent matching is already a maximal weakly disjoint matching due to the net structure.

For elementary Petri nets we only need one kernel rule and two multi rules to describe the complete firing semantics for all well-defined nets. We neither need infinite many rules, which are difficult to analyze, nor any control or helper structure when using amalgamation. This eases the modeling of the semantics and prevents errors.

4.2.2 Syntax of Statecharts

Before we specify the operational semantics for statecharts we introduce the represented features and define the syntax based on typed attributed graphs and constraints (see Chapter 3). We consider a simplified variant of UML statecharts [OMG09b]. In [Har87], Harel introduced statecharts by enhancing finite automata by hierarchies, concurrency, and some communication issues. Over time, many versions with slightly differing features and semantics have evolved. We restrict ourselves to the most interesting parts of the UML statechart diagrams, where amalgamation is useful for a suitable modeling of the semantical rules. We allow orthogonal regions as well as state nesting. But we do not handle entry and exit actions on states, do not allow extended state variables, and allow guards only to be conditions over active states.

In Fig. 4.21, an example statechart ProdCons is depicted modeling a producer-consumer system. When initialized, the system is in the state prod, which has three regions. There, in parallel the producer, a buffer, and the consumer may act. The producer alternates between the states produced and prepare, where the transition produce between the states prepare and produced models the actual production activity. It is guarded by a condition that the parallel state empty is also current, meaning that the buffer is empty and may receive a produce, which is then modeled by the action incbuff denoted after the /-dash. Similarly to the producer, the buffer alternates between the states empty and full, and the consumer

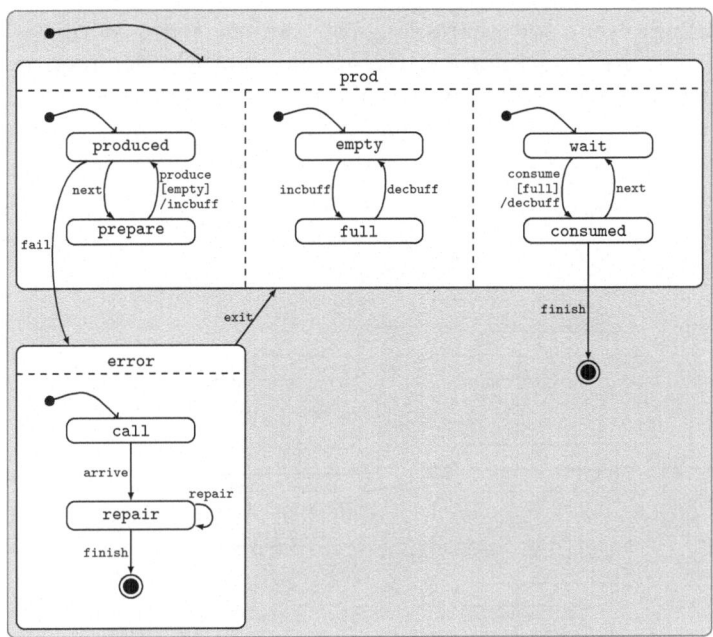

Figure 4.21: The example statechart ProdCons in concrete syntax

between the states wait and consumed. The transition consume is again guarded by the state full and followed by a decbuff-action emptying the buffer.

There are two possible events that may happen causing a state transition leaving the state prod. First, the consumer may decide to leave and finish the complete run. Second, there may be a failure detected after the production leading to the error-state. Then, a mechanic is called who has to repair the machine. When this is done, the error-state can be exited via the corresponding exit-transition and the standard behavior in the prod-state is executed again, where all three regions are set back to there initial behavior.

Note that for the states used as conditions in guards we assume to have unique names, but this is merely a problem of the concrete syntax. In the abstract syntax graph, this problem is solved by introducing a direct edge from the guard to this state, and not only a reference by name as done in the concrete statechart diagram.

For the modeling of our statecharts language, we use typed attributed graphs. Concerning the representation, the attributes of a node are given in a class diagram-like style. For the values of attributes in the rules we can also use variables. Note that for the typing of the edges, we omit the edge types if they are clear from the node types they are connecting.

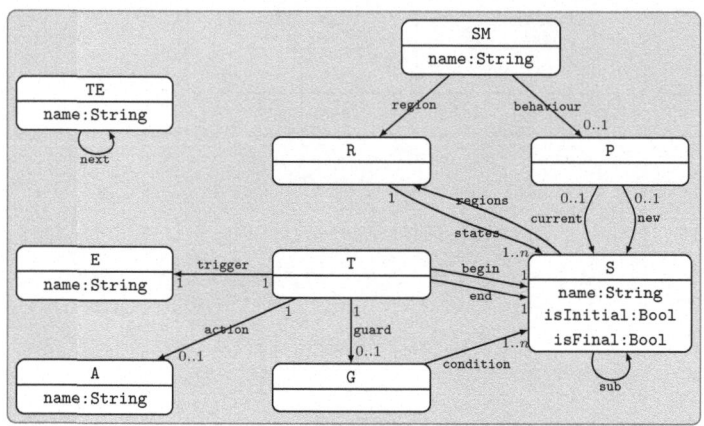

Figure 4.22: The type graph TG_{SC} for statecharts

The type graph TG_{SC} is given in Fig. 4.22. Note that we use multiplicities to denote some constraints directly in the type graph. This is only an abbreviation of the corresponding constraints and does not extend the expressiveness of typed graphs with constraints. Additional constraints are defined in Fig. 4.23 and explained in the following that have to be valid for well-defined statechart diagrams.

Each diagram consists of exactly one statemachine SM (constraint c_1) containing one or more regions R. A region contains states S, where state names are unique within one region. A state may again contain one or more regions. Constraint c_2 expresses in addition that each region is contained in either exactly one state or the statemachine. Moreover, states may be initial (attribute value isInitial = true) or final (attribute value isFinal=true), each region has to contain exactly one initial and at most one final state, and final states cannot contain regions (constraint c_3). Note that the edge type sub is only necessary to compute all substates of a state, which we need for the definition of the semantics. This relation is computed in the beginning using the states- and regions-edges.

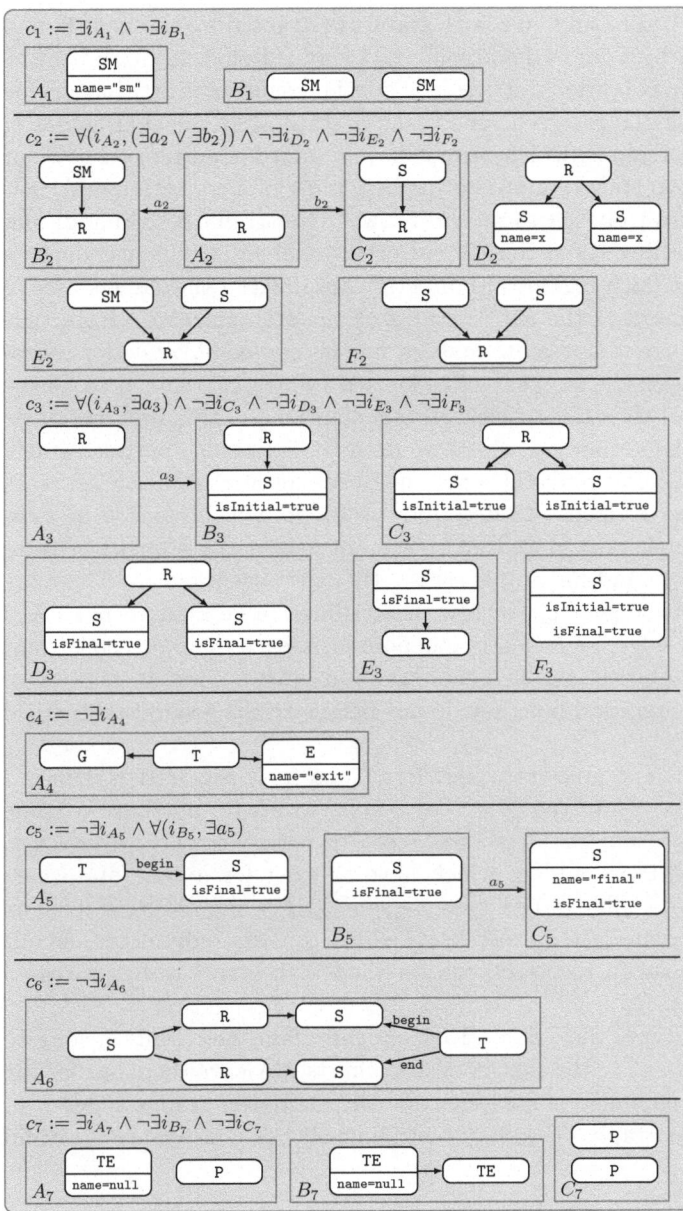

Figure 4.23: Constraints limiting the valid statechart diagrams

A transition T begins and ends at a state, is triggered by an event E, and may be restricted by a guard G and followed by an action A. A guard has one ore more states as conditions. There is a special event with attribute value name="exit" which is reserved for exiting a state after the completion of all its orthogonal regions, which cannot have a guard condition (constraint c_4). Moreover, final states cannot be the beginning of a transition and their name attribute has to be set to name="final" (constraint c_5). In addition, transitions cannot link states in different orthogonal regions (constraint c_6), which means that both regions are directly contained in the same state.

A pointer P describes the active states of the statemachine. Note that newly inserted current states are marked by the new-edge, while for established current states the current-edge is used (which is assumed to be the standard type and thus not marked in our diagrams). This differentiation is necessary for the semantics, where we need to distinguish between states that were current before and states that just became current in the last state transition. Trigger elements TE describe the events which have to be handled by the statemachine. Note that this is not necessarily a queue because of orthogonal states, but for simplicity we still call it event queue. There are at least the empty trigger element with attribute value name = null and no outgoing next-edge, and exactly one pointer in each diagram (constraint c_7). The pointer and trigger elements are used later for the description of the operational semantics, but they do not belong to the general syntactical description.

In Fig. 4.24, the example statechart ProdCons from Fig. 4.21 is depicted in abstract syntax. Note that for final states, which do not have a name in the concrete syntax, the attribute is set to name="final". Moreover, the nodes P and TE are added, which have to exist for a valid statechart model, but are not visible in the concrete syntax. For simulating statechart runs, the event queue of the statechart, which consists only of the default element named null in Fig. 4.24, can be filled with events to be processed as explained later.

Since edges of types sub, behavior, current, and next only belong to the semantics but not to the syntax of statecharts, we leave them out for the definition of the language of statecharts. All attributed graphs typed over this reduced type graph $TG_{SC,Syn}$ satisfying all the constraints are valid statecharts.

Definition 4.36 (Language VL_{SC})
Define the syntax type graph $TG_{SC,Syn} = TG_{SC} \backslash \{\text{sub}, \text{behavior}, \text{current}, \text{next}\}$ based on the type graph TG_{SC} in Fig. 4.22. The language VL_{SC} consists of all

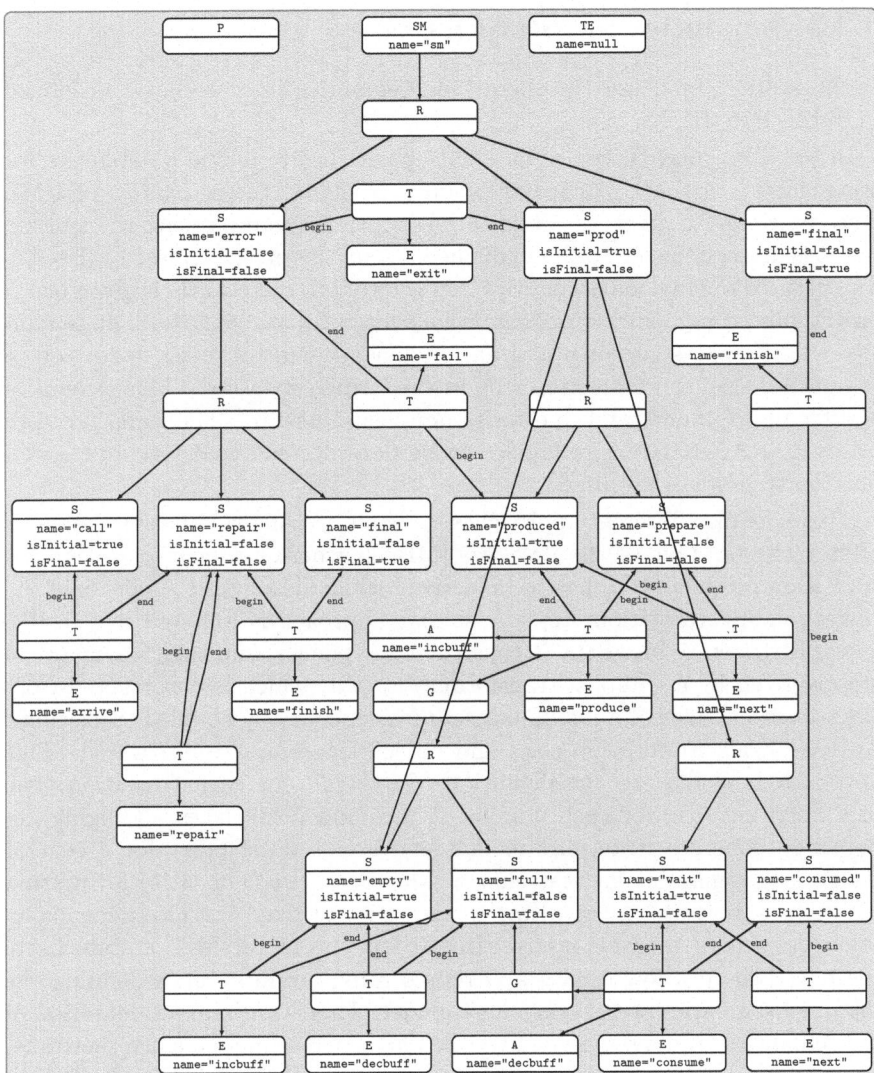

Figure 4.24: The example statechart ProdCons in abstract syntax

typed attributed graphs respecting the type graph $TG_{SC,Syn}$ and the constraints in Fig. 4.23, i.e. $VL_{SC} = \{(G, type) \mid type : G \to TG_{SC,Syn}, G \models c_1 \wedge \ldots \wedge c_7\}$.

4.2.3 Semantics for Statecharts

In this section, we define the operational semantics for statecharts as defined in Subsection 4.2.2.

In the literature, there are different approaches to define a semantics for statecharts. In the UML specification [OMG09b], the semantics of UML state machines is given as a textual description accompanying the syntax, but it is ambiguous and often explained essentially on examples. In [Bee02], a structured operational semantics (SOS) for UML statecharts is given based on the preceding definition of a textual syntax for statecharts. The semantics uses Kripke structures and an auxiliary semantics using deduction, a semantical step is a transition step in the Kripke structure. This semantics is difficult to understand due to its non-visual nature. The same problem arises in [RACH00], where labeled transitions systems and algebraic specification techniques are used.

There are also different approaches to define a visual rule-based semantics of statecharts. One of the first was [MP96], where for each transition t a transition production p_t has to be derived which describes the effects of the corresponding transition step. A similar approach is followed in [Kus01], where first a state hierarchy is constructed explicitly, and then a semantical step is given by a complex transformation unit, which is constructed from the transition rules of a maximum set of independently enabled transitions. In [KGKK02], in addition class and object diagrams are integrated. This approach is similar to the definition of one rule for each transition type of a Petri net, i.e. for each number of pre- and post-places. It highly depends on concrete statechart models and is not satisfactory for a general interpreter semantics for statecharts. Moreover, problems arise for nesting hierarchies, because the resulting situation is not fixed but also depends on other current or inactive states. In [GP98], the hierarchies of statecharts are flattened to a low-level graph representing an automaton defining the intended semantics of the statechart model. This is an indirect definition of the semantics, and again dependent on the concrete model, since the transformation rules have to be specified according to this model. In [EHHS00], the operational semantics of a fragment of UML statecharts is specified by UML collaboration diagrams formalized as graph transformation rules. But it is not clear if and how this approach can be extended for more complex statechart models.

In [Var02], a general interpreter semantics for statecharts is defined. Syntactical and static semantic concepts of statecharts like conflicts and priorities are separated from their dynamic operational semantics, which is specified by graph transformation rules. A control structure, so called model transition systems, controls the application of the rules. In this approach, a lot of additional control and helper structure is needed to encode when which transition is enabled or in conflict, and which states become current or inactive as the result of a state transition.

The main advantage of our solution explained in the following using amalgamation is that we do not need additional helper and control structure to cover the complex statechart semantics: we define a state transition mainly by one interaction scheme followed by some clean-up rules. Therefore, our model-independent definition based on rule amalgamation is not only visual and intuitive but allows us to show termination in Chapter 6 and forms a solid basis for applying further graph transformation-based analysis techniques.

The semantics of our statecharts is modeled by amalgamated transformations, but we apply the rules in a more restricted way, meaning that one step in the semantics is modeled by several applications of interaction schemes. For the application of an interaction scheme we use maximal weakly disjoint matchings. We assume to have a finite statechart with a finite event queue where all trigger elements are already given in the diagram as an initial event queue.

The rules are depicted in a more compact notation where we do not show the gluing object K. It can be infered by the intersection $L \cap R$ of the corresponding left- and right-hand sides. The mappings are given as numberings for the nodes and can be infered for the edges. As above, if the edge types are clear we do not explicitly state them.

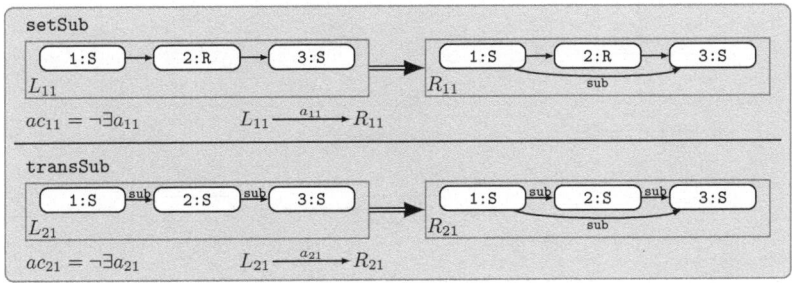

Figure 4.25: The rules setSub and transSub

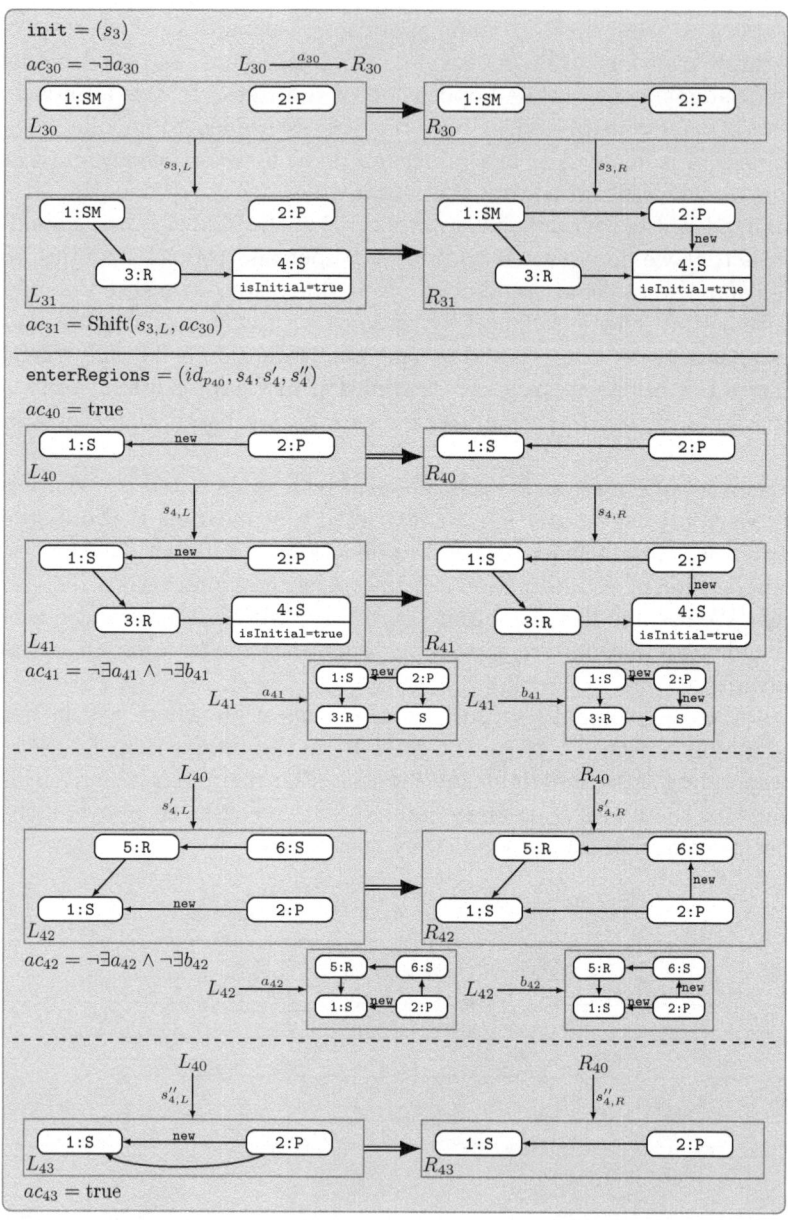

Figure 4.26: The interaction schemes init and enterRegions

For the *initialization step*, we first compute all substates of all states by applying the rules `setSub` and `transSub` given in Fig. 4.25 as long as possible. Then, the interaction scheme `init` is applied followed by the interaction scheme `enterRegions` applied as long as possible, which are depicted in Fig. 4.26. With `init`, the pointer is associated to the statemachine and all initial states of the statemachine's regions. The interaction scheme `enterRegions` handles the nesting and sets the current pointer also to the initial states contained in an active state. When applied as long as possible, this means that all substates are handled. Note that not all initial substates become active, but only these which are contained in a hierarchy of nested initial states. The interaction scheme `enterRegions` also contains the identical kernel morphism $id_{p_{40}} : p_{40} \to p_{40}$ to ensure that this kernel rule is also applied in the lowest hierarchy level changing the `new`- to a `current`-edge. For later use, also double edges are deleted and if the direct superstate is not marked by the pointer a `new`-edge is added to it.

A state transition representing a *semantical step*, i. e. switching from one state to another, is done by the application of the interaction scheme `transitionStep` shown in Fig. 4.27 followed by the interaction schemes `enterRegions!`, `leaveState1!`, `leaveState2!`, and `leaveRegions!` given in Figs. 4.26, 4.28, and 4.29 in this order, where ! means that the corresponding interaction scheme is applied as long as possible.

For such a semantical step, the first trigger element (or one of the first if more than one action of different orthogonal substates may occur next) is chosen and deleted, while the corresponding state transitions are executed. `exit`-trigger elements are handled with priority which is ensured by the application condition ac_{50}. Note that a transition triggered by its trigger element is active if the state it begins at is active, its guard condition state is active, and it has no active substate where a transition triggered by the same event is active. These restrictions are handled by the application conditions ac_{51} and ac_{52}. Moreover, if an action is provoked, this has to be added as one of the first next trigger elements. The two multi rules of `transitionStep` handle the state transition with and without action, respectively. The application condition ac_{52} is not shown explicitly, but the morphisms $a_{52}, \ldots, f_{52}$ are similar to $a_{51}, \ldots, f_{51}$ except that all objects contain in addition the node `8:A`.

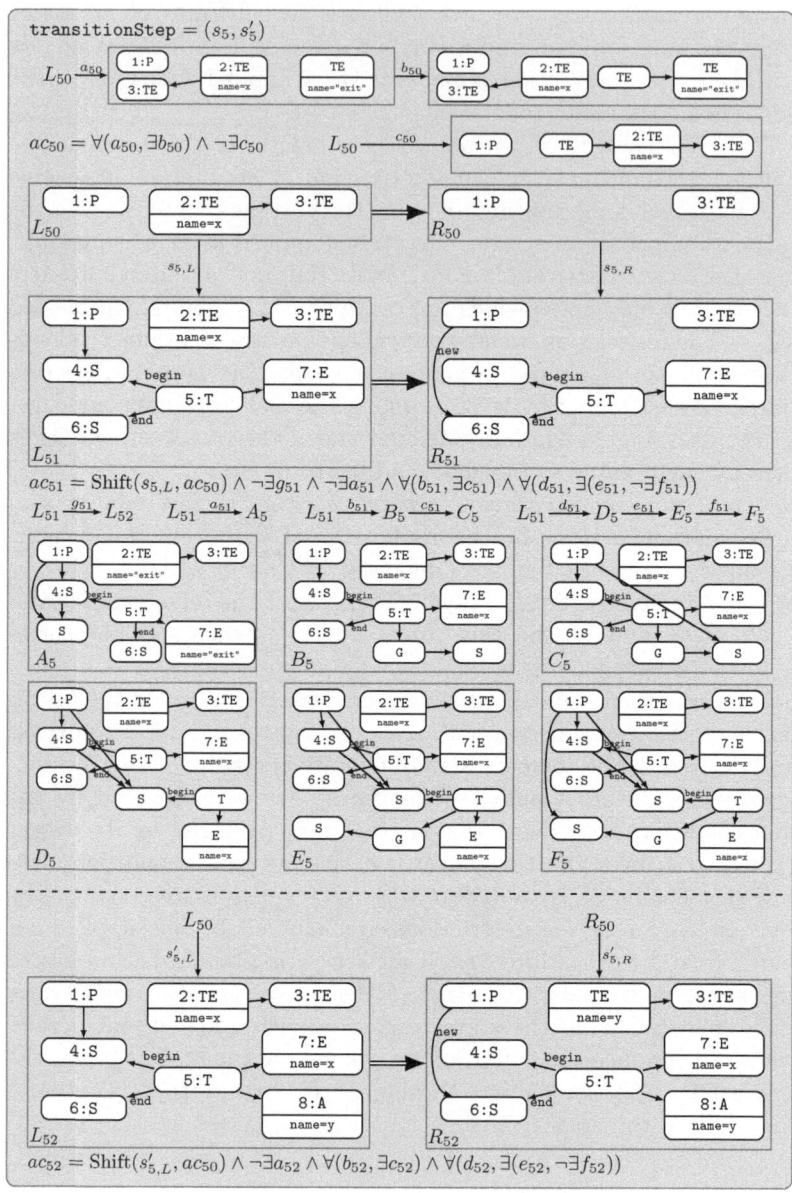

Figure 4.27: The interaction scheme transitionStep

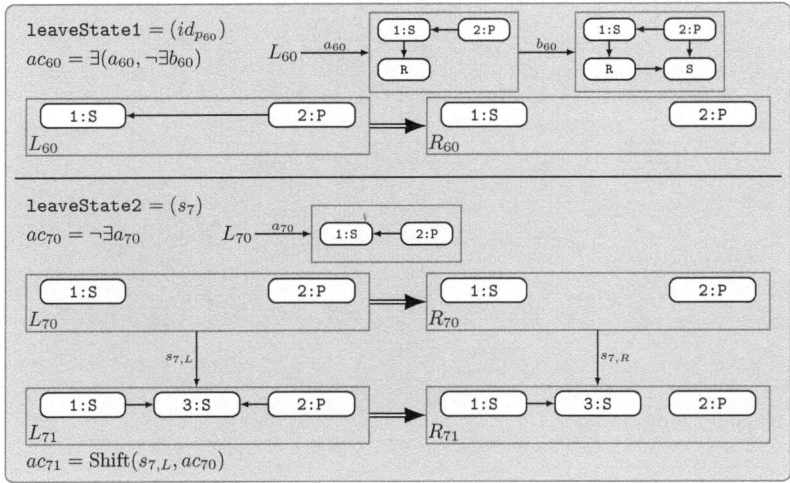

Figure 4.28: The interaction schemes `leaveState1` and `leaveState2`

The interaction schemes `leaveState1`, `leaveState2`, and `leaveRegions` handle the correct selection of the active states. When for a yet active state with regions, by state transitions all states in one of its regions are no longer active, also this superstate is no longer active, which is described by `leaveState1`. The interaction scheme `leaveState2` handles the case that, when a state become inactive by a state transition, also all its substates become inactive. If for a state with orthogonal regions the final state in each region is reached then these final states become inactive, and if the superstate has an `exit`-transition it is added as the next trigger element. This is handled by `leaveRegions`.

Combining these rules as explained above leads to the semantics of statecharts.

Definition 4.37 (Statechart semantics)
The operational semantics of statecharts consists of one initialization step followed by as many as possible semantical steps defined as follows:

- *Initialization step.* For a statechart model $M \in VL_{SC}$ (see Def. 4.36) we obtain a model $M_{initial}$ by applying the sequence `setSub!`, `transSub!`, `init`, `enterRegions!` to M.

- *Semantical step.* Consider a model M_1 with M_1 obtained by a finite number of semantical steps from a model $M_{initial}$ for some $M \in VL_{SC}$, then a semantical step from M_1 to M_2 is computed by applying the sequence

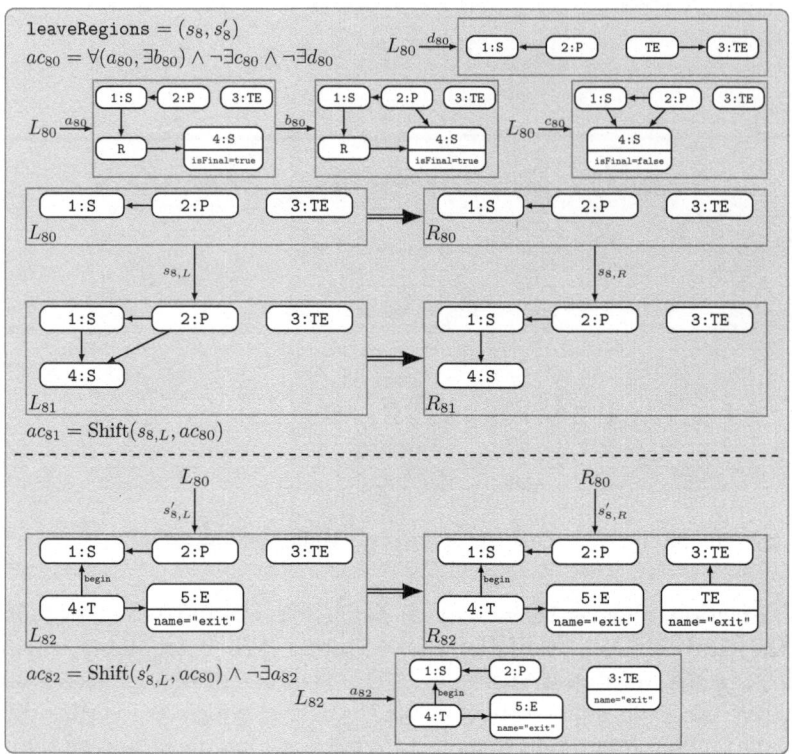

Figure 4.29: The interaction scheme `leaveRegions`

transitionStep, enterRegions!, leaveState1!, leaveState2!, leave-Regions! to M_1.

Example 4.38

Consider now some semantical steps in our statechart example from Fig. 4.21. After initialization, the initial state `prod` and its initial substates `produced`, `empty`, and `wait` are current. If the event `next` occurs, we switch from the state `produced` to the state `prepare`. The second `next`-transition does not allow a step because the state `consumed` is not active at the moment. Now the event `produce`, whose guard condition `empty` is valid, leads to the state transition from `prepare` back to `produced` triggering the action `incbuff`. This leads to the state transition from `empty` to `full`.

Now the event `consume` may occur, with valid guard condition `full`, and trigger the action `decbuff`. Afterwards, the states `prod`, `produced`, `empty`, and `consumed` are the current states. If now the event next occurs, two state transitions are executed in parallel, since both transitions of the producer and of the consumer are active. After an additional event chain produce – consume with a following decbuff-action we are back in the situation that the states prod, produced, empty, and consumed are current.

If a fail-event occurs, the prod-state is completely left, and only the states error and call become the current states. After the event chain arrive – repair – finish, the exit-action of the error-state leads back again to the initial situation.

In Fig. 4.30, the current states and their state transitions as described above are depicted, where the guard conditions enabling a transition are marked. In addition, we show the incoming event queue as needed for our system run to be processed. Note that the actions that are triggered by state transitions do not occur here because they are started internally, while the other events have to be supplied from the outside.

We want to simulate these semantical steps now using the rules for the semantics applied to the statechart in abstract syntax in Fig. 4.24, extended by the trigger element chain from Fig. 4.30.

First, the initialization has to be done. We compute all sub-edges by applying the rules setSub and transSub in Fig. 4.25 as long as possible. For the actual initialization, we apply the interaction scheme init from Fig. 4.26 followed by the application of enterRegions as long as possible. With init, we connect the state machine and the pointer node, and in addition set the pointer to the prod-state using a new-edge. Now the only available kernel match for enterRegions is the match mapping node 1 to the prod-state, and with maximal matchings we obtain the bundle of kernel morphisms $(id_{p_{40}}, s_4, s_4, s_4)$, where the node 4 in L_{41} is mapped to the states produced, empty, and wait, respectively. After the application of the corresponding amalgamated rule, the current pointer is now connected to the state machine and the state prod, and via new-edges to the states produced, empty, and wait. Further applications of enterRegions using these three states for the kernel matches, respectively, lead to the bundle $(id_{p_{40}})$ thus changing the new-edges to current-edges by its application. As a result, the states prod, produced, empty, and wait are current, which is the initial situation for the statemachine as shown in Fig. 4.30. We do not find additional matches for enterRegions, as we only have one level of nesting in our diagram, which means that the initialization is completed.

For a state transition, the interaction scheme transitionStep in Fig. 4.27 is applied, followed by the interaction schemes enterRegions!, leaveState1!, leaveState2!, and leaveRegions! given in Figs. 4.26, 4.28, and 4.29.

For the initial situation, the kernel rule p_{50} in Fig. 4.27 has to be matched such that the node 2 is mapped to the first trigger element next and the node 3 to produce, otherwise the application condition of the rule p_{50} would be violated.

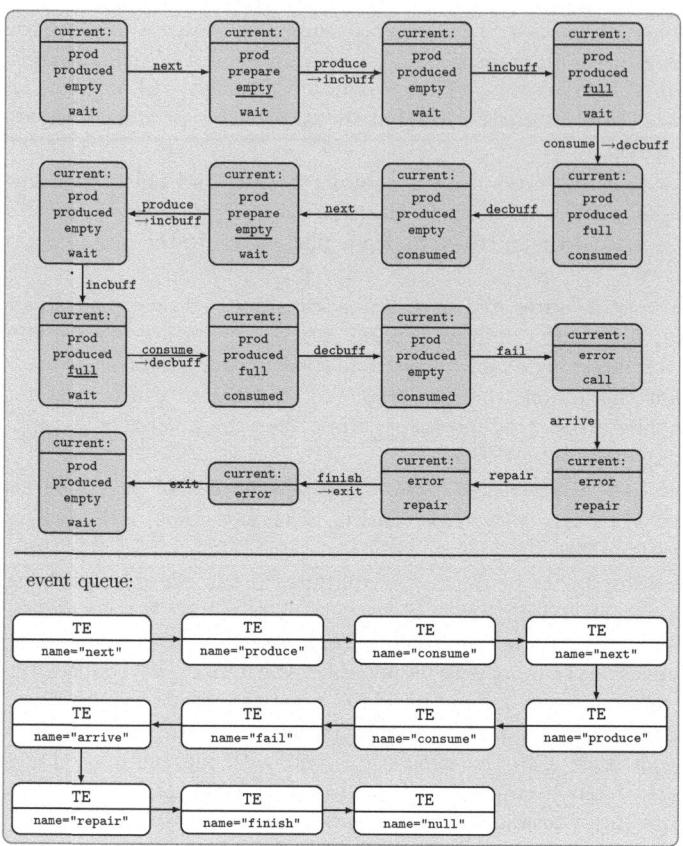

Figure 4.30: The state transitions and their corresponding event queue

For the multi rules, there are two events with the name next, but since the state consumed is not current, only one match for L_{51} is found mapping the nodes 4 to the current state produced and 6 to the state prepare. All application conditions are fulfilled, since this transition does not have a guard or action, and the state produced does not have any substates. Thus, the application of the bundle (s_5) deletes the first trigger element next, which is done by the kernel rule, and redirects the current pointer from produced to prepare via a new-edge. An application of the interaction scheme enterRegions using the bundle ($id_{p_{40}}$) changes this new-edge to a current-edge. Since we do not find further matches for L_{40}, L_{60}, L_{71}, L_{81}, and L_{82}, the other interaction schemes cannot be applied.

This means that the states prod, prepare, empty, and wait are now the current states, which is the situation after the state transition triggered by next as shown in Fig. 4.30.

For the next match of the kernel rule p_{50}, the node 2 is mapped to the new next trigger element produce and 3 is mapped to consume. Since the transition produce has an action, we cannot apply the multi rule p_{51} but p_{52} has a valid match. In particular, the application condition is fulfilled because the guard condition state empty is current and the state prepare does not have any substates. Thus, the bundle (s_5') leads to the deletion of the trigger element produce, the current pointer is redirected from prepare to produced, and a new trigger element incbuff is inserted with a next-edge to the trigger element consume. Again, enterRegions changes the new- to a current-edge and we do not find further matches for L_{40}, L_{60}, L_{71}, L_{81}, and L_{82}. This means that now the states prod, produced, empty, and wait are current.

We can process our trigger element queue step by step retracing the state transitions by the application of the rules. We do not explain all steps explicitly, but skip until after the last decbuff-trigger element, which leads to the current states prod, produced, empty, and consumed.

The next match of the kernel rule p_{50} maps the nodes 2 to the trigger element fail and 3 to arrive. The only match for the multi rules maps the nodes 4 and 6 in L_{51} to the states produced and error, respectively. Since the application condition is fulfilled, the application of the bundle (s_5) leads to the deletion of the trigger element fail, and the current pointer is redirected from produced to error. Now we find a match for the interaction scheme enterRegions mapping the node 1 to the state error and 4 to the state call. Thus the application of the bundle $(id_{p_{40}}, s_4)$ adds a new pointer to the state call, which is then changed from new to current. Afterwards, we find a match for leaveState1, where the kernel rule match maps the node 1 to the state prod. The application condition is fulfilled because there is a region - the one for the producer - where no state is current. Thus, the current-edge to prod is deleted. No more matches for L_{60} can be found, but there are two different matches for the multi rule p_{71} of leaveState2 matching the node 3 to the states empty and wait, respectively. The application of the bundle (s_7, s_7) then leads to the deletion of the current pointer for the states empty and wait. No more matches for L_{71}, L_{81}, and L_{82} can be found. Altogether, the states error and call are current now. This is exactly the situation as described in Fig. 4.30 after the state transition triggered by the fail-event.

Now we skip again two more trigger elements leading to the remaining trigger element queue finish $\rightarrow$ null and the current states error and repair. The kernel rule p_{50} is now matched to these two trigger elements, and the application of the bundle (s_5) deletes the trigger element finish and redirects the current pointer from repair to final, the final state within the error-state. With enterRegions, the corresponding new-edge is set to current. No matches for L_{60} and L_{71} can be found, but we find a match for the interaction scheme leaveRegions, where the kernel rule is matched such that the node 1 is mapped to the state error and 3 is mapped to the null-trigger element. The application condition is fulfilled because all current substates of error are final states - actually, there is only the one - and null is the first trigger element in the queue. Now there is a match for L_{81} mapping the node 4 to the state final and a match for L_{82} mapping the nodes 4 and 5 to the transition and the event between the stated error and prod. After the application of the bundle (s_8, s_8'), the current pointer is deleted from the final-state, and a new exit-trigger element is inserted before the null-trigger element. No more matches for L_{81} and L_{82} can be found, thus only the state error is current.

A last application of the interaction scheme transitionStep followed by enter-Regions leads back to the initial situation and completes our example, since the event queue is empty except for the default element null.

5 Model Transformation Based on Triple Graph Transformation

Triple graphs and triple graph grammars are a successful approach to describe model transformations. They relate the source and target models by some connection parts thereby integrating both models into one graph. This uniform description of both models allows to obtain a unified theory for forward and backward transformations.

As shown already for the specification of visual models by typed attributed graph transformation, the expressiveness of the approach can be enhanced significantly by using application conditions, which are known to be equivalent to first order logic on graphs. In this chapter, we introduce triple graphs and triple transformations with application conditions and show that the composition and decomposition property valid for the case without application conditions can be extended to transformations with application conditions. Mainly, we can reuse the proofs but have to show the properties for the application conditions in addition.

In Section 5.1, we define the category of triple graphs and show how triple rules without application conditions lead to forward and backward model transformations. This theory is extended in Section 5.2 to triple rules and triple transformations with application conditions, where we define S- and T-consistent application conditions and show the composition and decomposition result. All our results are illustrated by a small example model transformation. In Section 5.3, a more elaborated case study, a model transformation from statecharts to Petri nets, is shown to apply the theory in a larger setting.

5.1 Introduction to Triple Graph Transformation

In this section, we first introduce triple graphs as done in [EEE+07], show how to define triple transformations, and obtain the derived rules that lead to the actual model transformations. Note that the theory introduced in this section is without application conditions, which are introduced later in Section 5.2.

5.1.1 The Category of Triple Graphs

A triple graph consists of three components - source, connection, and target - together with two morphisms connecting the connection to the source and and target components. A triple graph morphism matches the single components and preserves the connection part.

Definition 5.1 (Triple graph)
A *triple graph* $G = (G_S \xleftarrow{s_G} G_C \xrightarrow{t_G} G_T)$ consists of three graphs G_S, G_C, and G_T, called source, connection, and target component, respectively, and two graph morphisms s_G and t_G mapping the connection to the source and target components.

Given triple graphs $G_i = (G_{i,S} \xleftarrow{s_{G_i}} G_{i,C} \xrightarrow{t_{G_i}} G_{i,T})$ for $i = 1, 2$, a *triple graph morphism* $f = (f_S, f_C, f_T) : G_1 \rightarrow G_2$ consists of graph morphisms $f_S : G_{1,S} \rightarrow G_{2,S}$, $f_C : G_{1,C} \rightarrow G_{2,C}$, and $f_T : G_{1,T} \rightarrow G_{2,T}$ between the three components such that $s_{G_2} \circ f_C = f_S \circ s_{G_1}$ and $t_{G_2} \circ f_C = f_T \circ t_{G_1}$.

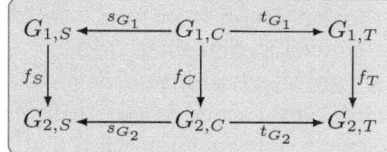

The typing of triple graphs is done in the same way as for standard graphs via a type graph - in this case a triple type graph - and typing morphisms into this type graph.

Definition 5.2 (Typed triple graph)
Given a triple type graph $TG = (TG_S \xleftarrow{s_{TG}} TG_C \xrightarrow{t_{TG}} TG_T)$, a *typed triple graph* $(G, type_G)$ is given by a triple graph G and a typing morphism $type_G : G \rightarrow TG$.

For typed triple graphs $(G_1, type_{G_1})$ and $(G_2, type_{G_2})$, a *typed triple graph morphism* $f : (G_1, type_{G_1}) \rightarrow (G_2, type_{G_2})$ is a triple graph morphism f such that $type_{G_2} \circ f = type_{G_1}$.

As for standard graphs, if the typing is clear we do not explicitly mention it.

Triple graphs and triple type graphs, together with the component-wise compositions and identities, form categories.

Definition 5.3 (Categories of triple and typed triple graphs)
Triple graphs and triple graph morphisms form the category **TripleGraphs**.

Typed triple graphs and typed triple graph morphisms over a triple type graph TG form the category **TripleGraphs$_{\mathbf{TG}}$**.

Moreover, the categories of triple graphs and typed triple graphs can be extended to $\mathcal{M}$-adhesive categories which allows us to instantiate the theory of transformations introduced in Section 3.1 also to transformations of triple graphs in the next section.

Theorem 5.4 (TripleGraphs as $\mathcal{M}$-adhesive categories)
The categories **TripleGraphs** and **TripleGraphs$_{TG}$** with the class $\mathcal{M}$ of monomorphisms, i.e. injective (typed) triple graph morphisms, are $\mathcal{M}$-adhesive categories.

PROOF See [EEE+07].

Moreover, all the additional properties stated in Def. 3.8 hold in the categories **Triple-Graphs** and **TripleGraphs$_{TG}$**.

5.1.2 Triple Graph Transformation

In this subsection, we introduce triple rules without application conditions [EEE+07]. They have been extended in [EHS09] to triple rules with negative application conditions. In the next section, we combine triple rules with general application conditions, but here we first restrict them to rules without application conditions for an overview. We consider both triple graphs and typed triple graphs, even if we do not explicitly mention the typing.

In general, triple rules and triple transformations are an instantiation of $\mathcal{M}$-adhesive systems. But for the special case of model transformations we only use triple rules that are non-deleting, therefore we can omit the first part of a rule, the rule morphism l which is in the non-deleting case always the identity (or an isomorphism).

Definition 5.5 (Triple rule without application conditions)
A *triple rule* $\overline{tr} = (tr : L \to R)$ without application conditions consists of triple graphs L and R, and an $\mathcal{M}$-morphism $tr : L \to R$.

A *direct triple transformation* $G \xRightarrow{\overline{tr},m} H$ of a triple graph G via a triple rule $\overline{tr}$ without

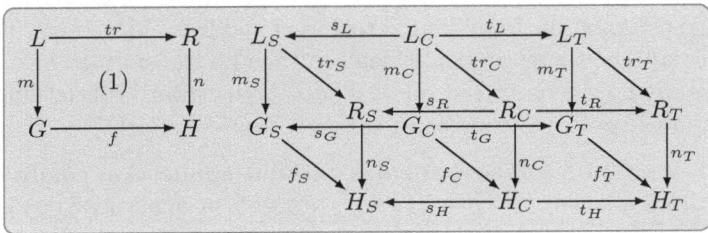

application conditions and a match $m : L \rightarrow G$ is given by the pushout (1), which is constructed as the component-wise pushouts in the S-, C-, and T-components, where the morphisms s_H and t_H are induced by the pushout of the connection component.

A triple graph transformation system is based on triple graphs and rules over them. A triple graph grammar contains in addition a start graph.

Definition 5.6 (Triple graph transformation system and grammar)
A *triple graph transformation system* $TGS = (TR)$ consists of a set of triple rules TR.

A *triple graph grammar* $TGG = (TR, S)$ consists of a set of triple rules TR and a start triple graph S.

For triple graph grammars, not only the generated language, but also the source and target languages are of interest. The source language contains all standard graphs that originate from the source component of a derived triple graph. Similarly, the target language contains all derivable target components.

Definition 5.7 (Triple, source, and target language)
The *triple language* VL of a triple graph grammar $TGG = (TR, S)$ is defined by
$$VL = \{G \mid \exists \text{ triple transformation } S \stackrel{*}{\Rightarrow} G \text{ via rules in } TR\}.$$
The *source language* VL_S is defined by $VL_S = \{G_S \mid (G_S \stackrel{s_G}{\leftarrow} G_C \stackrel{t_G}{\rightarrow} G_T) \in VL\}$.
The *target language* VL_T is defined by $VL_T = \{G_T \mid (G_S \stackrel{s_G}{\leftarrow} G_C \stackrel{t_G}{\rightarrow} G_T) \in VL\}$.

From a triple rule without application conditions, we can derive source and target rules which specify the changes done by this rule in the source and target components, respectively. Moreover, the forward resp. backward rules describe the changes done by the rule to the connection and target resp. source parts, assuming that the source resp. target rules have been applied already. Intuitively, the source rule creates a source model, which can then be transformed by the forward rules into the corresponding target model. This means that the forward rules define the actual model transformation from source to target models. Vice versa, the target rules create the target model, which can then be transformed into a source model applying the backward rules. Thus, the backward rules define the backward model transformation from target to source models.

Definition 5.8 (Derived rules without application conditions)
Given a triple rule $\overline{tr} = (tr : L \rightarrow R)$ without application conditions we obtain the following *derived rules* without application conditions:

- the *source rule* $\overline{tr}_S =$

$$
\begin{array}{ccccccc}
L_S & \xleftarrow{\varnothing} & \varnothing & \xrightarrow{\varnothing} & \varnothing \\
\downarrow{\scriptstyle tr_S} & & \downarrow{\scriptstyle \varnothing} & & \downarrow{\scriptstyle \varnothing} \\
R_S & \xleftarrow{\varnothing} & \varnothing & \xrightarrow{\varnothing} & \varnothing
\end{array}
$$

- the *target rule* $\overline{tr}_T =$

$$
\begin{array}{ccccccc}
\varnothing & \xleftarrow{\varnothing} & \varnothing & \xrightarrow{\varnothing} & L_T \\
\downarrow{\scriptstyle \varnothing} & & \downarrow{\scriptstyle \varnothing} & & \downarrow{\scriptstyle tr_T} \\
\varnothing & \xleftarrow{\varnothing} & \varnothing & \xrightarrow{\varnothing} & R_T
\end{array}
$$

- the *forward rule* $\overline{tr}_F =$

$$
\begin{array}{ccccccc}
R_S & \xleftarrow{tr_S \circ s_L} & L_C & \xrightarrow{t_L} & L_T \\
\downarrow{\scriptstyle id_{R_S}} & & \downarrow{\scriptstyle tr_C} & & \downarrow{\scriptstyle tr_T} \\
R_S & \xleftarrow{s_R} & R_C & \xrightarrow{t_R} & R_T
\end{array}
$$

- the *backward rule* $\overline{tr}_B =$

$$
\begin{array}{ccccccc}
L_S & \xleftarrow{s_L} & L_C & \xrightarrow{tr_T \circ t_L} & R_T \\
\downarrow{\scriptstyle tr_S} & & \downarrow{\scriptstyle tr_C} & & \downarrow{\scriptstyle id_{R_T}} \\
R_S & \xleftarrow{s_R} & R_C & \xrightarrow{t_R} & R_T
\end{array}
$$

The triple rule $\overline{tr}$ without application conditions can be shown to be the E-concurrent rule of both the source and forward as well as the target and backward rules, where the E-dependency relation is given by the domain of the forward and backward rules, respectively.

Fact 5.9
Given a triple rule $\overline{tr} = (tr : L \to R)$, then we have that $\overline{tr} = \overline{tr}_S *_{E_1} \overline{tr}_F = \overline{tr}_T *_{E_2} \overline{tr}_B$ with E_1 and E_2 being the domain of $\overline{tr}_F$ and $\overline{tr}_B$, respectively.

PROOF See [EEE$^+$07].

5.2 Triple Graph Transformation with Application Conditions

As introduced in Section 3.4, rules with application conditions are more expressive and allow to restrict the application of the rules. Thus, we enhance triple rules without to triple rules with application conditions. Since the categories of triple and typed triple graphs are $\mathcal{M}$-adhesive categories holding the additional properties from Def. 3.8, we can instantiate the main theory introduced in Section 3.4 to triple transformations with application conditions.

5.2.1 S- and T-Consistent Application Conditions

To introduce application conditions we combine a triple rule $\overline{tr}$ without application conditions with an application condition ac over L leading to a triple rule. Then a triple transformation is applicable if the match m satisfies the application condition ac.

Definition 5.10 (Triple rule and transformation)
A *triple rule* $tr = (tr : L \to R, ac)$ consists of triple graphs L and R, an $\mathcal{M}$-morphism $tr : L \to R$, and an application condition ac over L.

A *direct triple transformation* $G \xrightarrow{tr,m} H$ of a triple graph G via a triple rule tr and a match $m : L \to G$ with $m \models ac$ is given by the direct triple transformation $G \xrightarrow{\overline{tr},m} H$ via the corresponding triple rule $\overline{tr}$ without application conditions.

Example 5.11
We illustrate our definitions and results with a small example showing the simultaneous development of a graph and a Petri net representing clients and communication channels. The main motivation of this example is to illustrate the theory – for a more complex and realistic example see the case study from statecharts to Petri nets in Section 5.3.

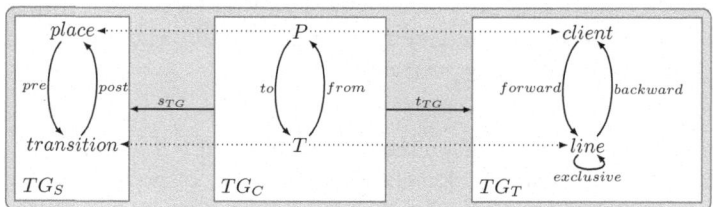

Figure 5.1: The triple type graph TG for the communication example

Our example uses typed triple graphs. The triple type graph TG is given in Fig. 5.1. The source component describes Petri nets (see Subsection 4.2.1), while the target component describes models containing clients which can be connected by lines. A line may be marked as exclusive by the corresponding loop. The connection component has two nodes P and T connecting places and clients resp. transitions and lines. The connection morphisms s_{TG} and t_{TG} are not explicitly shown, but can be easily deduced for the edges from the node mappings. For a useful model description, especially the target model should be restricted to valid models by suitable constraints, for example that exclusive edges always have to be loops, or that lines connect exactly two clients. Here we do not explicitly model these constraints but always assume to have reasonable models.

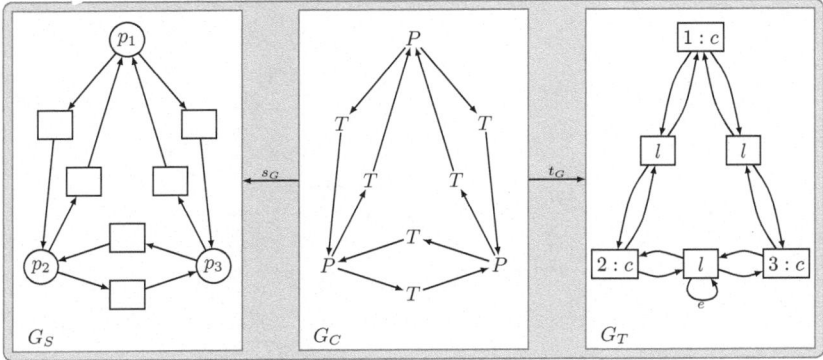

Figure 5.2: The triple graph G for the communication example

In Fig. 5.2, a corresponding triple graph G is shown. Note that we show the Petri net source model in concrete syntax for easier understanding. In the Petri net component, each client is represented by a place, and each line by two transitions connecting the corresponding places in both direction. Note that the Petri net does not differ between normal and exclusive lines. In the target model, the clients and lines are represented by boxes abbreviating the types by c and l, respectively. For each line between two nodes, forward and backward edges demonstrate that a line is bidirectional, and we also need them for the mapping from the connection component. The loop e marks the exclusive line between clients 2 and 3. The connection morphisms s_G and t_G are not explicitly shown, but can be deduced from the positions of the nodes and edges. Note that two T-nodes of the connection part are mapped to the same line in the target component.

In Figs. 5.3 and 5.4, the triple rules for creating these triple graphs are given. With the triple rule newClient, a new client and its corresponding place in the Petri net as well as their connection are created. The triple rule newConnection creates a new line between two clients as well as their corresponding connection nodes and transitions if there is no connection neither in the Petri net nor in the corresponding target model. While in the Petri net always just one communication connection is allowed, there may be multiple lines between the clients in the target model. These are created by the triple rule extendConnection if no already existing line is marked exclusive. With the triple rule newExclusive, such an exclusive line with the corresponding connections and transitions is created if there is no connection present in the Petri net part, no line between the clients, and if there is no intermediate client between these two clients that is already connected to both via exclusive lines.

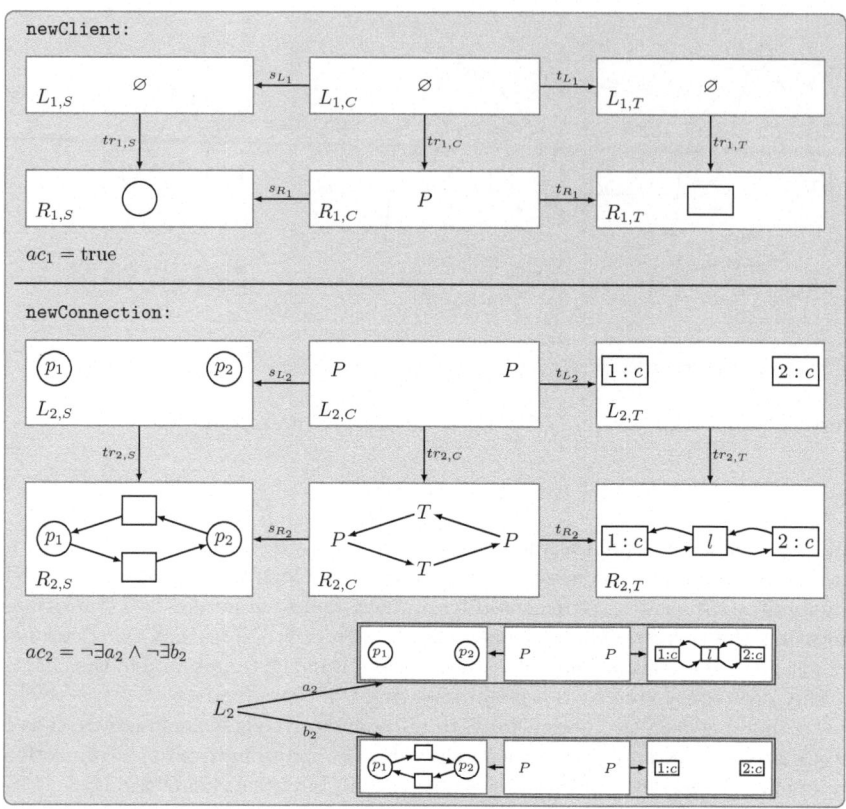

Figure 5.3: The triple rules newClient and newConnection for the communication example

We can apply the rule sequence newClient, newClient, newClient, newConnection, newConnection, newExclusive with suitable matches to obtain the triple graph G from the empty start graph. In G, neither newConnection nor newExclusive can be applied any more due to the application conditions. But we can extend G to a triple graph G' by applying the triple rule extendConnection. The direct triple transformation $G \xrightarrow{\text{extendConnection},m'} G'$ is depicted in Fig. 5.5. Note that the match m' maps the places p_1 and p_2 of the source part of the left-hand side $L_{3,S}$ to p_1 and p_2 of G, and respectively for the connection and target components. m' satisfies the application condition because the line between clients 1 and 2 is not marked as exclusive.

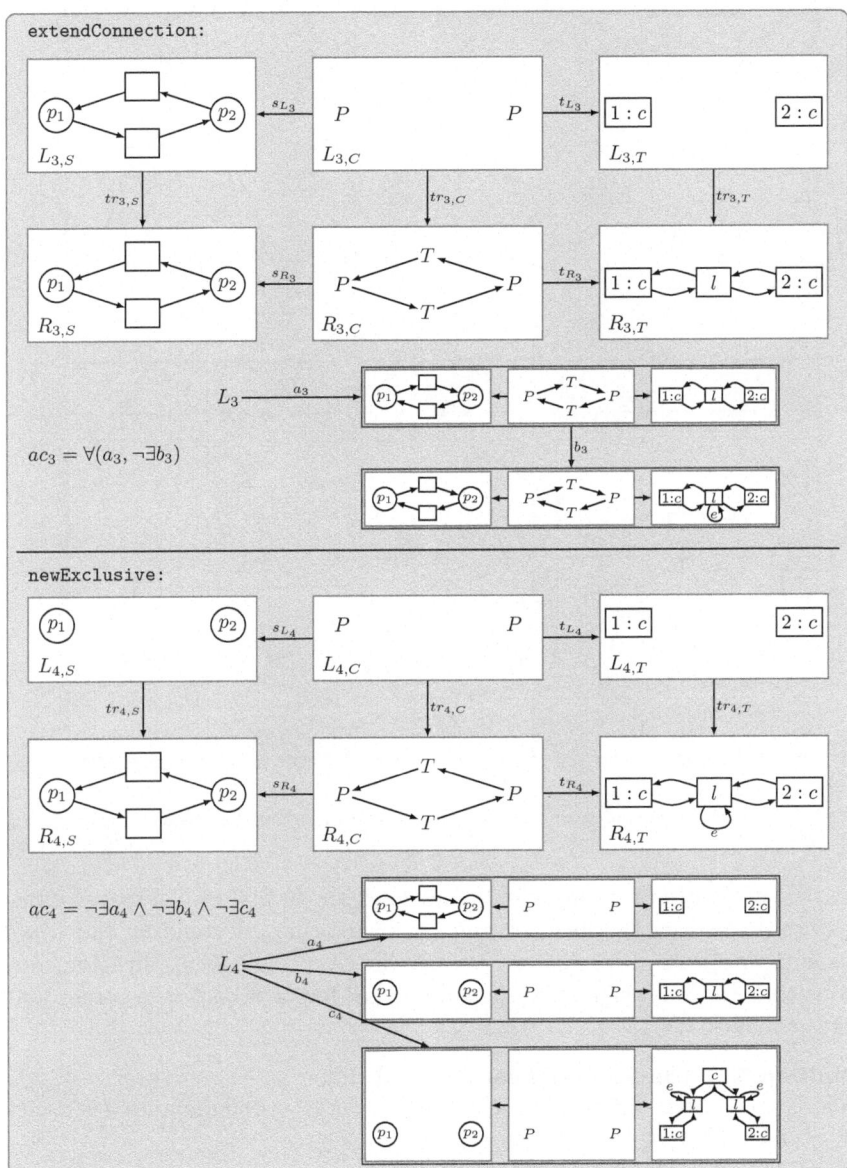

Figure 5.4: The triple rules **extendConnection** and **newExclusive** for the communication example

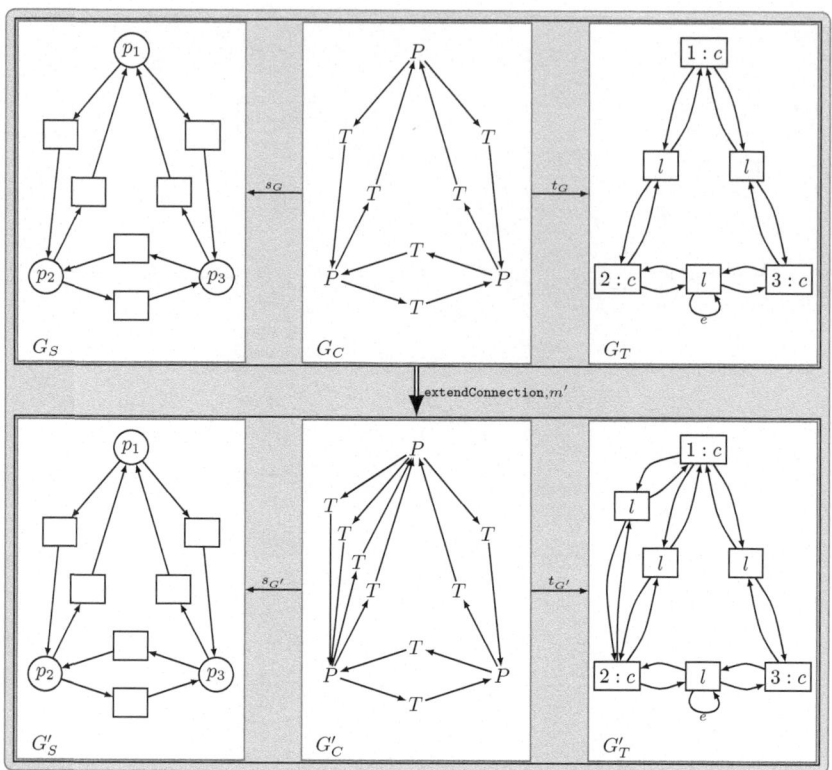

Figure 5.5: A triple transformation for the communication example

In the case without application conditions, the actual model transformations are defined by the forward and backward rules. Extending the triple rules with application conditions, we need more specialized application conditions that can be assigned to the source and forward resp. the target and backward rules.

Definition 5.12 (Special application conditions)

Given a triple rule $tr = (tr : L \to R, ac)$, the application condition $ac = \exists(a, ac')$ over L with $a : L \to P$ is an

- *S-application condition* if a_C, a_T are identities, i.e. $P_C = L_C$, $P_T = L_T$, and ac' is an *S*-application condition over P,

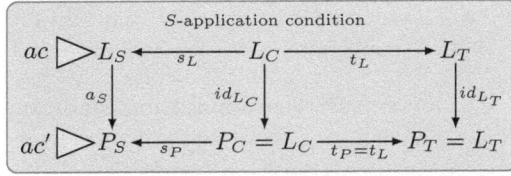

- *S-extending application condition* if a_S is an identity, i.e. $P_S = L_S$, and ac' is an *S*-extending application condition over P,

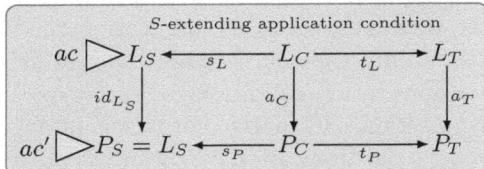

- *T-application condition* if a_S, a_C are identities, i.e. $P_S = L_S$, $P_C = L_C$, and ac' is a *T*-application condition over P,

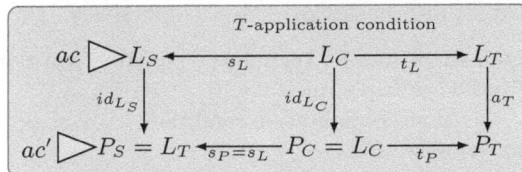

- *T-extending application condition* if a_T is an identity, i.e. $P_T = L_T$, and ac' is a *T*-extending application condition over P.

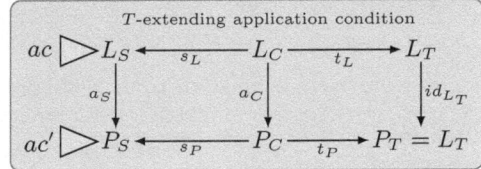

Moreover, true is an *S*-, *S*-extending, *T*-, and *T*-extending application condition, and if ac, ac_i are *S*-, *S*-extending, *T*-, *T*-extending application conditions so are $\neg ac$, $\wedge_{i \in \mathcal{I}} ac_i$, and $\vee_{i \in \mathcal{I}} ac_i$.

Remark 5.13
Note that any *T*-application condition is also an *S*-extending application condition, and vice versa an *S*-application condition is also a *T*-extending application condition.

For the assignment of the application condition ac to the derived rules, the application condition has to be consistent to the source/forward resp. target/backward rules, which means that we must be able to decompose ac into *S*- and *S*-extending resp. *T*- and *T*-extending application conditions.

Definition 5.14 (*S*- and *T*-consistent application condition)
Given a triple rule $tr = (tr : L \rightarrow R, ac)$, then ac is

- *S-consistent* if it can be decomposed into $ac \cong ac'_S \wedge ac'_F$ such that ac'_S is an *S*-application condition and ac'_F is an *S*-extending application condition,

- *T-consistent* if it can be decomposed into $ac \cong ac'_T \wedge ac'_B$ such that ac'_T is a T-application condition and ac'_B is a T-extending application condition.

For an S-consistent application condition, we obtain the application conditions of the source and forward rules from the S- and S-extending parts of the application condition, respectively. Given $ac \cong ac'_S \wedge ac'_F$ S-consistent we translate ac'_S to an application condition $toS(ac'_S)$ on $(L_S \leftarrow \varnothing \rightarrow \varnothing)$ using only the source morphisms of ac'_S. Similarly, ac'_F is translated to an application condition $toF(ac'_F)$ on $(R_S \leftarrow L_C \rightarrow L_T)$ using only the connection and target morphisms of ac'_F. Vice versa, this is done for a T-consistent application condition using the T- and T-extending parts for the target and backward rules, respectively.

Definition 5.15 (Translated application condition)
Consider a triple rule $tr = (tr : L \rightarrow R, ac)$.

Given an S-application condition ac'_S over L, we define an application condition $toS(ac'_S)$ over $(L_S \leftarrow \varnothing \rightarrow \varnothing)$ by

- $toS(\text{true}) = \text{true}$,
- $toS(\exists(a, ac''_S)) = \exists((a_S, id_\varnothing, id_\varnothing), toS(ac''_S))$, and
- recursively defined for composed application conditions.

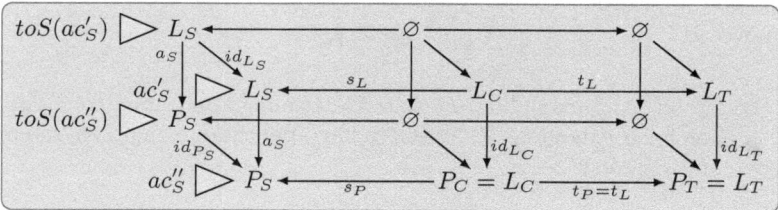

Given an S-extending application condition ac'_F over L, we define an application condition $toF(ac'_F)$ over $(R_S \xleftarrow{tr_S \circ s_L} L_C \xrightarrow{t_L} L_T)$ by

- $toF(\text{true}) = \text{true}$,
- $toF(\exists(a, ac''_F)) = \exists((id_{R_S}, a_C, a_T), toF(ac''_F))$, and
- recursively defined for composed application conditions.

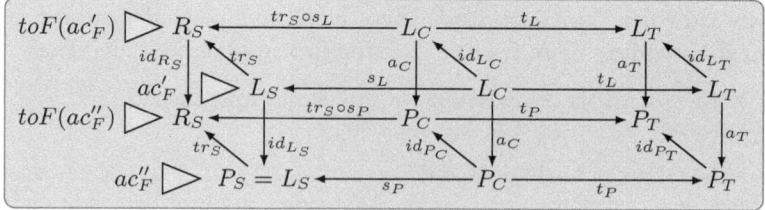

Given a T-application condition ac'_T over L, we define an application condition $toT(ac'_T)$ over $(\varnothing \leftarrow \varnothing \rightarrow L_T)$ by

- $toT(\text{true}) = \text{true}$,
- $toT(\exists(a, ac''_T)) = \exists((id_\varnothing, id_\varnothing, a_T), toT(ac''_T))$, and
- recursively defined for composed application conditions.

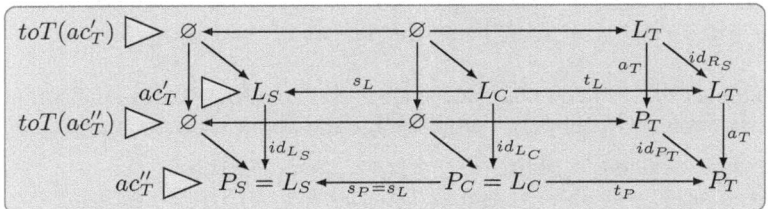

Given a T-extending application condition ac'_B over L, we define an application condition $toB(ac'_B)$ over $(L_S \xleftarrow{s_L} L_C \xrightarrow{tr_T \circ t_L} L_T)$ by

- $toB(\text{true}) = \text{true}$,
- $toB(\exists(a, ac''_B)) = \exists((a_S, a_C, id_{R_T}), toB(ac''_B))$, and
- recursively defined for composed application conditions.

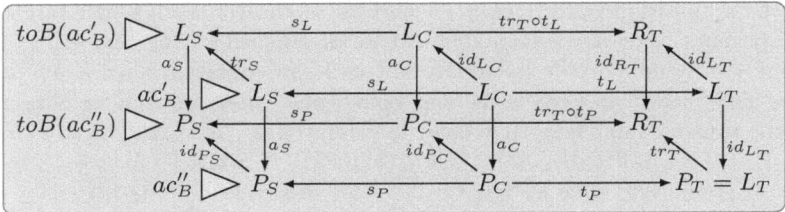

We combine these translated application conditions with the derived rules without application conditions leading to the derived rules of a triple rule with application conditions.

Definition 5.16 (Derived rules with application conditions)
Given a triple rule $tr = (tr : L \rightarrow R, ac)$ with S-consistent $ac \cong ac'_S \wedge ac'_F$ then we obtain the *source rule* $tr_S = (\overline{tr}_S, ac_S)$ with $ac_S = toS(ac'_S)$ and the *forward rule* $tr_F = (\overline{tr}_F, ac_F)$ with $ac_F = toF(ac'_F)$.

Given a triple rule $tr = (tr : L \rightarrow R, ac)$ with T-consistent $ac \cong ac'_T \wedge ac'_B$ then we obtain the *target rule* $tr_T = (\overline{tr}_T, ac_T)$ with $ac_T = toT(ac'_T)$ and the *backward rule* $tr_B = (\overline{tr}_B, ac_B)$ with $ac_B = toB(ac'_B)$.

With this notion of S- and T-consistency we can extend the result from Fact 5.9 to triple rules with application conditions. This means that in case of S-consistency each triple rule is the E-concurrent rule of its source and forward rules, and in case of T-consistency the E-concurrent rule of its target and backward rules.

Fact 5.17
Given a triple rule $tr = (tr : L \to R, ac)$ with S-consistent ac, then $tr = tr_S *_{E_1} tr_F$ with E_1 being the domain of the forward rule. Dually, if ac is T-consistent we have that $tr = tr_T *_{E_2} tr_B$ with E_2 being the domain of the backward rule.

PROOF From Fact 5.9 we know that this holds for triple rules without application conditions. It remains to show the property for the application conditions, i.e. we have to show that $ac \cong \mathrm{Shift}((id_{L_S}, \varnothing_{L_C}, \varnothing_{L_T}), ac_S) \wedge \mathrm{L}((L \overset{(tr_S, id_{L_C}, id_{L_T})}{\Rightarrow} E_1), \mathrm{Shift}(id_{E_1}, ac_F))$. We show this in two steps:

1. $\mathrm{Shift}((id_{L_S}, \varnothing_{L_C}, \varnothing_{L_T}), ac_S) \cong ac'_S$. With $ac_S = toS(ac'_S)$ this is obviously true for $ac'_S = $ true. Consider $ac'_S = \exists(a, ac''_S)$ and suppose $\mathrm{Shift}((id_{P_S}, \varnothing_{L_S}, \varnothing_{L_C}), toS(ac''_S)) \cong ac''_S$. Then we have that $(P_S \overset{s_P}{\leftarrow} P_C = L_C \overset{t_P = t_L}{\to} P_T = L_T)$ is the only square that we have to consider in the Shift-construction: for the connection and target components, (C) and (T) are the only jointly epimorphic extensions we have to consider because all morphisms in the application conditions are identities in the connection and target components. For any square (1) with a monomorphism b_S and (b_S, c_S) being jointly epimorphic it follows that b_S is an epimorphism, i.e. $P_S \cong Q_S$. This means that (S) is the only epimorphic extension that we obtain in the source component. It follows that $\mathrm{Shift}((id_{L_S}, \varnothing_{L_C}, \varnothing_{L_T}), toS(\exists(a, ac''_S))) \cong \exists(a, \mathrm{Shift}((id_{P_S}, \varnothing_{L_S}, \varnothing_{L_T}), toS(ac''_S)) \cong \exists(a, ac''_S) = ac'_S$. This can be recursively done leading to the result that indeed $\mathrm{Shift}((id_{L_S}, \varnothing_{L_C}, \varnothing_{L_T}), ac_S) \cong ac'_S$.

2. $\mathrm{L}((L \overset{(tr_S, id_{L_C}, id_{L_T})}{\Rightarrow} E_1), \mathrm{Shift}(id_{E_1}, ac_F)) \cong ac'_F$. With $ac_F = toF(ac'_F)$ this is obvious for $ac'_F = $ true. Consider $ac'_F = \exists(a, ac''_F)$ with $\mathrm{L}((L_S \leftarrow P_C \to P_T) \to (R_S \leftarrow P_C \to P_T), \mathrm{Shift}(id, toF(ac''_F))) \cong ac'_F$. Then $(P_S = L_S \overset{s_P}{\leftarrow} P_C \overset{t_P}{\to} P_T)$ is the pushout complement constructed for the left-shift-construction and we have that $\mathrm{L}((L \overset{(tr_S, id_{L_C}, id_{L_T})}{\Rightarrow} E_1), \mathrm{Shift}(id_{E_1}, toF(\exists(a, ac''_F)))) \cong \mathrm{L}((L \overset{(tr_S, id_{L_C}, id_{L_T})}{\Rightarrow} E_1), \exists((id_{R_S}, a_C, a_T), toF(ac''_F))) \cong \exists((id_{L_S}, a_C, a_T), \mathrm{L}(((L_S \leftarrow P_C \to P_T) \to (R_S \leftarrow P_C \to P_T)), toF(ac''_F)) \cong \exists(a, ac'_F)$

$= ac'_F$. This can be recursively done leading to the result that indeed $\mathrm{L}((L \overset{(tr_S, id_{L_C}, id_{L_T})}{\Rightarrow} E_1), \mathrm{Shift}(id_{E_1}, ac_F)) \cong ac'_F$.

It follows that $ac \cong ac'_S \wedge ac'_F \cong \mathrm{Shift}((id_{L_S}, \varnothing_{L_C}, \varnothing_{l_T}), ac_S) \wedge \mathrm{L}((L \overset{(tr_S, id_{L_C}, id_{L_T})}{\Rightarrow} E_1), \mathrm{Shift}(id_{E_1}, ac_F))$.

Dually, we can obtain the same result for a T-consistent application condition $ac \cong ac'_T \wedge ac'_B \cong \mathrm{Shift}((\varnothing_{L_S}, \varnothing_{L_C}, id_{L_T}), ac_T) \wedge \mathrm{L}((L \overset{(id_{L_S}, id_{L_C}, tr_T)}{\rightarrow} E_2), \mathrm{Shift}(id_{E_2}, ac_B))$.

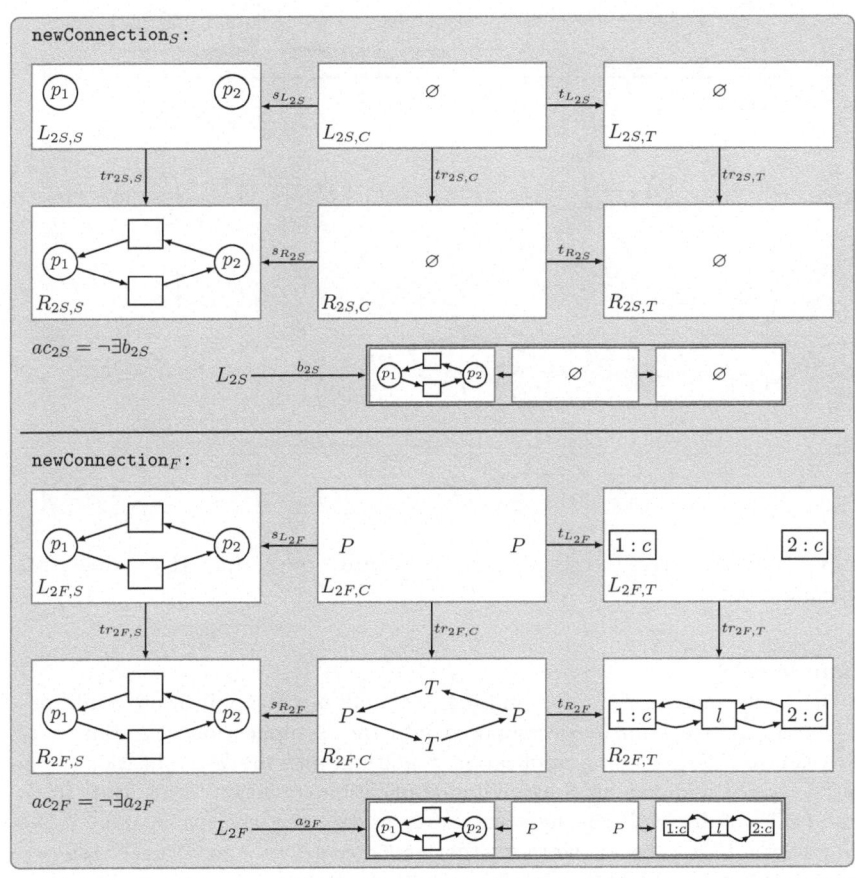

Figure 5.6: The derived source and forward rules for the triple rule newConnection

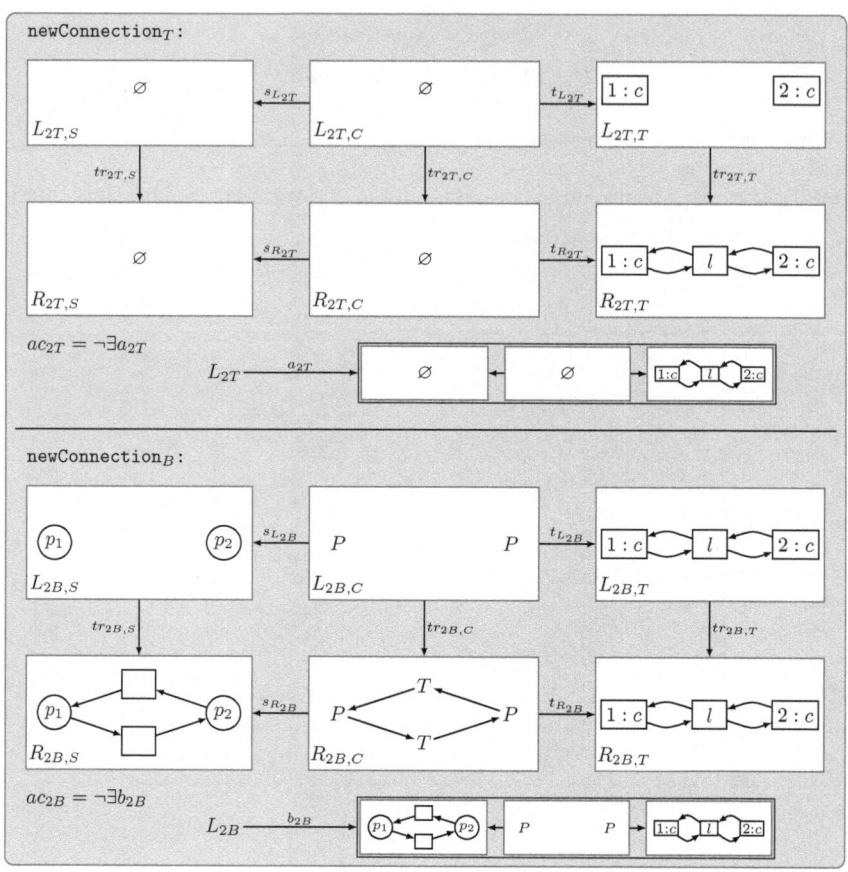

Figure 5.7: The derived target and backward rules for the triple rule
newConnection

Example 5.18

For the triple rules in Figs. 5.3 and 5.4, we analyze the application conditions.
$ac_2 = \neg\exists a_2 \wedge \neg\exists b_2$ can be decomposed into the S-application condition $\neg\exists b_2$,
which is also a T-extending application condition, and the T-application condi-
tion $\neg\exists a_2$, which is also an S-extending application condition. This leads to the
derived rules of the triple rule newConnection as depicted in Figs. 5.6 and 5.7. Applying Fact 5.17 we obtain the result that newConnection = newConnection$_S *_{E_1}$
newConnection$_F$ and newConnection = newConnection$_T *_{E_2}$ newConnection$_B$.

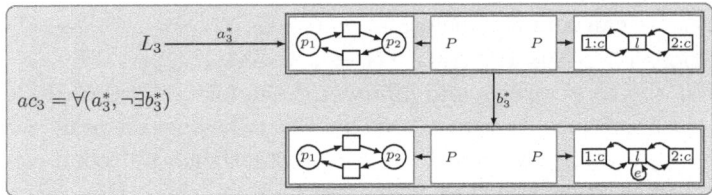

Figure 5.8: Alternative application condition for the triple rule `extendConnection`

Similarly, $ac_4 = \neg\exists a_4 \wedge \neg\exists b_4 \wedge \neg\exists c_4$ can be decomposed into the S-application condition $\neg\exists a_4$ and the T-application condition $\neg\exists b_4 \wedge \neg\exists c_4$. This means that both rules are S- and T-consistent. $ac_3 = \forall(a_3, \neg\exists b_3)$ is an S-extending application condition, but not a T-application condition. This means that the application condition ac_3 of the triple rule `extendConnection` is S-consistent but not T-consistent. Note that we could choose an alternative application condition $ac_3^* = \forall(a_3^*, \neg\exists b_3^*)$ as shown in Fig. 5.8 which is equally expressive for our example but leads to both S- and T-consistency of the rule `extendConnection`$^* = (tr_3, ac_3^*)$.

5.2.2 Composition and Decomposition of Triple Transformations

Now we want to analyze how a triple transformation can be decomposed into a transformation applying first the source rules followed by the forward rules. Match consistency of the decomposed transformation means that the co-matches of the source rules define the source parts of the matches of the corresponding forward rules. This helps us to define suitable forward model transformations which have to be source consistent to ensure a valid model. Note that we define the notions and obtain the results in this subsection only for decompositions into source and forward rules. Dually, all these notions and results can be shown for target and backward rules.

Definition 5.19 (Source and match consistency)
Consider a sequence $(tr_i)_{i=1,\ldots,n}$ of triple rules with S-consistent application conditions leading to corresponding sequences $(tr_{iS})_{i=1,\ldots,n}$ and $(tr_{iF})_{i=1,\ldots,n}$ of source and forward rules. A triple transformation sequence $G_{00} \xRightarrow{tr_S^*} G_{n0} \xRightarrow{tr_F^*} G_{nn}$ via first $tr_{1S},\ldots,tr_{nS}$ and then $tr_{1F},\ldots,tr_{nF}$ with matches m_{iS} and m_{iF} and co-matches n_{iS} and n_{iF}, respectively, is *match consistent* if the source component of the match m_{iF} is uniquely defined by the co-match n_{iS}.

A triple transformation $G_{n0} \xRightarrow{tr_F^*} G_{nn}$ is called *source consistent* if there is a match consistent sequence $G_{00} \xRightarrow{tr_S^*} G_{n0} \xRightarrow{tr_F^*} G_{nn}$.

Using Fact 5.17, we can split a transformation $G_0 \xrightarrow{tr_1} G_1 \Rightarrow \ldots \xrightarrow{tr_n} G_n$ into transformations $G_0 \xrightarrow{tr_{1S}} G'_0 \xrightarrow{tr_{1F}} G_1 \Rightarrow \ldots \xrightarrow{tr_{nS}} G'_{n-1} \xrightarrow{tr_{nF}} G_n$. But to apply first the source rules and afterwards the forward rules, these have to be independent in a certain sense. In the following theorem, we show that if the application conditions are S-consistent such a decomposition into a match consistent transformation can be found and, vice versa, each match consistent transformation can be composed to a transformation via the corresponding triple rules. This result is an extension of the corresponding result in [EEE$^+$07] for triple transformations without application conditions and in [EHS09] for triple transformations with negative application conditions.

Theorem 5.20 (De- and composition)
For triple transformation sequences with S-consistent application conditions the following holds:

1. **Decomposition:** For each triple transformation sequence $G_0 \xrightarrow{tr_1} G_1 \Rightarrow \ldots \xrightarrow{tr_n} G_n$ there is a corresponding match consistent triple transformation sequence $G_0 = G_{00} \xrightarrow{tr_{1S}} G_{10} \Rightarrow \ldots \xrightarrow{tr_{nS}} G_{n0} \xrightarrow{tr_{1F}} G_{n1} \Rightarrow \ldots \xrightarrow{tr_{nF}} G_{nn} = G_n$.

2. **Composition:** For each match consistent triple transformation sequence $G_{00} \xrightarrow{tr_{1S}} G_{10} \Rightarrow \ldots \xrightarrow{tr_{nS}} G_{n0} \xrightarrow{tr_{1F}} G_{n1} \Rightarrow \ldots \xrightarrow{tr_{nF}} G_{nn}$ there is a triple transformation sequence $G_{00} = G_0 \xrightarrow{tr_1} G_1 \Rightarrow \ldots \xrightarrow{tr_n} G_n = G_{nn}$.

3. **Bijective Correspondence:** Composition and Decomposition are inverse to each other.

PROOF This result has been shown in [EEE$^+$07] for triple rules without application conditions. We use the facts that $tr_i = tr_{iS} *_{E_i} tr_{iF}$, as shown in Fact 5.17, and that the transformations via tr_{iS} and tr_{jF} are sequentially independent for $i > j$, which is shown in [EEE$^+$07] for rules without application conditions and can be extended to triple rules with application conditions as shown in the following. Thus, the proof from [EEE$^+$07] can be done analogously for rules with application conditions.

It suffices to show that the transformations $G_{10} \xrightarrow{tr_{1F}, m_1} G_{11} \xrightarrow{tr_{2S}, m_2} G_{21}$ are sequentially independent. From the sequential independence without application conditions we obtain morphisms $i : R_{1F} \to G_{11}$ with $i = n_1$ and $j : L_{2S} \to G_{10}$ with $g_1 \circ j = m_2$.

It remains to show the compatibility with the application conditions:

- $j \models ac_{2S}$: $ac_{2S} = toS(ac'_{2S})$, where ac'_{2S} is an S-application condition. For $ac'_{2S} = $ true, also $ac_{2S} = $ true and therefore $j \models ac_{2S}$. Suppose $ac'_{2S} = $

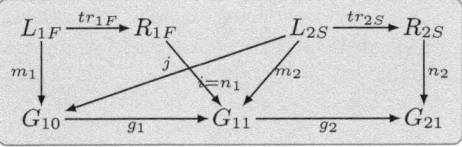

$\exists(a, ac''_{2S})$ leading to $ac_{2S} = \exists((a_S, id_\varnothing, id_\varnothing), toS(ac''_{2S}))$. Moreover, tr_{1F} is a forward rule, i. e. it does not change the source component and $G_{11,S} = G_{10,S}$.

We know that $m_2 = g_1 \circ j \models ac_{2S}$, which means that there exists $p : P \to G_{11}$ with $p \circ a = g_1 \circ j$, $p \models toS(ac''_{2S})$, and $p_C = \varnothing$, $p_T = \varnothing$. Then there exists $q : P \to G_{10}$ with $q = (p_S, \varnothing, \varnothing)$, $q \circ a = (p_S \circ a_S, \varnothing, \varnothing) = j$, and $q \models toS(ac''_{2S})$ because all objects occuring in $toS(ac''_{2S})$ have empty connection and target components. This means that $j \models ac_{2S}$ for this case, and can be shown recursively for composed ac_{2S}.

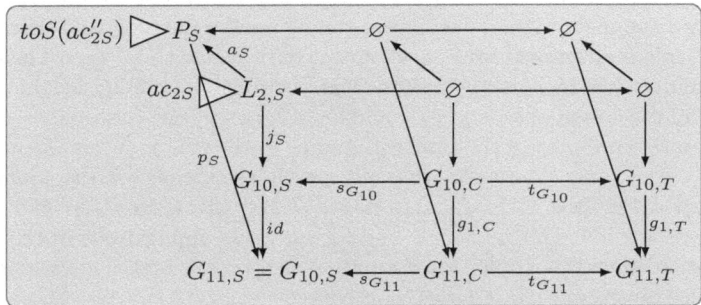

- $g_2 \circ n_1 \models ac_R := R(tr_{1F}, ac_{1F})$: $ac_{1F} = toF(ac'_{1F})$, where ac'_{1F} is an S-extending application condition. For $ac'_{1F} = $ true also $ac_{1F} = $ true and $ac_R = $ true, therefore $g_2 \circ n_1 \models ac_R$. Now suppose $ac'_{1F} = \exists(a, ac''_{1F})$ leading to $ac_{1F} = \exists((id_{R_{1,S}}, a_C, $

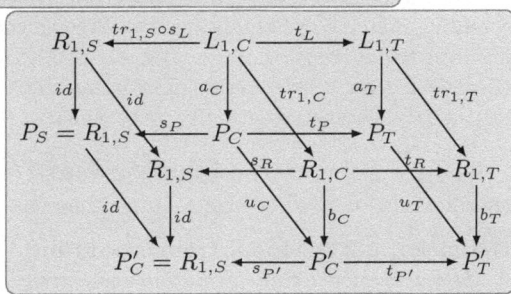

$a_T), toF(ac''_{1F}))$ and $ac_R = \exists((id_{R_{1_S}}, b_C, b_T), ac'_R)$ by component-wise push-out construction for the right-shift with $ac'_R = R(u, toF(ac''_{1F}))$. Moreover, tr_{2S} is a source rule which means that $g_{2,C}$ and $g_{2,T}$ are identities.

From Fact 3.41 we know that $n_1 \models ac_R$ using that $m_1 \models ac_{1F}$. This means that there is a morphism $p : P \to G_{11}$ with $p \circ a = n_1$, $p \models ac'_R$, and $p_S = n_{1,S}$. It follows that $g_2 \circ p \circ a = g_2 \circ n_1$ and $g_2 \circ p = (g_{2,S} \circ p_S, p_C, p_T) \models ac'_R$, because it only differs from p in the S-component, which is identical in all objects occuring in ac'_R. This means that $g_2 \circ n_1 \models ac_R = \exists(a, ac'_R)$, and can be shown recursively for composed ac_R.

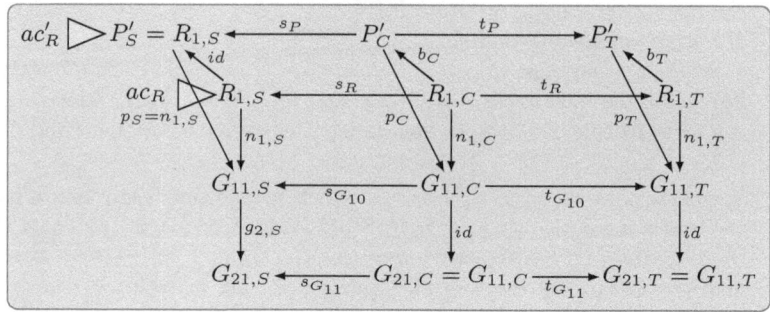

Example 5.21

Consider the transformation $G_{00} \overset{*}{\Rightarrow} G_{33} = G$ in Fig. 5.9, where we first apply the source rules $\mathtt{newConnection}_S$, $\mathtt{newConnection}_S$, $\mathtt{newExclusive}_S$ and afterwards the forward rules $\mathtt{newConnection}_F$, $\mathtt{newConnection}_F$, $\mathtt{newExclusive}_F$. The source parts of the matches m_{1F}, m_{2F}, and m_{3F} are completely defined by the source component of the co-matches n_{1S}, n_{2S}, and n_{3S}. For example, choosing $m_{1F,S}$ like $n_{1S,S}$ defines the mapping of the places p_1 and p_2 in the rule to p_1 and p_2 in $G_{30,S}$ and of the transitions. Moreover, the only possible matches for the connection and target parts are the corresponding nodes P and clients in $G_{30,C}$ and $G_{30,T}$, respectively. This holds for all source and forward rule applications in this triple transformation, thus this triple transformation sequence is match consistent.

The triple transformation $G_{30} \overset{*}{\Rightarrow} G_{33}$ is source consistent since we find a corresponding match consistent sequence. We can compose these transformations leading to a triple transformation $G_{00} \xrightarrow{\mathtt{newConnection}} G_1 \xrightarrow{\mathtt{newConnection}} G_2 \xrightarrow{\mathtt{newExclusive}} G$, and vice versa this triple transformation can be decomposed. This also holds for the triple transformation $\varnothing \overset{*}{\Rightarrow} G$ which we originally considered in Ex. 5.11.

Based on source consistent forward transformations we define model transformations, where we assume that the start graph is the empty graph.

Definition 5.22 (Model transformation)

A *(forward) model transformation sequence* $(G_S, G_0 \xrightarrow{tr_F^*} G_n, G_T)$ is given by a source graph G_S, a target graph G_T, and a source consistent forward transformation $G_0 \xrightarrow{tr_F^*} G_n$ with $G_0 = (G_S \xleftarrow{\varnothing} \varnothing \xrightarrow{\varnothing} \varnothing)$ and $G_{n,T} = G_T$.

A *(forward) model transformation* $MT_F : VL_S \Rightarrow VL_T$ is defined by all (forward) model transformation sequences.

Example 5.23

Our triple transformation $(G_S \leftarrow \varnothing \rightarrow \varnothing) \overset{*}{\Rightarrow} G_{33}$ with G_{33} shown in Fig. 5.9 is source consistent. Thus, it leads to a forward transformation sequence $(G_S, G_0$

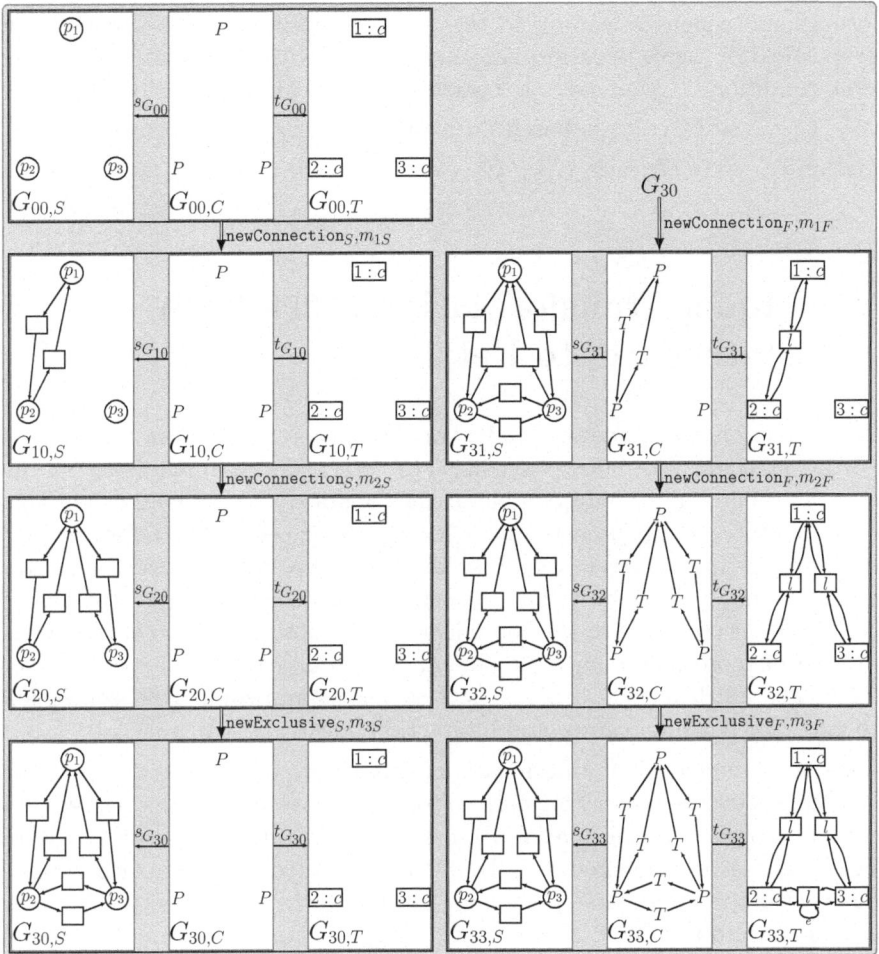

Figure 5.9: A match consistent triple transformation sequence

$\xrightarrow{tr_F^*} G_{33}, G_T$). Collecting all possible source consistent transformations defines the forward model transformation from Petri nets to our communication models.

For all notions and results concerning source and forward rules, we obtain the dual notions and results for target and backward rules. Thus, we have target and match consistency of the corresponding triple transformations sequences leading to the dual composition and decomposition properties for triple transformation sequences with T-consistent application conditions. Moreover, a backward model transformation sequence $(G_T, G'_0 \xrightarrow{tr_B^*} G'_n, G_S)$ is based on a target consistent backward transformation $G'_0 \xrightarrow{tr_B^*} G'_n$ with $G'_0 = (\varnothing \xleftarrow{\varnothing} \varnothing \xrightarrow{\varnothing} G_T)$ and $G'_{n,S} = G_S$.

5.3 Model Transformation SC2PN from Statecharts to Petri Nets

In this section, we define the model transformation SC2PN from a variant of UML statecharts (see Subsection 4.2.2) to Petri nets. We further restrict the statecharts and allow only two hierarchies of states, i.e the longest possible chain of states and regions is SM $\rightarrow$ R $\rightarrow$ S $\rightarrow$ R $\rightarrow$ S. The reason is that for more nesting of hierarchies, Petri nets are not a suitable target language to find a mapping to such that the semantical behavior of the statecharts can be preserved. Due to the complicated behavior of the current-pointer, in case of more hierarchies one should choose object Petri nets as target language, which may have Petri nets as tokens and some synchronization to allow for communication and interaction [Far01, KR04].

Existing model transformations from statecharts to Petri nets restrict the statecharts even more or transform into much more complex net classes. In [LV02], a model transformation from statecharts without any hierarchy to Petri nets is implemented in AToM^3, a meta-modelling tool using three different graph grammars applied one after the other. In [San00], the statecharts are also restricted and as target language stochastic reward nets are used, while the transformation is directly implemented.

Thus, we add an additional constraint c_8 depicted in Fig. 5.10. Moreover, we redefine the constraint c_6 which should ensure that transitions do not connect states in parallel regions. While this demand cannot be presented by a constraint for arbitrary hierarchy depth, it is shown as constraint c'_6 in Fig. 5.10 for the reduced hierarchy. Moreover, we allow only multi chains of trigger elements, meaning that trigger elements form a tree with root null and incoming edges. This constraint c_9 cannot be expressed by a finite constraint therefore we phrase it in its textual form. This leads to the restricted language VL_{SC2} for statecharts with only two hierarchy levels.

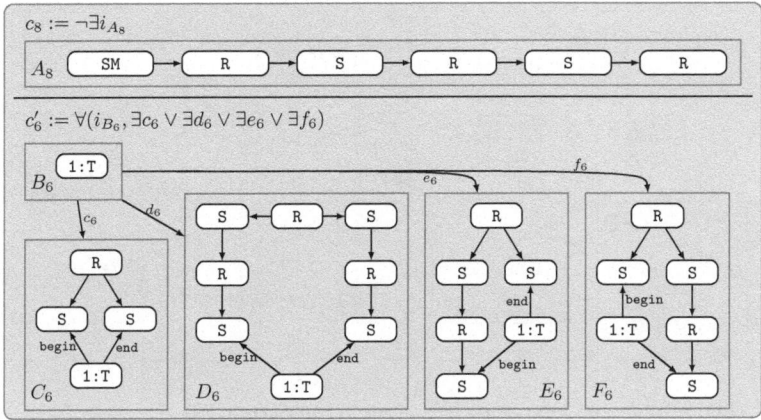

Figure 5.10: Additional constraints for the restricted number of state hierarchies

Definition 5.24 (Language VL_{SC2})
The language VL_{SC2} consists of all typed attributed graphs respecting the type graph $TG_{SC,Syn}$ (see Def. 4.36) and the constraints $c_1, \ldots, c_5, c_6', c_7, c_8, c_9$ in Figs. 4.23, 5.10, and desribed above, i. e. $VL_{SC2} = \{G \mid G \in VL_{SC}, G \models c_6' \wedge c_8 \wedge c_9\}$.

For the target language of Petri nets, we extend our elementary Petri nets from Subsection 4.2.1 with inhibitor arcs, contextual arcs, open places, and allow arbitrary many token on each place. A transition with an inhibitor arc from a place (denoted by a filled dot instead of an arrow head) is only enabled if there is no token on this place. A contextual arc between a place and a transition (denoted by an edge without arrow heads), also known as read arc in the literature, means that this token is required for firing, but remains on the place. Moreover, open places allow the interaction with the environment, i. e. tokens may appear or disappear without firing a transition within the net. We assume all places to be open.

In the following, we present the triple rules that create simultaneously the statechart model, the connection part, and the corresponding Petri net. In Fig. 5.11, the triple type graph is depicted, which has in the left the source component containing the type graph $VL_{SC,Syn}$ of statecharts as defined in Subsection 4.2.2, in the right the target component containing the type graph of elementary Petri nets extended by inhibitor and contextual arcs and a loop at the place denoting open places, and some connecting nodes

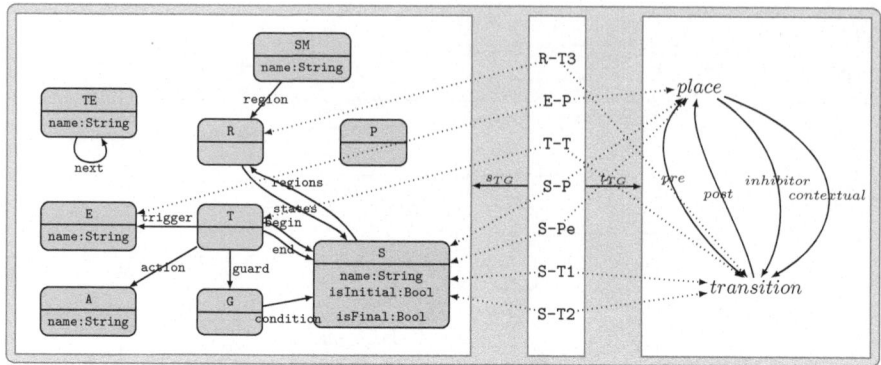

Figure 5.11: The triple type graph for the model transformation

in the connection component in between. As for the language, the edge types sub, behavior, current, and next in the statecharts and similarly the tokens in the Petri nets are only needed for the semantics but not for the model transformation, thus we leave them out here. For the mappings of the connection to the source and target parts, s_{TG} maps the nodes S-P, S-Pe, S-T1, and S-T2 to the state S, the node T-T to the transition T, the node R-T3 to the region R, and the node E-P to the event E, while t_{TG} maps S-P, S-Pe and E-P to *place* and S-T1, S-T2, T-T, and R-T3 to *transition*.

In general, each state of the statechart model is connected to a place in the Petri net, where a token on it represents that this state is current. Transitions between states are mapped to Petri net transitions and fire when the corresponding state transition occurs. Events are connected to open places, where all events with the same name share the same Petri net place. They are connected via a contextual arc to their corresponding transition thus enabling the simultaneous firing of all enabled Petri net transitions when a token is placed there. By using contextual arcs it is possible that all transitions connected to an event with this name are enabled simultaneously if also their other pre-places are marked. Otherwise, we would not be able to fire all these transitions concurrently. They would not be independent but compete for the token. For independence, we had to know in advance how many of these transitions will fire to allocate that number of tokens on the event's place. For a guard, the Petri net transition of its transition in the statechart diagram is the target of a pre- and post-arc from the place connected to the condition. Thus, we check also in the Petri net that this condition is fulfilled before firing the transition. Note that we use open places for modeling places connected to states and events.

Additional places and transitions make sure that the effects of a state transition concerning involved sub- or superstates can be simulated also in the Petri net part. Each state that may contain regions is connected via S-T1 to a transition that is the target of pre-arcs from all places of final states and inhibitor arcs from all other places in its regions, while the superstate's place is a contextual place. This makes sure that, when all substates are final, these substates are no longer current and, if it exists, the exit-action of the superstate can be initiated. Similarly, each substate is connected via S-T2 to a transition which is the target of a pre-arc from its superstate. This makes sure that, when a state transition leaves this superstate, also all substates are no longer current. Each region is connected via R-T3 to a transition which makes sure that, when no state inside this region is current, also the superstate is deactivated. For the handling of the special "exit"-events, each state which may be a superstate is connected via S-Pe to a place which handles the proper execution of this event regarding T1- and T3-transitions.

For the initialization and the semantical steps, all places corresponding to currently active states will be marked. For the handling of the hierarchical activation of initial states the corresponding open places may fire triggered by the corresponding semantical rules for the statecharts. When handling a trigger element of the event queue, the corresponding open place has to first add and later delete a token. These restrictions imply that the Petri net for itself shows different semantical behavior than the statechart, but every semantical statechart step can be simulated as shown later in Subsection 6.3.2.

The start graph is the empty graph, and the first rule to be applied is the triple rule start shown in Fig. 5.12 which creates the start graph of statecharts in the source component, and empty connection and target components. Due to its application condition it can only be applied once.

In Fig. 5.13, the triple rules newRegionSM and newRegionS are depicted which allow to create a new region of a statemachine or a state, respectively. Since each region has to have an initial state, this initial state is also created and connected to its corresponding place via S-P. With newRegionSM, the initial state is also connected to a T1-transition in the target component and another place via S-Pe. Moreover, if the new region is created inside a state by newRegionS the substate is the inhibitor of the superstate's T1-transition, the superstate inhibits a new T2-transition and the region and

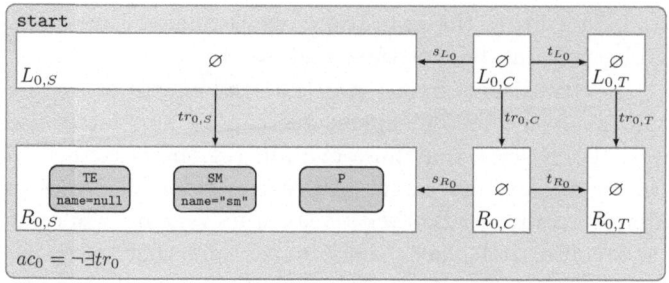

Figure 5.12: The triple rule start

the substate inhibit a new T3-transition. For the triple rule newRegionS, the application condition forbids that the superstate is final or already a substate of another state. newRegionSM has the application condition true which is not depicted. Note that we allow parameters for the rules to define the attributes. Thus, the user has to declare the name of the newly created state when applying these triple rules.

In Figs. 5.14 and 5.15, the triple rules for creating new states are shown. With newStateSM and newStateS, new states inside a region of the statemachine or a state are created, which are not final states. Similarly, final states are created by the triple rules newFinalStateSM and newFinalStateS. In all cases, a corresponding place is created in the target component. As in the case of a new region, if creating a state as a substate of another state, there is a new T2-transition with this superstate as inhibitor and the substate inhibits the T1-transition of the superstate. Moreover, the new place inhibits the region's T3-transition. For a final state created with newFinalStateSM, we do not have to create a T1-transition in the Petri net because final states are not allowed to contain regions. But a final state inside a state has to be connected to this superstate's T1-transition. The application conditions of these rules make sure that the new state name is unique within its region and that, for final states, only one final state per region is allowed.

For the creation of a new transition, the triple rules newTransitionNew-Event, newTransitionNewExit, newTransitionOldEvent, and newTransitionOldExit in Figs. 5.16 and 5.17 are used. A new transition in the source part connected with a new Petri net transition in the target part is created, and in case of a new event, this event is connected with a new place which is a contextual place for the transition. Otherwise, the transition is connected with the place of the already existing event. In case of an exit-

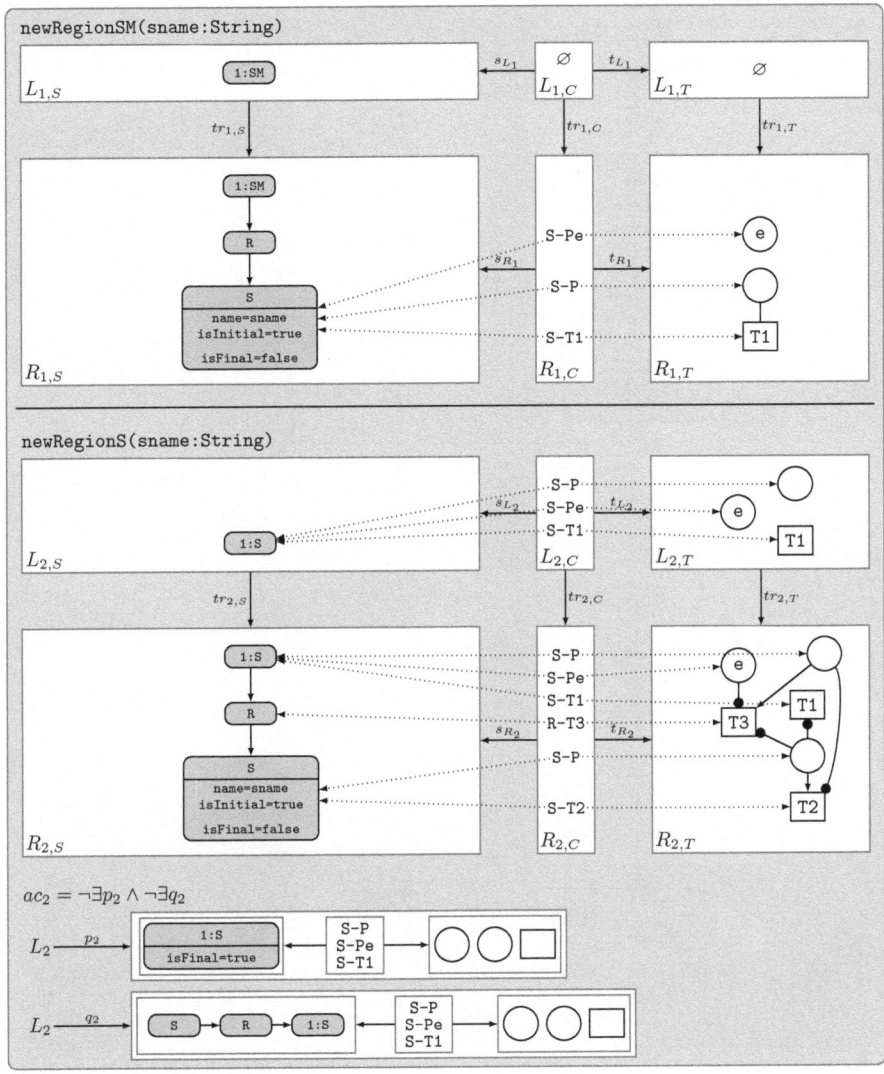

Figure 5.13: The triple rules newRegionSM and newRegionS

event, the place connected via S-Pe to the begin-state has to be connected to the new transition and the begin-state's T1-transition. The application

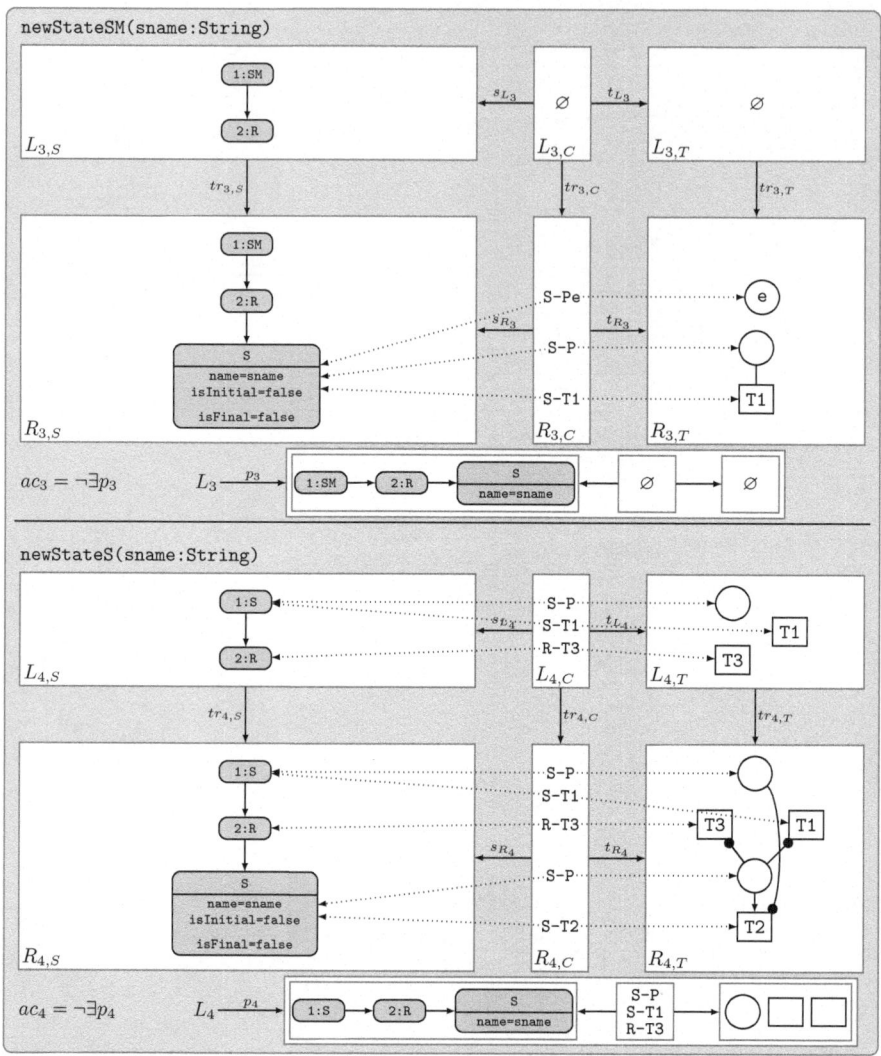

Figure 5.14: The triple rules newStateSM and newStateS

conditions forbid that the begin-state is a final state and that states over different regions are connected by a transition, and ensure that exit-events only begin at superstates. Note that the objects and morphisms used for

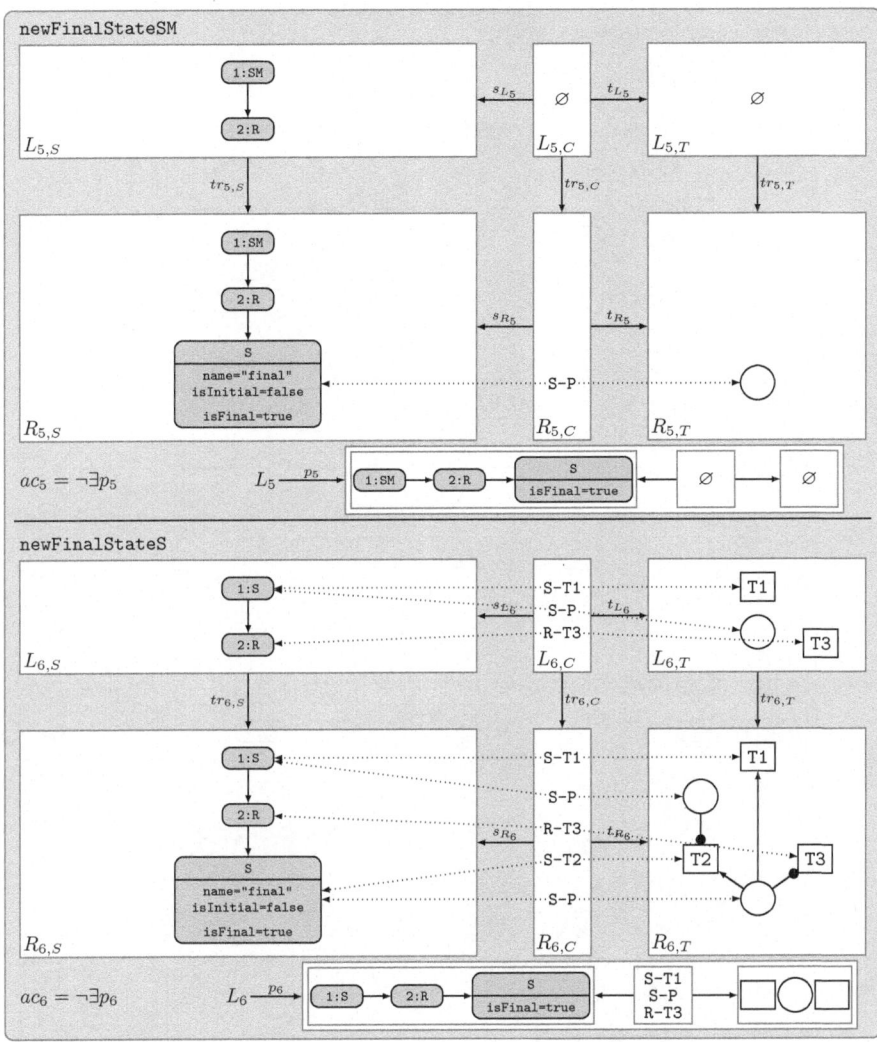

Figure 5.15: The triple rules `newFinalStateSM` and `newFinalStateS`

the application conditions ac_8, ac_9, and ac_{10} are not shown explicitly, but they correspond to the objects and morphisms used in ac_7.

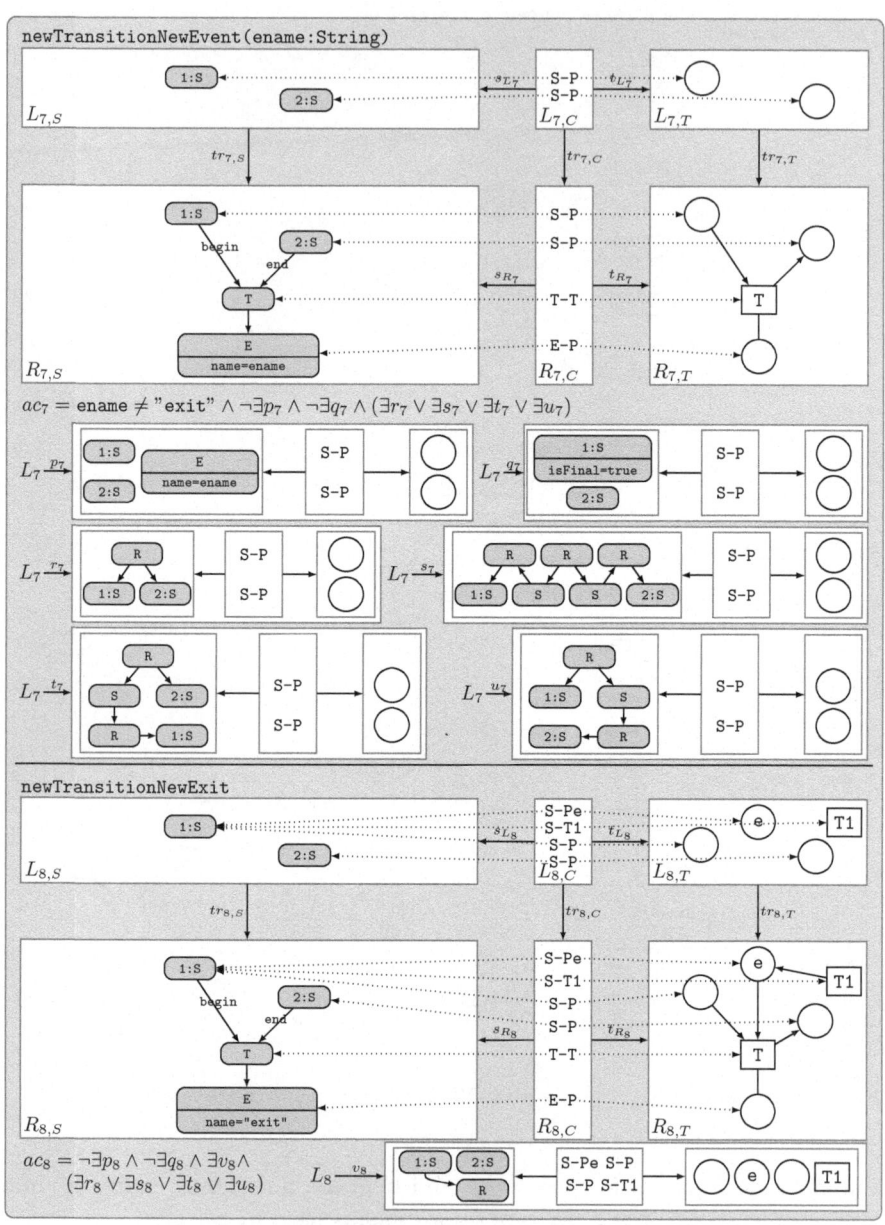

Figure 5.16: newTransitionNewEvent and newTransitionNewExit

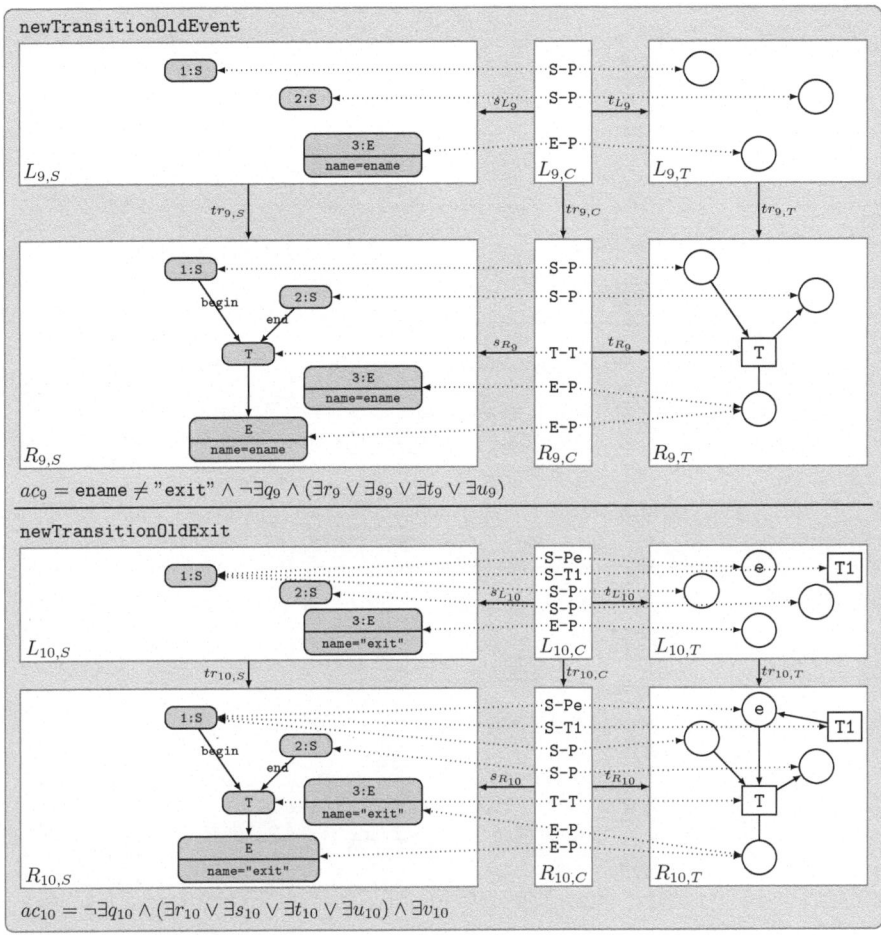

Figure 5.17: `newTransitionOldEvent` and `NewTransitionOldExit`

In Fig. 5.18, the triple rules `newGuard` and `nextGuard` are shown which create the guard conditions of a transition. The guard condition is a state whose corresponding place is connected via a contextual arc to the corresponding net transition. The application conditions ensure that only one guard per transition is allowed and that a transition with `exit`-event is not guarded at all. With the rule `newAction` in Fig. 5.19, an action is added to a transition in the statechart model if none is specified yet. Moreover, the

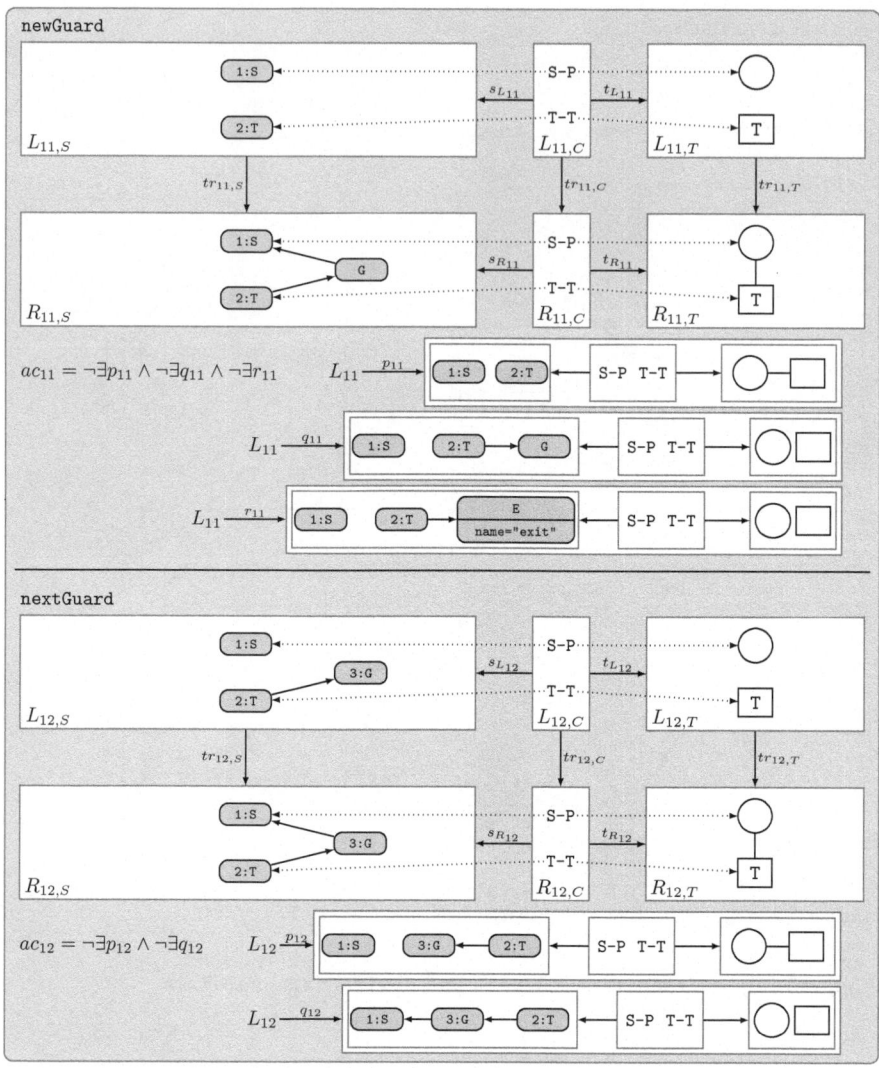

Figure 5.18: The triple rules newGuard and nextGuard

triple rule newTriggerElement in Fig. 5.19 adds a new TriggerElement
with a given name. Since the actions and trigger elements are handled by
the semantics they do not have a counterpart in the Petri net model.

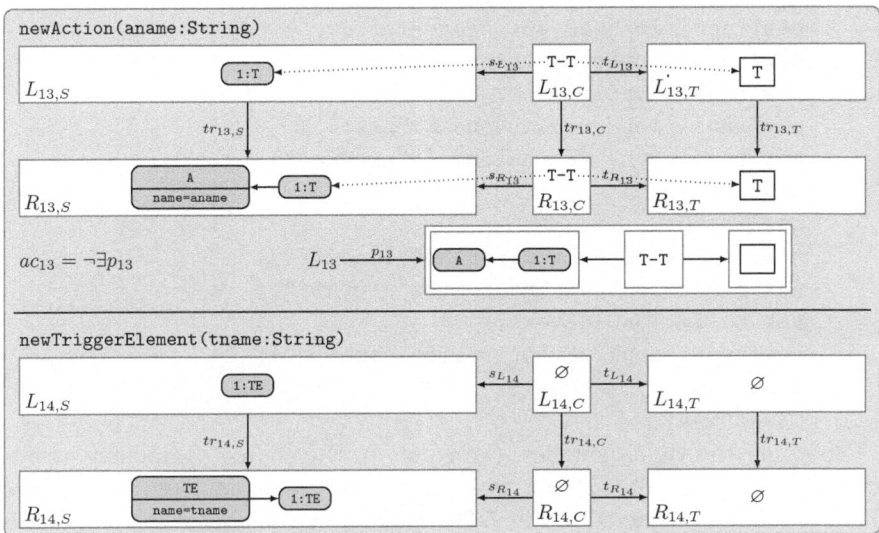

Figure 5.19: The triple rules `newAction` and `newTriggerElement`

The statechart example `ProdCons` can be constructed in the source component of a triple graph by the application of the following triple rule sequence `tr =`

```
start;
newRegionSM(sname="prod");
newRegionS(sname="produced");
newRegionS(sname="empty");
newRegionS(sname="wait");
newStateSM(sname="error");
newRegionS(sname="call");
newStateS(sname="prepare");
newStateS(sname="full");
newStateS(sname="consumed");
newStateS(sname="repair");
newFinalStateSM;
newFinalStateS;
newTransitionNewExit;
newTransitionNewEvent(ename="fail");
newTransitionNewEvent(ename="finish");
```

```
newTransitionNewEvent(ename="arrive");
newTransitionNewEvent(ename="repair");
newTransitionOldEvent;
newTransitionNewEvent(ename="next");
newTransitionNewEvent(ename="produce");
newGuard;
newAction;
newTransitionNewEvent(ename="incbuff");
newTransitionNewEvent(ename="decbuff");
newTransitionOldEvent;
newTransitionNewEvent(ename="consume");
newGuard;
newAction;
```

Choosing the right matches, the result in the source component is our statechart example ProdCons, while in the target component we find the Petri net PN_{PC} depicted in Fig. 5.20, where we have labeled the places and transitions with the names of the corresponding statechart elements and connection node names to denote the correspondence.

From the triple rules, we can derive the corresponding source and forward rules. All application conditions are S- or T-application conditions and thus S-consistent. For example, the application condition ac_{10} of the rule newGuard in Fig. 5.18 can be decomposed into the S-application condition $\neg \exists q_{10} \wedge \neg \exists r_{10}$ and the S-extending application condition $\neg \exists p_{10}$. In Fig. 5.21, the corresponding source and forward rules newGuard$_S$ and newGuard$_F$ are depicted. The S-application condition $\neg \exists q_{10} \wedge \neg \exists r_{10}$ is translated to the source rule, where the source parts of the original application conditions are kept, but the connection and target parts are empty now. The S-extending application condition $\neg \exists p_{10}$ is translated to the forward rule, where the source part is adapted to the new left-hand side.

The forward rules define the actual model transformation SC2PN from statecharts to Petri nets.

Definition 5.25 (Model transformation SC2PN)
For our triple transformations, the triple rules are given by the set $TR = \{$start, newRegionSM, newRegionS, newStateSM, newStateS, newFinalStateSM, newFinalStateS, newTransitionNewEvent, newTransitionNewExit, newTransitionOldEvent, newTransitionOldExit, newGuard, nextGuard, newAction, newTriggerElement$\}$.

The model transformation SC2PN from statecharts to Petri nets is defined by all forward model transformations using the forward rules TR_F.

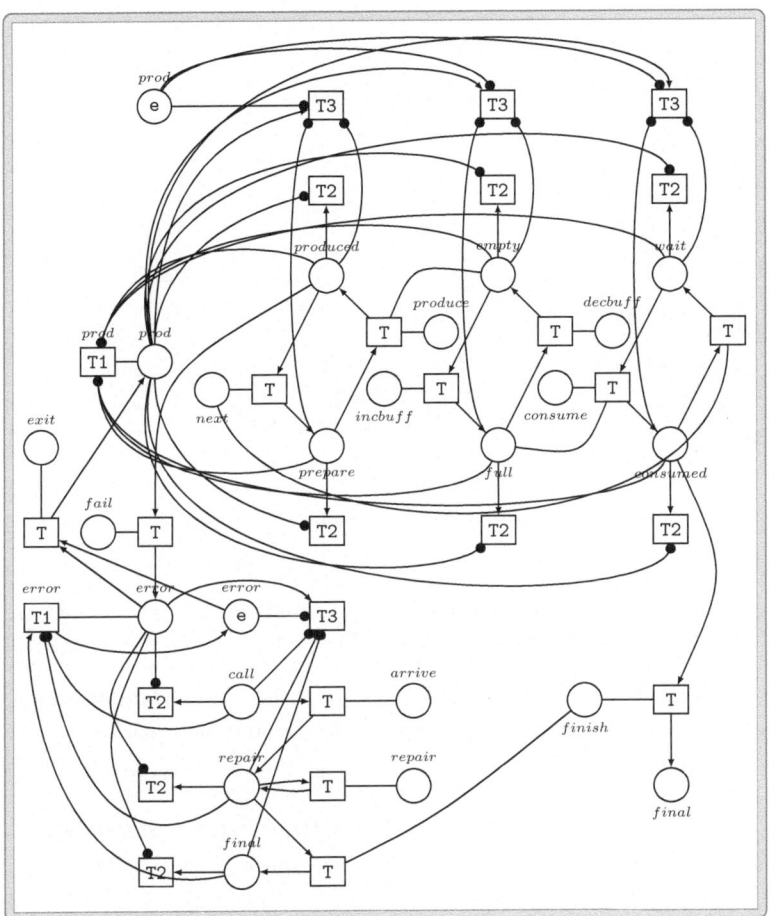

Figure 5.20: The Petri net PN_{PC} corresponding to the statechart example

The source rules represent a generating grammar for our statechart models. Moreover, the restriction of all derived triple graphs to their source part, the language constructed by the source rules, and the statechart language VL_{SC2} are equal.

Theorem 5.26 (Comparison of statechart languages)
Consider the languages $VL_S = \{G_S \mid \exists$ triple transformation $\emptyset \xRightarrow{\text{start}} \xRightarrow{tr^*} (G_S \leftarrow G_C \rightarrow G_T)$ via rules in $TR\}$, $VL_{S0} = \{G_S \mid \exists$ triple transformation $\emptyset \xRightarrow{\text{start}_S}$

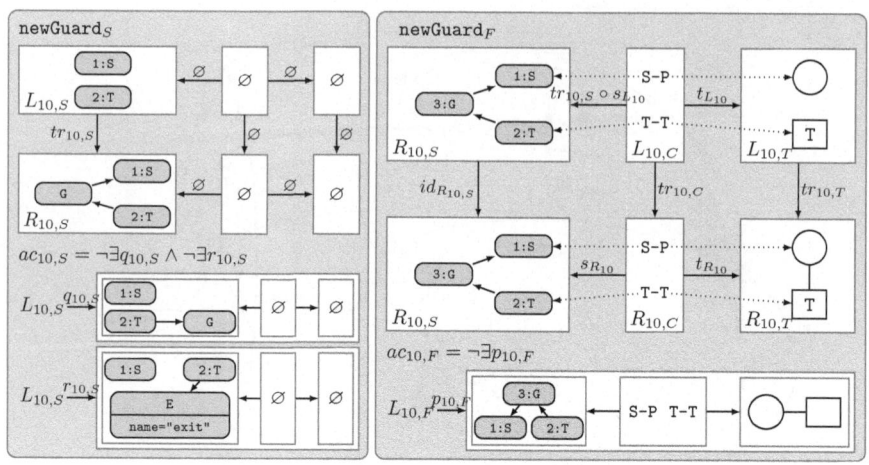

Figure 5.21: The source and forward rules of newGuard

$\xrightarrow{tr_S^*} (G_S \leftarrow \varnothing \rightarrow \varnothing)$ via source rules in TR_S}, and VL_{SC2} as defined in Def. 5.24. Then we have that $VL_S = VL_{S0} = VL_{SC2}$.

PROOF $VL_S \subseteq VL_{S0}$: For a statechart $G_S \in VL_S$ there is a transformation $\varnothing \xrightarrow{start} \xrightarrow{tr^*} (G_S \leftarrow G_C \rightarrow G_T) = G_n$, which can be decomposed with Thm. 5.20 into a corresponding sequence $\varnothing \xrightarrow{start_S} \xrightarrow{tr_S^*} (G_S \leftarrow \varnothing \rightarrow \varnothing) \xrightarrow{start_F} \xrightarrow{tr_F^*} G_n$. This means that $G_S \in VL_{S0}$.

$VL_{S0} \subseteq VL_{SC2}$: For a statechart $G_S \in VL_{S0}$ there is a transformation $\varnothing \xrightarrow{start_S} \xrightarrow{tr_S^*} (G_S \leftarrow \varnothing \rightarrow \varnothing)$. G_S is typed over the type graph $TG_{SC,Syn}$ and respects the multiplicities specified in the type graph and the constraints in Figs. 4.23 and 5.10, as shown in the following:

- c_1: The only source rules that may create SM-nodes is the rules $start_S$, which is applied once and only once due to its application condition. This means that there is exactly one SM-node with attribute name = "sm".

- c_2: The only source rules which may create regions are the rules newRegion-SM$_S$ and newRegionS$_S$. They ensure that each region is contained in exactly one state or the statemachine. Moreover, the rules newStateSM$_S$ and newStateS$_S$ guarantee that state names within one region are unique.

- c_3: The rules newRegionSM$_S$ and newRegionS$_S$ are the only rules creating initial states. When creating a region, also a corresponding initial state is generated, and initial states can only be created inside a new region. In addition, the attribute isFinal=false is set for this initial state. This means that $G_S \models \forall(i_{A_3}, \exists a_3) \wedge \neg \exists i_{C_3} \wedge \neg \exists i_{F_3}$. Moreover, the application condition $\neg \exists p_2$ of newRegionS$_S$ ensures that $\neg \exists i_{E_3}$ is satisfied. Final states can only be created by the rules newFinalStateSM$_S$ and newFinalStateS$_S$, where the application conditions make sure that only one final state exists in each region, i.e. $G_S \models \neg \exists i_{D_3}$.

- c_4: newGuard$_S$ is the only rule creating guards and the application condition $\neg \exists r_{11}$ ensures that an exit-transition is not connected to a guard.

- c_5: Final states can only be created by the rules newFinalStateSM$_S$ and newFinalStateS$_S$, where the attribute name = "final" is set. For the creation of begin-edges, only the rules newTransitionNewEvent, newTransitionNewExit, newTransitionOldEvent, and newTransitionOldExit can be used. The application conditions $\neg \exists q_i$ for $i = 7, \ldots, 10$ ensure that a final state cannot be the source of a begin-edge.

- c'_6: Similarly, for states 1 and 2 to be connected via a transition, the application conditions $(\exists r_i \vee \exists s_i \vee \exists t_i \vee u_i)$ for $i = 7, \ldots, 10$ have to hold, which directly correspond to this constraint.

- c_7: The only source rule that may create P-nodes is the rule start$_S$, which is applied once and only once due to its application condition. This means that there is exactly one P-node. Moreover, the rule creates the trigger element with name=null. Moreover, the only rule creating trigger elements is newTriggerElement$_S$, which has the name of the new trigger element as a parameter such that no additional null-trigger element may occur.

- c_8: The application condition $\neg \exists q_2$ of the rule newRegionS$_S$, which is the only rule that may create the forbidden situation, ensures that G_S satisfies this constraint.

- c_9: With newTriggerElement$_S$, only chains of trigger elements can be constructed and this constraint is satisfied.

- Multiplicities: The source rules also ensure the multiplicities defined in the type graph. For example, the rule newAction$_S$, which is the only rule introducing actions, makes sure that each action is connected to exactly one transition. Its application condition forbids more than one application for a certain transition. Similarly, this hold for guards analyzing the rules newGuard$_S$ and nextGuard$_S$, which may add $1, \ldots, n$ conditional states to the guard of a transition. Transitions and events are always constructed as pairs by the source rules ensuring their one-to-one correspondence. Also, each transition is connected to exactly one begin- and end-state.

$VL_{SC2} \subseteq VL_S$: Given a statechart model $M \in VL_{SC2}$ we have to show that we find a transformation sequence $\varnothing \xrightarrow{\text{start}} \xrightarrow{tr^*} G$ with $G_S = M$. We can show this by arguing about the composition of M.

Due to the constraints c_1 and c_7, M has to contain nodes of type SM, TE, and P. Moreover, also the attribute values are restricted to name = "sm" for the statemachine and name = null for the trigger element. This smallest model M_0 is exactly the result in the source component of the transformation $\varnothing \xrightarrow{\text{start}} G$.

If the statemachine contains a region, this region also has to contain exactly one initial state (constraint c_3). Both can be constructed using the rule newRegionSM. Additional states in this region can be constructed using the rule newStateSM, which is applicable because M satisfies the constraint c_2. The final state in this region, which has to be unique due to constraint c_3, is constructed by the rule newFinalStateSM. Similarly, if a state contains a region with states the rules for constructing regions, states, and final states inside a state can be applied. The application conditions and constraints correspond to each other such that all regions and states in M can be constructed.

A transition in M, which has to have a one-to-one correspondence to an event, one of the rules newTransitionNewEvent, newTransitionOldEvent, newTransitionNewExit, newTransitionOldExit can be applied. We analyze the case for a transition with an arbitrary, i. e. not an exit-event, which can be handled similarly. If the event name is unique, the rule newTransitionNewEvent is applied. It is applicable because M satisfies the constraints c_5' and c_6' and creates the transition and its event. Otherwise, we can apply one the rule newTransitionNewEvent and afterwards as often as necessary the rule newTransitionOldEvent.

Guards, actions, and trigger elements in M can be created using the rules newGuard, nextGuard, newAction, and newTriggerElement, where we can construct all multi chains of trigger elements with newTriggerElement.

For the target rules, only a subset of Petri nets can be generated, but all models obtained from transformations using the target rules are well-formed, because they are typed over the Petri net type graph and we cannot generate double arcs. This is due to the fact that the rules either create only arcs from or to a new element or the multiple application is forbidden as in the rule newGuard as part of the application condition.

Applying the corresponding source rule sequence, we obtain our statechart example ProdCons in Fig. 4.21. This statechart model can be transformed into the Petri net PN_{PC} in Fig. 5.20 via the forward rules. This triple transformation is source consistent, since the source parts of the matches of the forward rules are uniquely defined by the co-matches of the source rules. Thus, we actually obtain a model transformation sequence from the statechart model ProdCons to the Petri net PN_{PC}.

6 Analysis, Correctness, and Construction of Model Transformations

Model transformations from a source to a target language can be described by triple graph transformations as shown in Chapter 5. Important properties for the analysis and correctness of such model transformations are syntactical correctness, completeness, and functional behavior. Moreover, the semantics of the source and target models may be given by interaction schemes using amalgamation as done in Chapter 4. In this case, we are interested in analyzing the semantical correctness, i.e. the correctness of the model transformation with respect to the semantical behavior of the corresponding source and target models.

While we can analyze syntactical correctness, completeness, and functional behavior in general, this is more complicated for the semantical behavior and depends on the actual models, semantics, and model transformation. We show this exemplarily on our model transformation SC2PN from statecharts to Petri nets. In particular, we show that for this model transformation, each initialization and semantical step in the statechart model can be simulated in the corresponding Petri net.

For the construction of a model transformation sequence, source consistency does not directly guide the application of the forward rules but has to be checked for the complete forward sequence. This means that possible forward sequences have to be constructed until one is found to be source consistent. Additionally, termination of this search is not guaranteed in general. Therefore we introduce a more efficient construction technique for model transformation sequences on-the-fly, where correctness and completeness properties are ensured by construction.

In Section 6.1, we show results concerning syntactical correctness, completeness, and backward information preservation of model transformations based on triple graph transformation. Termination and functional behavior is analyzed in Section 6.2. In particular, we analyze termination on two levels: for the model transformation and also for the semantics. In Section 6.3, we analyze semantical correctness of our model transformation SC2PN. For a more efficient computation of model transformations, in Section 6.4 the on-the-fly construction is introduced.

6.1 Syntactical Correctness

In this section, we analyze the syntactical correctness, completeness, and backward information preservation of model transformations. We illustrate our results by analyzing the model transformation SC2PN from statecharts to Petri nets defined in Section 5.3.

Using triple graph transformations with application conditions, as for the case without application conditions [EEE$^+$07] the model transformation sequences (see Def. 5.22) are correct and complete with respect to the source and target languages. Correctness means that the source and target models actually belong to the source and target languages (see Def. 5.6), while completeness ensures that for each correct source or target model a model transformation sequence can be found.

Theorem 6.1 (Syntactical correctness w. r. t. VL_S, VL_T)
Each model transformation sequence $(G_S, G_0 \xdmapsto{tr_F^*} G_n, G_T)$ and $(G_T, G_0' \xdmapsto{tr_B^*} G_n', G_S)$ is syntactically correct with respect to the source and target languages, i. e. $G_S \in VL_S$ and $G_T \in VL_T$.

PROOF Consider a forward model transformation sequence $(G_S, G_0 \xdmapsto{tr_F^*} G_n, G_T)$. If $G_0 \xdmapsto{tr_F^*} G_n$ is source consistent we have a match consistent sequence $\varnothing \xdmapsto{tr_S^*} G_0 \xdmapsto{tr_F^*} G_n$ by Def. 5.19. By composition in Thm. 5.20 there is a triple transformation $\varnothing \xdmapsto{tr^*} G_n$ with $G_S = G_{n,S} \in VL_S$ and $G_T = G_{n,T} \in VL_T$ by Def. 5.7. Dually, this holds for a backward model transformation sequence $(G_T, G_0' \xdmapsto{tr_B^*} G_n', G_S)$.

Theorem 6.2 (Completeness w. r. t. VL_S, VL_T)
For each $G_S \in VL_S$ there is a corresponding $G_T \in VL_T$ such that there is a forward model transformation sequence $(G_S, G_0 \xdmapsto{tr_F^*} G_n, G_T)$.

Similarly, for each $G_T \in VL_T$ there is a corresponding $G_S \in VL_S$ such that there is a backward model transformation sequence $(G_T, G_0' \xdmapsto{tr_B^*} G_n', G_S)$.

PROOF For $G_S \in VL_S$ there exists a triple transformation $\varnothing \xdmapsto{tr^*} G$ which can be decomposed by Thm. 5.20 into a match consistent sequence $\varnothing \xdmapsto{tr_S^*} G_0 = (G_S \xleftarrow{\varnothing} \varnothing \xrightarrow{\varnothing} \varnothing) \xdmapsto{tr_F^*} G$, and by definition $(G_S, G_0 \xdmapsto{tr_F^*} G, G_T)$ is the required forward model transformation sequence with $G_T \in VL_T$. Dually, this holds for $G_T \in VL_T$.

Example 6.3

Since our example in Section 5.3 represents a well-defined model transformation sequence, our statechart ProdCons in Fig. 4.21 and the corresponding Petri net PN_{PC} in Fig. 5.20 are correct. Moreover, each valid statechart model is in VL_{SC2} (see Thm. 5.26) and thus can be transformed to a correct Petri net model. Note that for the backward transformation this only holds for Petri nets which are correct w.r.t. our target language, and not the language of all well-formed Petri nets. For example, Petri nets with only places but no transitions cannot be generated and are therefore not in VL_T.

A forward model transformation from G_S to G_T is backward information preserving concerning the source component if there is a backward transformation sequence from G_T leading to the same source graph G_S. This means that all information necessary to construct the source model is preserved in the target model.

Definition 6.4 (Backward information preserving)

A forward transformation sequence $G \xrightarrow{tr_F^*} H$ is *backward information preserving* if for the triple graph $H' = (\varnothing \xleftarrow{\varnothing} \varnothing \xrightarrow{\varnothing} H_T)$ there is a backward transformation sequence $H' \xrightarrow{tr_B^*} G'$ with $G'_S \cong G_S$.

Source consistency leads to backward information preservation and especially all forward model transformation sequences are backward information preserving. This fact is an extension of the corresponding result in [EEE$^+$07] to triple transformations with application conditions.

Fact 6.5

If all triple rules are S- and T-consistent a forward transformation sequence $G \xrightarrow{tr_F^*} H$ is backward information preserving if it is source consistent. Moreover, in this case each forward model transformation sequence $(G_S, G_0 \xrightarrow{tr_F^*} G_n, G_T)$ is backward information preserving.

PROOF If $G \xrightarrow{tr_F^*} H$ is a source consistent transformation sequence then by Def. 5.19 there exists a match consistent transformation sequence $\varnothing \xrightarrow{tr_S^*} G \xrightarrow{tr_F^*} H$ leading to the triple transformation sequence $\varnothing \xrightarrow{tr^*} H$ using Thm. 5.20. From the decomposition, we also obtain a match consistent transformation sequence $\varnothing \xrightarrow{tr_T^*} H' \xrightarrow{tr_B^*} H$ using the target and backward rules, with $H'_T = H_T$ and $H'_C = H'_S = \varnothing$. Thus, $G \xrightarrow{tr_F^*} H$ is backward information preserving. By

Def. 5.22, the forward transformation sequence $G_0 \xrightarrow{tr_F^*} G_n$ leading to a forward model transformation sequence is source consistent, and thus also backward information preserving.

Example 6.6
The Petri net PN_{PC} in Fig. 5.20 can be transformed into the statechart ProdCons in Fig. 4.21 using the backward rules of our model transformation in the same order as the forward rules were used for the forward transformation. Indeed, this holds for each Petri net obtained of a model transformation sequence from a valid statechart model.

6.2 Termination and Functional Behavior

Functional behavior describes that a model transformation MT behaves like a function, i. e. that for each source model a unique target model is found. For model transformations based on graph transformation, functional behavior can be obtained by showing termination and local confluence for the system. As described in Subsection 3.4.3, local confluence can be analyzed using critical pairs and strict AC-confluence of all critical pairs leads to local confluence of the transformation system.

6.2.1 Termination

Termination of a transformation means that no other rule can be applied any more. Then a system is terminating if all transformations terminate somewhen and no infinite transformations occur. In contrast to this definition, for triple graph transformations we can define SC-termination, which requires termination only for source consistent transformations.

Definition 6.7 (Termination)
Given an $\mathcal{M}$-adhesive transformation system $AS = (\mathbf{C}, \mathcal{M}, P)$ a transformation $G \xRightarrow{*} H$ is *terminating* if no rule $p \in P$ is applicable to H. AS is *terminating* if there are no infinite transformations.

Given a triple graph transformation system $TGS = (TR)$, a source consistent transformation $G_0 \xrightarrow{tr_F^*} G_n$ is *SC-terminating* if any extended sequence $G_0 \xrightarrow{tr_F^*} G_n \xrightarrow{tr_F'^+} G_m$ is not source consistent. Similarly, a target consistent transformation $G_0 \xrightarrow{tr_B^*} G_n$ is *TC-terminating* if any extended sequence $G_0' \xrightarrow{tr_B^*} G_n' \xrightarrow{tr_B'^+} G_m'$ is not target consistent. TGS is *SC-terminating* (*TC-terminating*) if there are no infinite source (target) consistent transformations.

For model transformations based on triple graph grammars, we can show SC-termination if the source or target rules are creating.

Theorem 6.8 (Termination of model transformation)
Consider a set of triple rules such that all rule components are finite on the graph part. If the triple rules are creating on the source component, for a source model $G_S \in VL_S$ which is finite on the graph part each model transformation sequence $(G_S, G_0 \xrightarrow{tr_F^*} G_n, G_T)$ is SC-terminating.

Dually, if the triple rules are creating on the target component, for a target model $G_T \in VL_T$ which is finite on the graph part each model transformation sequence $(G_T, G_0' \xrightarrow{tr_B^*} G_n', G_S)$ is TC-terminating.

PROOF Let $G_0 \xrightarrow{tr_F^*} G_n$ be a source consistent forward transformation sequence such that $\varnothing \xrightarrow{tr_S^*} G_0 \xrightarrow{tr_F^*} G_n$ is match consistent, i.e. each co-match $n_{i,S}$ determines the source component of the match $m_{i,F}$. Thus, also each forward match $m_{i,F}$ determines the corresponding co-match $n_{i,S}$. By uniqueness of pushout complements along $\mathcal{M}$-morphisms the co-match $n_{i,S}$ determines the match $m_{i,S}$ of the source step, thus $m_{i,F}$ determines $m_{i,S}$ (*).

If $G_0 \xrightarrow{tr_F^*} G_n \xrightarrow{tr_{(n+1,F)}, m_{(n+1,F)}} G_{n+1} \xrightarrow{tr_F''^*} G_m$ is a source consistent forward transformation sequence then there is a corresponding source sequence $\varnothing \xrightarrow{tr_S^*} G' \xrightarrow{tr_{n+1,S}} G'' \xrightarrow{tr_S''^*} G_0$ leading to match consistency of the complete sequence $\varnothing \Rightarrow^* G_m$. Using (*) it follows that $G' \cong G_0$, which implies that we have a transformation step $G_0 \xrightarrow{tr_{n+1,S}} G'' \subseteq G_0$, because triple rules are non-deleting. This is a contradiction to the precondition that each rule is creating on the source component implying that $G' \ncong G_0$. Therefore, the forward transformation sequence $G_0 \xrightarrow{tr_F^*} G_n$ cannot be extended and is SC-terminating.

Dually, this can be shown for backward model transformation sequences.

Example 6.9
All triple rules in our example model transformation SC2PN in Section 5.3 are finite on the graph part and source creating. Thus, all model transformation sequences based on finite statechart models are SC-terminating. Note that this does not hold for the backward direction, since the rule `newAction` is not target creating. Thus, the corresponding backward rule can be applied infinitely often leading to non-terminating target consistent backward transformation sequences.

6.2.2 Termination of Statecharts Semantics

Termination is not only interesting for model transformations, but also for the analysis of the semantics. In the following, we show that also our interpreter semantics for statecharts given in Subsection 4.2.3 is terminating for finite well-behaved statecharts with a finite event queue.

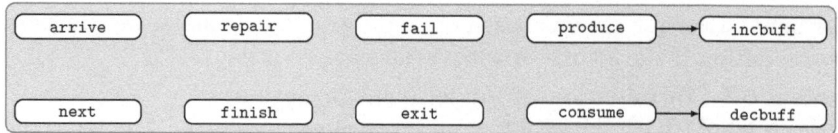

Figure 6.1: The action-event graph of our statechart example

The termination of the interpreter semantics of a statechart in general depends on the structural properties of the simulated statechart. A simulation will terminate for the trivial cases that the event queue is empty, that no transition triggers an action, or that there is no transition from any active state triggered by the current head elements of the event queue. Since transitions may trigger actions which are added as new events to the queue it is possible that the simulation of a statechart may not terminate even if all semantical steps do. Hence, it is useful to define structural constraints that provide a sufficient condition guaranteeing termination of the simulation in general for well-behaved statecharts, where we forbid cycles in the dependencies of actions and events.

Definition 6.10 (Well-behaved statecharts)
For a given statechart model, the *action-event graph* has as nodes all event names and an edge (n_1, n_2) if an event with name n_1 triggers an action named n_2.

A statechart is called *well-behaved* if it is finite, has an acyclic state hierarchy, and its action-event graph is acyclic.

Example 6.11
An example of a well-behaved statechart is our statechart model in Fig. 4.21. It is finite, has an acyclic state hierarchy, and its action-event graph is shown in Fig. 6.1. This graph is acyclic, since the only action-event dependencies in our statechart occur between produce triggering incbuff and consume triggering decbuff.

For the initialization step, we first compute the substates relation by applying the rules setSub and transSub as long as possible. These rule applications terminate because there could be at most one sub-edge between each pair of states due to the application conditions. Since no new states are created, these rules can only be applied finitely often. Then the interaction scheme init is applied once followed by the application of the interaction scheme enterRegions as long as possible. This also terminates because each application of enterRegions replaces one new-edge with a current-edge.

The multi rules p_{41} and p_{42} create new new-edges on the next lower and upper levels of a hierarchical state, but if the state hierarchy is acyclic this interaction scheme is only applicable a finite number of times. The same holds for the multi rule p_{43} which deletes double edges, since the number of current- and new-edges is decreased. Thus, the transformation terminates.

For the termination of a semantical step it is sufficient to show that the four interaction schemes enterRegions, leaveState1, leaveState2, and leaveRegions are only applicable a finite number of times. For the interaction scheme enterRegions we have already argued that above. The interaction schemes leaveState1, leaveState2 as well as the multi rule p_{81} of the interaction scheme leaveRegions reduce the number of active states in the statechart by deleting at least one current-edge. The application of the second multi rule p_{82} of the interaction scheme leaveRegions prevents another match for itself because it creates the situation forbidden by its application condition ac_{82}. It follows that the application of each of these four interaction schemes as long as possible terminates.

Combining these result we can conclude the termination of the statecharts semantics for well-behaved statecharts.

Theorem 6.12 (Termination of operational semantics)
For well-behaved statecharts with finite event queue, the operational semantics defined in Subsection 4.2.3 terminates.

PROOF According to the above considerations, each initialization step and each semantical step terminates. Moreover, each semantical step consumes an event from the event queue. If it triggers an action, the acyclic action-event graph ensures that there are only chains of events triggering actions, but no cycles, such that after the execution of this chain the number of elements in the event queue actually decreases. Thus, after finitely many semantical steps the event queue is empty and the operational semantics terminates.

6.2.3 Functional Behavior

Note that one source model $G_S \in VL_S$ constructed with a source transformation sequence $\varnothing \xrightarrow{tr_S^*} G_0 = (G_S \leftarrow \varnothing \rightarrow \varnothing)$ can be related to target models G_T and G'_T which are both constructed via the same sequence of forward rules with source consistent forward transformation sequences $G_0 \xrightarrow{tr_F^*} G_n$, $G_0 \xrightarrow{tr_F^*} G'_n$ and $G_{n,T} = G_T$, $G'_{n,T} = G'_T$. This may happen if the co-match of the source rule does not induce a unique match for the forward rule, but only for the source part of it, as shown in the following

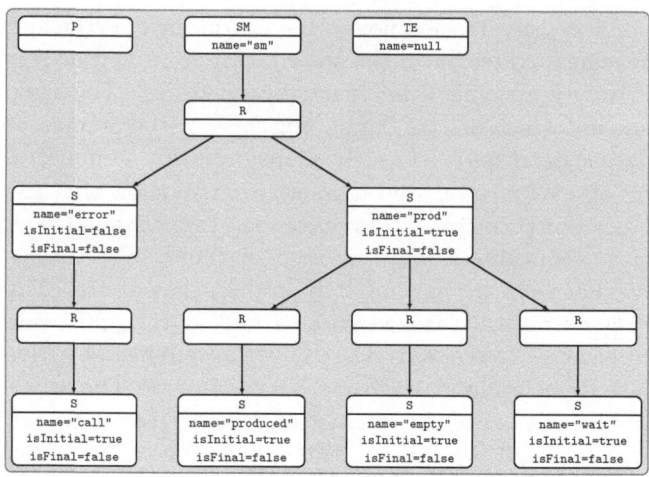

Figure 6.2: The statechart model after a partial model transformation

example. Moreover, there may be also different possibilities to construct the source models leading to different related target models.

Example 6.13

If we consider the backward model transformation from Petri nets to statecharts, this model transformation is not locally confluent. The Petri net PN_{PC} in Fig. 5.20 can be constructed by the corresponding target transformation sequence. When applying the backward rules to this Petri net, the following situation in Fig. 6.2 occurs, where we only show the source component which is the statechart model after the application of the first seven backward rules

$\quad$ start$_B$;
$\quad$ newRegionSM(sname="prod")$_B$;
$\quad$ newRegionS(sname="produced")$_B$;
$\quad$ newRegionS(sname="empty")$_B$;
$\quad$ newRegionS(sname="wait")$_B$;
$\quad$ newStateSM(sname="error")$_B$;
$\quad$ newRegionS(sname="call")$_B$;

Now we have to apply the backward rule newStateS(sname="prepare")$_B$, where the co-match of the target rule determines how the Petri net part is matched, which leads to the matching of the state 1 in the source component of the left-hand side of the backward rule to the prod-state. But it is not clear how to map the contained region - there are three regions available and we do not know which one to choose. Any choice leads to target consistency, but choosing the wrong match would lead to a different statechart model.

Functional behavior of a model transformation means that each model of the source language is transformed into a unique model of the target language.

Definition 6.14 (Functional behavior of model transformations)
A model transformation MT_F has *functional behavior* if each model G_S of the source language VL_S is transformed into a unique model G_T such that G_T belongs to the target language VL_T.

A well-known fact about graph transformation is that termination and local confluence imply confluence (see [EEPT06]), which means functional behavior on the level of model transformations. But for model transformations based on triple graphs, in general we do not have termination of the triple rules, but only SC-termination. It is future work to relate both concepts and obtain criteria for functional behavior. Nevertheless, the analysis of critical pairs may determine local confluence which is a necessary precondition for functional behavior.

Example 6.15
For our example model transformation SC2PN from statecharts to Petri nets we can analyze the critical pairs for the forward rules. All forward rules are non-deleting and the only application conditions are negative application conditions for the rules $\mathtt{newGuard}_F$ and $\mathtt{nextGuard}_F$, which are equal. Note that for non-deleting rules with negative application conditions only delete-use conflicts may appear. The conflict between $\mathtt{newGuard}_F$ and $\mathtt{nextGuard}_F$ can be trivially dissolved as confluent since both rule applications lead to the same result. No other conflicts occur, since the only other rules that create the forbidden contextual arc are the rules creating new transitions, where the types of the connection elements do not coincide. Thus, our model transformation is locally confluent. Moreover, the model transformation also has functional behavior, because due to our rules all source consistent transformation sequences of a source model lead to the same result.

6.3 Semantical Simulation and Correctness

In this section, we analyze the semantical correctness of our example model transformation from statecharts to Petri nets. For a formal definition of semantical correctness we use the well-known notion of labeled transition systems. For the case of transformations, a labeled transition system is given by recursively applying all rules to a graph, which is the initial state of its labeled transition system, where the states are graphs and the transitions are rule applications.

Definition 6.16 (Labeled transition system)

A *labeled transition system* is given by a tuple $LTS = \langle Q, L, \rightarrow, \iota \rangle$, where Q is a set of states, $\rightarrow \subseteq Q \times L \times Q$ is a transition relation with labels L, and $\iota \in Q$ is the initial state.

For a graph G and a set P of rules, where we have the set of rule names $\tilde{P}$ as labels, we obtain a labeled transition system $LTS(G)_{\tilde{P}} = \langle \{H \mid G \overset{*}{\Rightarrow} H\}, \tilde{P}, \rightarrow, G \rangle$.

Note that for a semantics described by graph transformation, in general the rules are to subtle to describe the transition labels. This means that the labels do not coincide with the rules names, but with more complex combinations of these leading to actual changes of the model's system states.

Example 6.17

For our model transformation SC2PN from Section 5.3, we have to main steps in the semantics in Def. 4.37 describing state changes: the initialization step and semantical steps defining state transitions. Thus, for a model $M \in VL_{SC2}$ we obtain a labeled transition system $LTS(M)_{L_S} = \langle Q, L_S = \{\text{init}, \text{sem}\}, \rightarrow, M \rangle$, where Q contains all semantical states of M and the labels init and sem denote initialization and semantical steps, respectively.

There are different notions of semantical correctness of model transformations, which correspond to the relations of the labeled transition systems. For a model transformation $MT : VL_S \Rightarrow VL_T$ we analyze the relationship between the labeled transition systems $LTS(G_S)$ and $LTS(G_T)$ for all model transformation sequences $(G_S, G_0 \overset{tr_F^*}{\Longrightarrow} G_n, G_T)$. In this thesis, we consider weak simulation where internal, unobservable steps may occur. Such internal steps are labeled by the special transition label τ. For states $q, q' \in Q$ we write $q \overset{a}{\Rightarrow} q'$ for $q \overset{\tau}{\rightarrow}^* \overset{a}{\rightarrow} \overset{\tau}{\rightarrow}^* q'$ and $q \overset{\tau}{\Rightarrow} q'$ for $q \overset{\tau}{\rightarrow}^* q'$.

Definition 6.18 (Weak simulation and bisimulation)

Given labeled transition systems $LTS_1 = \langle Q_1, L, \rightarrow_1, \iota_1 \rangle$ and $LTS_2 = \langle Q_2, L, \rightarrow_2, \iota_2 \rangle$ over the same labels L, a relation $\sim \subseteq Q_1 \times Q_2$ is a

- *weak simulation relation* from LTS_1 to LTS_2 if for all $q_1 \sim q_2$ we have that $q_1 \overset{a}{\rightarrow} q_1'$ implies that there exists $q_2 \overset{a}{\Rightarrow} q_2'$ with $q_1' \sim q_2'$.

- *weak bisimulation relation* if $\sim$ and $\sim^{-1}$ are weak simulation relations.

LTS_1 and LTS_2 are weakly (bi)similar if there exists a weak (bi)simulation relation $\sim$ between LTS_1 and LTS_2 with $\iota_1 \sim \iota_2$.

The semantical simulation and correctness of model transformations is based on the labeled transition systems of the source and target semantics, where we have to find common labels to compare them.

Definition 6.19 (Semantical correctness of model transformations)
Given source and target languages VL_S and VL_T with labeled transition systems $LTS(G_S)_{L_S}$ and $LTS(G_T)_{L_T}$ for models $G_S \in VL_S$ and $G_T \in VL_T$, respectively, a model transformation $MT : VL_S \Rightarrow VL_T$ is *semantics-simulating* if there are labeling functions $l_S : L_S \to L$ and $l_T : L_T \to L$ into some set of labels L with $\tau \in L$ such that for all model transformation sequences $(G_S, G_0 \xrightarrow{tr_F^*} G_n, G_T)$ we have that $LTS(G_S)_{l_S(L_S)}$ and $LTS(G_T)_{l_T(L_T)}$ are weakly similar.

$MT : VL_S \Rightarrow VL_T$ is *semantically correct* if $LTS(G_S)_{l_S(L_S)}$ and $LTS(G_T)_{l_T(L_T)}$ are weakly bisimilar for all model transformation sequences $(G_S, G_0 \xrightarrow{tr_F^*} G_n, G_T)$.

In general, the labeled transition systems for a semantical description are not finite, thus it is difficult to compute both labeled transition systems completely to directly analyze semantical simulation or correctness.

6.3.1 Simulation of Petri Nets

To analyze the semantical correctness of our model transformation SC2PN from statecharts to Petri nets defined in Section 5.3 we need to define suitable semantical rules. The semantics for statecharts is given in Subsection 4.2.3. But for our Petri nets, we have to extend the semantics in Subsection 4.2.1 for open places and inhibitor and contextual arcs. Moreover, we change the semantics to control which tokens are old and which ones are newly placed by marking these, and allow typed transitions using the types T, T1, T2, and T3 from the model transformation.

These extensions are necessary to obtain a semantics-simulating model transformation. The main idea of the model transformation was that states correspond to places and transitions in the statechart to transitions in the Petri net. But while our statechart semantics can handle concurrent transitions, in the Petri net only one transition may fire at a time. Thus, we have to remember which tokens have been newly created to forbid their use in the same semantical step.

The firing rules +p and −p are given in the top of Fig. 6.3, where +p creates and −p deletes a token on an open place. Similarly, there is a rule +pm which puts a marked, i. e. unfilled token on the places, which is not explicitly shown. The interaction scheme for firing a transition of type T is shown in the middle of Fig. 6.3.

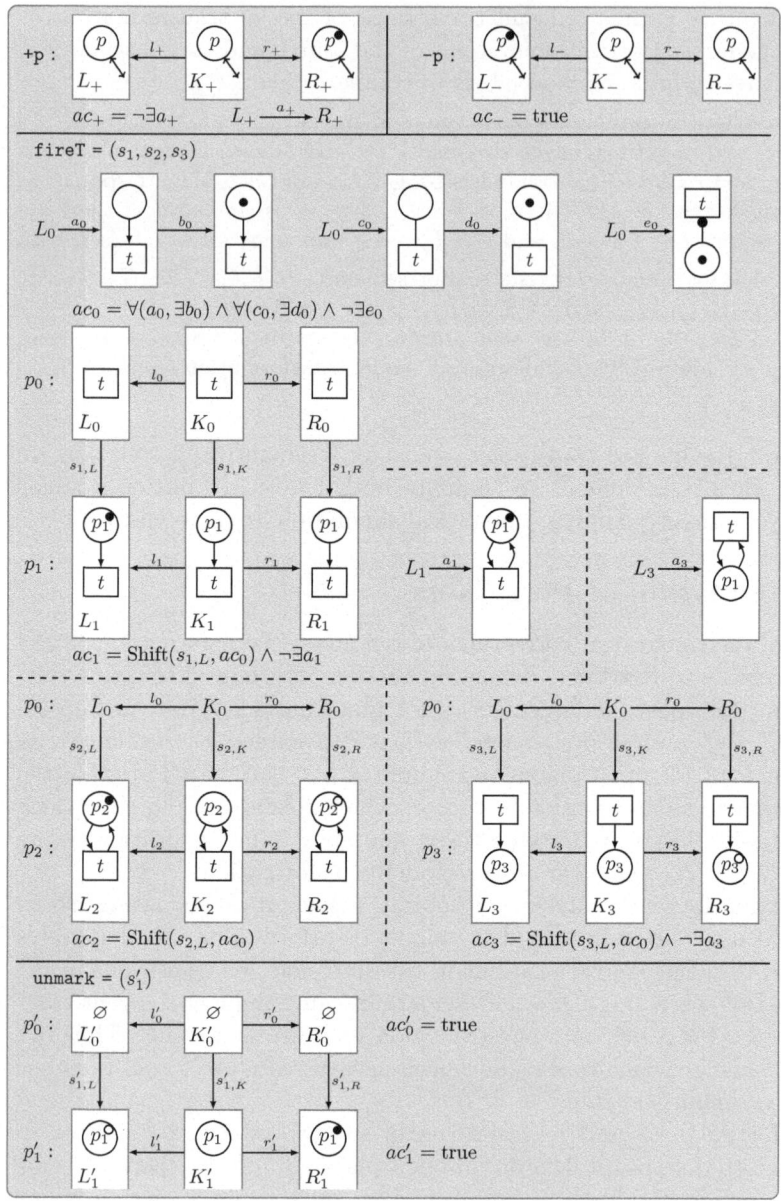

Figure 6.3: The rules for firing the extended Petri nets

As in the standard case described in Subsection 4.2.1, the kernel rule selects an activated transition, where the application condition ensures that all pre-places hold an old (full) token, all contextual places hold a token, and all inhibitor places are token-free. The multi rules handle the pre, post, and combined pre- and post-places, where newly created tokens are marked (unfilled). We have similar interaction schemes fireT1, fireT2, and fireT3 for the firing of the other transition types. Moreover, we need an interaction scheme unmark to unmark all marked tokens, which is depicted in the bottom of Fig. 6.3.

6.3.2 Semantical Correctness of the Model Transformation SC2PN

Both the semantical rules for the statecharts and the Petri nets keep the syntactic static structure of their models and only change the semantics: in case of statecharts the trigger elements and the current- and new-edges, and in case of Petri nets the tokens. Therefore we can analyze these rules independent of the actual models. For the analysis, we make use of the correspondence nodes which connect statechart and Petri net elements.

We want to show that our model transformation SC2PN is semantics-simulating. This means that each semantical step in a statechart can be simulated in its corresponding Petri net. First, we define the weak simulation relation $\sim$.

Definition 6.20 (Weak simulation relation)
Given a statechart M with states Q_1 in $LTS(M)_{L_S}$ and it corresponding Petri net P with states Q_2 in $LTS(P)_{L_T}$. The relation $\sim \subseteq Q_1 \times Q_2$ is defined as follows: A statechart with semantics $q_1 \in Q_1$ and a marked Petri net $q_2 \in Q_2$ are in correspondence, i.e. $q_1 \sim q_2$, if for each current- or new-edge to a state in q_1 there is a token or marked token, respectively, on this state's place in q_2 which is connected via an S-P-node. No other tokens are allowed to appear in the net except for tokens on e-nodes.

Note that the correspondence of states and places via S-P-nodes is unique: whenever an S-P-node is created with our triple rules, also the corresponding state and place are newly created. Obviously, for the initial states ι_1 and ι_2, i.e. the statechart without any current- and next-edges and the Petri net without tokens, these are in $\sim$.

In the following, we analyze the different semantical rules of the state-charts semantics and show their counterparts in the Petri net semantics.

For the different rules or their application as long as possible of the statecharts semantics we find a corresponding rule or rule sequence in the firing semantics of the Petri nets. In the following, we first analyze these correspondences and later put them together to show the semantical simulation in Thm. 6.21.

The rules setSub and transSub do not change the pointer edges, which means that for a state q_1 with $q_1 \sim q_2$ and any application of this rules leading to a state q_1' we have that $q_1' \sim q_2$. In the following, we assume that our considered statechart models are equipped with all sub-edges.

For the rule init, only new-edges are created by this rule while the behavior-pointer to the state machine has no counter part in the Petri net. All these states with new-edges have corresponding places that are open by construction. Thus, if we apply for each match m of the multi rule the rule +pm to the corresponding open place, all places corresponding to new-states hold a marked token. Thus, if we have a state q_1 with $q_1 \sim q_2$ and a transformation $q_1 \xrightarrow{\text{init}} q_1'$, the proper application of $q_2 \xRightarrow{\text{+pm}}{}^* q_2'$ leads to $q_1' \sim q_2'$.

With enterRegions!, all initial substates of a new-state as well as its superstates and their initial substates are set to current states, while double edges are deleted. With the kernel rule, a new-state is made current and using the multi rule p_{41} its directly contained initial states become new. Moreover, if the superstate of the new-state is not current or new, also this superstate is set to new. Applying enterRegions as long as possible sets all these new-states to current-states. As above, for all these states the corresponding places are open. Thus, we apply the rule +pm to the corresponding open places such that in the end all places corresponding to new- or current-states hold a marked or unmarked token. Applying the interaction scheme unmark unmarks all marked tokens. Now, double tokens are delete by -p. In the end, if we have a state q_1 with $q_1 \sim q_2$ and a transformation $q_1 \xrightarrow{\text{enterRegions!}} q_1'$, the proper application of $q_2 \xRightarrow{\text{+pm}}{}^* \xrightarrow{\text{unmark}} \xRightarrow{\text{-p}}{}^* q_2'$ leads to $q_1' \sim q_2'$.

Altogether, this means that we have for the initialization step:

(∗) if $q_1 \sim q_2$ with a transformation $q_1 \xrightarrow{\text{setSub!}} \xrightarrow{\text{transSub!}} \xrightarrow{\text{init}} \xrightarrow{\text{enterRegions!}} q_1'$ we find a transformation $q_2 \xRightarrow{\text{+pm}}{}^* \xRightarrow{\text{+pm}}{}^* \xrightarrow{\text{unmark}} \xRightarrow{\text{-p}}{}^* q_2'$ with $q_1' \sim q_2'$.

The rule leaveState1 deletes the current-edge to a state 1 which has a region R without current states. In the corresponding Petri net, the region R has a T3-transition with the state 1's place as a pre-place, which currently holds a token, and all its substates as inhibitors, which are currently token-free. A special case is the e-place: as described later, it can only hold a token if the exit-transition of the state 1 is activated. A token on the e-place can only be put there firing a T1-transition, which corresponds to the rule leaveRegions. But since the rule leaveState1 is applied before leaveRegions and exit-transitions are handled with priority, if leaveState1 is applicable this e-place cannot hold a token. Thus, leaveState1 is applicable if and only if fireT3 is applicable. For $q_1 \sim q_2$ this leads to the transformations $q_1 \xrightarrow{\text{leaveState1}} q_1'$ and $q_2 \xrightarrow{\text{fireT3}} q_2'$ with $q_1' \sim q_2'$. Moreover, leaveState1! and fireT3! correspond to each other, i. e. $q_1 \xrightarrow{\text{leaveState1!}} q_1'$ and $q_2 \xrightarrow{\text{fireT3!}} q_2'$ imply $q_1' \sim q_2'$.

With leaveState2, the current-edges of all current substates of a non-current state 1 are deleted. In the corresponding Petri net, each one of these substates is the pre-place of a T2-transition with the superstate 1 as inhibitor. Thus, if 1 is not current there is no token on this place and fireT2 is activated. A single application of fireT2 corresponds to one application of the multi rule. Thus, for $q_1 \sim q_2$ we have that $q_1 \xrightarrow{\text{leaveState2}} q_1'$ implies a transformation $q_2 \xrightarrow{\text{fireT2}}^{*} q_2'$ with $q_1' \sim q_2'$. Moreover, leaveState2! and fireT2! correspond to each other.

Using leaveRegions, for a current state 1 where no other but all final substates are current the current-edges to these final states are deleted. Note that the state itself stays current. If it has an exit-transition, a new trigger element is added to the event queue. Since the state 1 is a superstate, there is a corresponding T1-transition which has all non-final substates as inhibitors and all final substates as pre-places. If all final states are current, the corresponding places hold tokens. All non-final places are not current and their places are token-free. This means that this transition is activated. When firing, it deletes the tokens on the places of the final states and, in addition, adds a token to an eventual e-place of the state 1. Thus, for $q_1 \sim q_2$ leaveRegions can be applied to q_1 if and only if fireT1 can be applied to q_2. This leads to the transformations $q_1 \xrightarrow{\text{leaveRegions}} q_1'$ and $q_2 \xrightarrow{\text{fireT1}} q_2'$ with $q_1' \sim q_2'$, and moreover leaveRegions! and fireT1! correspond to each other.

For an application of the interaction scheme transitionStep, we find the first trigger element in the event queue and compute the corresponding state transitions. In the Petri net, we first have to fire +p to mark the place corresponding to this event, which is connected by an E-P-node. This place is uniquely constructed by the triple rule newTransitionNewEvent, which can only be applied once due to the application condition. Additional events with the same name can only be constructed using `newTransitionOld-Event`, which connects these new events to the same place. Now we have to show that each match m_i which is constructed for the interaction scheme leading to a maximal disjoint matching corresponds to an application of the rule `fireT`. Then, we delete the token on the event's place with `-p`. It follows that for a state q_1 with $q_1 \sim q_2$ and a transformation $q_1 \xrightarrow{\text{transitionStep}} q_1'$ the application of $q_2 \xrightarrow{+p} \xrightarrow{\text{fireT!}} \xrightarrow{-p} q_2'$ leads to $q_1' \sim q_2'$.

Now consider the construction of a weakly disjoint matching $(m_0, m_1, \dots, m_n)$. From Fact 4.16 and Thm. 4.17 we know that the application of the amalgamated rule $\tilde{p}_s$ to a graph G via a match $\tilde{m}$ is equivalent to the transformation $G \xrightarrow{p_0, m_0} G_0 \xrightarrow{\overline{p_1}, \overline{m_1}} G_1 \Rightarrow \dots \xrightarrow{\overline{p_n}, \overline{m_n}} G_n$, where $\overline{p_i}$ is the (weak) complement rule of p_i. We show that we find a corresponding firing sequence $P \xrightarrow{+p} P_0 \xrightarrow{\text{fireT}} P_1 \Rightarrow \dots \xrightarrow{\text{fireT}} P_n \xrightarrow{-p} P'$ such that $G \sim P$ implies that $G_n \sim P'$ and $G_i \sim_{te} P_i$ for $i = 0, \dots, n$, where $G \sim_{te} P$ means that $G \sim P_{te}$ and P_{te} emerges from p by deleting the token on the trigger element te's place.

If $G \sim P$ this means that all `current-` or `new-states` in G have a token or marked token on their corresponding places. As already described, the application of the kernel rule p_{50} leads to the transformation $G \xrightarrow{p_{50}} G_0$ and the deletion of the first trigger element in G_0. With `+p`, we add a token on this trigger element te's place. Thus, $G_0 \sim_{te} P_0$.

For $G_i \sim_{te} P_i$, consider the next match m_{i+1} which satisfies the application conditions ac_{51} or ac_{52}, respectively. The complement rules $\overline{p_{51}}$ and $\overline{p_{52}}$ are similar to p_{51} and p_{52} except for the trigger element 2 in the left-hand sides. With $G_i \xrightarrow{\overline{p_{i+1}}, \overline{m_{i+1}}} G_{i+1}$ we consider a state transition, delete the `current-edge` to the state $m_{i+1}(4)$ and add a `new-edge` to the state $m_{i+1}(6)$. We have to show that `fireT` is applicable to the T-transition t corresponding via a T-T-node to the considered transition in the statechart model. A T-transition together with its corresponding transition in the statechart model can only be created by one of the four `newTransition*` rules. Moreover, contextual places can be added with `newGuard` and `nextGuard`. The following places may appear in the environment of the transition t:

- t has exactly one pre-place corresponding to the `begin-state` and on post-place corresponding to the `end-state`. Since $G_i \sim_{te} P_i$ and m_{i+1} is a valid match, the `begin-state` is current and its place holds a token. When applying the rule, this `current-edge` is deleted and the `end-state` is connected to the pointer by a `new-edge`. With `fireT`, the token on the pre-place is deleted and a marked token is added to the post-place.

- The event te's place is a contextual place for t and holds a token as described above.

- A guard state 2 corresponds directly to its place being a contextual place of t. This place holds a token if the corresponding state is current, which is true due to the application condition $\forall(b_{51}, \exists c_{51})$ of transitionStep.

- If t is an exit-transition m_{i+1} is only applicable if no substates are current due to the application condition $\neg\exists a_{51}$. In this case, t has an e-place as a pre-place connected to its begin-state. An exit-trigger event can only be obtained by a previous application of the rule leaveRegions. This means that in the Petri net the corresponding T1-transition has fired and the e-place holds a token, which is deleted when firing t.

Altogether, t is activated and its firing corresponds to one application of the complement rules $\overline{p_{51}}$ or $\overline{p_{52}}$. This means that we have a transformation $P_i \xrightarrow{\text{fireT}} P_{i+1}$ with $G_{i+1} \sim_{te} P_{i+1}$. After n applications of fireT, we have that $G_n \sim_{te} P_n$. Moreover, no other T-transition is activated, otherwise we would find an additional match for the multi rules. With -p, we delete the token on the event's place, i.e. $P_n \xrightarrow{\text{-p}} P'$, and it follows that $G_n \sim P'$ as required.

Combining all these steps, we have for a semantical step that:

$(**)$ for $q_1 \sim q_2$ and the transition step $q_1 \xrightarrow{\text{transitionStep}} \xrightarrow{\text{enterRegions!}} \xrightarrow{\text{leaveState1!}} \xrightarrow{\text{leaveState2!}} \xrightarrow{\text{leaveRegions!}} q_1'$ we have a transformation $q_2 \xrightarrow{\text{+p}} \xrightarrow{\text{fireT!}} \xrightarrow{\text{-p}} \xrightarrow{\text{+pm}} \xrightarrow{\text{unmark}}^* \xrightarrow{\text{-p}}^* \xrightarrow{\text{fireT3!}} \xrightarrow{\text{fireT2!}} \xrightarrow{\text{fireT1!}} q_2'$ with $q_1' \sim q_2'$.

With these considerations we can show that our model transformation SC2PN is semantics-simulating.

Theorem 6.21 (Semantics-simulating model transformation)
The model transformation from statecharts to Petri nets defined in Section 5.3 is semantics-simulating w. r. t. the operational semantics of statecharts defined in Subsection 4.2.3 and the operational semantics for Petri nets in Subsection 6.3.1.

PROOF As shown in Ex. 6.17, for the labeled transition systems of statecharts semantics there are only two labels: the initialization and a semantical step. Both are mapped with the labeling function to the label step. For the Petri net rules, except for unmark, which is mapped to step, all rules are mapped to τ.

According to $(*)$, we have for the initialization step that, if $q_1 \sim q_2$ with a transformation $q_1 \xrightarrow{\texttt{setSub!}} \xrightarrow{\texttt{transSub!}} \xrightarrow{\texttt{init}} \xrightarrow{\texttt{enterRegions!}} q_1'$ we find a transformation $q_2 \xrightarrow{\texttt{+pm}}^* \xrightarrow{\texttt{+pm}}^* \xrightarrow{\texttt{unmark}} \xrightarrow{\texttt{-p}}^* q_2'$ with $q_1' \sim q_2'$ and $q_2 \xRightarrow{step} q_2'$. Similarly, according to $(**)$, for $q_1 \sim q_2$ and the semantical step $q_1 \xRightarrow{\texttt{transitionStep}} \xrightarrow{\texttt{enterRegions!}} \xrightarrow{\texttt{leaveState1!}}$ $\xrightarrow{\texttt{leaveState2!}} \xrightarrow{\texttt{leaveRegions!}} q_1'$ we have a transformation $q_2 \xrightarrow{\texttt{+p}} \xrightarrow{\texttt{fireT!}} \xrightarrow{\texttt{-p}} \xrightarrow{\texttt{+pm}}^*$ $\xrightarrow{\texttt{unmark}} \xrightarrow{\texttt{-p}}^* \xrightarrow{\texttt{fireT3!}} \xrightarrow{\texttt{fireT2!}} \xrightarrow{\texttt{fireT1!}} q_2'$ with $q_1' \sim q_2'$ and $q_2 \xRightarrow{step} q_2'$.

This means that the relation $\sim$ as constructed above is a weak simulation relation and our model transformation SC2PN from statecharts to Petri nets is semantics-simulating.

Obviously, this choice of labeling functions does not lead to weak bisimularity of our model transformation. While the firing of the transitions basically corresponds to rules in the statechart semantics, the main problem which prevents weak bisimilarity are the open places in the Petri net, which may get or loose tokens any time. But these are difficult to circumvent: while firing an open place corresponding to an event could be handled, we have to close the places corresponding to states. This means that we had to introduce new transitions which fire corresponding to the application of the interaction scheme enterRegions!.

Such transitions are difficult to construct, since the actual matches for enterRegions depend on the current states. Thus, we could either construct one transition for each possible current state situation – which is difficult to design and has to be constructed after all other items, because it depends on the whole superstate hierarchy – or we could construct smaller transitions whose firing is somehow controlled. Both ways are difficult to handle and do not necessarily lead to weak bisimilarity. In this case, it seems more reasonable to conclude that Petri nets are not an adequate target language for weak bisimilarity to statecharts. Nevertheless, the analysis of the Petri net model, for example regarding deadlocks, may be helpful for the analysis of the corresponding statechart model.

Example 6.22

We want to analyze the simulation of the statecharts semantics in the Petri net in more detail. Consider our example statechart ProdCons in Fig. 4.21 and the corresponding Petri net PN_{PC} in Fig. 5.20. We have that ProdCons $\sim PN_{PC}$ because we have no current- or new-edges in the statechart and no tokens in the Petri net. In Subsection 4.2.3, we have described some semantical steps in ProdCons as summarized in Fig. 4.30. These steps can be simulated in the Petri net as explained in the following.

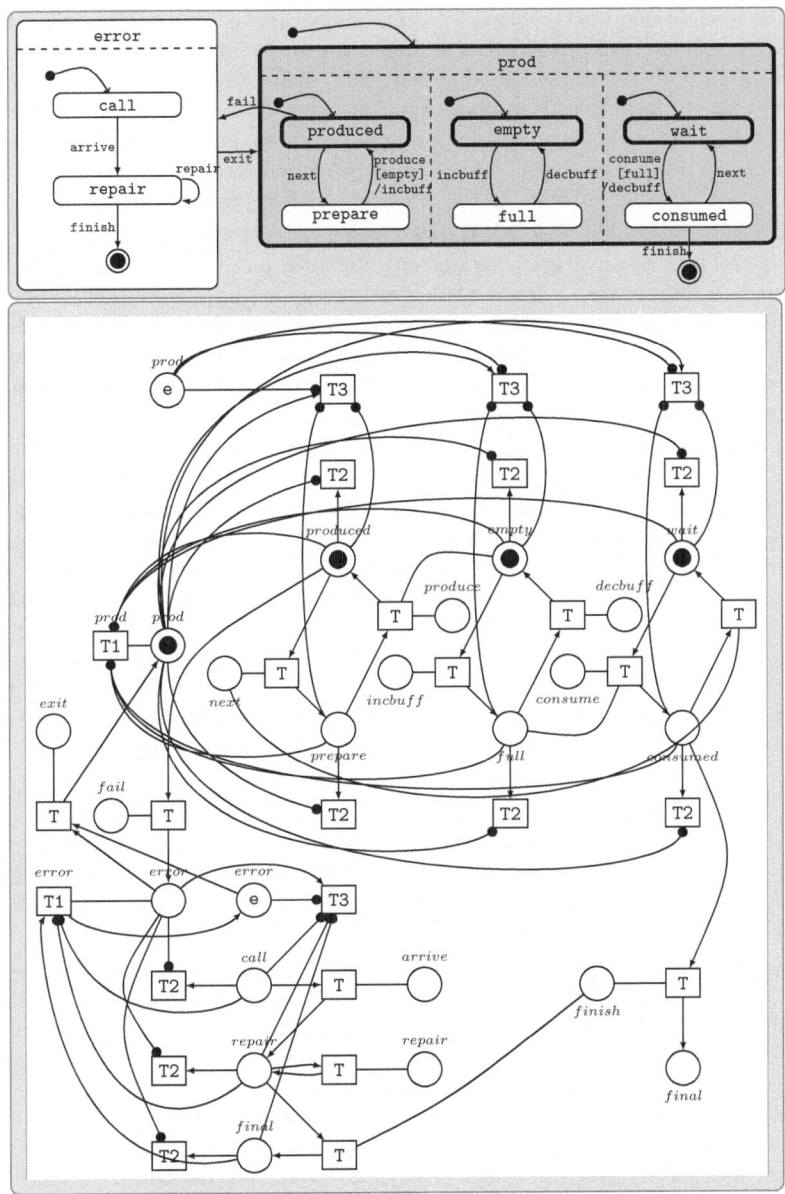

Figure 6.4: **ProdCons** and PN_{PC} after the initialization step

First, the initialization takes place. As mentioned above, the applications of setSub and transSub do not lead to a changed semantics of the statechart and thus no rules have to be applied in the Petri net. After the application of the interaction scheme init there is a new-pointer to the prod-state. Firing the rule +pm puts a marked token on the corresponding place. Now the interaction scheme enterRegions leads to new-edges to the states produced, empty, and wait, and the edge to prod becomes current. In the Petri net, we fire +pm three times leading to marked tokens in the places prod, produced, empty, and wait.

Applying the interaction scheme enterRegions three more times leads to current edges to all four states. With unmark, the corresponding places in the Petri net now hold unmarked tokens. This means that the statechart and the Petri net are actually in the simulation relation after this initialization step as shown in Fig. 6.4, where the current states in the statecharts are marked by thicker lines and darker background.

For the first semantical step using the trigger element next, the application of the interaction scheme transitionStep deletes this trigger element and the current-edge to the state produced, and creates a new-edge to the state prepare. In the end, this new-edge is changed to a current-edge by enterRegions leading to the current states prod, prepare, empty, and wait. In the Petri net, with +p we put a token on the next-place. Now the T-transition with next and produced as pre-places is activated and may fire using the interaction scheme fireT. This leads to a marked token on prepare and unchanged, unmarked tokens on the places next, prod, empty, and wait. No other T-transition is activated. Deleting the next-token and unmarking the token on prepare leads to the resulting Petri net simulation step with unmarked tokens on the places prod, prepare, empty, and wait corresponding to the statechart's current semantical state.

We could carry this on for the other semantical steps described in Subsection 4.2.3. Mainly, whenever one of the interaction schemes leaveState1, leaveState2, or leaveRegions is applied in the statechart semantics, the corresponding T3-, T2- or T1-transition is fired in the Petri net. To illustrate this, we skip until before the execution of the trigger element fail.

This trigger element and the current-edge to produced are deleted, and a new-edge is added to error. With enterRegions!, this new-edge becomes current and also the state call. Then there is a match for leaveState1 deleting the current-edge from prod, and leaveState2 deletes the current-edges to empty and consumed. The result is that only the states error and call are current now. In the Petri net, we first used +p to put a token on the fail-place. Now there is a T-transition whose firing puts a marked token on error and deleted the one from produced. No other T-transition is activated, thus we delete the token on fail. With +pm and unmark, we add a new token on the place call and unmark both new tokens. Now the T3-transition corresponding to the first region of pros as activated, since all inhibiting places are token-free and with fireT3 we delete the token on `prod`. Afterwards, the T2-transitions for `empty` and `consumed` fire using `fireT2` twice, which leads to tokens on `error` and `call`. No more transitions are activated, and the marking of the Petri net corresponds to the semantical state of the statechart.

6.4 On-the-Fly Construction of Model Transformations

Up to now, the construction of correct model transformation sequences is very complex. In order to construct a model transformation sequence $(G_S, G_0 \xrightarrow{tr_F^*} G_n, G_T)$ from a given source model G_S there are two alternatives [EEE[+]07, EHS09]: Either we construct a parsing sequence $\varnothing \xrightarrow{tr_S^*} G_0$ with $G_{0,S} = G_S$ first and then try to extend it to a match consistent transformation sequence $\varnothing \xrightarrow{tr_S^*} G_0 \xrightarrow{tr_F^*} G_n$, or we construct a forward transformation sequence $G_0 \xrightarrow{tr_F^*} G_n$ directly and check afterwards whether it is source consistent. Even though source consistency is a sufficient and necessary condition for the correctness and completeness of model transformations based on triple graph grammars, this means that many candidates of forward transformation sequences may have to be constructed before a source consistent one is found.

Therefore, we introduce the notion of partial source consistency which enables us to construct consistent model transformations on-the-fly instead of analyzing consistency of completed transformations. Partial source consistency of a forward transformation sequence, which is necessary for a complete model transformation, requires that there has to be a corresponding source transformation sequence such that both transformation sequences are partially match consistent. This means that the source components of the matches of the forward transformation sequence are defined by the co-matches of the source transformation sequence.

Definition 6.23 (Partial match and source consistency)

Consider a set of triple rules TR with S-consistent application conditions. A transformation sequence $\varnothing = G_{00} \xrightarrow{tr_S^*} G_{n0} \xrightarrow{g_n}$

$$
\begin{array}{ccccccc}
L_{i,S} & \xrightarrow{tr_{i,S}} & R_{i,S} \hookleftarrow & \longrightarrow & L_{i,F} & \xrightarrow{tr_{i,F}} & R_{i,F} \\
\downarrow{m_{i,S}} & (1_i) & \downarrow{n_{i,S}} & (2_i) & \downarrow{m_{i,F}} & (3_i) & \downarrow{n_{i,F}} \\
G_{i-1\,0} & \xrightarrow{t_{i,S}} & G_{i\,0} \hookleftarrow_{g_i} & G_0 \hookrightarrow & G_{i-1} & \xrightarrow{t_{i,F}} & G_i
\end{array}
$$

$G_0 \xrightarrow{tr_F^*} G_n$ defined by the pushout diagrams (1_i) and (3_i) for $i = 1 \dots n$ with $G_{0,C} = G_{0,T} = \varnothing$ and inclusion $g_n : G_{n0} \hookrightarrow G_0$ is called *partially match consistent* if the diagram (2_i) commutes for all i, which means that the source component of the forward match $m_{i,F}$ is determined by the co-match $n_{i,S}$ of the corresponding step of the source transformation sequence with $g_i = g_n \circ t_{n,S} \dots t_{i-1,S}$.

A forward transformation sequence $G_0 \xrightarrow{tr_F^*} G_n$ is partially source consistent if there is a source transformation sequence $\varnothing = G_{00} \xrightarrow{tr_S^*} G_{n0}$ with inclusion $G_{n0} \xoverset{g_n}{\hookrightarrow} G_0$ such that $G_{00} \xrightarrow{tr_S^*} G_{n0} \xoverset{g_n}{\hookrightarrow} G_0 \xrightarrow{tr_F^*} G_n$ is partially match consistent.

Example 6.24
Consider as G_0 the triple graph with our statechart model depicted in Fig. 4.21 in concrete and in Fig. 4.24 in abstract syntax in the source component and with empty connection and target components. Consider the first seven rules of our example transformation in Section 5.3:

```
start;
newRegionSM(sname="prod");
newRegionS(sname="produced");
newRegionS(sname="empty");
newRegionS(sname="wait");
newStateSM(sname="error");
newRegionS(sname="call");
```

If we apply the corresponding source rule sequence to the start graph $G_{00} = \varnothing$, we obtain a graph G_{70} with the statechart in Fig. 6.2 in the source component.

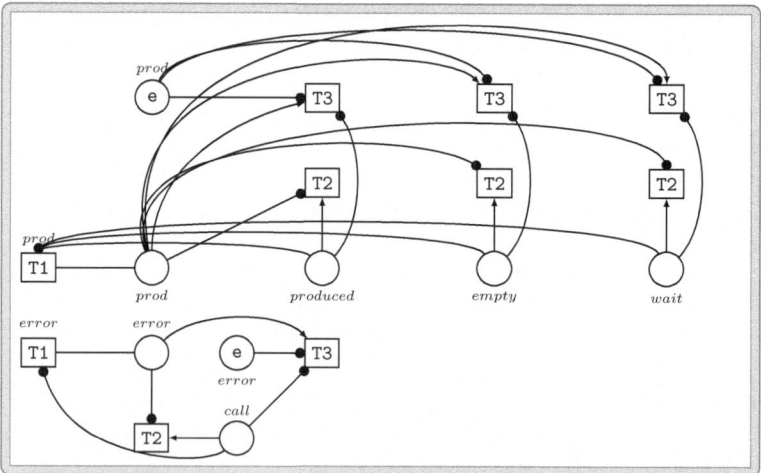

Figure 6.5: The Petri net corresponding to the partial transformation

In addition, we can apply the corresponding forward rule sequence to the triple graph G_0 leading to the triple graph G_7 with $G_{7,S} = G_{0,S}$ and the Petri net in the target component depicted in Fig. 6.5.

All diagrams (2_i) commute for $i = 1, \ldots, 7$ because the matches of the source components of the forward rules are determined by the co-matches of the source rules. Thus, $\varnothing = G_{00} \overset{tr_S^*}{\Longrightarrow} G_{70} \overset{g7}{\hookrightarrow} G_0 \overset{tr_F^*}{\Longrightarrow} G_7$ for the above rule sequence is partially match consistent, and therefore $G_0 \overset{tr_F^*}{\Longrightarrow} G_7$ is partially source consistent.

In order to provide an improved construction of source consistent forward transformation sequences we characterize valid matches by introducing the following notion of forward consistent matches. The formal condition of a forward consistent match is given by a pullback diagram which, intuitively, specifies that the effective elements of the forward rule are matched for the first time in the forward transformation sequence.

Definition 6.25 (Forward consistent match)

Given a partially match consistent transformation sequence $\varnothing = G_{00} \overset{tr_S^*}{\Longrightarrow} G_{n-10}$ $\overset{g_{n-1}}{\hookrightarrow} G_0 \overset{tr_F^*}{\Longrightarrow} G_{n-1}$ then a match $m_{n,F}$: $L_{n,F} \to G_{n-1}$ for $tr_{n,F} : L_{n,F} \to R_{n,F}$ is called *forward consistent* if there is a source match $m_{n,S}$ such that diagram (1) is a pull-

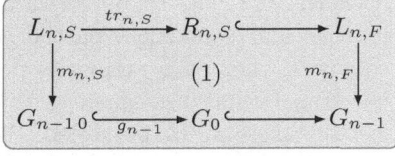

back and the matches $m_{n,F}$ and $m_{n,S}$ satisfy the corresponding application conditions.

Remark 6.26

The pullback property of (1) means that the intersection of the match $m_{n,F}(L_{n,F})$ and the source graph G_{n-10} constructed so far is equal to $m_{n,F}(L_{n,S})$, the match restricted to $L_{n,S}$, i.e. we have

$$(2) : m_{n,F}(L_{n,F}) \cap G_{n-10} = m_{n,F}(L_{n,F}).$$

This condition can be checked easily and $m_{n,S} : L_{n,S} \to G_{n-10}$ is uniquely defined by the restriction of $m_{n,F} : L_{n,F} \to G_{n-1}$. Furthermore, as a direct consequence of (2) we have

$$(3) : m_{n,F}(L_{n,F} \setminus L_{n,S}) \cap G_{n-10} = \varnothing.$$

On the one hand, the source elements of $L_{n,F} \setminus L_{n,S}$ – called effective elements – are the elements to be transformed by the next step of the forward transformation sequence. On the other hand, G_{n-10} contains all elements that were matched by the preceding forward steps, because matches of the forward transformation sequence coincide on the source part with co-matches of the source transformation sequence. Hence, condition (3) means that the effective elements were not matched before, i.e. they do not belong to G_{n-10}.

Example 6.27

Consider the partially match consistent transformation sequence $\varnothing = G_{00}$ $\overset{tr_S^*}{\Longrightarrow} G_{70} \overset{g7}{\hookrightarrow} G_0 \overset{tr_F^*}{\Longrightarrow} G_7$ from Ex. 6.24. For the application of the next rule newStateS(name= "prepare") we find a match $m_{8,F}$ for the corresponding forward rule mapping the state 1 to the prod-state and the other state in $R_{4,S}$ to the prepare-state in the source component of G_7, the place and transition in $L_{4,T}$ to the place connected to prod and the T3-transition of produced in the target component, and corresponding mappings of the S-P- and R-T3-nodes in $L_{4,C}$. For this match, we can find a corresponding match $m_{8,S}$ of the source rule of newStateS mapping 1 to the prod-state and 2 to the region which already contains the state produced. The corresponding diagram is a pullback and the matches satisfy the application conditions. Thus, $m_{8,F}$ is a forward consistent match and leads to the partially match consistent transformation sequence $\varnothing = G_{00} \overset{tr_S^*}{\Longrightarrow} G_{70} \xrightarrow{\text{newStateS}_S} G_{80} \overset{g8}{\hookrightarrow} G_0 \overset{tr_F^*}{\Longrightarrow} G_7 \xrightarrow{\text{newStateS}_F} G_8$.

In the following improved construction of model transformations, we check the matches to be forward consistent. The construction proceeds stepwise and constructs partial source consistent forward transformation sequences. For each step, the possible matches of rules are filtered such that transformation sequences that will not lead to source consistency are rejected as soon as possible. Simultaneously, the corresponding source transformation sequences of the forward transformation sequences are constructed on-the-fly. Intuitively, this can be seen as an on-the-fly parsing of the source model. This means that the matches of the forward transformation sequence are controlled by an automatic parsing of the source model, which can be deduced by inverting the source sequence. This allows us to incrementally extend partially source consistent transformation sequences and we can derive complete source consistent transformation sequences, which ensure that all elements of the source model are translated exactly once. Thus, re-computations of model transformations may be avoided. We extend the results from [EEHP09], where triple rules with NACs are handled, to the case of triple rules with arbitrary S-consistent application conditions.

Theorem 6.28 (On-the-fly construction of model transformations)
Given a triple graph G_0 with $G_{0,C} = G_{0,T} = \varnothing$, execute the following steps:

1. Start with $G_{00} = \varnothing$ and $g_0 : G_{00} \hookrightarrow G_0$.

2. For $n > 0$ and an already computed partially source consistent transformation sequence $s = (G_0 \overset{tr_F^*}{\Longrightarrow} G_{n-1})$ with $\varnothing = G_{00} \overset{tr_S^*}{\Longrightarrow} G_{n-10}$ and embedding $g_{n-1} : G_{n-10} \hookrightarrow G_0$ find a (not yet considered) forward consistent match for some $tr_{n,F}$ leading to a partially source consistent transformation

sequence $G_0 \xrightarrow{tr_F^*} G_{n-1} \xrightarrow{tr_{n,F}} G_n$ with $G_{00} \xrightarrow{tr_S^*} G_{n-1\,0} \xrightarrow{tr_{n,S}} G_{n\,0}$ and embedding $g_n : G_{n\,0} \hookrightarrow G_0$. If there is no such match, s cannot be extended to a source consistent transformation sequence. Repeat until $g_n = id_{G_0}$ or no new forward consistent matches can be found.

3. If the procedure terminates with $g_n = id_{G_0}$ then $G_0 \xrightarrow{tr_F^*} G_n$ is source consistent leading to a model transformation sequence $(G_S, G_0 \xrightarrow{tr_F^*} G_n, G_T)$ with G_S and G_T being the source and target models of G_0 and G_n.

PROOF This follows directly from the proof in [EEHP09].

If the on-the-fly construction terminates in Step 3, we obtain a source consistent transformation sequence $G_0 \xrightarrow{tr_F^*} G_n$ and therefore the resulting model transformation sequence $(G_S, G_0 \xrightarrow{tr_F^*} G_n, G_T)$ is correct, complete, and in the case that all source rules are creating also terminating. The construction does not restrict the choice of a suitable n, $tr_{n,F}$, and match in Step 2. Hence, different search algorithms are possible, e.g.

- *Depth First:* If we increase n after every iteration, and only decrease n by 1 if no more new forward consistent matches can be found, a depth-first search is performed.

- *Breadth First:* If we increase n only after all forward consistent matches for n are considered, the construction performs a breadth-first search.

Depending on the type of the model transformation, other search strategies may be reasonable.

In the following, we describe how to improve efficiency by analyzing parallel independence of extensions. Two partially match consistent transformation sequences which differ only in the last rule application are parallel independent if the last rule applications are parallel independent both for the source and forward transformation sequence, and, in addition, if the embeddings into the given graph G_0 are compatible.

Definition 6.29 (Parallel independence of extensions)
Two partially match consistent transformation sequences $\varnothing = G_{00} \xrightarrow{tr_S^*} G_{n\,0}$ $\xrightarrow{tr_{1,S}} G_{n+1\,0} \overset{g_{n+1}}{\hookrightarrow} G_0 \xrightarrow{tr_F^*} G_n \xrightarrow{tr_{1,F}} G_{n+1}$ and $\varnothing = G_{00} \xrightarrow{tr_S^*} G_{n\,0} \xrightarrow{tr_{2,S}}$ $G'_{n+1\,0} \overset{g'_{n+1}}{\hookrightarrow} G_0 \xrightarrow{tr_F^*} G_n \xrightarrow{tr_{2,F}} G'_{n+1}$ are *parallel independent* if $G_{n\,0} \xrightarrow{tr_{1,S}}$ $G_{n+1\,0}$ and $G_{n\,0} \xrightarrow{tr_{2,S}} G'_{n+1\,0}$ as well as $G_n \xrightarrow{tr_{1,F}} G_{n+1}$ and $G_n \xrightarrow{tr_{2,F}} G'_{n+1}$

are parallel independent leading to the diagrams (1_S) and (1_F), and the diagram (2) is a pullback.

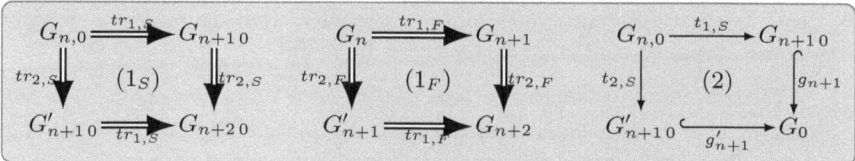

In this case of parallel independence, both extensions can be extended both in the source and forward transformation sequences leading to two longer partially match consistent transformation sequences which are switch-equivalent.

Theorem 6.30 (Partial match consistency with parallel independence)
If two partially match consistent transformation sequences $\varnothing = G_{00} \overset{tr_S^*}{\Longrightarrow} G_{n\,0}$ $\overset{tr_{1,S}}{\Longrightarrow} G_{n+1\,0} \overset{g_{n+1}}{\hookrightarrow} G_0 \overset{tr_F^*}{\Longrightarrow} G_n \overset{tr_{1,F}}{\Longrightarrow} G_{n+1}$ and $\varnothing = G_{00} \overset{tr_S^*}{\Longrightarrow} G_{n\,0} \overset{tr_{2,S}}{\Longrightarrow} G'_{n+1\,0} \overset{g'_{n+1}}{\hookrightarrow} G_0 \overset{tr_F^*}{\Longrightarrow} G_n \overset{tr_{2,F}}{\Longrightarrow} G'_{n+1}$ are parallel independent then the following upper and lower transformation sequences are partially match consistent and called *switch equivalent*.

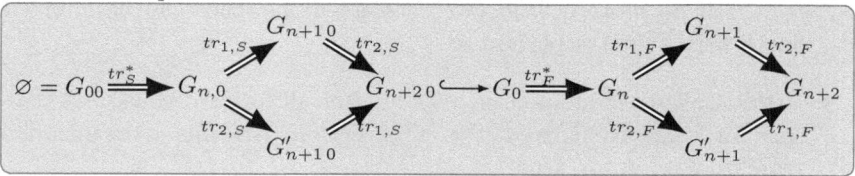

PROOF This follows directly from the proof in [EEHP09].

Example 6.31
In analogy to the partially match consistent transformation sequence $\varnothing = G_{00}$ $\overset{tr_S^*}{\Longrightarrow} G_{7\,0} \overset{\text{newStateS}_S}{\Longrightarrow} G_{8\,0} \overset{g_8}{\hookrightarrow} G_0 \overset{tr_F^*}{\Longrightarrow} G_7 \overset{\text{newStateS}_F}{\Longrightarrow} G_8$ in Ex. 6.27, for the rule newStateS(sname="full") we also find a forward consistent match $m'_{8,F}$ leading to the partially match consistent transformation sequence $\varnothing = G_{00} \overset{tr_S^*}{\Longrightarrow}$ $G_{7\,0} \overset{\text{newStateS}_S}{\Longrightarrow} G'_{8\,0} \overset{g'_8}{\hookrightarrow} G_0 \overset{tr_F^*}{\Longrightarrow} G_7 \overset{\text{newStateS}_F}{\Longrightarrow} G'_8$, where in contrast to the first transformation sequence not the prepare- but the full-state is added and translated. Both applications of newStateS are parallel independent for the source and forward rules, since they do not interfere and only overlap at the super-state prod. Also the corresponding diagram (2) is a pullback, thus both partially match consistent transformation sequences are parallel independent. Applying Thm. 6.30 we obtain partially match consistent transformation sequences

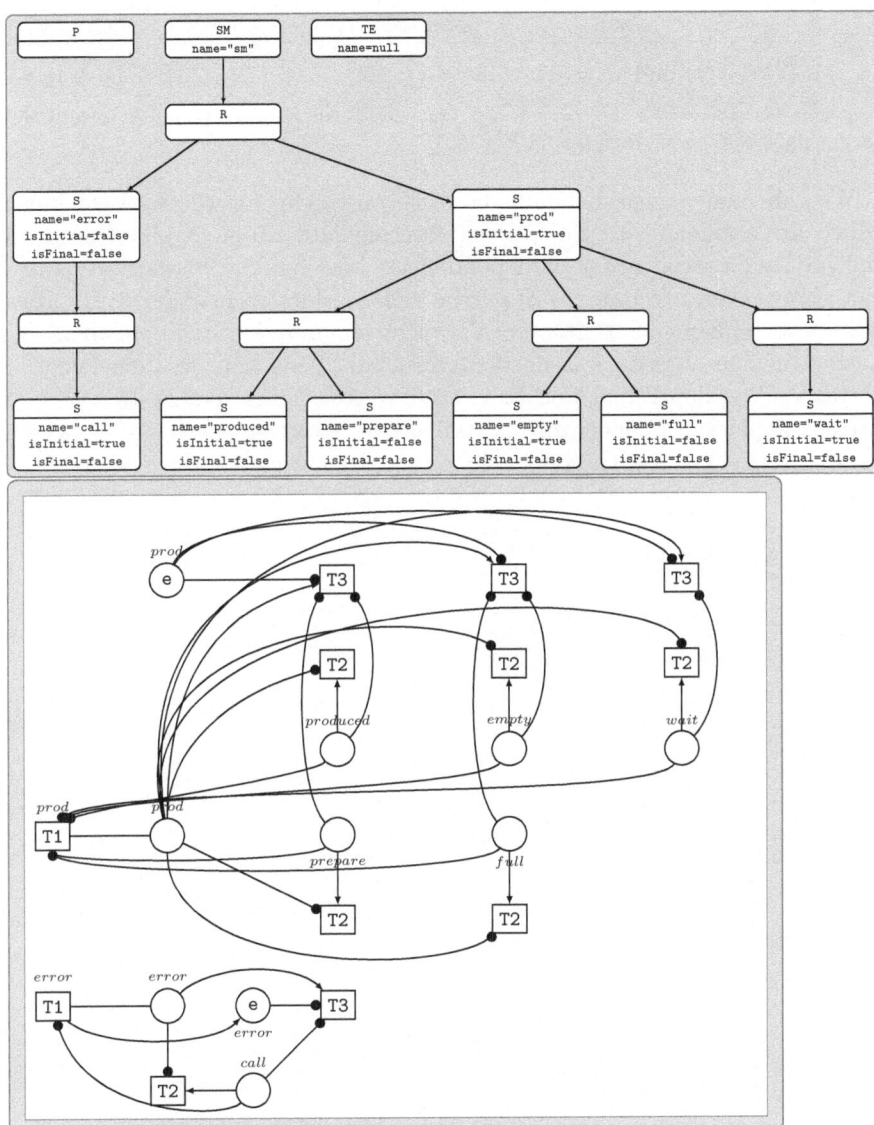

Figure 6.6: The partial models after two more steps

$\varnothing = G_{00} \xrightarrow{tr_S^*} G_{70} \xrightarrow{\text{newStateS}_S} G_{80} \xrightarrow{\text{newStateS}_S} G_{90} \xrightarrow{g9} G_0 \xrightarrow{tr_F^*} G_7 \xrightarrow{\text{newStateS}_F}$
$G_8 \xrightarrow{\text{newStateS}_F} G_9$ and $\varnothing = G_{00} \xrightarrow{tr_S^*} G_{70} \xrightarrow{\text{newStateS}_S} G'_{80} \xrightarrow{\text{newStateS}_S} G_{90} \xrightarrow{g9}$
$G_0 \xrightarrow{tr_F^*} G_7 \xrightarrow{\text{newStateS}_F} G'_8 \xrightarrow{\text{newStateS}_F} G_9$, where the source part of G_{90} and the
target part of G_9 are depicted in Fig. 6.6.

We can analyze parallel independence on-the-fly for the forward steps
which are applicable to the current intermediate triple graph. Based on
the induced partial order of dependencies between the forward steps we
can apply several techniques of partial order reduction in order to improve
efficiency. This means that we can neglect remaining switch-equivalent sequences if one of them has been constructed. This improves efficiency of
corresponding depth-first and breadth-first algorithms. For an overview of
various approaches concerning partial order reduction see [God96], where
benchmarks show that these techniques can dramatically reduce complexity.

7 Conclusion and Future Work

Graphs are a very natural way to explain complex situations on an intuitive level. Hence, they are useful for the visual specification of systems. Nevertheless, it is still complicated to combine an easy, intuitive approach with a formal description leading to a wide range of analysis techniques for complex structures. Graph transformation with its formal background in category theory and its broad theoretical results concerning the behavior of models constitutes a suitable foundation for the description of system behavior and model transformations.

In Section 7.1, we summarize our theoretical results concerning the theory as a formal foundation for model transformations and their analysis. In Chapter 7.2, we analyze how this theory can be used in software engineering and model-driven software development. In Section 7.3, we present different case studies for model transformations. Tools supporting our theory and facilitating the specification and analysis of model transformations are presented in Section 7.4. In Section 7.5, we conclude with future work.

7.1 Theoretical Contributions

In this thesis, we have improved and adapted the theory of graph transformations based on $\mathcal{M}$-adhesive categories in different directions:

In Chapter 3, we have first introduced different kinds of graphs and $\mathcal{M}$-adhesive categories including additional properties that are significant for the theory. Then we extended the Construction Theorem in [EEPT06] to general comma categories which are a suitable foundation to represent different kinds of low- and high-level Petri nets as categorical constructions. Using this theorem we have shown that algebraic high-level schemas, nets, and net systems are $\mathcal{M}$-adhesive categories, as already published in [Pra07, Pra08]. Moreover, we have analyzed how far these additional properties are preserved under different categorical constructions as shown in [PEL08]. In contrast to [EEPT06], where only negative and simple positive applications conditions are considered, we utilize the theory of $\mathcal{M}$-adhesive systems for rules with general application conditions [HP09]. These application conditions are equivalent to first-order logic on graphs and significantly enhance the expressiveness of graph transformations and broaden the application areas of transformations. All the main results for graph transformation are also valid in this framework.

In Chapter 4, we have generalized the theory of amalgamation in [BFH87] to multi-amalgamation in $\mathcal{M}$-adhesive categories. More precisely, the Complement Rule and Amalgamation Theorems in [BFH87] were presented on a set-theoretical basis for pairs of plain graph rules without any application conditions. The Complement Rule and Multi-Amalgamation Theorems in this thesis and published in [GEH10] are valid in $\mathcal{M}$-adhesive categories for n rules with application conditions. Moreover, we have shown a characterization of parallel independence of amalgamable transformations, published in [BEE+10], and introduced interaction schemes and maximal matchings. These generalizations are non-trivial and important for applications of parallel graph transformations to communication-based systems [Tae96], to model transformations from BPMN to BPEL [BEE+10], and for the modeling of the operational semantics of visual languages like Petri nets and statecharts as shown in Section 4.2, where interaction schemes are used to generate multi-amalgamated rules and transformations based on suitable maximal matchings.

In Chapter 5, we have introduced the theory of model transformations based on TGGs for rules with application conditions. This enhances the expressiveness of model transformations including that of the generation of source and/or target languages. As the main result we have shown the composition and decomposition property for triple graph transformations based on rules with S-consistent application conditions. We have discussed in detail a model transformation from statecharts to Petri nets, where the use of application conditions allows to specify and translate more general statecharts then those considered in [EEPT06] using an inplace model transformation.

In Chapter 6, we have presented main results for syntactical correctness, completeness, information preservation, termination, and functional behavior for model transformations based on triple graph transformations extending those for the case without NACs in [EEE+07] and with NACs in [EHS09]. Although the confluence results for $\mathcal{M}$-adhesive systems cannot be assigned directly to triple graph transformations, we have the main advantage that correctness, completeness, and termination results can be shown in general for triple graph transformations. Moreover, triple graphs are a somewhat natural choice for exogenous model transformations, since they explicitly integrate both models which have to be distinguished otherwise by inplace transformations. We have analyzed our example model transformation regarding these properties, and have shown that the operational semantics for statecharts terminates for well-behaved statecharts. Moreover, we have shown how to analyze the semantical correctness of the model transformation based on the semantics defined using amalgamation. The on-the-fly construction of model transformations, already published in [EEHP09], allows a more efficient construction of model transformations based on our results for partial match consistency and forward consistent matches, which can be further improved by using shift-equivalent sequences.

7.2 Relevance for Model-Driven Software Development

As already introduced in Section 2.1, model transformations play a central role in model-driven software development. Different model transformation tasks like refactoring, translation of models to intermediate models, or generating code appear in this context. Since it is natural to consider graphs as the underlying structure of visual models, graph transformation is a natural means to describe the manipulation of graph structures. This is not only true for model-to-model transformation, but also for model-to-text transformations where the code or text parts are described by meta-models. For example, the Java Model Parser and Printer (JaMoPP) [HJSW09] specifies a meta-model for Java which can be used for code generation from UML diagrams to Java code using graph transformation.

While other transformation approaches are often weakly structured, untyped, and do not even guarantee syntactical correctness, graph transformation offers features like typing and node type inheritance [LBE+07] leading automatically to well-typed, consistent models. In [Tae10], the usefulness of graph transformations for model transformation is analyzed in more detail.

In praxis, model transformations are often tested, but seldom verified. The key properties for verification are the following:

- *Consistency.* Models should be structurally and type consistent. This corresponds to syntactical correctness, which is directly implied by model transformations based on triple graph grammars (see Thm. 6.1) and can be checked for other graph transformations using characteristics for well-formedness expressed by graph constraints, which can also be translated to application conditions of rules in many cases.

- *Termination.* Model transformations should be terminating, which cannot be guaranteed for model transformations based on graph transformations in general. But this property can be shown for triple graph grammars (see Thm 6.8) or using several termination criteria [EEPT06, VVE+06].

- *Uniqueness of Results.* The model transformation of a source model should lead to a unique target model, either with respect to isomorphisms of target models or semantical equivalence. While the semantical equivalence of target models is often difficult to analyze, there are practical results to show the isomorphism of models. A local confluence analysis of the model transformations rules using critical pairs leads, together with termination, to confluence of the model transformation and thus to functional behavior.

- *Preservation of Semantics.* Model transformations should preserve certain semantical properties of the source model in the target model. While some approaches use model checking [RSV04] oder theorem provers [Str08], a more promising approach seems to be to discover a relation between the semantical rules of the source and target models as shown for our case study in Subsection 6.3.2 or proposed in [EE08] for a very restricted set of rules and models.

Graph transformation offers a broad range of analysis methods for the verification of model transformations. With the Eclipse Modeling Framework (EMF) [SBPM08], a quasi-standard modeling technology has evolved as an implementation approach, where EMF models can be considered as graphs with a spanning tree or forest defining special containment relations. EMF model transformations can be seen as graph transformations with special kinds of rules that do not destroy the spanning containment tree or forest. As already shown in [BET10], also amalgamated rules can be implemented for EMF transformations.

Altogether, the EMF framework reveals that the formal concepts of graph transformation can be well applied in a practical setting for model-driven software development. They are an essential foundation including a mature theory for a consistent analysis and correctness of software systems based on algebraic graph and model transformations.

7.3 Case Studies

In this thesis, we have deliberately chosen a very complex and difficult main example, the model transformation SC2PN from UML statecharts to Petri nets, for a feasibility study to show that our theory can even be applied in such challenging cases. In our work, other case studies based on triple graph transformations occur, which could be analyzed accordingly, where the analysis is easier since the model transformations can be defined more direct and the semantics have a closer relation.

- SC2PN. For the definition of statecharts, which are a variant of UML statecharts including orthogonal regions and nested states, we have introduced their syntax in Subsection 4.2.2 and their operational semantics using the concept of amalgamated graph transformation in Subsection 4.2.3. For this semantics, we have shown that a semantical step is terminating for well-behaved statecharts in Thm. 6.12. While a general operational semantics for elementary Petri nets is defined in Subsection 4.2.1, a more specific one adapted for the model transformation is used for Petri nets with inhibitor and contextual arcs and open places in Subsection 6.3.1. Both specifications use amalgamated graph transformation.

  In Section 5.3, we have specified the model transformation SC2PN using triple graph transformations with application conditions. First, the triple rules are defined that construct both the source and target models simultaneously. The derived forward rules express the actual model transformation. In Section 6.1, we have shown that this model transformation is syntactically correct and complete w. r. t. the target language of Petri nets, and moreover backward information preserving. We have shown SC-termination and functional behavior of the model transformation SC2PN in Section 6.2 and have argued for semantical simulation in Thm. 6.21. While all other results are general results for a certain class of triple graph transformations, this last result heavily depends on a thorough investigation of the involved semantical rules and cannot be easily generalized to other model transformations.

- CD2RDBM. In [BRST05], a case study from class diagrams to relational database models is introduced. This case study has become well-established in the model transformation community, with lots of different implementations and analysis results. In [TEG⁺05], we have implemented this case study with our tool AGG and compared this solution to other implementations. In [EEHP09], the optimization of the construction of model transformations based on the on-the-fly construction has been demonstrated on this example. Moreover, it has been shown that the model transformation is syntactically correct, complete, and SC-terminating.

- AD2CSP. In [BEH07], a case study from a simplified version of activity diagrams with only actions, binary decisions, and merges to communicating sequential processes (CSP) was proposed in a tool contest. We have implemented this case study in [EP08] using triple graph grammars. Moreover, with the use of special *kernel elements* and derived negative application conditions we were able to show that this model transformation is terminating and confluent, i. e. has functional behavior. Both source and target models could be equipped with semantics, where it should be possible to show bisimilarity with the methods proposed in this thesis.

- BPMN2BPEL. In [ODHA06], a case study from the Business Process Modeling Notation (BPMN) to executable processes formulated in the Business Process Execution Language (BPEL) for Web Services is specified. In [BEE$^+$10], we have implemented this model transformation in our tool AGG. For the translation of certain BPMN-elements, namely Split- and Join-constructs, amalgamation is used, because an arbitrary number of branches may occur. We have shown parallel independence of the amalgamated transformations leading to functional behavior of this model transformation.

7.4 Tool Support

The comprehensive theory of typed attributed graph transformation can be used to describe and analyze visual model transformations. Most of this theory has already been implemented by our TFS group at Technische Universität Berlin in the integrated tool environment Attributed Graph Grammar (AGG) system, developed in Java, that supports the development of graph grammars, as well as their testing and analysis. AGG provides a comprehensive functionality for the input and modification of typed attributed graph grammars by a mouse/menu-driven visual user interface. The theoretical concepts are implemented as directly as possible – but, naturally, respecting necessary efficiency considerations – such that AGG offers clear concepts and sound behavior concerning the graph transformation part. Owing to its formal foundation, AGG offers validation support in the form of graph parsing, consistency checking of graphs and graph transformation systems, critical pair analysis, and analysis of the termination of graph transformation systems.

AGG supports attributed type graphs with multiplicity constraints and attribution by use of Java objects. An attribute is declared just like a variable in a conventional programming language: by specifying its name and type and assigning a value of this type. In contrast to the theory, each attribute has at most one value. While Java attributes allow a large variety of applications to graph transformation, it is clear that the Java semantics is not covered by the formal foundation.

Internally, AGG follows the single-pushout approach, but the double-pushout approach can be simulated with proper system settings. For rules, negative application conditions can be defined. Moreover, global constraints can be checked after each transformation to decide whether this transformation is valid. For a simple control flow, layers may be assigned to rules that fix an order on how the rules are applied.

Lately, AGG has been equipped with amalgamated graph transformation. As introduced in Chapter 4, a kernel and different multi rules can be specified in AGG leading to interaction schemes. With maximal disjoint matching, the amalgamated rule is constructed and applied leading to an amalgamated transformation. It is ongoing work to implement application conditions with arbitrary levels of nesting for standard and amalgamated rules to allow the complete expressiveness of this approach.

Also, AGG offers different analysis techniques for graph transformations:

- Graph constraints allow to check for certain properties.

- Critical pair and dependency analysis detects conflicts and dependencies of transformations.

- Graph parsing allows to decide whether a given graph belong to a language defined by a graph grammar.

- Termination criteria allow to decide for termination.

To integrate graph and model transformation into the development toolset Eclipse [Gro09], the EMF Henshin project provides an in-place model transformation language for EMF. The framework supports endogenous transformations of EMF model instances as well as exogenous transformations generating instances of a target language from given instances of a source language. It offers a graphical syntax and some support for static analysis of transformations.

For a more efficient application of triple graph rules, a tool environment based on the well-known Mathematica software is currently under work [Ada09]. This seems to be a promising approach for a fast and efficient model transformation tool.

7.5 Future Work

For future work, the categorical foundation of $\mathcal{M}$-adhesive categories should be further analyzed and adapted to our needs. One interesting field of investigation are finite objects. In many application areas, infinite objects do not play a role and only finite objects are considered for transformations. Results concerning the preservation of finiteness and the availability of the additional properties would be of importance [BEGG10].

Moreover, it would be interesting to investigate how far the definition of $\mathcal{M}$-adhesive categories and especially the weak van Kampen squares are necessary for the complete theory. An interesting approach in [Hei09] redefines van Kampen squares in a way that we do not have to require all $\mathcal{M}$-morphisms, but some have to be induced by the van Kampen property. This may allow to ease or directly induce efficient pushouts and other relevant properties.

To analyze local confluence, the critical pair analysis for rules with application conditions should be made more efficient. Up to now, to rule out that a pair is actually a critical pair all extensions have to be checked. Suitable conditions for extensions as well as for strict AC-confluence should help to improve the analysis.

The theory of multi-amalgamation is a solid mathematical basis to analyze interesting properties of the operational semantics, like termination, local confluence, and functional behavior. However, it is left open for future work to generalize the corresponding results in [EEPT06] like the Concurrency, the Embedding and Extension, and the Local Confluence Theorem to results for multi-amalgamated rules based on the underlying kernel and multi rules. These results are of special interest in the case of maximal matchings, where they do not hold in general even for amalgamated transformations. Properties which ensure the local Church-Rosser or Extension

Theorem and a critical pair analysis optimized for maximal matchings would be of great importance.

For the analysis of functional behavior, an important approach could be the use of forward translation rules [HEOG10], where additional attributes keep track which source elements have been translated already by the model transformation. While triple rules are no longer non-deleting in this approach, we can apply the main results of the theory in Section 3.4 directly to the model transformation, especially the local confluence and termination analysis.

A main challenge for future work is to obtain a more general theory to show the semantical correctness of model transformations. While we have shown the semantical simulation based on a comparison of the semantical rules, it would be a great improvement to have a formalism to directly integrate the semantical rules for the source and target languages into the triple graph formalism and to show there directly their correspondence.

Graph transformation and several analysis techniques have been implemented in our tool AGG. While the basic mechanisms for negative application conditions, amalgamated transformations, and maximal disjoint matchings are already implemented there, it is future work to extend AGG with arbitrary application conditions and the corresponding analysis possibilities. Moreover, up to now the computing of triple graph grammars is mainly accomplished by first flattening the triple graphs to plain graphs with special edge types for the connection morphisms. This could be improved for a more direct implementation and an automatic construction of the derived rules. With these extensions, our examples and the case study in this thesis can be the input for AGG, where the corresponding analysis can be done automatically or semi-automatically.

Appendix

A Categorical Results

In this Appendix, we show different results and extensions of the theory in the main part that are necessary for the full proofs of our theory.

In Section A.1, lemmas for the categorical construction of $\mathcal{M}$-adhesive categories are shown. Results concerning the functors used for the definition of generalized AHL Schemas are proven in Section A.2. In Section A.3, the category of markings is introduced used for the proof that AHL systems are an $\mathcal{M}$-adhesive category. In Section A.4, different lemmas for the theory of amalgamated transformations are shown.

A.1 Proofs for Construction of $\mathcal{M}$-Adhesive Categories

In this section, we show how pushouts in general comma categories are constructed and how to define product, slice, coslice, and comma categories as general comma categories, which eases the proof for Thm. 3.11.

In a general comma category, pushouts can be constructed component-wise in the underlying categories if the domain functors of the operations preserve pushouts. This is a generalization of the corresponding result in [PEL08] for comma categories.

Lemma A.1

Consider a general comma category $\mathbf{G} = GComCat((\mathbf{C}_j)_{j\in\mathcal{J}}, (F_i, G_i)_{i\in\mathcal{I}}; \mathcal{I}, \mathcal{J})$ based on $\mathcal{M}$-adhesive categories $(\mathbf{C}_j, \mathcal{M}_j)$, where F_i preserves pushouts along $\mathcal{M}_{k_i}$-morphisms.

For objects $A = ((A_j), (op_i^A))$, $B = ((B_j), (op_i^B))$, and $C = ((C_j), (op_i^C)) \in \mathbf{G}$ and morphisms $f = (f_j) : A \to B$, $g = (g_j) : A \to C$ with $f \in \times_{j\in\mathcal{J}} \mathcal{M}_j$ we have: The diagram (1) is a pushout in $\mathbf{G}$ iff for all $j \in \mathcal{J}$ $(1)_j$ is a pushout in $\mathbf{C}_j$, with $D = ((D_j), (op_j^D))$, $f' = (f_j')$, and $g' = (g_j')$.

$$
\begin{array}{ccc}
A_j \xrightarrow{\;f_j\;} B_j & \quad & A \xrightarrow{\;f\;} B \\
\downarrow{g_j} \quad (1)_j \quad \downarrow{g_j'} & \quad & \downarrow{g} \quad (1) \quad \downarrow{g'} \\
C_j \xrightarrow{\;f_j'\;} D_j & \quad & C \xrightarrow{\;f'\;} D
\end{array}
$$

PROOF "$\Leftarrow$" Given the morphisms f and g in (1), and the pushouts $(1)_j$ in $\mathbf{C}_j$ for $j \in \mathcal{J}$. We have to show that (1) is a pushout in $\mathbf{G}$.

Since F_i preserves pushouts along $\mathcal{M}_{k_i}$-morphisms, with $f_{k_i} \in \mathcal{M}_{k_i}$ the diagram $(2)_i$ is a pushout for all $i \in \mathcal{I}$. Then $D = ((D_j), (op_i^D))$ is an object in $\mathbf{G}$, where, for $i \in \mathcal{I}$, op_i^D is induced by pushout $(2)_i$ and $G_i(f'_{\ell_i}) \circ op_i^C \circ F_i(g_{k_i}) = G_i(f'_{\ell_i}) \circ G_i(g_{\ell_i}) \circ op_i^A = G_i(g'_{\ell_i}) \circ G_i(f_{\ell_i}) \circ op_i^A = G_i(g'_{\ell_i}) \circ op_i^B \circ F_i(f_{k_i})$. It holds that $op_i^D \circ F_i(f'_{k_i}) = G_i(f'_{\ell_i}) \circ op_i^C$ and $op_i^D \circ F_i(g'_{k_i}) = G_i(g'_{\ell_i}) \circ op_i^B$. Therefore $f' = (f'_j)$ and $g' = (g'_j)$ are morphisms in **G** such that (1) commutes.

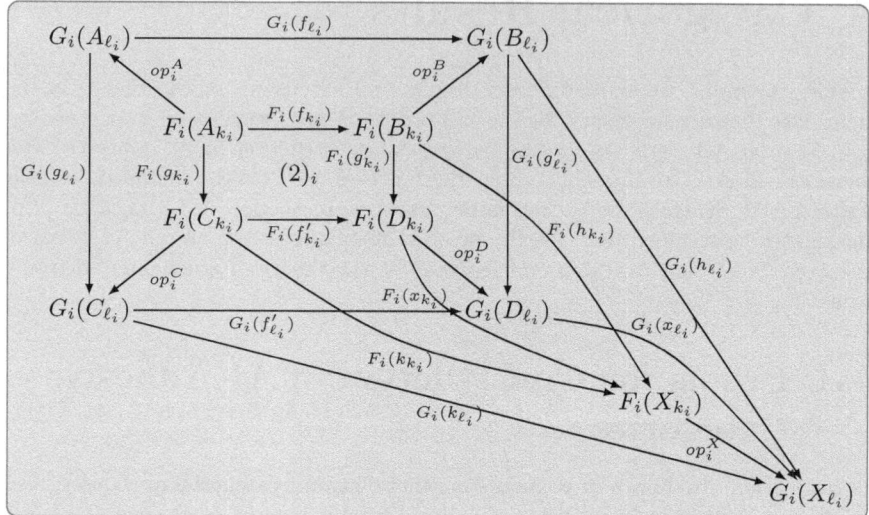

It remains to show that (1) is a pushout. Given an object $X = ((X_j), (op_i^X))$ and morphisms $h = (h_j) : B \to X$ and $k = (k_j) : C \to X$ in **G** such that $h \circ f = k \circ g$. From pushouts $(1)_j$ we obtain unique morphisms $x_j : D_j \to X_j$ such that $x_j \circ g'_j = h_j$ and $x_j \circ f'_j = k_j$ for all $j \in \mathcal{J}$. Since $(2)_i$ is a pushout, from $G_i(x_{\ell_i}) \circ op_i^D \circ F_i(g'_{k_i}) = G_i(x_{\ell_i}) \circ G_i(g'_{\ell_i}) \circ op_i^B = G_i(h_{\ell_i}) \circ op_i^B = op_i^X \circ F_i(h_{k_i}) = op_i^X \circ F_i(x_{k_i}) \circ F_i(g'_{k_i})$ and $G_i(x_{\ell_i}) \circ op_i^D \circ F_i(f'_{k_i}) = G_i(x_{\ell_i}) \circ G_i(f'_{\ell_i}) \circ op_i^C = G_i(k_{\ell_i}) \circ op_i^C = op_i^X \circ F_i(k_{k_i}) = op_i^X \circ F_i(x_{k_i}) \circ F_i(f'_{k_i})$ it follows that $G_i(x_{\ell_i}) \circ op_i^D = op_i^X \circ F_i(x_{k_i})$. Therefore $x = (x_j) \in$ **G**, and x is unique with respect to $x \circ g' = h$ and $x \circ f' = k$.

"$\Rightarrow$" Given the pushout (1) in **G** we have to show that $(1)_j$ are pushouts in $\mathbf{C}_j$ for all $j \in \mathcal{J}$. Since $(\mathbf{C}_j, \mathcal{M}_j)$ is an $\mathcal{M}$-adhesive category there exists a pushout $(1')_j$ over $f_j \in \mathcal{M}_j$ and g_j in $\mathbf{C}_j$.

Therefore (using "$\Leftarrow$") there is a corresponding pushout $(1')$ in **G** over f and g with $E = ((E_j), (op_i^E))$, $f^* = (f_j^*)$ and $g^* = (g_j^*)$. Since pushouts are unique up to isomorphism it follows that $E \cong D$, which means $E_j \cong D_j$ and therefore $(1)_j$ is a pushout in $\mathbf{C}_j$ for all $j \in \mathcal{J}$.

$$
\begin{array}{ccc}
A_j \xrightarrow{f_j} B_j & \qquad & A \xrightarrow{f} B \\
\downarrow{g_j} \quad (1')_j \quad \downarrow{g_j^*} & & \downarrow{g} \quad (1') \quad \downarrow{g^*} \\
C_j \xrightarrow{f_j^*} E_j & & C \xrightarrow{f^*} E
\end{array}
$$

A standard comma category is an instantiation of a general comma category.

Lemma A.2

A comma category $\mathbf{A} = ComCat(F : \mathbf{C} \to \mathbf{X}, G : \mathbf{D} \to \mathbf{X}, \mathcal{I})$ is a special case of a general comma category.

PROOF With $\mathcal{I}$ as given, $\mathcal{J} = \{1, 2\}$, $\mathbf{C}_1 = \mathbf{C}$, $\mathbf{C}_2 = \mathbf{D}$, $\mathbf{X}_i = \mathbf{X}$, $F_i = F$ and $G_i = G$ for all $i \in \mathcal{I}$ the resulting general comma category is obviously isomorphic to $\mathbf{A}$.

Product, slice and coslice categories are special cases of comma categories.

Lemma A.3

For product, slice and coslice categories, we have the following isomorphic comma categories:

1. $\mathbf{C} \times \mathbf{D} \cong ComCat(!_{\mathbf{C}} : \mathbf{C} \to \mathbf{1}, !_{\mathbf{D}} : \mathbf{D} \to \mathbf{1}, \varnothing)$,

2. $\mathbf{C}\backslash X \cong ComCat(id_{\mathbf{C}} : \mathbf{C} \to \mathbf{C}, X : \mathbf{1} \to \mathbf{C}, \{1\})$ and

3. $X\backslash\mathbf{C} \cong ComCat(X : \mathbf{1} \to \mathbf{C}, id_{\mathbf{C}} : \mathbf{C} \to \mathbf{C}, \{1\})$,

where $\mathbf{1}$ is the final category, $!_{\mathbf{C}} : \mathbf{C} \to \mathbf{1}$ is the final morphism from $\mathbf{C}$, and $X : \mathbf{1} \to \mathbf{C}$ maps $1 \in \mathbf{1}$ to $X \in \mathbf{C}$.

PROOF This is obvious.

A.2 Proofs for Generalized AHL Schemas as an $\mathcal{M}$-Adhesive Category

In this section, we give the additional proofs used in Thm. 3.23 to show that the category of generalized HLR schemas is an $\mathcal{M}$-adhesive category.

Lemma A.4

The functor $H : \mathbf{Specs} \times \mathbf{Sets} \to \mathbf{Sets} : (SP, M) \mapsto M, (f_{SP}, f_M) \mapsto f_M$ preserves pushouts along $\mathcal{M}_1 \times \mathcal{M}_2$-morphisms.

PROOF In a product category, a square is a pushout if and only if the component-wise squares are pushouts in the underlying categories. Thus, if (1) is a pushout in $\mathbf{Specs} \times \mathbf{Sets}$ also (2) is a pushout in $\mathbf{Sets}$,

$$
\begin{array}{ccc}
(SP_0, M_0) & \xrightarrow{(f_{SP}, f_M)} & (SP_1, M_1) \\
\downarrow{\scriptstyle (g_{SP}, g_M)} & (1) & \downarrow{\scriptstyle (g'_{SP}, g'_M)} \\
(SP_2, M_2) & \xrightarrow[(f'_{SP}, f'_M)]{} & (SP_3, M_3)
\end{array}
\qquad
\begin{array}{ccc}
M_0 & \xrightarrow{f_M} & M_1 \\
\downarrow{\scriptstyle g_M} & (2) & \downarrow{\scriptstyle g'_M} \\
M_2 & \xrightarrow[f'_M]{} & M_3
\end{array}
$$

which means that H preserves pushouts.

Lemma A.5

The functor $H : \mathbf{Specs} \times \mathbf{Sets} \to \mathbf{Sets} : (SP = (S, OP, E), M) \mapsto S$, $(f_{SP}, f_M) \mapsto f_{SP,S}$ preserves pullbacks along $\mathcal{M}_1 \times \mathcal{M}_2$-morphisms.

PROOF In a product category, a square is a pullback if and only if the component-wise squares are pullbacks in the underlying categories. Thus, if (3) is a pullback in **Specs** × **Sets** also (4) is a pullback in **Specs**. In **Specs**, pullbacks are constructed component.wise on the signature part (with some special treatment of the equations). Thus, also (5) is a pullback in **Sets**, which means that H preserves pullbacks.

$$
\begin{array}{ccc}
(SP_0, M_0) \xrightarrow{(f_{SP}, f_M)} (SP_1, M_1) & SP_0 \xrightarrow{f_{SP}} SP_1 & S_0 \xrightarrow{f_{SP,s}} S_1 \\
\downarrow{(g_{SP}, g_M)} \ (3) \ \downarrow{(g'_{SP}, g'_M)} & g_{SP}\downarrow \ (4) \ \downarrow g'_{SP} & g_{SP,s}\downarrow \ (5) \ \downarrow g'_{SP,s} \\
(SP_2, M_2) \xrightarrow{(f'_{SP}, f'_M)} (SP_3, M_3) & SP_2 \xrightarrow{f'_{SP}} SP_3 & S_2 \xrightarrow{f'_{SP,s}} S_3
\end{array}
$$

Lemma A.6

The functor H : **Specs** × **Sets** → **Sets** : $(SP, M) \mapsto (T_{SIG}(X) \times M)^{\oplus}$, $(f_{SP}, f_M) \mapsto (f_{SP}^{\#} \times f_M)^{\oplus}$ preserves pullbacks along $\mathcal{M}_1 \times \mathcal{M}_2$-morphisms.

PROOF The product functor × preserves general pullbacks and, as shown in [EEPT06], the functor $\Box^{\oplus}$ preserves pullbacks along injective morphisms. Thus, it lasts to show that T : **Specs** → **Sets** : $SP \mapsto T_{SIG}(X)$, where we forget the type information of the terms, preserves pullbacks.

In **Specs**, the pullback (4) is constructed component-wise on the sorts, operations and variables, which means that $S_0 = \{(s_1, s_2) \mid g'_{SP,S}(s_1) = f'_{SP,S}(s_2)\}$, $OP_0 = \{(op_1, op_2) : (s_1^1, s_2^1)...(s_1^n, s_2^n) \rightarrow (s_1, s_2) \mid g'_{SP,OP}(op_1 : s_1^1...s_1^n \rightarrow s_1) = f'_{SP,OP}(op_2 : s_2^1...s_2^n \rightarrow s_2)\}$ and $X_0 = \{(x_1, x_2) \mid g'_{SP,X}(x_1) = f'_{SP,X}(x_2)\}$. Therefore, the terms in $T_{SIG_0}(X_0)$ are defined by $T_{SIG_0,s}(X_0) = X_{0,s} \cup \{(c_1, c_2) \mid (c_1, c_2) :\rightarrow s \in OP_0\} \cup \{(op_1, op_2)(t_1, .., t_n) \mid (op_1, op_2) : s_1...s_n \rightarrow s \in OP_0, t_i \in T_{SIG_0,s_i}(X_0)\}$.

We have to show that $T_{SIG_0}(X_0)$ is isomorphic to the pullback object P over $f'^{\#}_{SP}$ and $g'^{\#}_{SP}$ with $P = \{(t_1, t_2) \mid g'^{\#}_{P}(t_1) = f'^{\#}_{P}(t_2)\}$. Since P is a pullback, with $f'^{\#}_{SP} \circ g^{\#}_{SP} = g'^{\#}_{SP} \circ f^{\#}_{SP}$ we get an induced morphism $i : T_{SIG_0}(X_0) \rightarrow P$ with $i(t) = (f^{\#}_{SP}(t), g^{\#}_{SP}(t))$, which means that i is inductively defined by $i(c_1, c_2) = (c_1, c_2)$ for constants, $i(x_1, x_2) = (x_1, x_2)$ for variables and $i((op_1, op_2)(t_1, ..., t_n)) = (op_1(i(t_1)_1, ..., i(t_n)_1), op_2(i(t_1)_2, ..., i(t_n)_2))$ for complex terms.

f'_{SP}, g'_{SP} are specification morphisms and $f'^{\#}_{SP}$, $g'^{\#}_{SP}$ are inductively defined on terms. This means that, for a pair $(t_1, t_2) \in P$, the terms t_1 and t_2 have to have the same structure. Define $j : P \rightarrow T_{SIG_0}(X_0)$ inductively by $j(c_1, c_2) = (c_1, c_2)$ for constants, $j(x_1, x_2) = (x_1, x_2)$ for variables and $j(op_1(t_1^1, ..., t_1^n), op_2(t_2^1, ..., t_2^n)) = (op_1, op_2)(j(t_1^1, t_2^1), ...,$

$$
\begin{array}{ccc}
T_{SIG_0}(X_0) & \xrightarrow{f^{\#}_{SP}} & T_{SIG_1}(X_1) \\
g^{\#}_{SP}\downarrow & (6) & \downarrow g'^{\#}_{SP} \\
T_{SIG_2}(X_2) & \xrightarrow{f'^{\#}_{SP}} & T_{SIG_3}(X_3)
\end{array}
$$

$j(t_1^n, t_2^n))$ for complex terms.

By induction, it can be shown that $i \circ j = id_P$ and $j \circ i = id_{T_{SIG_0}(X_0)}$. This means that i and j are isomorphisms and (6) is a pullback in **Sets**.

Lemma A.7
The functor $H : \mathbf{Specs} \times \mathbf{Sets} \to \mathbf{Sets} : (SP, M) \mapsto \mathcal{P}_{fin}(Eqns(SIG, X)), (f_{SP}, f_M) \mapsto \mathcal{P}_{fin}(f_{SP}^{\#})$ preserves pullbacks along $\mathcal{M}_1 \times \mathcal{M}_2$-morphisms.

PROOF In [EEPT06], it is shown that $\mathcal{P}$ preserves pullbacks along injective morphisms. Analogously, this can be shown for $\mathcal{P}_{fin}$, since if we start the construction for finite sets, this property is preserved. Thus, it lasts to show that $Eqns$ preserves pullbacks, which can be proven similar to the proof for sets of terms in Lemma A.6 above.

A.3 Proofs for AHL Systems as an $\mathcal{M}$-adhesive Category

In this section, we define the category **Markings** of markings and show that this category is an $\mathcal{M}$-adhesive category. Moreover, we combine nets with markings and show under which conditions the resulting category of net systems is also an $\mathcal{M}$-adhesive category.

A.3.1 The Category of Markings

In general, a marking of a net can be seen as a multiset, i.e. an element of a free commutative monoid – in the case of P/T nets of $P^{\oplus}$, in the case of AHL nets of $(A \otimes P)^{\oplus}$, where $\otimes$ means the type-correct product. As a consequence, we could use the category **FCMonoids** of free commutative monoids for our markings. Unfortunately, in many cases the morphisms between P/T or AHL systems should not be marking-strict, which means that the marking on each place p has to be equal in both nets, as is the case for morphisms in **FCMonoids**.

For this reason, we define the category **Markings**, where the objects are sets combined with a function to natural numbers defining the quantity of each element of the set. For morphisms, we only require a mapping between the sets that at least preserves these quantities.

Definition A.8 (Category Markings)
The category **Markings** consists of

- objects (S, s) with a set S and a function $s : S \to \mathbb{N}$,
- morphisms $f : (S, s) \to (T, t)$ with a function $f : S \to T$ such that $\forall s_1 \in S : s(s_1) \leq t(f(s_1))$,
- a composition $g \circ f$ of $f : (S, s) \to (T, t)$, $g : (T, t) \to (U, u)$ with $\forall s_i \in S : g \circ f(s_1) = g(f(s_1))$ as in **Sets**,
- identities $id_{(S,s)} : (S, s) \to (S, s)$ with $id_{(S,s)} = id_S$ as in **Sets**.

This category is well-defined since the morphisms are basically morphisms in **Sets**, and for the composition we have $\forall s_1 \in S : s(s_1) \leq t(f(s_1)) \leq u(g(f(s_1)))$, which means $g \circ f$ is a valid **Markings**-morphism.

Now we shall show that the category of markings with a suitable morphism class $\mathcal{M}_{strict}$ of strict morphisms is an $\mathcal{M}$-adhesive category. First we define this morphism class $\mathcal{M}_{strict}$, and then we prove some lemmas which are necessary to show the desired result.

Definition A.9 (strict morphism)
A morphism $f : (S, s) \rightarrow (T, t)$ in **Markings** is marking-strict if $\forall s_1 \in S : s(s_1) = t(f(s_1))$. A morphism $f : (S, s) \rightarrow (T, t)$ in **Markings** is strict, if f is injective and marking-strict. All strict morphisms form the morphism class $\mathcal{M}_{strict}$.

The category **FCMonoids** of free commutative monoids is a subcategory of **Markings**, where the morphisms in **FCMonoids** are exactly the marking-strict morphisms.

Lemma A.10
$\mathcal{M}_{strict}$ is a class of monomorphisms closed under composition and decomposition.

PROOF Given morphisms $f : (S, s) \rightarrow (T, t)$, $g : (T, t) \rightarrow (U, u)$ in **Markings** the following properties hold:

1. If f is strict, then it is injective and we inherit from **Sets** that it is a monomorphism.
2. Injective morphisms in **Sets** are closed under composition and decomposition. This holds also in **Markings**.
3. If f, g are strict we have $\forall s_1 \in S : s(s_1) \stackrel{f \text{ strict}}{=} t(f(s_1)) \stackrel{g \text{ strict}}{=} u(g(f(s_1)))$, which means that also $g \circ f$ is strict.
4. If g, $g \circ f$ are strict we have $\forall s_1 \in S : s(s_1) \stackrel{g \circ f \text{ strict}}{=} u(g(f(s_1))) \stackrel{g \text{ strict}}{=} t(f(s_1))$, which means that also f is strict.

The next proofs are very similar to the proofs for P/T systems being an $\mathcal{M}$-adhesive category in [PEHP08]. We generalize these proofs to the category of markings. First we shall show that pushouts along $\mathcal{M}_{strict}$-morphisms exist and preserve $\mathcal{M}_{strict}$-morphisms.

Lemma A.11

In **Markings**, pushouts along $\mathcal{M}_{strict}$-morphisms exist and preserve $\mathcal{M}_{strict}$, i.e. given morphisms f and m with m strict, then the pushout (1) exists and n is also a strict morphism.

$$
\begin{array}{ccc}
(A, a) & \xrightarrow{\ m\ } & (B, b) \\
{\scriptstyle f}\downarrow & (1) & \downarrow{\scriptstyle g} \\
(C, c) & \xrightarrow{\ n\ } & (D, d)
\end{array}
$$

PROOF Given f, m with $m \in \mathcal{M}_{strict}$ we construct D as pushout object in **Sets**, which means $D = (C \mathbin{\dot{\cup}} B)\backslash m(A)$ with inclusion $n : C \to D$, and $g : B \to D :$ $b_1 \in B\backslash m(A) \mapsto b_1, m(a_1) \mapsto f(a_1)$. For $d_1 \in D$, d is defined by

(1) $d_1 = b_1 \in B\backslash m(A)$: $d(b_1) = b(b_1)$,
(2) $d_1 = c_1 \in C$: $d(c_1) = c(c_1)$.

Obviously, $d : D \to \mathbb{N}$ is well-defined. First we shall show that g, n are **Markings**-morphisms and n is strict.

1. $\forall b_1 \in B$ we have:
    1. $b_1 \in B\backslash m(A)$ and $b(b_1) \overset{(1)}{=} d(b_1) = d(g(b_1))$ or
    2. $\exists a_1 \in A$ with $b_1 = m(a_1)$ and $b(b_1) = b(m(a_1)) \overset{m \text{ strict}}{=} a(a_1) \le c(f(a_1))$ $\overset{(2)}{=} d(f(a_1)) = d(g(m(a_1))) = d(g(b_1))$.
    This means that $g \in$ **Markings**.
2. $\forall c_1 \in C$ we have:
    1. $c(c_1) \overset{(2)}{=} d(c_1) = d(n(c_1))$.
    This means that $n \in$ **Markings** and n is strict.

It remains to show the pushout property. Given **Markings**-morphisms $h : (C,c) \to (E,e)$, $k : (B,b) \to (E,e)$ with $h \circ f = k \circ m$, we have a unique induced morphism x in **Sets** with $x \circ n = h$ and $x \circ g = k$. We shall show that $x \in$ **Markings**, i.e. $\forall d_1 \in D : d(d_1) \le e(x(d_1))$.

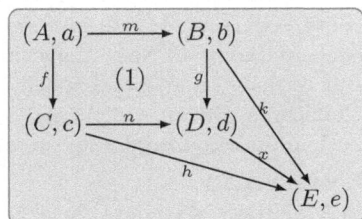

1. For $d_1 = b_1 \in B\backslash m(A)$ we have
$$d(b_1) \overset{(1)}{=} b(b_1) \le e(k(b_1)) = e(x(g(b_1))) = e(x(b_1)).$$
2. For $d_1 = c_1 \in C$ we have $d(c_1) \overset{(2)}{=} c(c_1) \le e(h(c_1)) = e(x(n(c_1))) = e(x(c_1))$.

As next property, we shall show that pullbacks along $\mathcal{M}_{strict}$-morphisms exist and preserve $\mathcal{M}_{strict}$-morphisms.

Lemma A.12
In **Markings**, pullbacks along $\mathcal{M}_{strict}$-morphisms exist and preserve $\mathcal{M}_{strict}$, i.e. given morphisms g and n with n strict, then the pullback (1) exists and m is also a strict morphism.

PROOF Given g, n with $n \in \mathcal{M}_{strict}$ we construct A as pullback object in **Sets**, which means $A = g^{-1}(n(C))$ with inclusion $m : A \to B$ and $f : A \to C : a \mapsto n^{-1}(g(a))$. For all $a_1 \in A$, a is defined by

$$(*)\quad a(a_1) = b(m(a_1)).$$

Obviously, a is a well-defined marking. f is a well-defined function since n is injective. We have to show that f, m are **Markings**-morphisms and m is strict.

1. $\forall a_1 \in A$ we have: $a(a_1) \overset{(*)}{=} b(m(a_1)) \leq d(g(m(a_1)) = d(n(f(a_1)) \overset{n \text{ strict}}{=} c(f(a_1))$.
   This means $f \in$ **Markings**.
2. $\forall a_1 \in A$ we have: $a(a_1) \overset{(*)}{=} b(m(a_1))$.
   This means $m \in$ **Markings** and m is strict.

To show the pullback property, for given **Markings**-morphisms $h : (E,e) \to (C,c)$, $k : (E,e) \to (B,b)$ with $n \circ h = g \circ k$, we have a unique induced morphism x in **Sets** with $f \circ x = h$ and $m \circ x = k$. We shall show that $x \in$ **Markings**, i.e. $\forall e_1 \in E : e(e_1) \leq a(x(e_1))$. For $e_1 \in E$ we have $e(e_1) \leq b(k(e_1))$ $= b(m(x(e_1))) \overset{m \text{ strict}}{=} a(x(e_1))$.

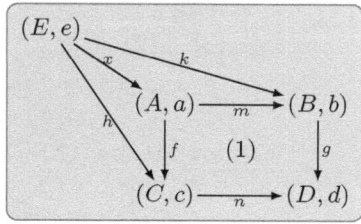

It remains to show the $\mathcal{M}$-van Kampen property for **Markings**. We know that (**Sets**, $\mathcal{M}$) is an $\mathcal{M}$-adhesive category for the class $\mathcal{M}$ of injective morphisms, hence pushouts in **Sets** along injective morphisms are $\mathcal{M}$-van Kampen squares. But we have to give an explicit proof for the markings, because a square (1) in **Markings** with $m, n \in \mathcal{M}_{strict}$, which is a pushout in **Sets**, is not necessarily a pushout in **Markings**, since we may have $d(g(b_1)) > b(b_1)$ for some $b_1 \in B \backslash m(A)$.

Lemma A.13

In **Markings**, pushouts along $\mathcal{M}_{strict}$-morphisms are $\mathcal{M}$-van Kampen squares.

PROOF Given the following commutative cube (2) with $m \in \mathcal{M}_{strict}$ and ($f \in \mathcal{M}_{strict}$ or $t, u, v \in \mathcal{M}_{strict}$), where the bottom face is a pushout and the back faces are pullbacks, we have to show that the top face is a pushout if and only if the front faces are pullbacks.

"$\Rightarrow$" If the top face is a pushout then the front faces are pullbacks in **Sets**, since all squares are pushouts or pullbacks in **Sets**, where the $\mathcal{M}$-van Kampen property holds. For a pullback (1) with $m, n \in \mathcal{M}_{strict}$, the function a of A is completely determined by the fact that $m \in \mathcal{M}_{strict}$ as shown in the

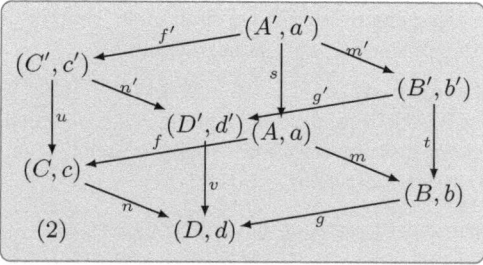

proof of Lemma A.12. Hence a diagram (1) in **Markings** with $m, n \in \mathcal{M}_{strict}$ is a pullback in **Markings** if and only if it is a pullback in **Sets**. This means, the front faces are also pullbacks in **Markings**.

"$\Leftarrow$" If the front faces are pullbacks we know that the top face is a pushout in **Sets**. To show that it is also a pushout in **Markings** we have to verify the conditions (1) and (2) from the construction in Lemma A.11.

(1) For $b_1' \in B' \backslash m'(A')$ we have to show that $d'(g'(b_1')) = b'(b_1')$.

If f is strict then also g and g' are strict, since the bottom face is a pushout and the right front face is a pullback, and $\mathcal{M}_{strict}$ is preserved by both pushouts and pullbacks. This means that $b'(b_1') = d'(g'(b_1'))$.

Otherwise t and v are strict. Since the right back face is a pullback and $b_1' \in B' \backslash m'(A')$ we have $t(b_1') \in B \backslash m(A)$. With the bottom face being a pushout we have by (1) in Lemma A.11

$$(*) \quad d(g(t(b_1'))) \overset{(1)}{=} b(t(b_1')).$$

It follows that $d'(g'(b_1')) \overset{v \text{ strict}}{=} d(v(g'(b_1'))) = d(g(t(b_1'))) \overset{(*)}{=} b(t(b_1')) \overset{t \text{ strict}}{=} b'(b_1')$.

(2) For $c_1' \in C'$ we have to show that $d'(n'(c_1')) = c'(c_1')$.

With m being strict also n and n' are strict, since the bottom face is a pushout and the left front face is a pullback, and $\mathcal{M}_{strict}$ is preserved by both pushouts and pullbacks. This means that $c'(c_1') = d'(n'(c_1'))$.

Theorem A.14
The category (**Markings**, $\mathcal{M}_{strict}$) is an $\mathcal{M}$-adhesive category.

PROOF By Lemma A.10, the morphism class $\mathcal{M}_{strict}$ has the required properties. Moreover, we have pushouts and pullbacks along $\mathcal{M}_{strict}$-morphisms in **Markings**, as shown in Lemma A.11 and Lemma A.12, respectively. By Lemma A.13, pushouts along strict morphisms are $\mathcal{M}$-van Kampen squares. Hence all properties of $\mathcal{M}$-adhesive categories are fulfilled.

A.3.2 From Nets to Net Systems

Now we combine nets with markings and show that under certain conditions the category of the corresponding net systems is also an $\mathcal{M}$-adhesive category. The term *net* means any variant of Petri nets, for example place/transition nets, AHL nets or generalized AHL nets.

The general idea is to define for a net N a marking set $M(N)$ dependent on N, where the actual marking is a function $m : M(N) \rightarrow \mathbb{N}$. For place/transition nets this marking set is the set P of places, for AHL nets and generalized AHL nets this marking set is the set $(A \otimes P)$. Then the category of the corresponding net systems can be seen as a subcategory of a comma category of nets and markings, where the marking set is compatible with the net.

Definition A.15 (Net system)
Given a category **Nets** of nets, a net system $S = (N, m)$ is given by a net $N \in$ **Nets** and a function $m : M(N) \to \mathbb{N}$, where $M :$ **Nets** $\to$ **Sets** is a functor assigning a marking set to each net N.

For net systems $S = (N, m)$ and $S' = (N', m')$, a net system morphism $f_S : S \to S'$ is a net morphism $f_N : N \to N'$ such that $M(f_N) : (M(N), m) \to (M(N'), m')$ is a **Markings**-morphism.

Net systems and net system morphisms form the category **Systems**.

Theorem A.16
Given an $\mathcal{M}$-adhesive category (**Nets**, $\mathcal{M}'$) of nets with a marking set functor $M :$ **Nets** $\to$ **Sets** that preserves pushouts and pullbacks along $\mathcal{M}'$-morphisms, then the category (**Systems**, $\mathcal{M}$) of net systems over these nets is an $\mathcal{M}$-adhesive category, where $\mathcal{M}$ is the class of all morphisms $f_S = (f_N)$ with $f_N \in \mathcal{M}'$ and $M(f_N) \in \mathcal{M}_{strict}$.

PROOF First we define the category $\mathbf{C} = ComCat(M, V, \{1\})$ with $V :$ **Markings** $\to$ **Sets**, $V(T, t) = T, V(f) = f$. We can apply Thm. 3.11 Item 6 using that M preserves pushouts along $\mathcal{M}'$ and V preserves pullbacks along $\mathcal{M}_{strict}$, which follows from the construction in the proof of Lemma A.12. It follows that $(\mathbf{C}, \mathcal{M}_C)$ with $\mathcal{M}_C = (\mathcal{M}' \times \mathcal{M}_{strict})|_{\mathbf{C}}$ is an $\mathcal{M}$-adhesive category.

Now we only consider objects $(N, (T, t), op^1) \in \mathbf{C}$ where $op^1 : M(N) \to T$ is an identity, i. e. $M(N) = T$. This restriction leads to the full subcategory $\mathbf{D}$ of $\mathbf{C}$. By construction, the category $\mathbf{D}$ is isomorphic to the category **Systems**:

- For an object $D = (N, (T, t), op^1) \in \mathbf{D}$ we have $op^1 : M(N) \to T$ is an identity, i. e. $D = (N, (M(N), t : M(N) \to \mathbb{N}), id_{M(N)})$, which is a one-to-one correspondence to the net system $(N, t) \in$ **Systems**.

- For a morphism $f = (f_N, f_M) : D \to D'$ with $D = (N, (T, t), op^1)$ and $D' = (N', (T', t'), op^{1'})$ we have $D = (N, (M(N), t : M(N) \to \mathbb{N}), id_{M(N)})$ and $D' = (N', (M(N'), t' : M(N') \to \mathbb{N}), id_{M(N')})$, and by the definition of morphisms in a comma category $id_{M(N')} \circ M(f_N) = V(f_M) \circ id_{M(N)}$. This means that $M(f_N) = V(f_M)$, which corresponds to the morphism $f_S = (f_N) \in$ **Systems**, where $M(f_N)$ is a **Markings**-morphism.

To apply Thm. 3.11 Item 1 we have to show that $\mathbf{D}$ has pushouts and pullbacks along $\mathcal{M}_D$-morphisms with $\mathcal{M}_D = \mathcal{M}_C|_{\mathbf{D}}$ that are preserved by the inclusion functor. Given objects $(N_i, (M(N_i), m_i), op_i^1 = id_{M(N_i)})$ for $i = 0, 1, 2$ and morphisms $f_S = (f_N, f_M) : (N_0, (M(N_0), m_0), op_0^1) \to (N_1, (M(N_1), m_1), op_1^1)$ and $g_S = (g_N, g_M) : (N_0, (M(N_0), m_0), op_0^1) \to (N_2, (M(N_2), m_2), op_2^1)$ with $f_S \in \mathcal{M}_D$ we can construct the pushout (1) of f_N, g_N in **Nets** with $f_N \in \mathcal{M}'$. Since M preserves pushouts along $\mathcal{M}'$-morphisms, (2) is a pushout in **Sets**. By assumption, we have $M(f_N) \in \mathcal{M}_{strict}$. Now we can use the construction in the proof of Lemma A.11 to construct a marking $m_3 : M(N_3) \to \mathbb{N}$ leading to the pushout (3) in **Markings**. By the construction of pushouts in comma categories, $(N_3, (M(N_3), m_3), op_3^1 = id_{M(N_3)})$ is a pushout in **C** and **D**.

$$
\begin{array}{ccc}
N_0 \xrightarrow{f_N} N_1 & \quad M(N_0) \xrightarrow{M(f_N)} M(N_1) & \quad (M(N_0), m_0) \xrightarrow{M(f_N)} (M(N_1), m_1) \\
{\scriptstyle g_N}\downarrow \quad (1) \quad \downarrow{\scriptstyle g'_N} & \quad {\scriptstyle M(g_N)}\downarrow \, (2) \, \downarrow{\scriptstyle M(g'_N)} & \quad {\scriptstyle M(g_N)}\downarrow \qquad (3) \qquad \downarrow{\scriptstyle M(g'_N)} \\
N_2 \xrightarrow{f'_N} N_3 & \quad M(N_2) \xrightarrow{M(f'_N)} M(N_3) & \quad (M(N_2), m_2) \xrightarrow{M(f'_N)} (M(N_3), m_3)
\end{array}
$$

Analogously, this can be done for pullbacks using the fact that M preserves pullbacks along $\mathcal{M}'$-morphisms and the construction of pullbacks in **Markings**.

This means that we can apply Thm. 3.11 and $(\textbf{Systems}, \mathcal{M}) \cong (\textbf{D}, \mathcal{M}_D)$ is an $\mathcal{M}$-adhesive category.

A.4 Proofs for Amalgamated Transformations

In this section, we formulate and proof different properties of diagrams concerning pullbacks, pushouts, pushout complements, and colimits in $\mathcal{M}$-adhesive categories where the additional properties hold.

Lemma A.17

If (1) is a pushout, (2) is a pullback, and $n' \in \mathcal{M}$ then there exists a unique morphism $c : C' \to C$ such that $c \circ f' = f$, $n \circ c = n'$, and $c \in \mathcal{M}$.

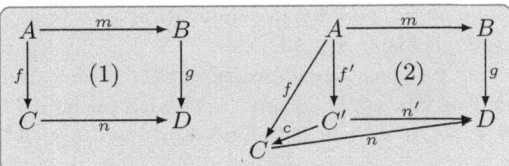

PROOF Since (2) is a pullback, $n' \in \mathcal{M}$ implies that $m \in \mathcal{M}$, and then also $n \in \mathcal{M}$ because (1) is a pushout.

Construct the pullback (3) with $v, v' \in \mathcal{M}$, and since $n' \circ f = g \circ m = n \circ f$ there is a unique morphism $f^* : A \to C''$ with $v \circ f^* = f'$ and $v' \circ f^* = f$. Now consider the following cube (4), where the bottom face is pushout (1), the back left face is a pullback because $m \in \mathcal{M}$, the front left face is pullback (2), and the front right face is pullback (3).

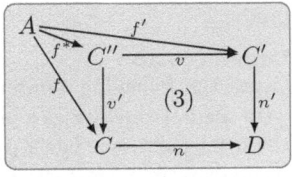

By pullback composition and decomposition also the back right face is a pullback, and then the VK property implies that the top face is a pushout. Since (5) is a pushout and pushout objects are unique up to isomorphism this implies that v is an isomorphism and $C'' \cong C'$. Now define $c := v' \circ v^{-1}$ and we have that $c \circ f' = v' \circ v^{-1} \circ f' = v' \circ f^* = f$, $n \circ c = n \circ v' \circ v^{-1} = n'$, and $c \in \mathcal{M}$ by decomposition of $\mathcal{M}$-morphisms.

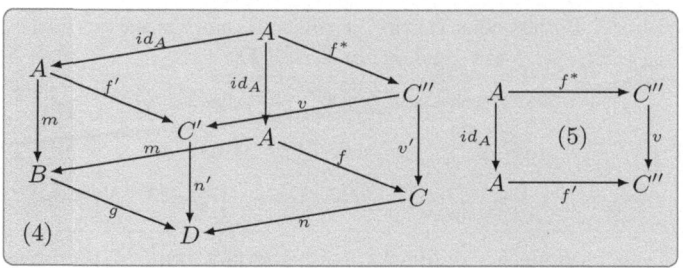

(4)   (5)

Lemma A.18

If $(1) + (2)$ is a pullback, (1) is a pushout, (2) commutes, and $o \in \mathcal{M}$ then also (2) is a pullback.

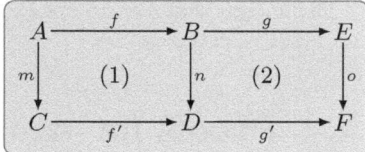

PROOF With $o \in \mathcal{M}$, $(1) + (2)$ being a pullback, and (1) being a pushout we have that $m, n \in \mathcal{M}$. Construct the pullback (3) of o and g', it follows that $\overline{n} \in \mathcal{M}$ and we get an induced morphism $b : B \to \overline{B}$ with $\overline{g} \circ b = g$, $\overline{n} \circ b = n$, and by decomposition of $\mathcal{M}$-morphisms $b \in \mathcal{M}$.

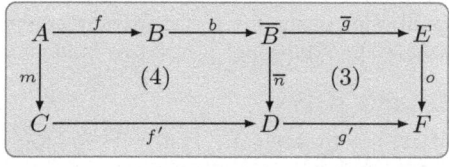

By pullback decomposition, also (4) is a pullback and we can apply Lemma A.17 with pushout (1) and $\overline{n} \in \mathcal{M}$ to obtain a unique morphism $\overline{b} \in \mathcal{M}$ with $n \circ \overline{b} = \overline{n}$ and $\overline{b} \circ b \circ f = f$. Now $n \in \mathcal{M}$ and $n \circ \overline{b} \circ b = \overline{n} \circ b = n$ implies that $\overline{b} \circ b = id_B$, and similarly $\overline{n} \in \mathcal{M}$ and $\overline{n} \circ b \circ \overline{b} = n \circ \overline{b} = \overline{n}$ implies that

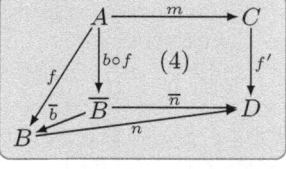

$b \circ \overline{b} = id_{\overline{B}}$, which means that B and $\overline{B}$ are isomorphic such that also (2) is a pullback.

Lemma A.19

Given the following commutative cube with the bottom face as a pushout, then the front right face has a pushout complement over $g \circ b$ if the back left face has a pushout complement over $f \circ a$.

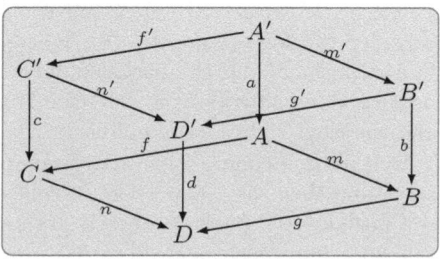

PROOF Construct the initial pushout (1) over f. Since the back left face has a pushout complement there is a morphism $b^* : B_f \to A'$ such that $a \circ b^* = b_f$.

The bottom face being a pushout implies that (2) as the composition is the initial pushout over g. Now $b \circ m' \circ b^* = m \circ a \circ b^* = m \circ b_f$, and the pushout complement of $g \circ b$ exists.

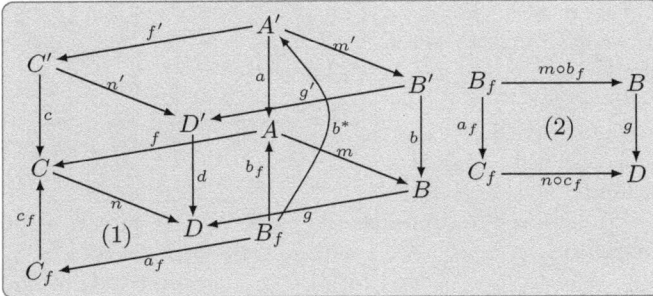

Lemma A.20

Given pullbacks (1) and (2) with pushout complements over $f' \circ m$ and $g' \circ n$, respectively, then also $(1)+(2)$ has a pushout complement over $(g' \circ f') \circ m$.

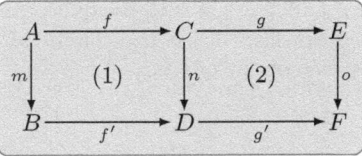

PROOF Let C' and E' be the pushout complements of (1) and (2), respectively.

By Lemma A.17 there are morphisms c and e such that $c \circ f = f^*$, $n^* \circ c = n$, $e \circ g = g*$, and $o^* \circ e = o$. Now $(2')$ can be decomposed into pushouts (3) and (4), and $(1') + (4)$ is also a pushout and the pushout complement of $(g' \circ f') \circ m$.

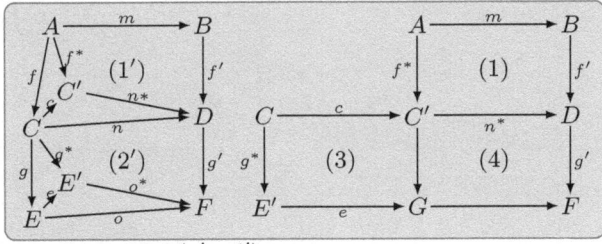

Lemma A.21

Given the following pushouts (1_i) and (3_i) with $b_i \in \mathcal{M}$ for $i = 1, \ldots, n$, morphisms $f_{ij} : B_i \to C_j$ with $c_j \circ f_{ij} = d_i$ for all $i \neq j$, and the limit (2) such that g_i is the induced morphism into E using $c_j \circ f_{ij} \circ b_i = d_i \circ b_i = c_i \circ a_i$, then (4) is the colimit of $(h_i)_{i=1,\ldots,n}$, where l_i is the induced morphism from pushout (3_i) compared with $\bar{e} \circ g_i = c_i \circ e_i \circ g_i = c_i \circ a_i = d_i \circ b_i$.

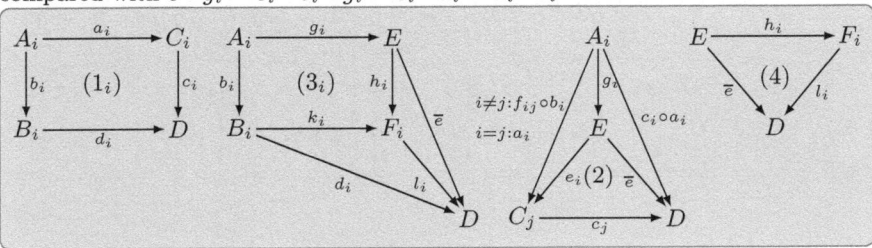

PROOF We prove this by induction over n.

I.B. $n = 1$: For $n = 1$, we have that C_1 is the limit of c_1, i.e. $E = C_1$, it follows that $F_1 = C_1$ for the pushout $(3_1) = (1_1)$, and obviously (4_1) is a colimit.

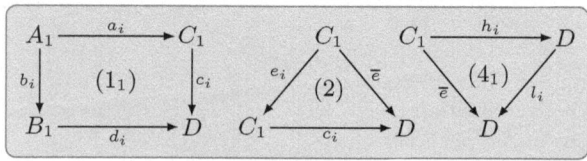

I.S. $n \to n + 1$: Consider the pushouts (1_i) with $b_i \in \mathcal{M}$ for $i = 1, \ldots, n + 1$, morphisms $f_{ij} : B_i \to C_j$ with $c_j \circ f_{ij} = d_i$ for all $i \neq j$, the limits (2_n) and (2_{n+1}) of $(c_i)_{i=1,\ldots,n}$ and $(c_i)_{i=1,\ldots,n+1}$, respectively, leading to pullback (5_{n+1}) by construction of limits. Moreover, g_{in} and g_{in+1} are the induced morphisms into E_n and E_{n+1}, respectively, leading to pushouts (3_{in}) and (3_{in+1}). By induction hypothesis, (4_n) is the colimit of $(h_{in})_{i=1,\ldots,n}$, and we have to show that (4_{n+1}) is the colimit of $(h_{in+1})_{i=1,\ldots,n+1}$.

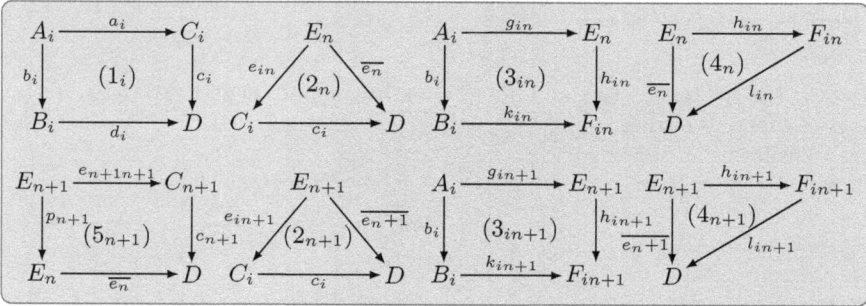

Since (2_n) is a limit and $c_i \circ f_{n+1i} = d_{n+1}$ for all $i = 1, \ldots, n$, we obtain a unique morphism m_{n+1} with $e_{in} \circ m_{n+1} = f_{n+1i}$ and $\overline{e_n} \circ m_{n+1} = d_{n+1}$. Since (1_{n+1}) is a pushout and (5_{n+1}) is a pullback, by $\mathcal{M}$-pushout-pullback decomposition also (5_{n+1}) and (6_{n+1}) are pushouts, and it follows that $F_{n+1n+1} = E_n$. From pushout $(3_{in+1}$ and $h_{in} \circ p_{n+1} \circ g_{in+1} = h_{in} \circ g_{in} = k_{in} \circ b_i$ we get an induced morphism q_{in+1} with $q_{in+1} \circ h_{in+1} = h_{in} \circ p_{n+1}$ and

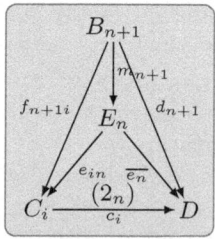

$q_{in+1} \circ k_{in+1} = k_{in}$, and from pushout decomposition alsy (7_{in+1}) is a pushout.

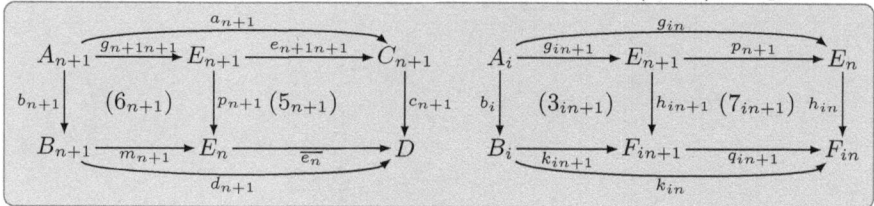

To show that (4_{n+1}) is a colimit, consider an object X and morphisms (x_i) and y with $x_i \circ h_{in+1} = y$ for $i = 1, \ldots, n$ and $x_{n+1} \circ p_{n+1} = y$. From pushout (7_{in+1})

we obtain a unique morphism z_i with $z_i \circ q_{in+1} = x_i$ and $z_i \circ h_{in} = x_{n+1}$. Now colimit (4_n) induces a unique morphism z with $z \circ \overline{e_n} = x_{n+1}$ and $z \circ l_{in} = z_i$. It follows directly that $z \circ l_{in+1} = z \circ l_{in} \circ q_{in+1} = z_i \circ q_{in+1} = x_i$ and $z \circ \overline{e_{n+1}} = z \circ \overline{e_n} \circ p_{n+1} = x_{n+1} \circ p_{n+1} = y$. The uniqueness of z follows directly from the construction, thus (4_{n+1}) is the required colimit.

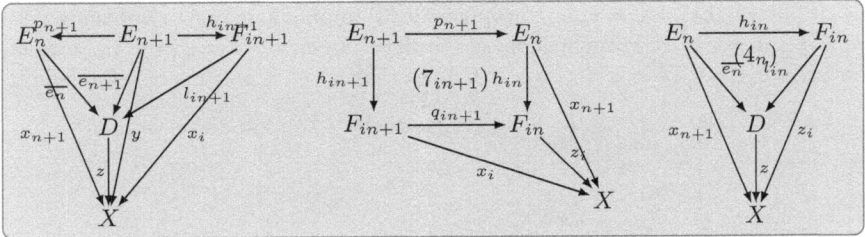

Lemma A.22

Given the following diagrams (1_i) for $i = 1, \ldots, n$, (2), and (3), with $b = +b_i$, and a and e induced by the coproducts $+A_i$ and $+B_i$, respectively, then we have:

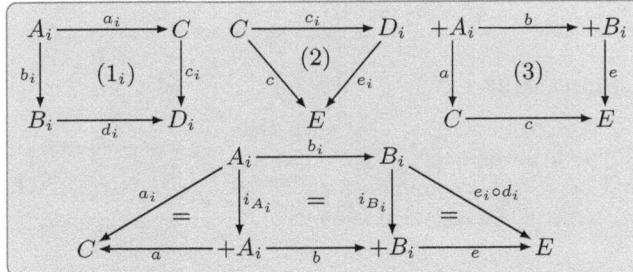

1. If (1_i) is a pushout and (2) a colimit then also (3) is a pushout.

2. If (3) is a pushout then we find a decomposition into pushout (1_i) and colimit (2) with $e_i \circ d_i = e \circ i_{B_i}$

PROOF 1. Given an object X and morphisms y, z with $y \circ a = z \circ b$. From pushout (1_i) we obtain with $z \circ i_{B_i} \circ b_i = z \circ b \circ i_{A_i} = y \circ a \circ i_{A_i} = y \circ a_i$ a unique morphism x_i with $x_i \circ c_i = y$ and $x_i \circ d_i = z \circ i_{B_i}$. Now colimit (2) implies a unique morphism x with $x \circ c = y$ and $x \circ e_i = x_i$. It follows that $x \circ e \circ i_{B_i} = x \circ e_i \circ d_i = x_i \circ d_i = z \circ i_{B_i}$, and since z is unique w.r.t. $z \circ i_{B_i}$ it follows that $z = x \circ e$. Uniqueness of x follows from the uniqueness of x and x_i, and hence (3) is a pushout.

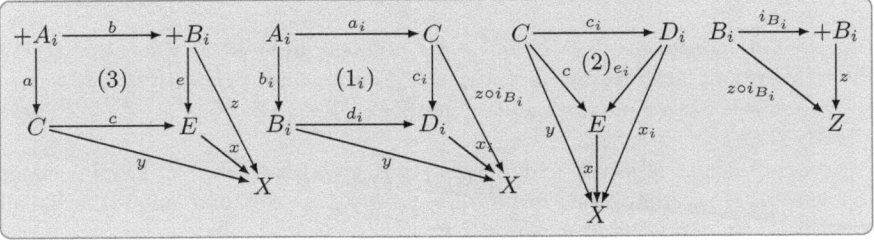

2. Define $a_i := a \circ i_{A_i}$. Now construct pushout (1_i). With $e \circ i_{B_i} \circ b_i = e \circ b \circ i_{A_i} = c \circ a_i$ pushout (1_i) induces a unique morphism e_i with $e_i \circ d_i = e \circ i_{B_i}$ and $e_i \circ c_i = c$. Given an object X and morphisms y, y_i with $y_i \circ c_i = y$ we obtain a morphism z with $z \circ i_{B_i} = y_i \circ d_i$ from coproduct $+B_i$. Then we have that $y \circ a \circ i_{A_i} = y_i \circ c_i \circ a_i = y_i \circ d_i \circ b_i = z \circ i_{B_i} \circ b_i = z \circ b \circ i_{A_i}$, and from coproduct $+A_i$ it follows that $y \circ a = z \circ b$. Now pushout (3) implies a unique morphism x with $x \circ c = y$ and $x \circ e = z$. From pushout (1_i) using $x \circ e_i \circ d_i = x \circ e \circ i_{B_i} = z \circ i_{B_i} = y_i \circ d_i$ and $x \circ e_i \circ c_i = x \circ c = y = y_i \circ c_i$ it follows that $x \circ e_i = y_i$, thus (2) is a colimit.

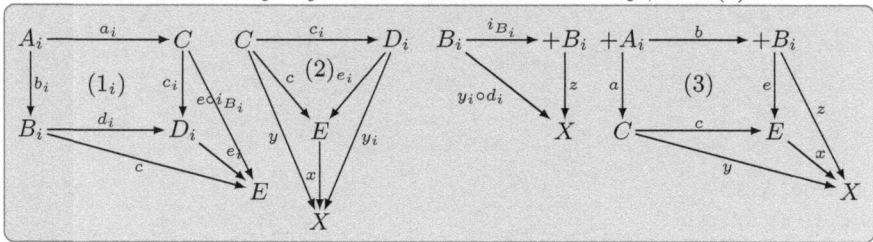

Lemma A.23

Consider colimits $(1) - (4)$ such that (5_i) is a pushout for all $i = 1, \ldots, n$ and $(7_k) - (9_k)$ commute for all $k = 1, \ldots, m$. Then also (10) is a pushout.

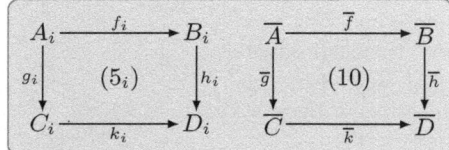

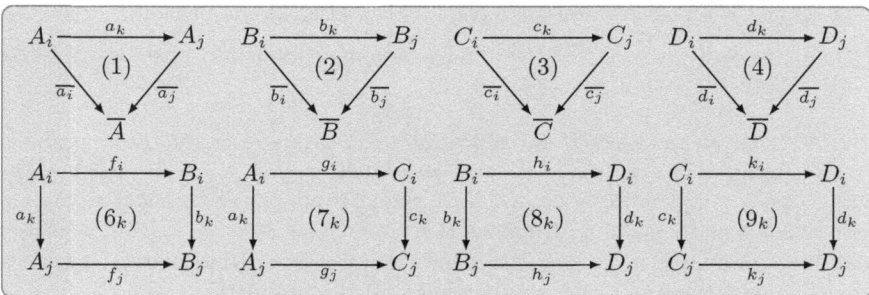

PROOF The morphisms $\overline{f}$, $\overline{g}$, $\overline{h}$, and $\overline{k}$ are uniquely induced by the colimits. We show this examplarily for the morphism $\overline{f}$: From colimit (1), with $\overline{b_j} \circ f_j \circ a_k = \overline{b_j} \circ b_k \circ f_i = \overline{b_i} \circ f_i$ we obtain a unique morphism $\overline{f}$ with $\overline{f} \circ \overline{a_i} = \overline{b_i} \circ f_i$. It follows directly that $\overline{k} \circ \overline{h} = \overline{h} \circ \overline{f}$.

Now consider an object X and morphisms y, z with $y \circ \overline{g} = z \circ \overline{f}$. From pushout (5_i) with $y \circ \overline{c_i} \circ g_i = y \circ \overline{g} \circ \overline{a_i} = z \circ \overline{f} \circ \overline{a_i} = z \circ \overline{b_i} \circ f_i$ we obtain a unique morphism x_i with $x_i \circ k_i = y \circ \overline{c_i}$ and $x_i \circ h_i = z \circ \overline{b_i}$.

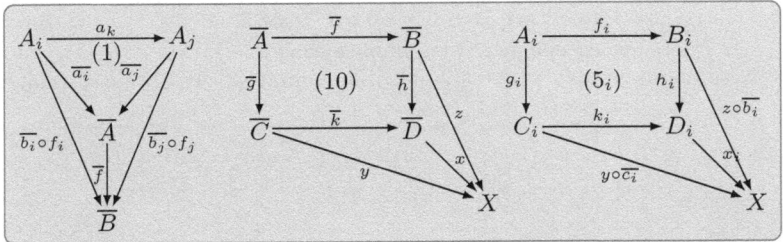

For all $k = 1, \ldots, m$, $x_j \circ d_k \circ k_i = x_j \circ k_j \circ c_k = y \circ \overline{c_j} \circ c_k = y \circ \overline{c_i}$ and $x_j \circ d_k \circ h_i = x_j \circ h_j \circ b_k = z \circ \overline{b_j} \circ b_k = z \circ \overline{b_i}$, and pushout (5_i) implies that $x_i = x_j \circ d_k$. This means that colimit (4) implies a unique x with $x \circ \overline{d_i} = x_i$. Now consider colimit (2), and $x \circ \overline{h} \circ \overline{b_i} = x \circ \overline{d_i} \circ h_i = x_i \circ h_i = z \circ \overline{b_i}$ implies that

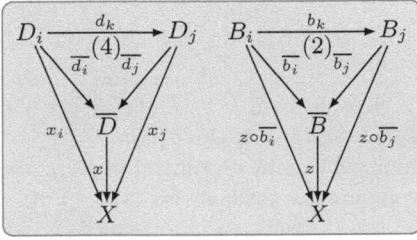

$x \circ \overline{h} = z$. Similarly, $x \circ \overline{k} = y$, and the uniqueness follows from the uniqueness of x with respect to (4). Thus, (10) is indeed a pushout.

Lemma A.24

Consider colimits (1) and (2) such that (3_i) commutes for all $i = 1, \ldots, n$, f is an epimorphism, and (4) is a pushout with $\overline{f}$ induced by colimit (1). Then also (5) is a pushout, where c and d are induced from the coproducts.

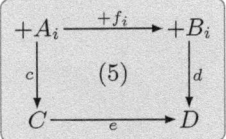

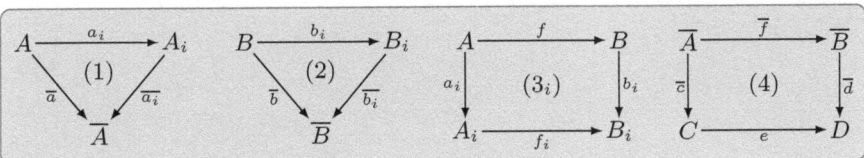

PROOF Since (1) is a colimit and $\overline{b_i} \circ f_i \circ a_i = \overline{b_i} \circ b_i \circ f = \overline{b} \circ f$, we actually get

an induced $\overline{f}$ with $\overline{f} \circ \overline{a_i} = \overline{b_i} \circ f_i$ and $\overline{f} \circ \overline{a} = \overline{b} \circ f$. From the coproducts, we obtain induced morphisms c with $c \circ i_{A_i} = \overline{c} \circ \overline{a_i}$ and d with $d \circ i_{B_i} = \overline{d} \circ \overline{b_i}$. Moreover, for all $i = 1, \ldots, n$ we have that $d \circ (+f_i) \circ i_{A_i} = d \circ i_{B_i} \circ f_i = \overline{d} \circ \overline{b_i} \circ f_i = \overline{d} \circ \overline{f} \circ \overline{a_i} = e \circ \overline{c} \circ \overline{a_i} = e \circ c \circ i_{A_i}$. Uniqueness of the induced coproduct morphisms leads to $d \circ (+f_i) = e \circ c$, i.e. (5) commutes.

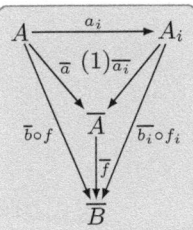

We have to show that (5) is a pushout. Given morphisms x, y with $x \circ c = y \circ (+f_i)$, we have that $y \circ i_{B_i} \circ b_i \circ f =$

$y \circ i_{B_i} \circ f_i \circ a_i = y \circ (+f_i) \circ i_{A_i} \circ a_i = x \circ c \circ i_{A_i} \circ a_i = x \circ \overline{c} \circ \overline{a_i} \circ a_i = x \circ \overline{c} \circ \overline{a}$ for all $i = 1, \ldots, n$. f being an epimorphisms implies that $y \circ i_{B_i} \circ b_i = y \circ i_{B_j} \circ b_j$ for all i, j. Now define $y' := y \circ i_{B_i} \circ b_i$, and from colimit (2) we obtain a unique morphism $\overline{y}$ with $\overline{y} \circ \overline{b_i} = y \circ i_{B_i}$ and $\overline{y} \circ \overline{b} = y'$.

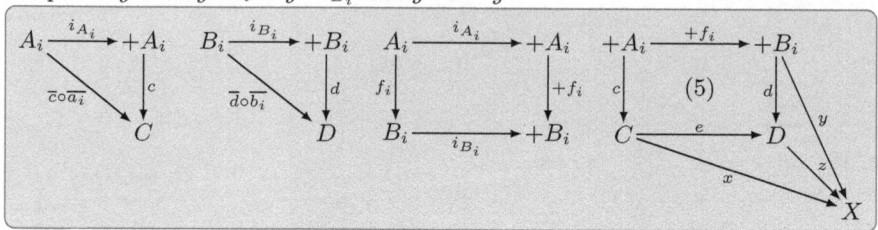

Now $x \circ \overline{c} \circ \overline{a_i} = x \circ c \circ i_{A_i} = y \circ (+f_i) \circ i_{A_i} = y \circ i_{B_i} \circ f_i = \overline{y} \circ \overline{b_i} \circ f_i = \overline{y} \circ \overline{f} \circ \overline{a_i}$ and $x \circ \overline{c} \circ \overline{a} = x \circ \overline{c} \circ \overline{a_i} \circ a_i = \overline{y} \circ \overline{f} \circ \overline{i} \circ a_i = \overline{y} \circ \overline{f} \circ \overline{a}$, and the uniqueness of the induced colimit morphism implies that $\overline{y} \circ \overline{f} = x \circ \overline{c}$. This means that X can be compared to pushout (4), and we obtain a unique morphism z with $z \circ \overline{d} = \overline{y}$ and $z \circ e = x$. Now $z \circ d \circ i_{B_i} = z \circ \overline{d} \circ \overline{b_i} = \overline{y} \circ \overline{b_i} = y \circ i_{B_i}$, and it follows that $z \circ d = y$. Similarly, the uniqueness of z w. r. t. to the pushout propert of (5) follows, thus (5) is a pushout.

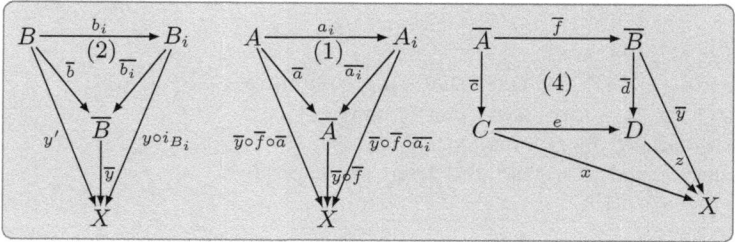

Bibliography

[Ada09]   ADAMEK, J.: *Konzeption und Implementierung einer Anwendung-sumgebung für attributierte Graphtransformation basierend auf Mathematica*. Diplomarbeit, Technische Universität Berlin, 2009.

[AGG]   AGG: *The AGG Homebase*. URL: http://tfs.cs.tu-berlin.de/agg/.

[AHS90]   ADÁMEK, J., H. HERRLICH and G. STRECKER: *Abstract and Concrete Categories*. Wiley, 1990.

[BBG05]   BEYDEDA, S., M. BOOK and V. GRUHN (editors): *Model-Driven Software Development*. Springer, 2005.

[BDE+07]   BATORY, D., O. DIAZ, H. EHRIG, C. ERMEL, U. PRANGE and G. TAENTZER: *Model Transformations Should be Functors*. Bulletin of the EATCS, 92:75–81, 2007.

[Bee02]   BEECK, M. VON DER: *A Structured Operational Semantics for UML-statecharts*. Software and Systems Modeling, 1:130–141, 2002.

[BEE+10]   BIERMANN, E., H. EHRIG, C. ERMÈL, U. GOLAS and G. TAENTZER: *Parallel Independence of Amalgamated Graph Transformations Applied to Model Transformation*. In ENGELS, G., C. LEWERENTZ, W. SCHÄFER, A. SCHÜRR and B. WESTFECHTEL (editors): *Graph Transformations and Model-Driven Engineering. Essays Dedicated to M. Nagl on the Occasion of his 65th Birthday*, volume 5765 of *LNCS*, pages 121–140. Springer, 2010.

[BEGG10]   BRAATZ, B., H. EHRIG, K. GABRIEL and U. GOLAS: *Finitary M-Adhesive Categories*. In EHRIG, H., A. RENSINK, G. ROZENBERG and A. SCHÜRR (editors): *Graph Transformations. Proceedings of ICGT 2010*, volume 6372 of *LNCS*, pages 234–249. Springer, 2010.

[BEH07]   BISZTRAY, D., K. EHRIG and R. HECKEL: *Case Study: UML to CSP Transformation*. In *Proceedings of AGTIVE 2007 Graph Transformation Tool Contest*, 2007.

[BELT04]   BARDOHL, R., H. EHRIG, J. DE LARA and G. TAENTZER: *Integrating Meta Modelling with Graph Transformation for Efficient Visual Language Definition and Model Manipulation*. In WERMELINGER, M. and T. MARGARIA-STEFFENS (editors): *Fundamental Approaches to Software Engineering. Proceedings of FASE 2004*, volume 2984 of *LNCS*, pages 214–228. Springer, 2004.

212 Bibliography

[BET10]   BIERMANN, E., C. ERMEL and G. TAENTZER: *Lifting Parallel Graph Transformation Concepts to Model Tranformations based on the Eclipse Modeling Framework.* Electronic Communications of the EASST, 26:1–19, 2010.

[BFH87]   BÖHM, P., H.-R. FONIO and A. HABEL: *Amalgamation of Graph Transformations: A Synchronization Mechanism.* Journal of Computer and System Sciences, 34(2-3):377–408, 1987.

[BKMW09] BORONAT, A., A. KNAPP, J. MESEGUER and M. WIRSING: *What Is a Multi-modeling Language?* In CORRADINI, A. and U. MONTANARI (editors): *Recent Trends in Algebraic Development Techniques. Proceedings of WADT 2008*, volume 5486 of *LNCS*, pages 71–87. Springer, 2009.

[BKS04]   BALDAN, P., B. KÖNIG and I. STÜRMER: *Generating Test Cases for Code Generators by Unfolding Graph Transformation Systems.* In EHRIG, H., G. ENGELS, F. PARISI-PRESICCE and G. ROZENBERG (editors): *Graph Transformations. Proceedings of ICGT 2004*, volume 3256 of *LNCS*, pages 194–209. Springer, 2004.

[BNBK06]   BALASUBRAMANIAN, D., A. NARAYANAN, C. VAN BUSKIRK and G. KARSAI: *The Graph Rewriting and Transformation Language: GReAT.* Electronic Communications of the EASST, 1:1–8, 2006.

[BRST05]   BÉZIVIN, J., B. RUMPE, A. SCHÜRR and L. TRATT: *Model Transformation in Practice Workshop Announcement.* 2005.

[CH03]   CZARNECKI, K. and S. HELSEN: *Classification of Model Transformation Approaches.* In *Proceedings of the GTMDA Workshop at OOPSLA 2003*, 2003.

[DF05]   DENNEY, E. and B. FISCHER: *Certifiable Program Generation.* In GLÜCK, R. and M. LOWRY (editors): *Generative Programming and Component Engineering. Proceedings of GPCE 2005*, volume 3676 of *LNCS*, pages 17–28. Springer, 2005.

[EE08]   ERMEL, C. and K. EHRIG: *Visualization, Simulation and Analysis of Reconfigurable Systems.* In SCHÜRR, A., M. NAGL and A. ZÜNDORF (editors): *Applications of Graph Transformations with Industrial Relevance. Proceedings of AGTIVE 2007*, volume 5088 of *LNCS*, pages 265–280. Springer, 2008.

[EEE+07]   EHRIG, H., K. EHRIG, C. ERMEL, F. HERMANN and G. TAENTZER: *Information Preserving Bidirectional Model Transformations.* In DWYER, M.B. and A. LOPES (editors): *Fundamental Approaches to Software Engineering. Proceedings of FASE 2007*, volume 4422 of *LNCS*, pages 72–86. Springer, 2007.

[EEE09] EHRIG, H., K. EHRIG and C. ERMEL: *Refactoring of Model Transformations*. Electronic Communications of the EASST, 18:1–19, 2009.

[EEEP07] EHRIG, H., K. EHRIG, C. ERMEL and U. PRANGE: *Model Transformations by Graph Transformation are Functors*. Bulletin of the EATCS, 93:134–142, 2007.

[EEHP09] EHRIG, H., C. ERMEL, F. HERMANN and U. PRANGE: *On-the-Fly Construction, Correctness and Completeness of Model Transformations Based on Triple Graph Grammars*. In SCHÜRR, A. and B. SELIC (editors): *Model Driven Engineering Languages and Systems. Proceedings of MODELS 2009*, volume 5795 of *LNCS*, pages 241–255. Springer, 2009.

[EEKR99] EHRIG, H., G. ENGELS, H.-J. KREOWSKI and G. ROZENBERG (editors): *Handbook of Graph Grammars and Computing by Graph Transformation, Volume 2: Applications, Languages and Tools*. World Scientific, 1999.

[EEL⁺05] EHRIG, H., K. EHRIG, J. DE LARA, G. TAENTZER, D. VARRÓ and S. VARRÓ-GYAPAY: *Termination Criteria for Model Transformation*. In CERIOLI, M. (editor): *Fundamental Approaches to Software Engineering. Proceedings of FASE 2005*, volume 3442 of *LNCS*, pages 214–228. Springer, 2005.

[EEPT06] EHRIG, H., K. EHRIG, U. PRANGE and G. TAENTZER: *Fundamentals of Algebraic Graph Transformation*. EATCS Monographs. Springer, 2006.

[EHHS00] ENGELS, G., J.H. HAUSMANN, R. HECKEL and S. SAUER: *Dynamic Meta Modeling: A Graphical Approach to the Operational Semantics of Behavioral Diagrams in UML*. In EVANS, A., S. KENT and B. SELIC (editors): *The Unified Modeling Language. Proceedings of UML 2000*, volume 1939 of *LNCS*, pages 323–337. Springer, 2000.

[EHKP91a] EHRIG, H., A. HABEL, H.-J. KREOWSKI and F. PARISI-PRESICCE: *From Graph Grammars to High Level Replacement Systems*. In EHRIG, H., H.-J. KREOWSKI and ROZENBERG G. (editors): *Graph Grammars and Their Application to Computer Science*, volume 532 of *LNCS*, pages 269–291. Springer, 1991.

[EHKP91b] EHRIG, H., A. HABEL, H.-J. KREOWSKI and F. PARISI-PRESICCE: *Parallelism and Concurrency in High-Level Replacement Systems*. Mathematical Structures in Computer Science, 1(3):361–404, 1991.

[EHL10a] EHRIG, H., A. HABEL and L. LAMBERS: *Parallelism and Concurrency Theorems for Rules with Nested Application Conditions*. Electronic Communications of the EASST, 26:1–23, 2010.

[EHL+10b] EHRIG, H., A. HABEL, L. LAMBERS, F. OREJAS and U. GOLAS: *Local Confluence for Rules with Nested Application Conditions*. In EHRIG, H., A. RENSINK, G. ROZENBERG and A. SCHÜRR (editors): *Graph Transformations. Proceedings of ICGT 2010*, volume 6372 of *LNCS*, pages 330–345. Springer, 2010.

[EHPP04] EHRIG, H., A. HABEL, J. PADBERG and U. PRANGE: *Adhesive High-Level Replacement Categories and Systems*. In EHRIG, H., G. ENGELS, F. PARISI-PRESICCE and G. ROZENBERG (editors): *Graph Transformations. Proceedings of ICGT 2004*, volume 3256 of *LNCS*, pages 144–160. Springer, 2004.

[EHS09] EHRIG, H., F. HERMANN and C. SARTORIUS: *Completeness and Correctness of Model Transformations based on Triple Graph Grammars with Negative Application Conditions*. Electronic Communications of the EASST, 18:1–18, 2009.

[EK76] EHRIG, H. and H.-J. KREOWSKI: *Parallelism of Manipulations in Multidimensional Information Structures*. In MAZURKIEWICZ, A. (editor): *Mathematical Foundations of Computer Science. Proceedings of MFCS 1976*, volume 45 of *LNCS*, pages 285–293. Springer, 1976.

[EKMR99] EHRIG, H., H.-J. KREOWSKI, U. MONTANARI and G. ROZENBERG (editors): *Handbook of Graph Grammars and Computing by Graph Transformation, Volume 3: Concurrency, Parallelism and Distribution*. World Scientific, 1999.

[EKR+08] ENGELS, G., A. KLEPPE, A. RENSINK, M. SEMENYAK, C. SOLTENBORN and H. WEHRHEIM: *From UML Activities to TAAL - Towards Behaviour-Preserving Model Transformations*. In SCHIEFERDECKER, I. and A. HARTMAN (editors): *Model Driven Architecture – Foundations and Applications. Proceedings of ECMDA-FA 2008*, volume 5095 of *LNCS*, pages 94–109. Springer, 2008.

[EKTW06] EHRIG, K., J.M. KÜSTER, G. TAENTZER and J. WINKELMANN: *Generating Instance Models from Meta Models*. In GORRIERI, R. and H. WEHRHEIM (editors): *Formal Methods for Open Object-Based Distributed Systems. Proceedings of FMOODS 2006*, volume 4037 of *LNCS*, pages 156–170. Springer, 2006.

[EP06] EHRIG, H. and U. PRANGE: *Weak Adhesive High-Level Replacement Categories and Systems: A Unifying Framework for Graph and Petri Net Transformations*. In FUTATSUGI, K., J.-P. JOUANNAUD and J. MESEGUER (editors): *Algebra, Meaning and Computation. Essays Dedicated to J.A. Goguen on the Occasion of His 65th Birthday*, volume 4060 of *LNCS*, pages 235–251. Springer, 2006.

[EP08]   EHRIG, H. and U. PRANGE: *Formal Analysis of Model Transfor-mations Based on Triple Graph Rules with Kernels*. In EHRIG, H., R. HECKEL, G. ROZENBERG and G. TAENTZER (editors): *Graph Transformations*. Proceedings of ICGT 2008, volume 5214 of *LNCS*, pages 178–193. Springer, 2008.

[EPS73]   EHRIG, H., M. PFENDER and H.J. SCHNEIDER: *Graph Grammars: an Algebraic Approach*. In *Foundations of Computer Science*. Proceedings of FOCS 1973, pages 167–180. IEEE, 1973.

[EPT04]   EHRIG, H., U. PRANGE and G. TAENTZER: *Fundamental Theory for Typed Attributed Graph Transformation*. In EHRIG, H., G. ENGELS, F. PARISI-PRESICCE and G. ROZENBERG (editors): *Graph Transfor-mations*. Proceedings of ICGT 2004, volume 3256 of *LNCS*, pages 161–177. Springer, 2004.

[Erm06]   ERMEL, C.: *Simulation and Animation of Visual Languages based on Typed Algebraic Graph Transformation*. PhD thesis, Technische Universität Berlin, 2006.

[Erm09]   ERMEL, C.: *Visual Modelling and Analysis of Model Tranformations Based on Graph Tranformation*. Bulletin of the EATCS, 99:135–152, 2009.

[Far01]   FARWER, B.: *Comparing Concepts of Object Petri Net Formalisms*. Fundamenta Informaticae, 47(3-4):247–258, 2001.

[FSB04]   FLEUREY, F., J. STEEL and B. BAUDRY: *Validation in Model-Driven Engineering: Testing Model Transformations*. In *Model, Design and Validation*. Proceedings of MoDeVa 2004, pages 29–40. IEEE, 2004.

[GBG+06]   GEISS, R., G.V. BATZ, D. GRUND, S. HACK and A.M. SZALKOWSKI: *GrGen: A Fast SPO-Based Graph Rewriting Tools*. In CORRADINI, A., H. EHRIG, U. MONTANARI, L. RIBEIRO and G. ROZENBERG (ed-itors): *Graph Transformations*. Proceedings of ICGT 2006, volume 4178 of *LNCS*, pages 383 – 397. Springer, 2006.

[GEH10]   GOLAS, U., H. EHRIG and A. HABEL: *Multi-Amalgamation in Ad-hesive Categories*. In EHRIG, H., A. RENSINK, G. ROZENBERG and A. SCHÜRR (editors): *Graph Transformations*. Proceedings of ICGT 2010, volume 6372 of *LNCS*, pages 346–361. Springer, 2010.

[GGL+06]   GIESE, H., S. GLESNER, J. LEITNER, W. SCHFER and R. WAGNER: *Towards Verified Model Transformations*. In BAUDRY, B., D. HEARN-DEN, N. RAPIN and J.G. SÜSS (editors): *Proceedings of MoDeV²a 2006*, pages 78–93, 2006.

[GKM09]   GRØNMO, R., S. KROGDAHL and B. MØLLER-PEDERSEN: *A Col-lection Operator for Graph Transformation*. In PAIGE, R. (editor):

Theory and Practice of Model Transformations. Proceedings of ICMT 2009, volume 5563 of *LNCS*, pages 67–82. Springer, 2009.

[God96]   GODEFROID, P.: *Partial-Order Methods for the Verification of Concurrent Systems – An Approach to the State-Explosion Problem*, volume 1032 of *LNCS*. Springer, 1996.

[GP98]   GOGOLLA, M. and F. PARISI-PRESICCE: *State Diagrams in UML: A Formal Semantics Using Graph Transformations*. In *Software Engineering. Proceedings of ICSE 1998*, pages 55–72. IEEE, 1998.

[Gro09]   GRONBACK, R.C.: *Eclipse Modeling Project: A Domain-Specific Language (DSL) Toolkit*. Addison-Wesley, 2009.

[GZ06]   GEIGER, L. and A. ZÜNDORF: *Tool Modeling with Fujaba*. Electronic Notes in Theoretical Computer Science, 148(1):173–186, 2006.

[Har87]   HAREL, D.: *Statecharts: A Visual Formalism for Complex Systems*. Science of Computer Programming, 8:231–274, 1987.

[Hei09]   HEINDEL, T.: *A Category Theoretical Approach to the Concurrent Semantics of Rewriting*. PhD thesis, Universität Duisburg-Essen, 2009.

[HEOG10]   HERMANN, F., H. EHRIG, F. OREJAS and U. GOLAS: *Formal Analysis of Functional Behaviour for Model Transformations based on Triple Graph Grammars*. In EHRIG, H., A. RENSINK, G. ROZENBERG and A. SCHÜRR (editors): *Graph Transformations. Proceedings of ICGT 2010*, volume 6372 of *LNCS*, pages 155–170. Springer, 2010.

[HJE06]   HOFFMANN, B., D. JANSSENS and N. VAN EETVELDE: *Cloning and Expanding Graph Transformation Rules for Refactoring*. Electronic Notes in Theoretical Computer Science, 152:53–67, 2006.

[HJSW09]   HEIDENREICH, F., J. JOHANNES, M. SEIFERT and C. WENDE: *JaMoPP: The Java Model Parser and Printer*. Technical Report TUD-FI09-10, Technische Universität Dresden, 2009.

[HKR⁺10]   HÜLSBUSCH, M., B. KÖNIG, A. RENSINK, M. SEMENYAK, C. SOLTENBORN and H. WEHRHEIM: *Verifying Full Semantic Preservation of Model Transformation is Hard*. Electronic Communications of the EASST, 2010. To appear.

[HMTW95]   HECKEL, R., J. MÜLLER, G. TAENTZER and A. WAGNER: *Attributed Graph Transformations with Controlled Application of Rules*. Technical Report B-19, Universitat de les Illes Balears, 1995.

[HP05]   HABEL, A. and K.-H. PENNEMANN: *Nested Constraints and Application Conditions for High-Level Structures*. In KREOWSKI, H.-J., U. MONTANARI, F. OREJAS, G. ROZENBERG and G. TAENTZER (editors): *Formal Methods in Software and Systems Modeling. Essays*

Dedicated to H. Ehrig on the Occasion of His 60th Birthday, volume 3393 of *LNCS*, pages 293–308. Springer, 2005.

[HP09]   HABEL, A. and K.-H. PENNEMANN: *Correctness of High-Level Transformation Systems Relative to Nested Conditions*. Mathematical Structures in Computer Science, 19(2):245–296, 2009.

[Hue80]   HUET, G.: *Confluent Reductions: Abstract Properties and Applications to Term Rewriting Systems*. Journal of the ACM, 27(4):797–821, 1980.

[JAB⁺06] JOUAULT, F., F. ALLILAIRE, J. BÉZIVIN, I. KURTEV and P. VALDURIEZ: *ATL: a QVT-like TransformationLanguage*. In TARR, P.L. and W.R. COOK (editors): *OOPSLA Companion*, pages 719–720. ACM, 2006.

[JABK08] JOUAULT, F., F. ALLILAIRE, J. BÉZIVIN and I. KURTEV: *ATL: A Model Transformation Tool*. Science of Computer Programming, 72(1-2):31–39, 2008.

[JLS07]   JOHNSTONE, P.T., S. LACK and P. SOBOCIŃSKI: *Quasitoposes, Quasiadhesive Categories and Artin Glueing*. In MOSSAKOWSKI, T., U. MONTANARI and M. HAVERAAEN (editors): *Algebra and Coalgebra in Computer Science. Proceedings of CALCO 2007*, volume 4626 of *LNCS*, pages 312–326. Springer, 2007.

[KA06]   KÜSTER, J.M. and M. ABD-EL-RAZIK: *Validation of Model Transformations - First Experiences Using a White Box Approach*. In KÜHNE, T. (editor): *Models in Software Engineering. Proceedings of MoDELS Workshops 2006*, volume 4364 of *LNCS*, pages 193–204. Springer, 2006.

[KGKK02] KUSKE, S., M. GOGOLLA, R. KOLLMANN and H.-J. KREOWSKI: *An Integrated Semantics for UML Class, Object and State Diagrams Based on Graph Transformation*. In BUTLER, M., L. PETRE and K. SERE (editors): *Integrated Formal Methods. Proceedings of IFM 2002*, volume 2335 of *LNCS*, pages 11–28. Springer, 2002.

[KN07]   KARSAI, G. and A. NARAYANAN: *On the Correctness of Model Tranformations in the Development of Embedded Systems*. In KORDON, F. and O. SOKOLSKY (editors): *Composition of Embedded Systems. Scientific and Industrial Issues. Monterey Workshop 2006*, volume 4888 of *LNCS*, pages 1–18. Springer, 2007.

[KR04]   KÖHLER, M. and H. RÖLKE: *Properties of Object Petri Nets*. In CORTADELLA, J. and W. REISIG (editors): *Applications and Theory of Petri Nets. Proceedings of ICATPN 2004*, volume 3099 of *LNCS*, pages 278–297. Springer, 2004.

Bibliography

[KS06]   KÖNIG, A. and A. SCHÜRR: *Tool Integration with Triple Graph Grammars - A Survey*. Electronic Notes in Theoretical Computer Science, 148(1):113–150, 2006.

[Kus01]   KUSKE, S.: *A Formal Semantics of UML State Machines Based on Structured Graph Transformation*. In GOGOLLA, M. and C. KOBRYN (editors): *The Unified Modeling Language. Modeling Languages, Concepts, and Tools. Proceedings of UML 2001*, volume 2185 of *LNCS*, pages 241–256. Springer, 2001.

[LBE⁺07]   LARA, J. DE, R. BARDOHL, H. EHRIG, K. EHRIG, U. PRANGE and G. TAENTZER: *Attributed Graph Transformation with Node Type Inheritance*. Theoretical Computer Science, 376(3):139–163, 2007.

[Lei06]   LEITNER, J.: *Verifikation von Modelltransformationen basierend auf Triple Graph Grammatiken*. Diplomarbeit, Universität Karlsruhe, 2006.

[LEO08]   LAMBERS, L., H. EHRIG and F. OREJAS: *Efficient Conflict Detection in Graph Transformation Systems by Essential Critical Pairs*. Electronic Notes in Theoretical Computer Science, 211:17–26, 2008.

[LEOP08]   LAMBERS, L., H. EHRIG, F. OREJAS and U. PRANGE: *Parallelism and Concurrency in Adhesive High-Level Replacement Systems with Negative Application Conditions*. Electronic Notes in Theoretical Computer Science, 203(6):43–66, 2008.

[LEPO08]   LAMBERS, L., H. EHRIG, U. PRANGE and F. OREJAS: *Embedding and Confluence of Graph Transformations with Negative Application Conditions*. In EHRIG, H., R. HECKEL, G. ROZENBERG and G. TAENTZER (editors): *Graph Transformations. Proceedings of ICGT 2008*, volume 5214 of *LNCS*, pages 162–177. Springer, 2008.

[LG08]   LARA, J. DE and E. GUERRA: *Pattern-Based Model-to-Model Transformation*. In EHRIG, H., R. HECKEL, G. ROZENBERG and G. TAENTZER (editors): *Graph Transformations. Proceedings of ICGT 2008*, volume 5214 of *LNCS*, pages 426–441. Springer, 2008.

[Löw93]   LÖWE, M.: *Algebraic Approach to Single-Pushout Graph Transformation*. Theoretical Computer Science, 109:181–224, 1993.

[LPE07]   LEVENDOVSZKY, T., U. PRANGE and H. EHRIG: *Termination Criteria for DPO Transformations with Injective Matches*. Electronic Notes in Theoretical Computer Science, 175(4):87–100, 2007.

[LS04]   LACK, S. and P. SOBOCIŃSKI: *Adhesive Categories*. In WALUKIEWICZ, I. (editor): *Foundations of Software Science and Computation Structures. Proceedings of FOSSACS 2004*, volume 2987 of *LNCS*, pages 273–288. Springer, 2004.

[LS05]   LACK, S. and P. SOBOCIŃSKI: *Adhesive and Quasiadhesive Categories*. Theoretical Informatics and Applications, 39(3):511–545, 2005.

[LV02]   LARA, J. DE and H. VANGHELUWE: *Computer Aided Multi-Paradigm Modelling to Process Petri-Nets and Statecharts*. In CORRADINI, A., H. EHRIG, H.-J. KREOWSKI and G. ROZENBERG (editors): *Graph Transformation. Proceedings of ICGT 2002*, volume 2505 of *LNCS*, pages 239–253. Springer, 2002.

[Mac71]   MACLANE, S.: *Categories for the Working Mathematician*. Number 5 in *Graduate Texts in Mathematics*. Springer, 1971.

[MB03]   MARSCHALL, F. and P. BRAUN: *Model Transformations for the MDA with BOTL*. In RENSINK, A. (editor): *Proceedings of MDAFA 2003*, pages 25–36, 2003.

[MG06]   MENS, T. and P. VAN GORP: *A Taxonomy of Model Transformation*. Electronic Notes in Theoretical Computer Science, 152:125–142, 2006.

[MP96]   MAGGIOLO-SCHETTINI, A. and A. PERON: *A Graph Rewriting Framework for Statecharts Semantics*. In CUNY, J., H. EHRIG, G. ENGELS and G. ROZENBERG (editors): *Graph Grammars and Their Application to Computer Science*, volume 1073 of *LNCS*, pages 107–121. Springer, 1996.

[NK08a]   NARAYANAN, A. and G. KARSAI: *Towards Verifying Model Transformations*. Electronic Notes in Theoretical Computer Science, 211:191–200, 2008.

[NK08b]   NARAYANAN, A. and G. KARSAI: *Verifying Model Transformations by Structural Correspondence*. Electronic Communications of the EASST, 10:1–14, 2008.

[ODHA06]   OUYANG, C., M. DUMAS, A.H.M. TER HOFSTEDE and W.M.P VAN DER AALST: *From BPMN Process Models to BPEL Web Services*. In *Web Services. Proceedings of ICWS 2006*, pages 285–292. IEEE, 2006.

[OMG05]   OMG: *MOF QVT Final Adopted Specification*, 2005.

[OMG08]   OMG: *Systems Modeling Language (OMG SysML), Version 1.1*, 2008.

[OMG09a]   OMG: *Business Process Model and Notation (BPMN), Version 1.2*, 2009.

[OMG09b]   OMG: *Unified Modeling Language (OMG UML), Superstructure, Version 2.2*, 2009.

[OW09] OREJAS, F. and M. WIRSING: *On the Specification and Verification of Model Transformations*. In PALSBERG, J. (editor): *Semantics and Algebraic Specification. Essays Dedicated to Peter D. Mosses on the Occasion of His 60th Birthday*, volume 5700 of *LNCS*, pages 140–161. Springer, 2009.

[PE07] PRANGE, U. and H. EHRIG: *From Algebraic Graph Transformation to Adhesive HLR Categories and Systems*. In BOZAPALIDIS, S. and G. RAHONIS (editors): *Algebraic Informatics. Proceedings of CAI 2007*, volume 4728 of *LNCS*, pages 122–146. Springer, 2007.

[PEHP08] PRANGE, U., H. EHRIG, K. HOFFMANN and J. PADBERG: *Transformations in Reconfigurable Place/Transition Systems*. In DEGANO, P., R. DE NICOLA and J. MESEGUER (editors): *Concurrency, Graphs and Models. Essays Dedicated to U. Montanari on the Occasion of His 65th Birthday*, volume 5065 of *LNCS*, pages 96–113. Springer, 2008.

[PEL08] PRANGE, U., H. EHRIG and L. LAMBERS: *Construction and Properties of Adhesive and Weak Adhesive High-Level Replacement Categories*. Applied Categorical Structures, 16(3):365–388, 2008.

[PER95] PADBERG, J., H. EHRIG and L. RIBEIRO: *Algebraic High-Level Net Transformation Systems*. Mathematical Structures in Computer Science, 5(2):217–256, 1995.

[Plu93] PLUMP, D.: *Hypergraph Rewriting: Critical Pairs and Undecidability of Confluence*. In SLEEP, M.R, M.J. PLASMEIJER and M.C.J.D. VAN EEKELEN (editors): *Term Graph Rewriting*, pages 201–214. Wiley, 1993.

[Plu95] PLUMP, D.: *On Termination of Graph Rewriting*. In NAGL, M. (editor): *Graph-Theoretic Concepts in Computer Science. Proceedings of WG 1995*, volume 1017 of *LNCS*, pages 88–100. Springer, 1995.

[PR69] PFALTZ, J.L. and A. ROSENFELD: *Web Grammars*. In WALKER, D.E. and L.M. NORTON (editors): *Proceedings of IJCAI 1969*, pages 609–620. William Kaufmann, 1969.

[Pra71] PRATT, T.W.: *Pair Grammars, Graph Languages and String-to-Graph Translations*. Journal of Computer and System Sciences, 5(6):560–595, 1971.

[Pra07] PRANGE, U.: *Algebraic High-Level Nets as Weak Adhesive HLR Categories*. Electronic Communications of the EASST, 2:1–13, 2007.

[Pra08] PRANGE, U.: *Towards Algebraic High-Level Systems as Weak Adhesive HLR Categories*. Electronic Notes in Theoretical Computer Science, 203(6):67–88, 2008.

[RACH00]   REGGIO, G., E. ASTESIANO, C. CHOPPY and H. HUSSMANN:
            *Analysing UML Active Classes and Associated State Machines - A
            Lightweight Formal Approach.* In MAIBAUM, T. (editor): *Fundamen-
            tal Approaches to Software Engineering. Proceedings of FASE 2000*,
            volume 1783 of *LNCS*, pages 127–146. Springer, 2000.

[RK09]   RENSINK, A. and J.-H. KUPERUS: *Repotting the Geraniums: On
            Nested Graph Tranformation Rules.* Electronic Communications of
            the EASST, 18:1–15, 2009.

[Roz97]   ROZENBERG, G. (editor): *Handbook of Graph Grammars and Com-
            puting by Graph Transformation, Volume 1: Foundations.* World
            Scientific, 1997.

[RSV04]   RENSINK, A., Á. SCHMIDT and D. VARRÓ: *Model Checking Graph
            Transformations: A Comparison of Two Approaches.* In EHRIG,
            H., G. ENGELS, F. PARISI-PRESICCE and G. ROZENBERG (editors):
            Graph Transformations. Proceedings of ICGT 2004, volume 3256 of
            LNCS, pages 226–241. Springer, 2004.

[San00]   SAND, M.: *Design und Implementierung einer Komponente zur
            Transformation von UML-Statecharts in stochastiche Petrinetze.* Stu-
            dienarbeit, Universität Erlangen, 2000.

[SBPM08]   STEINBERG, S., F. BUDINSKY, M. PATERNOSTRO and E. MERKS:
            EMF: Eclipse Modeling Framework, 2nd Edition. Addison-Wesley,
            2008.

[Sch94]   SCHÜRR, A.: *Specification of Graph Translators With Triple Graph
            Grammars.* In TINHOFER, G. (editor): *Graph-Theoretic Concepts in
            Computer Science. Proceedings of WG 1994*, volume 903 of *LNCS*,
            pages 151–163. Springer, 1994.

[Ste08a]   STEVENS, P.: *A Landscape of Bidirectional Model Transformations.*
            In LÄMMEL, R., J. VISSER and J. SARAIVA (editors): *Generative and
            Transformational Techniques in Software Engineering II. Proceedings
            of GTTSE 2007*, volume 5235 of *LNCS*, pages 408–424. Springer,
            2008.

[Ste08b]   STEVENS, P.: *Towards an Algebraic Theory of Bidirectional Trans-
            formations.* In EHRIG, H., R. HECKEL, G. ROZENBERG and
            G. TAENTZER (editors): *Graph Transformations. Proceedings of
            ICGT 2008*, volume 5214 of *LNCS*, pages 1–17. Springer, 2008.

[Str08]   STRECKER, M.: *Modeling and Verifying Graph Transformations in
            Proof Assistants.* Electronic Notes in Theoretical Computer Science,
            203(1):135–148, 2008.

[SV06]   STAHL, T. and M. VÖLTER: *Model-Driven Software Development.*
            Wiley, 2006.

[Tae96]   TAENTZER, G.: *Parallel and Distributed Graph Transformation -*
             Formal Description and Application to Communication Based Sys-
             tems. PhD thesis, TU Berlin, 1996.

[Tae10]   TAENTZER, G.: *Why Model Tranformations Should be Based on Al-*
             gebraic Graph Tranformation Concepts. Electronic Communications
             of the EASST, 30:1–10, 2010.

[TB94]   TAENTZER, G. and M. BEYER: *Amalgamated Graph Transforma-*
             tions and Their Use for Specifying AGG - an Algebraic Graph Gram-
             mar System. In SCHNEIDER, H.-J. and H. EHRIG (editors): *Graph*
             Transformations in Computer Science, volume 776 of *LNCS*, pages
             380–394. Springer, 1994.

[TEG⁺05]   TAENTZER, G., K. EHRIG, E. GUERRA, J. DE LARA, L. LENGYEL,
             T. LEVENDOVSKY, U. PRANGE, D. VARRÓ and S. VARRÓ-GYAPAY:
             Model Transformation by Graph Transformation: A Comparative
             Study. In *Proceedings of the MTP workshop at MoDELS 2005*, 2005.

[TR05]   TAENTZER, G. and A. RENSINK: *Ensuring Structural Constraints in*
             Graph-Based Models with Type Inheritance. In CERIOLI, M. (edi-
             tor): *Fundamental Approaches to Software Engineering. Proceedings*
             of FASE 2005, volume 3442 of *LNCS*, pages 64–79. Springer, 2005.

[Var02]   VARRÓ, D.: *A Formal Semantics of UML Statecharts by Model Tran-*
             sition Systems. In CORRADINI, A., H. EHRIG, H.-J. KREOWSKI
             and G. ROZENBERG (editors): *Graph Transformation. Proceedings*
             of ICGT 2002, volume 2505 of *LNCS*, pages 378–392. Springer, 2002.

[VB07]   VARRÓ, D. and A. BALOGH: *The Model Transformation Language*
             of the VIATRA2 Framework. Science of Computer Programming,
             68(3):214–234, 2007.

[VP03]   VARRÓ, D. and A. PATARICZA: *Automated Formal Verification of*
             Model Tranformations. In JÜRJENS, J., B. RUMPE, R. FRANCE and
             E.B. FERNANDEZ (editors): *Proceedings of Critical Systems Develop-*
             ment with UML 2003, volume TUM-I0323, pages 63–78. Technische
             Universität München, 2003.

[VVE⁺06]   VARRÓ, D., S. VARRÓ-GYAPAY, H. EHRIG, U. PRANGE and
             G. TAENTZER: *Termination Analysis of Model Transformations*
             by Petri Nets. In CORRADINI, A., H. EHRIG, U. MONTANARI,
             L. RIBEIRO and G. ROZENBERG (editors): *Graph Transformations.*
             Proceedings of ICGT 2006, volume 4178 of *LNCS*, pages 260–274.
             Springer, 2006.

[W3C07]   W3C: *XSL Transformations (XSLT) Version 2.0*, 2007.

Index